NANCY LANCASTER

Nancy Lancaster

HER LIFE, HER WORLD, HER ART

Robert Becker

ALFRED A. KNOPF

NEW YORK

1996

THIS IS A BORZOI BOOK
PUBLISHED BY ALFRED A. KNOPF, INC.

Copyright © 1996 by Robert Becker and the Estate of Nancy Lancaster
All rights reserved under International and Pan-American Copyright Conventions.
Published in the United States by Alfred A. Knopf, Inc., New York, and
simultaneously in Canada by Random House of Canada Limited, Toronto.
Distributed by Random House, Inc., New York.

Grateful acknowledgment is made to the following for permission to reprint
previously published material:

Curtis Brown Ltd.: Excerpts from *I Saw England* by Ben Robertson, copyright © 1941
by Ben Robertson, copyright renewed (London: Jarrolds). Reprinted by permission
of Curtis Brown Ltd.

Macmillan General Books: Excerpts from *When the Moon Was High* by Ronald Tree
(London: Macmillan General Books, 1975). Reprinted by permission of Macmillan
General Books.

Library of Congress Cataloging-in-Publication Data
Becker, Robert.
Nancy Lancaster : her life, her world, her art/Robert Becker.
p.   cm.
Includes bibliographical references and index.
ISBN 0-394-56791-9
1. Lancaster, Nancy, d. 1994. 2. Interior decorators—United States—Biography.
I. Title.
NK2004.3.L36B43   1996
747.213—dc20
[B]   95-34170   CIP

Manufactured in the United States of America
FIRST EDITION

FOR

MR. AND MRS. LOYALL ALLEN OSBORNE

AND

MR. AND MRS. ROBERT LOUIS BECKER,

MY GRANDPARENTS,

THROUGH WHOM I LEARNED TO RESPECT AND

ADMIRE THE GENERATION BORN AT THE TURN

OF THE TWENTIETH CENTURY

ACKNOWLEDGMENTS

The author would like to gratefully acknowledge the help and support of the following people:

Patricia Osborne Smith, Robert Louis Becker, Jr., Anne Becker Hulley, Emily Becker Naunheim.

Victoria Wilson.

Alice Winn, Anne and Michael Tree, Jeremy Tree, Isabella Burrell, Esther Cayzer-Colvin, Elizabeth Winn, Melissa Wyndham, Sir John Jacob Astor, David Astor, Phyllis Langhorne Draper, Langhorne Gibson, Jr., Chiswell Perkins, Elizabeth Perkins Varner.

Ruby Hill, Fred Field, Sophie Morrison, George Oakes, Imogen Taylor, Andy Menzies, Vernon Russell-Smith, Mary, Duchess of Buccleuch; Valencia Lancaster, John Cornforth, Sir Geoffrey Jellicoe, the Duke and Duchess of Devonshire, Jessica Gould, Hugo Vickers, Gervase Jackson-Stops, Lady Soames, Sir John Martin, Cecily Borwick, Edith Bridges, Fiona Heyward, Barrie McIntyre, Sir Reginald Hibbert, Baroness D'Erlanger, Sarah Baring, Christopher Hamel Cooke, Eric Beck, Simon Blow, Philip Hoare, Amanda Fry, Maria Seed, Mr. and Mrs. Duncan Clark, Trevor Humphries, Lady Alexandra Metcalfe, John Bowes-Lyon, Colonel Sir Rupert and Lady Hardy, Captain and Mrs. John Macdonald Buchannan, Valerie Finnis, Elizabeth Shonnard, Lady Bolker, Patsy Whetstone, Lord Wilton, Laura, Duchess of Marlborough; Catherine Pauson, Helen Cooper, Horst Horst, Catherine Fairweather, Camilla Costello, Alan S. Bell and the staff of the London Library, Lady Mary-rose Williams.

Emily Bailey, Mark Bailey, Tania Compton, Sophie Hicks, Daniel Moynihan, William Seighart, Duncan Ward, Anna Corbero, Xavier Corbero, Peter Fleisig, Selina Fellows, Nathalie Hambro, Edward St. Aubyn, Simon Rendel, Victoria Belfrage.

Roberta Bocock, Sara Lee Barnes, Anne Rafferty Barnes, Mr. and Mrs. Robert Carter, Mr. and Mrs. Joseph Johnston, Virginius Dabney, James Scott,

Mr. and Mrs. Lawrence Lewis, Mary Tyler McClenehan, Mr. and Mrs. Calvin Satisfield, Vernon Edenfield, Kitty Abbott Johnson, Teresa Roane.

Daniel M. Young, Howard Read, Fredrick W. Hughes, Fayette B. Hickox, Stanley Barrows, Galen Lee, Barton H. Miller, Fleming P. Rutlege, Richard Gradkowski, Paul Mellon, Mrs. Suydam Cutting, William Paley, Wallace W. Smith, Jr., Annette W. Becker, Lee Buttala, W. Howard Adams, Carol R. Irving.

CONTENTS

Full-color illustrations follow pages 110 and 366.

"Whenever Nancy comes into a room," said an admirer from Virginia, "men sit up and straighten their ties. She's the sexiest ninety-year-old you'll ever meet."

Nancy Lancaster wanted to write a book about her houses, to give an account of how she transformed the string of manor homes she kept in England and Virginia and to create a chronicle of the body of work that has so influenced contemporary taste and the character of the interior design profession. I went to England to help her for five months in 1988 but ended up staying for three years and, as we mutually agreed, writing the book myself. During that time, when I drove up to her Coach House at Haseley Court in Oxfordshire, she would jump to her feet to greet me with much of the same vitality that had always driven her: the sporting woman, politician's wife, chatelaine of immense houses and estates, and, most notably, one of the twentieth century's paramount decorators and garden designers. Though she professed to look like "old Mr. Ford," she remained a very attractive woman, alluring, exhilarating, dressed in pants suits, skirts and jackets, wearing rubber Wellingtons on rainy days, a gardening hat cocked at a jaunty tilt when the sun was shining. We talked as we strolled around Haseley's gardens, along gravel paths crowded by unruly flowers and unexpected scents, or when ensconced in armchairs by the fireplace in her sitting room. At lunch—game fowl and fresh vegetables in rich sauces, soufflés, and a sangria whose recipe came from the Spanish embassy in London, all brought to the table by her butler—I kept a notepad and pencil on the chair next to me or a tape recorder running under a napkin in my lap.

Nancy claimed to love houses more than people. By saying so she was being typically offhanded because her family and a few intimate friends, including men and women who had worked for her over the years, meant more to her than anything. But when Nancy looked back at the nine decades of her life, it was indeed the houses that peaked in her wistful and romantic nostalgia: big old houses, the surviving antebellum plantation mansions in

Virginia, where she was born in 1897; the Palladian masterpieces along the Brenta in northeastern Italy which had long ago succumbed to a dereliction that mesmerized her; the courts, halls, castles and châteaux of England and France, houses where generation after generation of the same family had lived for centuries, each superimposing its narratives onto the buildings. Throughout her life these houses served as lightning rods for her imagination and boundless creative gifts and as wellsprings of ideas for her work. Her uncanny ability to gather together their essence—the "stamp of history" as she called it, the antithesis of Modernism—and bring it so convincingly to the houses she decorated was at the center of her genius. John Fowler, Nancy's partner in the years she owned the firm of Colefax and Fowler, called interior decorating her "root and passion." Actually, the houses themselves, especially her own, were Nancy's passion—their very stone, mortar and wooden beams.

In the years during which I spent time with her, Nancy continually insisted that the book be only about houses, not herself. The artist, however, was inseparable from the art; inevitably, a picture of life, her life and that of the English and American upper classes of which she was a part, emerged alongside the decoration. Mirador in Virginia; Kelmarsh Hall, Ditchley Park and Haseley Court in England—names synonymous with *haute style* and comfort—would be as soulless as house museums without Nancy, her family and friends residing in colorful drawing rooms and dining rooms. Spurred by her innate clannishness and sense of family, it was for her remarkable "kin," from Lady Astor and Irene Gibson to Admiral Beatty and Joyce Grenfell, and for house guests like Winston Churchill, Anthony Eden, Edward, Prince of Wales, Diana Cooper and their very fast international society that Nancy composed these settings: luxurious, welcoming backdrops for the lives they lived.

Nancy's "voice" in this book, in bold type, comes mostly from transcriptions of our conversations tape recorded at Haseley. Nancy spoke with a distinctly aristocratic British accent, having moved permanently to England in the mid-1920s, although it was spiced with the earthy and succint expressions and pronunciations of turn-of-the-century Virginia. (Yellow was "yellah," window, "windah," and the Civil War, "the wah." She described a countess who refused to follow her advise on decoration as having the "taste of a balloon"; the artist Andy Warhol "looked like he had been pressed in a book"; the pregnant Duchess of York, who was taken to Haseley in 1988 to see Nancy's gardens, filled her sitting room "like a sofa and two chairs"; while the Labor MP Roy Jenkins, who went to lunch at the Coach House with one of Nancy's Astor relatives, was "stuffed like a Christmas stocking.") Occasionally she told me several versions of the same story, in which case I gleaned from each and edited them together. Other times I included notes I had taken during our telephone conversations and Nancy's written responses to specific questions into the transcriptions. In a few instances I used phrases and sentences from a short manuscript Nancy wrote in the mid-1980s and from articles she had published.

Among many other things, Nancy Lancaster was a raconteur and conversationalist whose timing was perfect, wit and sense of humor unabashed and poignant, and whose laugh was infectious; she punctuated her speech with a wry smile and a raised eyebrow. She also commanded a remarkable memory, could be racy and demure in the same sentence, was well-versed in history, literature and politics, and possessed a natural instinct for self-editing, the hallmark of great storytelling. Next to Nancy's acknowledged achievements as a decorator and gardener, and her position as having been one of the twentieth century's most extolled hostesses, she was, as Lord Carrington put it, "the best company . . . ever."

ROBERT BECKER

NANCY LANCASTER

MIRADOR

"Mirador, Mirth and Misery," my aunts used to say. Mirador is deep in me, I feel it in my bones even now. Nothing else has ever been as important. I'm not really interested in England or America, only in Virginia and Mirador. They're my roots and my soul.

A GUEST PASSED under a classical archway at the end of a footpath to reach the front steps of Mirador. Mr. Langhorne built the arch from field-stones when he bought the house and farm in Albemarle County, Virginia, in 1893. His workmen used an icing-thin layer of concrete to smooth over the chipped and pitted brick path that led from the bullring to the house, and the youngest Langhorne child's footprints were embedded in the wet cement near the steps. But Virginia's unrelenting summer heat and damp, penetrating winter chill cracked and broke apart the paving. Before too long, thick trumpet vines buried the triumphal arch. So within a few years of the Langhorne family's moving into Mirador, most of what was new seemed not the least bit out of character with a house built three quarters of a century before.

Mr. Langhorne added wings to either side of the original block and slightly enlarged the front porch for practical reasons, but they too suited the old house, melded right in. The family would have burst Mirador at the seams without them. Chiswell Langhorne and his wife, Nancy, had three sons and five daughters, with only one daughter married by then, not to mention the coterie of indoor and outdoor servants. When he bought Mirador it had only three bedrooms, a "spare room" and one bathroom. Providing a new kitchen and a bigger dining room, more bedrooms and bathrooms, and some privacy for Mr. and Mrs. Langhorne, the wings were an absolute necessity. His larger front porch, on the other hand, was more of a

The Langhorne family and their guests at Mirador. On the porch, left to right, are cousin Edna Hutter, Keene Langhorne, cousin Lucy Lewis, Mirador neighbor Dr. Oasley, Chiswell Langhorne and Buck Langhorne; on the steps Babs Gibson is sitting above Langhorne Gibson and Nancy Perkins. The dogs were called Bob and Tuck.

traditional imperative: Virginian custom dictated that no country house was complete without this perch, a spot for rocking in the evening after supper. Here Mr. Langhorne smoked his ever present cigar, sipped his whiskey, laughed with neighbors and listened proudly to his beautiful daughters playing the guitar and singing to him.

Once the porch and the wings were in place, it was hard to imagine the house without them. They added balance and presence, permanence and stature. The broad new facade, the elegant, whitewashed cornice of the main block echoed in the new wings, the porch with handsome turned balusters—these transformed Mirador into a true Virginia gentleman's countryseat.

Ever since I was old enough to reason, all of the fun and glamour and excitement in life came from Mirador and my mother's family. To "feel poorly" as a little girl and to be sent away by the doctor from Richmond, where my family lived, to the cool air and never-ending adventure of Grandfather's care was my idea of heaven. My

Chiswell Dabney Langhorne, veteran of the Army of Northern Virginia, railroad tycoon, "gentleman of the Old School" and patriarch of the Langhorne family at Mirador

suitcase was packed and I was taken by streetcar to Richmond's Main Street Station. The railway was the Chesapeake and Ohio, and the distance from Richmond to Greenwood, the town Mirador was in, was one hundred miles. The trip took four hours.

I was allowed to travel on my own from the age of four in the charge of the colored Pullman porters Ed or Wash and the conductor Captain Mickey. The three of them were virtually members of our family after so many trips back and forth and were entrusted with my safety. They were also entrusted once or twice a week with the safety of fresh Chesapeake Bay oysters or Virginia spots for Grandfather.

The Pullman car I traveled in had swiveling armchairs covered in green plush. The porters, whose jobs were to brush off passengers with a stiff whisk broom upon arriving at their destination, and placing a stool on the station platform to ease the step down, used to play with me and my paper dolls as the train steamed and whistled along.

Gordonsville was the waistline of the trip. It was when the mountains first came into sight, and it was the biggest stop on our route. There was a hotel near the station in Gordonsville where colored waiters in white suits carrying trays on their heads sold lemon pies and fried chicken to the passengers through the windows. Later came Charlottesville, the last big station; then the train had only three stops, Ivy, Mechum River and Crozet, before we came to Greenwood. Those last eighteen miles seemed an eternity.

A crisp blast of cold mountain air always met me at Greenwood in the winter, or fresh scented breezes in springtime. John Pate, Grandfather's coachman, was sent to the station to fetch me in the patent-leather-covered Black Maria pulled by Carry and Lena. The brakes creaked the entire way downhill from Greenwood Station to Mirador as John Pate negotiated the carriage over the rutted red clay road. We were home when we turned into the Mirador arch, rounded the circle and stepped down at the stone mounting blocks at the foot of the walk. The lamps were lit if it was getting dark; log fires burned if it was cold, even in early spring. If we arrived at Mirador as hot weather approached, I saw the periwinkles blossoming in the lawn surrounding the house. I remember most arriving to my Grandmother Nanere's warm greeting and Grandfather's clean, good smell. There was always a plate of cinnamon tea cakes on the table in the middle of the sitting room and in the hall a basket full of small lady apples picked in the orchard.

If I was sent up to Mirador on my own I stayed in the house, but in the summer, when I was with my mother, we lived in the cottage at the end of the path leading from my grandparents' wing. I was born in that cottage in 1897. Nobody knew how old it was, but it was at least as old as the main house and may have been the farm's original kitchen. It was very simple and small, with two rooms downstairs and two rooms upstairs in the attic. It had a porch in the back looking over the road and a brick walk to the house. Mother slept in one bedroom and I slept in the other with my mammie, Aunt Liza Pie, and my sister, Alice; Alice was born five years after me.

I woke up so excited at Mirador, always to the calls of catbirds sounding as if they were sucking their teeth. You knew it was going to be a long day, but you never knew what was going to happen. One uncle or another was always coming over the mountain in a Ford car, or an aunt was arriving from England with chic maids and trunks. They brought husbands, beaux and friends from every country in the world. People gravitated to them and to Grandfather; Mirador was always filled with people of all ages. Grandfather had his weekends of old Virginian gentlemen and fellow Confederate veterans when no one else was welcomed. Other times he might have someone like General Fitzhugh Lee down to stay, or his sister Aunt Liz Lewis and her husband; then my Aunt Irene and Uncle Dana would come with their children and maybe friends of theirs from New York; my aunts Phyllis and Nannie filled the house with admirers; so there would be a great mixture of ages and shapes, everyone doing things together. It was fascinating to watch them.

At the foot of Mirador Hill was an old millpond. Mr. Bowen, who built Mirador, was a miller. There my mother's younger sisters Nancy, who was called Nannie, and Phyllis and her youngest brother Buck shot bullfrogs. Grandfather and the older boys shot quail with the two pointers Bob and Tuck over by Avon and Batesville; they often got into trouble shooting over Miss Maria Bailey's land, now Tiverton. On warm September evenings everybody shot the migrating bullbats from the lawn.

Grandfather and all his children were fearless riders. He had them school their own horses from an early age regardless of the danger and would always shout, "Let go its head!" Nannie and Phyllis both rode in horse shows. Nannie used to jump her horse Queen Bee over the high fences in the orchard. I remember seeing Nanere come running out of the house one day crying, "Oh my god, oh my god." Nannie had fallen and was being carried in on a gate. And Grandfather kept hunters and a kennel of hounds for foxhunting. In those days there were only old snake fences, no wire.

Sometimes after breakfast Grandfather would take up his megaphone and call from the front porch to John Pate in the coach house for his horses and everybody would go riding. The grandchildren who came from up North got the good ponies and the good hunters: old reliable Nellie, or Punch, the mean chestnut; Aunt Nora's riding horse was called Dusk. I always got stuck on Pickles the donkey, who had to be beaten going and ran away coming home. The aunts and uncles and their friends rode or went along in the tandems, and Grandfather drove his four-in-hand or rode Blackbird, the five-gaited pacer he hunted on. The big group of us, grandparents, parents, children and guests, would go around our land and over to neighbors' farms visiting and inspecting. Often it was so hot we could only walk or ride at night.

Nancy Perkins' aunt, Nancy Langhorne, as a teenager. Nannie, as she was known, won dressage and show jumping competitions on her horse Queen Bee. She credited her outspokenness as a politician later in life to the fearlessness her father instilled in her as a rider.

Another jaunt was driving to fetch the mail at the station in Greenwood in the late afternoon. Everybody met everybody there, so the three-mile trip up the mountain turned into a social excursion. Near the railroad platform was a weatherboard hotel that had been used as a hospital in the Civil War. Across from there was Mr. Henderson's house. He was the station master and a permanent fixture in our lives. He used to let us watch him taking telegraph messages. Bruce's store was near the station. Every person in the county, white or colored, dealt there because anything at all could be bought there. We adored that store because we could buy hats and dress material, dolls with sawdust bodies and china heads and legs, bags of pink-and-white-striped peppermint sticks to suck lemons through, and all-day suckers on sticks. Mr. Bruce married Miss Dinwiddie, whose father ran the hotel. Mr. Fleming was Mr. Bruce's clerk. He bought one acre of land on Yellow Mountain and built a little shack for himself that housed a life-sized portrait of his grandmother.

A longer trip we would take was from Mirador to see my Uncle Keene, who lived in Buckingham County. It meant that we drove over the foothills of the Blue Ridge and crossed the James River. It was such rough terrain we had to have two horses pulling the spring wagon and a colored driver. We used to call one part of the road "Devil's Acre." All the roads in Virginia were bad in those days; there weren't even hard roads in Charlottesville. As we drove along you could look across to the mountain on the other side and see little white cabins where the poor whites lived. They saw so few people they'd come out to wave.

Phyllis, the fourth Langhorne sister, jumping a gate at Mirador. She was as cavalier on horseback as her father, and after moving abroad, she was considered one of the finest horsewomen in England.

We'd spend the night at my Uncle Buck's, who lived three miles from the James River at a farm called Greenfield that Grandfather had given him, then start off again the next day to the river, where horses, carriage and family crossed on a log ferry poled by colored men. The country on the other side of the James was quite different. It was flat, no longer the cool hills and the mountains, and it seemed to me that we'd drive for hours and hours through thick woods, surrounded by huge oak trees. That sort of country doesn't exist anymore.

There were no televisions or radios or cars then; people entertained themselves and each other and were extremely hospitable and generous. Families had "at home" days once a week. We had Wednesday at Mirador; the Browns from Baltimore who came down for the summer had Monday. You'd have to drive or ride to them, so out came Grandfather's four-in-hand. We'd play tennis and croquet; there'd be ice cream and cake and watermelons and iced tea. The Lees at Bloomfield had a day; they were from Philadelphia and were also in Virginia just for the summer.

The Lamberts from St. Louis had a place like Mirador. Mr. Lambert's wife was a Virginian. When she died, her sister raised her children. The Lamberts originally came from Staunton, then he went out to St. Louis and discovered Listerine, something to do with Lord Lister. They came for the summer with eight children, a Lambert to match every Langhorne. Bunny Mellon's father was one of the Lambert boys.

When I was little, most afternoons the grown-ups would play tennis on the grass court in back of the house. The court was at an odd angle to catch the right light, and it had a tree practically in the middle of one side, but whenever anyone complained about it, Grandfather would tell them if they weren't good enough to avoid the tree they shouldn't be playing. The court's tall wire fence was covered with sweet honeysuckle vine, which had a delicious scent but also ate tennis balls. If they didn't play tennis, they sat under the wonderful old sugar maples, where they rocked, did their fancy sewing and talked to whichever neighbor had dropped by.

The grandchildren had an enormous yard and garden to play in. On the other side of the house from the maple trees was a huge hemlock tree, where we all skinned-the-cat, turning inside-out somersaults low to the ground. Next to the hemlock was a huge oak. The roots of it made wonderful doll's houses for our paper dolls. Both of those trees are gone now from being struck by lightning.

It was so hot in the summer all of the grandchildren used to run around in drawers and underbodies. Button-down drawers. There were so many grandchildren they used to put little pink bows on the girls' underbodies to tell the girls from the boys. The first was my brother Chillie. Aunt Irene and Uncle Dana Gibson had Babs and Langhorne, and Nannie had Bobbie Shaw with her first husband. Me, Bobbie, Babs and Lang were all about the same age. The next batch was my sister Alice and the three boys Aunt Phyllis had with Reggie Brooks. Uncle Buck had two children; Phyllis had three more with her second husband, Bob Brand; Nancy had one daughter and five sons in England with Waldorf Astor, her second husband; and Nora had two children with Paul Phipps.

The family always ate in the dining room, although the children had their supper before the grown-ups had theirs. All the grandchildren were crazy about finding a turkey egg in the afternoon because then you could have it scrambled for supper. And I remember never getting the breast of the chicken as a child: The adults always told us the dark meat was the best part.

After supper I was put to bed in the cottage. Liza Pie would sit out on the porch smoking her corncob pipe. I always had a jar of fireflies that I'd caught next to my bed as a night light, and I would try to fall asleep listening to my grandparents, parents, aunts, uncles and their guests on the front porch of Mirador. They would be waiting, all dressed in their evening clothes, for their supper. Grandfather would always say "God bless us" whenever a meal was announced by the butler, no matter where he was at the time. If I was still awake later I would hear the doors open when they were finished, and they would all come back out to the porch, where one of my uncles would play the banjo, Aunt Nora would play the guitar and they would all sing together in close harmony. They'd laugh and laugh and tell stories and play games. One game they all played together was called Truth. One would ask another an embarrassing question and the other was obliged to answer truthfully. "Do you think Mary has a pretty face?" "No." "Do you think she's a liar?" "Yes, I do." There would be more laughter and sometimes tears, but in the end everybody made up. It sounded like such fun.

On quieter nights sometimes I heard Mr. Goodlow's hounds in the mountains above Mirador. It was a lovely sound. In the summer when it was too hot to exercise the hounds, he'd let them loose at dusk. I lay in bed going to sleep listening to them barking way up in the mountains.

Nancy Perkins in the foreground of a Mirador group portrait, which included her brother, Chiswell Perkins, on the far left and her uncles Harry and Buck Langhorne to the far right. Nancy said, "When I was growing up in Virginia, a gentleman always wore a jacket. Even on the hottest summer day he would sooner take off his trousers than his jacket."

Mirador was a clearing in the wilderness, a tiny corner of order carved out of the foothills of the Blue Ridge and the vast, tree-covered western Virginian landscape. The name Mirador meant, to all who visited, a home, a farm, a family, inseparable, one from the others. The brick house, a picture of classical refinement, was at the center of a civility that radiated outward over the land like ripples in a lake, diminishing as it traveled away from its source. Mirador was most formal in the dining and drawing rooms. Just a few paces outside of the house, although still buttoned up in jackets or dresses that swept the ground, the family and their friends sat relaxed on steps or the ground, with hounds, tongues hanging out, stretched at their feet. The mown lawns gave way to longer, tougher grass the farther they were from the house; the longer the grass, the more alive it was with the perpetual din of crickets and bees. To the west, the trees thickened abruptly and Humpback Mountain shot up. To the east, footpaths led downhill to the millpond; a footbridge traversed the stream, and tall shade trees, willows and oaks, surrounded the pond. Beyond the lawns, the gardens, the paddock and the outbuildings, Mirador's fields, pastures and orchard reached right up to where this bastion of civilization stopped, to where clearing had ceased and the hard Virginian countryside remained untouched and unpredictable.

Grandfather was very much the kingpin at Mirador and in the lives of all his children and the grandchildren. He was a huge presence. When all of us grandchildren were talking together once, somebody asked who we would most like to see in heaven. One answered for us all when she said, "Umpty, then I'd feel safe." He cast a very large shadow. Nancy Astor's strong outspokenness and teasing sense of humor came from Grandfather. She was the most like him. Some of it rubbed off from him, and some of it must have come from being one of five daughters competing for his attention. Irene's sensitivity and grace came from Nanere, but her confidence and ease with people were inherited from Grandfather.

He had a charm and a strength that drew people to him. Everybody at Mirador, in Greenwood or in Richmond, all of the family or the people who worked for him, always sat up in his presence. They came to him for advice and help. He had that sort of effect on people. Even when I was a little girl I sensed the respect and admiration he commanded; one somehow knew it was a particular privilege to be his grandchild.

We loved Grandfather, but we also respected his ire and stepped quickly when he called and quietly when he napped. This didn't mean he was overly stern; in fact, his wit, his sense of amusement, his love of fun, are what stand out about him. He was just never a saccharine or doting sort of man. You always knew where you stood, and you knew he was behind you, but there was never any "Come here, my dear, pretty, little girl." It was always "Come here, you little devil you," or even "Get over here." And you went. He never pampered us. We used to have to rub his head or fan him with a big palm fan while he napped in the hall in the afternoon. We thought it was frightfully funny to see a fly try to walk across his head, and we'd start to giggle. He'd say, "Go on out on the porch and finish your laugh, then come back." If we got tired and tried to sneak off before he was done with us, he'd snap, "Where are you going?"

He was an active man, even in his later years, and was always the center of things: the riding, the hunting, teaching us how to break our own horses, picnics and outings. He set the pace. He was particularly partial to four-in-hands. He could be spirited at the reins.

Once he upset all his grandchildren in one while driving to the Charlottesville Horse Show. Another time he upset one over Mechum River Bridge, and a friend of his who had come to spend a week stayed at Mirador invalided for six months.

Chiswell Langhorne—known as Chillie by his peers, Dab by his wife and Mr. Langhorne, Colonel Langhorne or Sir by everyone else, including his children and grandchildren (except Babs Gibson, who called him Umpty)— was born in Lynchburg in 1843 into the bosom of Virginia's gentry, the son of a prosperous miller. His full name was Chiswell Dabney Langhorne, after his mother's father, Chiswell Dabney, a descendant of Cornelius D'Aubigny, an Englishman who emigrated to Virginia in 1649. Birth and blood contributed a good part to the measure of a man in antebellum Virginia: Chiswell Langhorne's lines stretched long and straight, with plantation owners, governors, members of the House of Burgesses and Colonial Army officers in his ancestry. And his upbringing was steeped in Old Dominion traditions: A decade and a half before the Civil War, there was little reason to believe things would ever change in Virginia. Raised in the same rural, rough-and-tumble fashion as were the six previous generations of Langhornes and every other Virginian gentleman of his day, he was mammied and served, though hardly spoiled or softened. His people grew tobacco and presided over large, self-sufficient estates. They owned slaves. They lived simply and comfortably in shaded houses with graceful Georgian furniture and family portraits, married other Virginians of the same class and ate like kings from their own livestock or from the wild game they shot for sport on their land. Gun in hand, Virginians stalked abundant rabbit, deer, partridge, pigeon, quail, geese and bear. Many kept packs of hounds to chase fox in autumn and early winter. As a rule, Virginians were excellent horsemen who rode as much for amusement as for transportation. Langhorne's grandfather, who owned a plantation just outside Lynchburg, taught him to school his own riding horses; he remained an exceptional horseman until well into his seventies.

My grandmother Nanere ran Mirador, but it was Grandfather who ordered the special Virginian delicacies that he loved. He was a tremendous gourmet. He knew a lot about food and how it ought to be cooked. Whenever he had Virginia spots, he'd invite neighbors around for supper. Uncle Harry would come for supper and always say under his breath, "Another miracle of the loaves and fishes." He thought his father was peculiar when it came to hospitality.

Grandfather was fond of terrapin from Baltimore and Spanish mackerel; I liked the mackerel better because it didn't have as many bones. When Captain Mickey brought the oysters up from the

Chesapeake on Saturdays, he also brought up a quart of oyster crabs. You can't get oyster crabs now because they open the oysters by machine, but in those days they were opened by hand and in them they found tiny pink crabs not much bigger than fleas that would crackle when you ate them. They were cooked in sherry and cream or crisped, and you'd have them over waffles. Oh god, they were good.

We also had delicacies like pickled watermelon rinds and black bean soup. Nanere was famous for her Virginia ham: They cut it like smoked salmon, frightfully thin. Grandfather made something called garlic sherry. He'd take a bottle of sherry, fill it full of garlic and leave it for a time until the garlic got into the sherry. He'd put it on soups and greens. And he ate joel, which was pig's face, with turnip salad. Grandfather was mad about squirrels' brains, too: He always said they were a great delicacy. There was a colored man at Mirador whom Grandfather gave shot to to go out and shoot squirrels for him.

Before luncheon Grandfather would allow us sips of cherry bounce to give us an appetite. If he had friends around he made mint juleps on the sideboard in the hall. He was famous for these. The ice was wrapped in a napkin and beaten into snow with a hammer. They drank them under the trees. We children carried the empty glasses into the pantry and, no matter what mustache had been there before us, sipped the remains to taste the sugar and the mint in the bottom of the glass.

Grandfather was devoted to hospitality, and he always shared what he had. He once told me that Southern hospitality started because people lived deep in the country, separated from each other by miles and miles of impassable roads. They were so lonely that when they saw people going by they'd say, "Damn it, stranger, stop and have a drink or I'll shoot you." Nobody had cars, so nobody got out much. Other than "at homes" you never had arranged parties. But if people dropped in—the door was always open—what you had for supper was good enough for them, you just put more water in the soup. It was why people always came back to Mirador. Lord Antrim's son, Angus McDonnell, came to dine at Mirador once, and as he left, Grandfather said, "I hope you'll come again." Angus replied, "I think I will . . . next week." He did. Algy and Ned Craven from Northamptonshire used to come almost every night to Mirador for supper; a lot of young Englishmen were sent out to Albemarle County in those days because it was good fruit-growing country.

Virginians are brought up to pull their own weight; we were always told by Grandfather it was self-conscious to be shy. If you are asked to a party, you must try and add something to the party. Believe you me, Virginians have been pulling their own weight and boring people since the day they arrived from England. It is a thing ingrained in most of us that you must throw your hat over the fence and try to make it an enjoyable time. You can't just sit back and expect to be entertained. When my cousin Charlotte Noland came to visit me at Kelmarsh in the 1920s to hunt, she never stopped talking. She was still pulling her own weight.

Chillie (pronounced "Shilly"), raised in the twilight of the Old Dominion, possessed all the attributes of the perfect Virginian gentleman. Full of zest and zeal, polite yet plainspoken, he was stalky, athletic and quick to smile. As a boy he had the proper amount of disdain for book learning; the huge Virginian landscape was his for a playground, untouched beyond the acres put to plow. He was as free as a bird in the woods and hills, scrambling alongside rivers, through briars, up trees and over rocks. This idyllic boyhood ended abruptly, however, at the news of the abolitionist John Brown's raid at Harper's Ferry, Virginia, in 1859. A chapter of Chillie's legend in the eyes of his children and grandchildren began with his quickstep march into the Lynchburg Home Guard at the age of sixteen. The Home Guard, together with the Fincastle Rifles, the Rockbridge and Alleghany Regulators, the Rough and Ready Rifles from Fauquier County and a few other companies, formed the 11th Virginia Infantry.

Chillie saw action at the first battle of Manassas. Then the 11th Infantry, serving under Generals James Longstreet and A. P. Hill, fought in the Peninsular campaign at Williamsburg and Seven Pines; supported Stonewall Jackson at Gainesville; and was at Antietam, the most horrific battle of the war. While Mr. Langhorne never talked to anyone but his fellow veterans about his days in the Confederate Army, his family knew that one battle in particular affected him for the rest of his life. The 11th was under the command of General George E. Pickett at Gettysburg, where his company's attack ranks with the Charge of the Light Brigade as a notoriously suicidal maneuver. But Chillie missed the battle of Gettysburg: He had been sent back to Virginia a few days earlier to recuperate from a severe bout of carbuncles. Each of his children visited Gettysburg with him at one time or another, and each came away with the same feeling: Mr. Langhorne believed he had missed his fate that day.

Grandfather was the cock of the walk in Greenwood. In church on Sundays he sat in the third pew instead of the first because he

liked to signal to the parson if the sermon was too long or to the
choir if the music was too slow. He also chewed tobacco in church
and kept a cuspidor in the third pew. The parson was never very
pleased with Grandfather's chewing because Grandfather would spit
during his sermon and the parson would have to pause mid-
sentence. Grandfather always said he'd damn well chew his tobacco
whether the parson liked it or not. Once he wanted to hunt his pack
of hounds on a day a local man was supposed to be buried. Grandfather had the funeral postponed. But he did have a beautiful
singing voice, so he sang out the hymns on Sunday, and he always
supported the church.

Buying Mirador—the large, genteel plantation and plantation house—
was a victory over considerable odds. Mr. Langhorne's family, along with
most Virginians, had been left very poor by the Civil War. He told a friend on
the porch at Mirador years later, "There was nothing left of the old
life . . . the country was decimated; there was practically no stock of any kind
on the farms, neither horses, mules, cattle or sheep; they were using parched
corn for coffee, if they could get it." Of his own predicament he added, "I had
nothing but a wife, two children, a ragged seat to my pants and a barrel of
whiskey."[1] And no prospects. None existed in 1865.

Family legend continued that Mr. Langhorne talked his way into prosperity over the next twenty-five years, cajoling a living out of destitution. His
father's mill, Chillie's legacy, was a ruin; it had been a hospital for the four
years of the war. But he possessed his "gift of gab." He was the sort of man
who could make people do things they might not otherwise do, by sheer force
of personality, magnetism and pure charm. People wanted to get close to
Chillie Langhorne, to give him what he wanted; and he could be trusted,
because he came through with what he promised. His children inherited that
quality from him. His middle daughter, Nancy, turned it into votes and a
long, active career in the British House of Commons; his youngest, Nora,
could make you feel as though you were the only person on earth and
received over fifty wedding proposals—two of them in one day. His son Buck
was eulogized as the most popular man in Virginia of his day. Mr. Langhorne
was confident, curious, universally attractive and, most important, the same
to everyone, rich or poor, young or old. Nothing seemed put on. His temper
and barbed teasing just made him all the more appealing.

After attempts to support his family through door-to-door sales and auc-
tioneering—desperate steps for a Virginian gentleman—he finally built a substantial fortune through railroad contracting. He was no engineer, didn't own
a steam shovel or tractor, but he convinced investors he knew the men who

Nanere with her youngest child, Nora. Nancy Witcher Keene was the daughter of Virginia State Senator Colonel Elisha Keene and grew up on a plantation in Pittsylvania County. She married Chiswell Langhorne at the age of sixteen in the last year of the Civil War. Her granddaughter Alice Perkins Winn wrote, "From her came the famed beauty of her daughters, their love of gardens . . . a sense of the ridiculous and a basic simplicity" (Winn, p. 10).

could do the work. There was a con man in Langhorne, but a pragmatist as well. He embraced the possibilities of a new South and "Yankee notions" of progress; he recognized that the bitterness that mired most of Virginia couldn't put a roof over the Langhorne family's heads. His loyalty to his background and the "Lost Cause" never quit him—his children, his manners and Mirador attested to that—but he recognized faster than most that survival demanded assimilation, rather than an obsession with what was irretrievable.

Grandfather was someone I counted on, listened to and trusted. It was Grandfather who saw that Alice and I were taken care of after Mother and Father died. He saw to it that one of our aunts took us in. When I was older, before I was married, I would come and stay with him in the summer. I would sometimes go into Charlottesville to meet a beau or spend the afternoon, and often I'd stay quite late. Because I was terrified of the two-mile journey in the dark, Grandfather would have to send someone to the station for me. Whenever

I was late I used to bring him calves' liver, which he loved, from the butcher. "I brought you some calves' liver, Sir." He didn't fall for that, though; he was on to me.

I'm named for my Grandmother Langhorne, Nancy Witcher Keene. We called her Nanere. She was small like my mother, very beautiful, with wonderful little feet, marvelous blue eyes and a little bang. Nanere and Grandfather complemented each other. She was much quieter than he, but she had a very funny sense of humor like Grandfather. When Grandfather got too rambunctious once, she said to him, "I had a dream last night. I dreamt that a young lady came to me and said, 'I'm going to marry Mr. Langhorne. Can you tell me what I should wear?' I answered, 'Knowing the gentleman as I do, I suggest sackcloth and ashes.'" This got roars of laughter.

Nanere never really wanted to have children, she hated it, but she had twelve babies for Grandfather and eight survived. Her children all adored her, and each of the eight thought they were her favorite. She was always shielding the boys from Grandfather's quick temper and strictness; the girls didn't need her help with him because they each had her beauty and charm. All eight of her children, they spanned a number of years, had strong personalities and were entirely different.

Nanere also hated the idea of leaving Richmond to live in the country at Mirador. She had spent her entire childhood at Cottage Hill, a plantation in Pittsylvania County, but had grown to love the city and all her neighbors in Richmond. When they did move, though, Nanere made Mirador the place it was, decorating it, running the house, gardening.

The house emitted an air of stateliness and dignity without being stuffy or exaggerated. It stood erect and confident, a redbrick Rock of Ages against the hazy gray backdrop of the mountains, its line simple if not severe. Wooden shutters, twinned pillars supporting the portico, and the carved cornice saved Mirador from spartan austerity; without this minimal elaboration, all that was left was a cold, clean box. It was virtually as tall as it was wide, its windows and doors perfectly symmetrical and its walls capped by a hipped roof. Mirador was of a standard in Virginian architecture from the early nineteenth century Federal style, which mimicked in miniature houses built a century or so previously for the landowning gentlemen of England. In Virginia, however, as opposed to England, sunlight and cool breezes were priorities and influenced architecture almost as much as the promotion of the owner's

Chiswell Langhorne
and Irene, his second
daughter

status. The brick was pierced to let in fresh air—the doorways and windows
made large and wide, and the doors crowned with fanlights. Yet these varia-
tions never compromised the house's sturdy appearance.

Mrs. Langhorne decorated the house in the heavy fabrics and dark woods
fashionable in the late nineteenth century, solid as the house itself. All of the
dining room furniture—a table long enough to accommodate the whole family, the chairs, the sideboard, the corner cupboards for china—was made of
mahogany. Moved upstairs from the basement, where it had been in the original house, the dining room was in one of the new wings. It led into what was
called the back parlor, where an upright piano Irene and Nora Langhorne
played stood between the two windows and was draped in the same fabric—
cretonne with a bird-of-paradise pattern—as the curtains.

The sitting room was in front of the back parlor, to the right of the front
door. Mr. Langhorne had the wall dividing the room from the hall pulled
down to open the room up to the draft from the front door, replacing it with

thick velvet curtains that could be pulled in winter to keep the warmth from the fireplace in. Here again Mrs. Langhorne used Victorian furniture. She placed a "Napoleonic style" mahogany sofa with huge carved feet between the windows. To the left of the fireplace was a "half-a-sofa." **It was as if you took a typical Victorian sofa with curving arms and a high back and cut it in two. You leaned on its very high back and you could put your feet up, like a** *chaise longue*. **It was frightfully comfortable and everybody in the family always fought for it.** In the middle of the room opposite the fireplace she placed a table, with a stuffed leather chair on either side.

There's a picture of me in the wood-paneled library with very short hair that my brother, Chillie, took when I was about seven years old. I had got bugs in my hair from Fanny Brody. Fanny Brody used to bathe me when I was a child. She was madly in love with Stewart Wood, who became our butler at Mirador. One day she said to me, "If you hurry up I'll give you this pin I have"; she was in a rush to get finished so she could see Stewart. She'd bought the pin at the store in Greenwood; it looked like a strawberry with strawberry leaves. So I hurried up and she put the pin in my hair. Back then I had a tremendous lot of hair, long, curly, golden hair. My mother used to cut great wedges out of it to give her friends for Psyche knots. So Fanny pinned it up with this strawberry pin she had taken from her naps. Because Fanny had bugs I got them too. Our doctor in Richmond sent up this colored woman, who shaved all my hair off and wrapped my head in a cloth soaked in kerosene. I remember that distinctly. That awful summer. I wasn't really decent again until about the time of my seventh birthday, in September. All summer long, every week, that kerosene was wrapped around my head like a turban. They were very careful.

The downstairs rooms opened onto the wide, cool hallway where Colonel Langhorne rested every afternoon in high summer on a black-leather-covered sofa. Within arm's reach was the megaphone he used to call down to his coachman. This hall was more than a passageway; the Langhornes used it, and Mrs. Langhorne decorated it, as another room. She hung framed prints of Napoleon on the walls; her father-in-law had collected them, fancying a resemblance between himself and the emperor. Opposite the leather sofa was a mahogany table with a basket filled with the Mirador orchard's lady apples, and farther down, near the stairs, was a sideboard where Mr. Langhorne mixed his mint juleps. Above the sideboard hung an elk trophy with a child-sized Confederate cap stuck on its horn. A carved wooden rocking chair with lemon-shaped knobs, another spot where Chillie waited out hot afternoons in the shade, rested near the back door. Just inside the back door, a telephone was mounted to the wall, a great luxury in rural Virginia. The party line rang two longs and a short for Mirador.

Opposite the sitting room was the spare room. Mirador's guests slept there in the four-poster bed in which Mrs. Funsten—the previous owner of the house and the daughter of the Colonel Bowen who built Mirador in 1825— had died. **Her ghost haunted guests in the spare room. It used to slap their faces in the middle of the night or pull off the bedcovers.** When Charles Dana Gibson, the New York illustrator, came to court Irene Langhorne, the Virginian beauty, he slept in the spare room. Perhaps because the house was full at the time, but more likely because an old-school Virginian father was livid that his favorite daughter was falling for a "Yankee house painter," as Chillie called him, Gibson found himself sharing Mrs. Funsten's bed with Lilburn Myers, who had also come to court Irene. **No one in Virginia thought anything of that sort of arrangement. People had been sharing beds in crowded houses since the beginning of time. But Uncle Dana, being a Yankee, was horrified.**

The four unmarried Langhorne daughters lived in the four bedrooms on the second floor of the house. Three of the rooms had high, plaster-decorated ceilings, large windows on two sides of the house, fireplaces and draped four-poster beds. In the cooler months Callie, the housemaid, crept into the rooms in the early morning to clean the fireplace grates and lay a new fire so the rooms would be warm when the girls awoke; a hired man kept the wood baskets filled. Guests or grandchildren slept in the upstairs rooms when one of the daughters was away. Smaller bedrooms for the Langhorne boys were in one of the new wings, below Mr. and Mrs. Langhorne's own bedroom, bathroom and sitting room. These rooms, as well as the estate office, which could sleep a guest or two, had windows facing the garden and the Blue Ridge.

Mirador was pretty much self-sufficient. Getting supplies was still a chore because there were few shops and a great distance to get to them, so most things were grown and cured right there. There was a storeroom at Mirador for flour and sugar and coffee . . . things they didn't make; I remember that my grandmother carried the key to it on a very long chain. Whenever she went to the storeroom all the grandchildren followed her down in a line. We wanted the little sponge cakes she had in there. She'd take Aunt Ann Brody, who was the cook at Mirador, and give out the flour and the sugar, and then she'd lock the door again.

At Mirador they used to make their own soap from lye. They made jams and pickled fruits and vegetables; they butchered their own pigs. Pig killing was somewhat of an event. They'd put the hams and the bacon in the smokehouse to cure, and they'd make

Mirador's indoor and outdoor staff at the turn of the century included Aunt Ann Brody, the Langhornes' cook, pictured second from left, and her daughter Fanny, a housemaid, standing next to her. The oldest Mirador servants had been born slaves, while those younger were the children or grandchildren of slaves.

sausage meat from what was left. The colored people who worked for us would come and take the fixin's; they'd get their share. They got the feet.

The Langhorne place was a stage setting as much as anything else, an almost fantastic combination of the past and the present. The welcoming house and its beautiful surroundings embodied Mr. and Mrs. Langhorne's nostalgia for the simplicity, surety and enchantment of the Virginia they had known as children, rather than of anything they had discovered in the late nineteenth century. As soon as they could afford to, the two of them took their sons and daughters and leapt backward to what they remembered as a better moment. The rooms of Mirador, decorated in the contemporary, Victorian manner, were somewhat richer than others of the same era, instilled as they were with memories of the dreamlike time and culture made extinct a quarter-century before by the Civil War. The children's and grandchildren's generations brought a vitality of their own to Mirador, but the lives they all

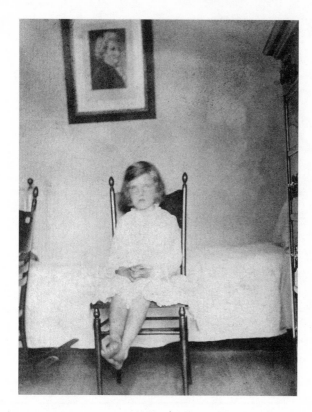

Nancy Keen Perkins at Mirador on September 10, 1904, her seventh birthday

lived there were very much set in motion by the patriarch and matriarch and their generosity and playfulness. Northern-style business practices had made the fantasy possible, not the slavery-driven agriculture of their youth, but the place's spirit came straight from the Old Dominion.

Nanere died suddenly when I was only seven years old. It was a huge blow to everybody, especially Grandfather, who had never even looked at another woman his entire life. She died at the Lynchburg Horse Show one evening, where they had gone to watch Nannie jump her horse Queen Bee. She had had a big dinner party beforehand, and Grandfather said she looked particularly pretty that night, but as she stood up to get out of the buggy she just collapsed. Nanere always said, "If Nancy doesn't stop jumping horses it will be the death of me." What was really sad was that she never got a good chance to enjoy Mirador and her daughters' successes.

I remember being in Richmond when my mother got the telegram. She'd have to go on the Southern Railroad to get to Lynchburg, and the Southern was notorious for accidents. I remember telling her, "Please don't go on the Southern Railroad." But she had to go. She said to me, "We've talked to the engineer and he's going to be particularly careful." And I remember the dress Mother had on—it sounds like a tablecloth to describe it—white linen with embroidered leaves. It was firm over the stomach, a little bustle behind, and she wore a pink sash.

Nanere was the first person I was close to who died. After that, whenever I've heard a train going "ooooooo-oooooo," like the C & O trains through the tunnel by Mirador, I think, "They've got Nanere's body on board." It used to make such a mournful sound. I'd like to have that at my funeral.

Nanere and Grandfather's eight children were my mother Elizabeth, Keene, Irene, Harry, Nancy, Phyllis, Buck and Nora. I never was as close to my two older uncles as I was to my aunts, but both Keene and Harry were as charming and entertaining as their sisters. It must have been easier to have been one of Grandfather's daughters, whom he doted on, than one of his sons, whom he demanded a great deal from and was very strict with. They never had the same large canvas to paint on that their sisters had. The boys stayed at home in Virginia and made a living; men worked in those days. They either went into the contracting business with Grandfather or they farmed. They never went away to live after they got married, as the girls did. Harry and Keene went up in the mountains of West Virginia to build railroads.

I think the real trouble was what my grandfather did with Harry and Keene and later my older brother, Chillie. Instead of letting them drink if they wanted to, Grandfather forbade it and told them he'd give them $1,000 if they didn't drink until they were twenty-one. People drank whiskey in America then, never wine. When they reached twenty-one, Keene and Harry became spree drinkers, dissipated. I think that's a bad thing, to forbid your children from drinking. My children were brought up to take it whenever they wanted to. The Langhorne women never drank, I think because the men went on sprees. My grandfather used to tell them that with all their natural high spirits, if anyone saw them even take a sip they would say they drank. The boys had the same high spirits, and they did drink.

I remember Nanere going to the telephone and answering, "Oh my god, oh my god." If it wasn't Nannie and Queen Bee it was either Harry or Keene on a spree. Keene was the sweeter of the two

Keene was the eldest of the three Langhorne sons. "Once when Keene had earned a lot of money from his contracting business," remembered his niece Nancy, "he went on a spree and hired a whole circus. We had our own circus set up right in Greenwood. Keene went to extremes."

in nature; he was near my mother's age and closest of all the others to her. He had tremendous ability in contracting like his father and was frightfully funny. He once bet he could charm his way across America on one dollar. He did it. He went all the way to California and back on charm alone.

Uncle Harry was very, very clever and handsome, but he had an unkind twist to his tongue that made all us grandchildren jump. He also had TB and couldn't come down from the mountain where he lived. They thought it very contagious. He lived in a little house way up the mountain above Mirador that Grandfather bought him. Grandfather would ride up to visit him, and we would follow on our ponies and wave to Uncle Harry from a distance, but we weren't allowed inside the house. He died from the TB at thirty-three.

I knew the third Langhorne brother, Buck, the best because as the second youngest of the Langhorne children he was still a boy when I was born. At Mirador I used to hear him calling "Oh, Nancy" from across the field, just like he was calling a cow or a dog.

Harry Langhorne with his wife, Genevieve. He was "the handsomest and most intelligent son," wrote Alice Winn. "Harry had his father's fiery temperament without his sense of purpose" (Winn, p. 40).

He called me "Sug" like in sugar. He'd say, "I'll tell you what, Sug, you and me got a little gyp in us. We like going places." *He* liked going places. One of his children was saying the Lord's Prayer before going to sleep once and said, "'Our Father, Who art in heaven' . . . where is our father anyway?"

Buck used to say to me, "Come on, Sug, I'll take you somewhere you've never been before," and he'd take me for days driving through the mountains, up and down dirt roads, telling me stories about people he knew and places he'd seen and showing me old isolated cabins where he'd stayed. Everywhere we went, people knew Buck. He had gone bear hunting with all the mountaineers. Buck was wiry and towheaded. He was handsome like his brothers, and like Grandfather he was considered the most popular man in Virginia in his day.

Despite being thrown out of V.M.I. [Virginia Military Institute], Buck was the only one of Grandfather's sons who made something of himself. He had a beautiful house and a farm in Albemarle

William Henry "Buck" Langhorne, seated between Nancy Perkins and his sister Phyllis. Called the most popular man in Virginia in his day, "Buck could get on chatty terms with a tombstone," said his friend Holman Willis of Roanoke.

County and served on Governor Stuart's staff; Governor Stuart was another cousin. Eventually Buck was elected to the state legislature for a term. When he stood for election, people came from all over the state to vote for him even if they weren't from the county he was running in. He won handily with a distinct campaign style: Whenever asked a pressing question, he answered confidently, "That's a question each man will have to decide for himself." His sister, my Aunt Nannie, who was by then in the British House of Commons, sent a telegram to the Speaker of the Virginia state legislature, whom she knew, that he read aloud to a packed house: "What has

Virginia come to that Buck Langhorne can belong to the Legislature and my Aunt Liz Lewis can't even vote." Aunt Liz Lewis was a rather brilliant sister of Grandfather's who was an early suffragette. Buck was always the brunt of the family's teasing, even then.

One of the Chiswell Langhornes' grandchildren, Michael Astor, described Mirador as "Mr. Langhorne's Circus."[2] Chillie was cast as ringmaster; the Langhorne boys were part of the entertainment, but the main attraction was his daughters, "the beautiful Langhorne sisters of Virginia," as they were known both North and South. The girls were all poised, all petulant and outspoken, all witty and sought after. Elizabeth, the eldest, was only seventeen years younger than her mother, to whom she was "as close as a sister."[3] Lizzie and her mother even had babies at the same time. She was the most old-fashioned, the one from old-school Virginia, like her parents, almost another generation from her sisters. Born one year after the end of the Civil War, she came of age just after the Langhornes moved to Richmond and just before her father made his fortune. She was the only one of the five to marry into another prominent Virginian family, the Perkinses, and the only daughter to remain in the state. Like her sisters, Lizzie was a sight and a presence; as a young woman, she was said to be the most stunning of the brood.

The fame of the family, though, began with Irene, the second daughter; the three youngest Langhorne girls, when their time came, debuted in her shadow. Even on her wedding day and in the preceding engagement notices, Nancy Langhorne was referred to as "the beautiful Irene Langhorne's sister."[4] Everyone who knew Irene testified that she was a glowing beacon who **filled a room with sunlight** every time she entered, be it the small Episcopal church in Greenwood, one of the ballrooms at the White Sulphur Springs resort in West Virginia or the dining room at Delmonico's in New York.

Irene was renowned for her singing voice. **She would exercise it every morning, singing "Ah . . . ah . . . ah . . . ah" with a match clamped between her teeth, just as Jean de Reszke, her voice teacher in Paris, had taught her.**[5] People also remarked on her disarming ease in conversation. But above all, she was majestically beautiful to look at. With her high cheekbones, long neck, cleft chin, thick hair piled atop her head and her pinched figure, she uncannily mirrored the fictitious "Gibson Girls," the unrivaled standard of feminine attractiveness in the 1890s as depicted in *Collier's Weekly* and *Life* magazines.

When Irene was a schoolgirl, newspaper articles declared that a "raving beauty was growing up in Richmond, Virginia, who would become the talk of the country."[6] Irene, May Handy from Richmond, Lela Harrison of Leesburg and Louise Morris of Baltimore were named by Southern writers the "Four

Chiswell Langhorne with three of his five daughters, Phyllis, Nancy and Irene

Graces," the most perfect and "beautiful embodiments of the American Girl."[7] All this publicity infuriated her protective father, who threatened to shoot at least one New York gossip writer. But the predictions came true when, after Irene's debut in Richmond, Mrs. Langhorne was asked if she would permit Irene to lead the Grand March at the Patriarch's Ball in New York, past Astors, Morgans, Winthrops, Fishes, Burdens, Rhinelanders, Cuttings, Roosevelts and other members of New York's Four Hundred. Prior to film stars, debutantes were the darlings of the public's imagination. Descriptions of them, their travels and their nuptial "successes" filled column after column in newspapers and magazines, and young girls fashioned themselves diligently from what they read or what they saw in the accompanying drawings. At eighteen, Irene Langhorne possessed one of the most celebrated faces and figures in the land.

I was closest to Aunt Irene; no one was like Renie to me. Aunt Irene would dive in and look perfectly lovely. It was like sunshine when she came into a room; she lit it up. Very few people have got that. Neither Nancy Astor nor Nora had it, attractive as they were, but Aunt Irene had it. The only other person I've ever known with it was Diana Cooper.

Aunt Irene had golden hair, violet, almost hyacinth eyes, the most beautiful teeth and the prettiest mouth in the world. She had a perfect figure with a tiny waist. I used to say to her, "You hold your bosom as though you're the only person who's ever had one." She was tall, five foot eleven. My mother once said to me, "If I could ask God for one thing, I'd like another foot to my height." Everybody in the family other than Irene was small. I think it's the Irish from the Keenes. My father was tall and used to think it was good breeding.

Aunt Irene was Grandfather's favorite. My mother and Aunt Nancy were too much like Grandfather for him to get along well with them, but Aunt Irene soft-soaped him. Even after she married she wrote him every day. Grandfather had a cousin who lived at Seven Oaks called Marion Langhorne, and the two would sit there at Mirador, these two old men, with tears streaming down their faces as Aunt Irene played the piano and sang, "Silver threads amongst the gold, Darling, I am growing old. . . ."

With Irene's fame came proposals of marriage from society's most eligible bachelors. She received over sixty. The man she did marry and with whom she remained in love her entire life was, in an oblique way, the man who helped "create" her. Charles Dana Gibson, the illustrator, cartoonist and painter, invented the Gibson Girl Irene so closely resembled. Perhaps it was a coincidence; more likely Irene and her sisters were as caught up in the Gibson Girl's allure as every other teenager was. Gibson's fictitious women, whom he "drew with bustled foreheads and posteriors . . . hourglass shapes and peek-aboo waists . . . and archly proper poses, so that young men breathed 'By Gad!,' "[8] became the mannikin of attitude and fashion of the age. The image of the Gibson Girl was so popular she was reproduced on everything from pillowcases to ashtrays and wallpaper. Later a radio used by downed pilots at sea was named for her because of its narrow "waist."

Dana and Irene's wedding was held in Richmond at St. Paul's in Capitol Square, the same cathedral where Confederate leaders worshiped during the war. The couple was the toast of the city, and the wedding like the marriage of royalty. Crowds swarmed around the brand-new Jefferson Hotel on Franklin Street—opened weeks ahead of schedule to accommodate the hundreds of out-of-town guests—to watch the comings and goings of their most lauded belle, her celebrated fiancé and all his glamorous friends from up North who had arrived in Richmond in private railcars. Among the ten ushers were Richard Harding Davis, then managing editor of *Harper's Weekly*; Algy Craven, a friend of the Langhorne family; Lilburn Myers, the former suitor of Irene's; and Harry Langhorne. Nannie and Phyllis Langhorne were maids of honor. Irene wore a gown "of rich ivory satin *en traine*, with high corsage of chiffon and satin sleeves, the shoulders and sleeves gracefully festooned in Renaissance lace of exquisite pattern," reported the November 8, 1895, edition of *The New York Times*, which gave two full columns to the story. "A cluster of orange blossoms adorned the left shoulder. Her tulle veil was fastened by a crescent of diamonds."

Dana Gibson really was the most delightful man. He always used to say, because Irene had so many beaux, "If you've got a songbird, you've got to let her sing." She always had a great many admirers. She had one once who was rather deaf; Uncle Dana said, "It's all right, I can go upstairs to take a nap and leave them alone in the garden and still hear every word they say." And there was Lord Geddes, who was the ambassador from London, who came to stay and was keen on Aunt Irene. When he went back to London after finishing his time as ambassador, Aunt Irene went to see him off at the ship. When Uncle Dana insisted on going too, Aunt Irene said, "Oh, Dana, how could you? I wanted to have a romantic farewell." Uncle Dana said, "Hon, I didn't want you to be disappointed." With all of Grandfather's objections in the beginning, Irene was the only Langhorne sister who married happily the first time.

The Gibson Girl of the magazines remained in vogue right up to the First World War, but she was no longer a figment of Dana Gibson's fantasies. Irene became his living model. After a honeymoon in Europe, which included a presentation to Queen Victoria at Buckingham Palace, the couple moved into a house on East Seventy-third Street in New York that Mr. Langhorne gave them as a wedding present and Gibson's friend Stanford White designed. Their home became a meeting place for American and European socialites, businessmen, writers, artists, architects, actors and Virginians, people from every corner of the couple's eclectic but polite backgrounds. Their summer house on Seven Hundred Acre Island, near Islesboro in Maine, was visited by intimate friends but was mostly reserved for the Gibsons, their three children and other kin.

Aunt Irene kept a beautiful garden, mostly annuals, and used to arrive in early May to supervise its planting. It was enclosed from the wind by a hedge of *arborvitae*, and the beds were set off from the grass paths by white, inch-wide boards attached lengthwise to four-inch stakes. She always had the entrance beds planted with

heliotrope and lemon verbena. The sea air made monkshood, rasp-berries and green peas grow enormous.[9]

After Irene's triumphs there was not much left for the other Langhorne girls to achieve. Nancy, the next daughter, seemed destined to spend her life as "the beautiful Irene Langhorne's sister." On the surface she followed the same course: small private finishing schools, a debut in Richmond, a marriage at the age of eighteen to a Northerner from a good background. But Irene and Nancy possessed entirely different characters, and what suited one so perfectly could never satisfy the other. If Irene was pious and thoughtful, Nancy was downright religious to the extent that at fourteen she followed an English clergyman into the impoverished mountain communities around Greenwood and helped him preach Christianity to the illiterate poor whites. "She knew her Bible," a friend later wrote, "and would on the most untoward occasions quote scripture at us in a manner only she could and not offend us."[10] Whereas Irene held an audience with her glowing aura, Nancy grabbed attention, hitting people over the head with her boisterous temperament and fearless opinions. She was a born showoff with an unquenchable will to shock. Irene gently "soft-soaped" her father, always abiding and fawning; her sister Nancy fought him word for word with a vigor matching his own. Packed into her lovely, small frame was all of her father's explosiveness and confidence, coupled with a sharp mind that tended "none too much along conventional lines, yet [was] always brilliant, alert, witty . . . and made up in natural flash what it lacked in serious training."[11] Nancy did not remain long in the beautiful Irene's shadow.

Bad falls never made Nannie afraid or stopped her from being saucy and cheeky when she competed in the horse shows. She would play to her audience. One thing she would do was jump the gate going out of the ring at the end of her turn instead of waiting for it to be opened. Her greatest rival was Mrs. Allen Potts, who was a neighbor in Albemarle County. She was a Rives, a sister of Princess Troubetzkoy's. At one show Nannie shouted for everybody there to hear, "Wake up your horse, Gertrude, and tell him the show is on." Mrs. Potts's horse, being well-schooled, had quite good manners. But Nannie and Queen Bee were more apt to make the spectators hold their breath.

Aunt Nannie was the only one of my aunts who, when I was young, would make me feel small. The others were all charming and warm, which Nannie could be too, but she was also quick and merciless with her tongue, sparing no one. She'd arrive from wherever she was and I'd have a large bow in my hair, thinking myself fright-

The first time Charles Dana Gibson called on Irene Langhorne in Virginia, he hired a horse and buggy to get him from the train station to the house. While he was paying the driver at the front steps of Mirador, Chiswell Langhorne told him not to bother— "You're not staying." Gibson replied, "Is this what they mean by Virginian hospitality, Mr. Langhorne?" and won a reprieve from the possessive father.

fully stylish, and she'd say, "Oh, look at that silly bow in your hair. It's the tackiest thing I've ever seen. Take it right off." I was deeply offended. I was crazy about hair ribbons.

Like all of my aunts and my mother, Nannie was very beautifully made. She had beautiful bones in her face . . . wonderful bones and figure and shaped legs and all that. She and Aunt Phyllis always kept themselves thin. At Mirador one of the first things that was built was a squash court so they could keep fit. They were tremendous exercise enthusiasts and would don innumerable sweaters to play squash and tennis in. And they both had these belts, like bridles made of canvas, that they'd pull tight around their waists to keep their waists tiny. When they rode they wore smart linen suits, straw sailor hats or Panamas turned up in front, with brown harem-veils to protect their complexions.

After a false start—a brief marriage to Robert Gould Shaw II of Massachusetts—Nancy married Waldorf Astor, the son of William Waldorf

Irene Langhorne, soon after her marriage to Charles Dana Gibson. Her sister Nancy said of her, "From the start she was the acknowledged family beauty, and none of us ever questioned it, and were quite satisfied to be the beautiful Irene Langhorne's sisters" (Sykes, p. 28).

Astor of the New York Astors, who had moved his family to England to set-tle in among its quiet landscapes and its landed gentry. Nancy met Waldorf while she and Phyllis were in Britain foxhunting for the season, on horses they had shipped over from Mirador, living in a hunting "box" rented by their father. For a wedding present, Nancy's father-in-law gave her a tiara with one of the world's largest diamonds, the Sancy, set into its crown. But it was his present to his son that Nancy most coveted and put to good use: Cliveden, Astor's countryseat in Buckinghamshire. A huge Palladian house resting on a rise overlooking the River Thames and surrounded by hun-dreds of acres of pleasure gardens and carriage paths, Cliveden had been variously owned or occupied by the Duke of Buckingham, the Earl of Orkney, Frederick, Prince of Wales, the Duke of Sutherland and the Duke of Westminster before William Waldorf bought it from Westminster in 1893. It was not the most picturesque of English country houses, but Clive-den made up in grandeur what it lacked in poetry. Classical ornaments—urns, pilasters and pedimented windows—accentuated the entrance and garden facades. A formal parterre stretched away from an arcaded terrace

Nancy Astor holding her daughter Wissy while Bobbie Shaw, her son by her first husband, stands next to her. Waldorf Astor holds their son William.

toward the Thames, and antiquities William Waldorf collected from crumbling Italian villas dotted the grounds.

The house, the park and the thirty or so indoor servants, including liveried footmen who powdered their hair and wore yellow stockings, gave the former Miss Langhorne a suitable *mise en scène.* Running such a palace, comparable with overseeing a small corporation, inspired her and proved an ideal outlet for her vitality. The rest is part of twentieth-century English history: Cliveden under the Astors became one of Britain's last "power houses," hosting such guests as King Edward VII and his court; Prime Ministers Asquith, Balfour and Lloyd George and future Prime Ministers Chamberlain and Churchill; colonialists Kitchener and Curzon; heroes Lawrence and Lindbergh; writers Shaw, Kipling and James; painters Sargent and Munnings; and an assortment of sporting men, press magnates, U.S. senators, MPs, Ph.D.'s, debutantes, socialists, communists, evangelists and Christian Scientists, at least one Nazi, and always a Langhorne or two. They all came because of the

Nannie and Phyllis Lang-
horne, dressed to ride

house, the food and the hospitality; they came because of the other guests; they came especially to spar and to laugh with Nancy Langhorne Astor.

This kind of entertaining was a labor of love and second nature to her. She thrived when she had an audience, or was herself the audience of someone who fascinated or amused her. She was curious and quick to assimilate; interested and hungry for experience. "She enjoyed intellectual people and natural talent wherever she met it, and she often enjoyed drawing out some expert on his particular form of expertise . . . ," wrote her son Michael. "[B]ut her view was tempered by her contempt for earnest intellectual people . . . who became so carried away by their knowledge that they ignored what was to her the point of living. . . . The point of life was always to be found out at the point of contact with people."[12] She rarely suffered fools for the sake of being polite or tactful, and liked nothing more than to pull the rug out from under pretensions. This otherwise exceedingly generous hostess kept her guests on their toes.

Nancy's pleasure was also her business. Never completely fulfilled by the role of chatelaine, she had a specific "higher" agenda. "Friday-to-Mondays" at Cliveden and dinners for one hundred in the Astors' London town house in St. James's Square were to her as much platform as social event. Since her days in the mountains with the Episcopal cleric, her concern for people from "the other side" stuck to her conscience. Feminism, suffrage and women's rights were constant themes, but her favorite cause—perhaps a result of her brothers' dissipation—was temperance. Nancy Astor loathed the power that drink had over the people she loved and especially felt for those whom she saw as the victims of drink, the wives and children of drunks. She herself was a life-long teetotaler. To the relief of her guests, however, she did not impose abstinence on them; Cliveden had an excellent wine cellar.

Strong convictions or not, public office was never a consideration for Nancy Astor until circumstances pushed her in that direction. There was no precedent for women in British politics at the turn of the century. Women couldn't vote, let alone run for office; they were wives of politicians and wives of voters. When Waldorf Astor stood for Parliament, his wife dutifully stumped by his side. She rode with him in his landau and sat beside him on the podium in church refectories and village halls. They shared moral and political values, so it was easy for her to speak from the heart on his behalf. Indeed, Nancy threw herself into Waldorf's career as if it were her own and even claimed to have visited more than twenty thousand homes looking for votes before he won a seat for the city of Plymouth in 1910. In campaigning, Nancy found the "point of contact with people" she lived for.

Two coincidental factors led Nancy Astor to stand herself in 1919. The first was the 1918 act of Parliament granting women suffrage. The second was the involuntary termination of Waldorf's career in the House of Commons. In 1916 William Waldorf accepted a hereditary peerage from the king and with it a place on the benches of the House of Lords. In 1919, when the 1st Viscount Astor died, Waldorf, the 2nd Viscount Astor, was obliged by law to take his father's seat in the Lords, precipitating a by-election to fill his vacant Commons seat. Lady Astor, a familiar voice and presence in Plymouth, was chosen as the Conservative Party's candidate to replace him.

Now Waldorf sat by Nancy's side in the carriage and on the podium. Her campaign was simple and direct and appealed to emotion rather than sophisticated political intellect: "If you want an MP who will be a repetition of the six hundred other MPs, don't vote for me. If you want a lawyer or if you want a pacifist, don't elect me. If you can't get a fighting man, take a fighting woman."[13] She made statements the English press termed "Astorisms" as reporters followed her campaign much as they would a general election. "Mr. Gay, the Labour candidate represents the shirking classes, but I represent the working classes."[14] And when faced with an impossibly detailed or politically intricate question she was ill-equipped to answer, she brushed it aside with little damage done. "I am not a paid politician, therefore I can afford to speak the truth and declare straightforwardly: I don't know."[15] Her technique in disarming such situations bore a striking resemblance to that of her younger brother Buck. But she was best when campaigning on street corners, literally standing on a soapbox, improvising before a gathering crowd. Banter was her genius. Hecklers *made* her candidacy for her. When at one stop a loudmouth shouted, "Go back to America," she snapped her return and kept up the volley. "Go back to Lancashire." "I'm an Irishman." "I knew it, an imported interrupter." "If I'd imported you I'd drown myself in the sea." "More likely in drink." "I'm a teetotaller." Nancy had the last shot: "Well go and have a drink today, it might sweeten you."[16] This kind of back-and-forth took place with no microphones, in an age before television enslaved politicians. It won her votes and respect.

It won her the by-election as well. On the first day of December, 1919, Nancy Astor became the first elected woman to take a seat in the British House of Commons, an exclusively male institution for centuries. She kept that seat, winning reelection over and over again, until 1945. In those twenty-five years Lady Astor was famous for her exchanges on the floor with other MPs, especially Winston Churchill, and infamous for her avid support of Neville Chamberlain and his policy of appeasing Adolf Hitler. She was also responsible for writing and seeing through the Commons dozens of bills related to women's rights, child protection and pub laws. She was no quiet back-bench yes-man, and her career was as successful as that of any politician, man or woman.

> **Here was this woman, extremely beautiful, extremely witty and extremely rich, who put everything she had into the House of Commons. It was very important to her. Most people like her spent their time dining out, but she gave up all those years working in the Commons for women and children. It was really quite extraordinary that she pushed all that aside.**

Phyllis Langhorne was only eighteen months younger than Nancy, and when the two were schoolgirls, they were thought of more as inseparable twins than as older and younger sisters. They shared friends, went to the same school—Miss Jennie Ellett's in Richmond—and both rode like the devil, charging sidesaddle across the fields around Mirador spring, summer and autumn, over impossible fences and jumps and up the steep, narrow trails ascending Humpback Mountain. Both were champion eventers as teenagers; decades later, after Nancy had given up hunting for her seat in Parliament, Phyllis was still considered one of the best horsewomen on either side of the Atlantic.

Phyllis expressed all the Langhorne flash in her riding. Besides eventing, foxhunting, the most physically demanding of sports, "gave Phyllis many exhilarating thrills," wrote her niece Alice Winn, "but also some hard knocks, especially when she had a bad fall with the Meadowbrook which compelled her to lie in a New York hospital completely blind, not knowing that eventually her sight would come back after six months."[17] She was hunting again the following season. "When hounds went there were none to excel her, for she allied with beautiful horsemanship that extra touch of quickness, decision and courage which characterizes the brilliant rider to hounds."[18]

On her own two feet, however, Phyllis did not seem a Langhorne. She was as beautiful as her sisters—"Her hair was dark, her eyes vivid and gay, her coloring the most glorious combination of rose and white"[19]—and she could be as witty and biting. But her demeanor was quiet, introverted, even melancholic. "She had a wistful nature," wrote Alice Winn, "for she was made in a minor key. She loved tough little boys and horse-coping men, but as she developed she took to intellectuals and musicians. . . . There was an aura of tragedy and romance around her."[20] While her family and their guests sat on the porch at Mirador singing and flinging gibes at each other, Phyllis stayed in her bedroom cleaning her bridles and stirrups hour after hour or reading poetry. **Everybody in the family thought that very peculiar, that Phyllis liked being alone. She was special, a much gentler person than the other Langhornes. When her younger brother Buck was asked which of his sisters he liked best, he replied, "Phyllis, 'cause she never made me feel small."**

Aunt Phyllis was not beautiful but she was lovely. She wasn't well-made like Nannie, she didn't have those bones. Phyllis had a rather Irish look. She had a rather long upper lip, which none of the Langhornes had. She was more a Keene like her mother. She also had a very long back and rather short legs. But she had the most lovely eyes like my grandmother. And she had tremendous allure for gentlemen. She was very calm and alluring and quiet, not at all like the Langhornes, who were firecrackers.

Following in the footsteps of Irene and Nannie, Phyllis married a Yankee, Reggie Brooks. They had three children, but the marriage didn't last. He was a marvelous golfer and a marvelous tennis player and rather good looking. But he had no responsibility. He was very rich and very idle. His mother would rent a house for them on Long Island so he could play polo or one in Palm Beach in the winter, but that was terrible because they never had their own home.

Grandfather gave Mirador to Phyllis as her share of his estate. Aunt Irene had houses in New York and Islesboro, Nannie was in England by then, Keene had a place in Buckingham County, Harry

was dead, and Buck had his house in Albemarle County, one thousand acres and all that. Grandfather hoped Mirador would settle Reggie down. Of course it didn't. There was nobody for him to play tennis or polo with. Phyllis sat in one room and wept and Reggie sat in another. She eventually got a divorce in New York, where you could be divorced for desertion after three years.

There was no end of men who wanted to marry Phyllis after Reggie. Geoffrey Dawson of the London *Times* wanted to marry her, and both of the Wyndham twins. Mirador was always filled with people attracted to her charm. The great violinist Zimbalist used to stay at Mirador and the pianist John Powell from Virginia. Walter Lippmann was a young man in his early twenties writing and editing for the *New Republic;* he spent a great deal of time at Mirador, as did the other editor Herbert Crowley. Mirador was full of people like that. Phyllis would sit at the piano in the back parlor with her hair all wrapped up in a turban and sing to them.

Before her divorce was final and just before the outset of the 1914 War, Phyllis fell very in love with Henry Douglas-Pennant, who was very handsome and who was a captain in the Grenadier Guards. Like Phyllis, he was a marvelous rider and loved hunting. Her divorce from Reggie was to come through in September and Phyllis was then to marry Captain Douglas-Pennant, but he was killed in France that August. I don't think she ever completely got over him. I remember writing a letter to someone in the family saying "Poor Phyllis, she's too old to ever marry again." Years later, after she married Bob Brand and had two daughters and a son with him, I remember looking out into the garden and seeing our children playing together and saying to her, "Oh, isn't it extraordinary how life is. Look how happy you are now with this young family. . . ." She must have had a nursery for about fifty-five years with all her children. She said, "Yes, it's true . . . but if the Captain came down the mountain I'd leave the lot of them."

She was very happy with Bob Brand, though, whom she married in 1917. He had been frightfully in love with her for years. She once gave me a pound to stay in the room with her so he wouldn't propose to her. "I can't marry him. His eyes are so close together he reminds me of a monkey." But Bob was a brilliant man. He was the younger son of Lord Hampden, a Fellow of All Souls at Oxford and had been one of Lord Milner's "kindergarten" in South Africa. He eventually became a director at Lazard Brothers and Lloyd's and was always in the thick of politics and the government. If I

Chiswell Langhorne gave Mirador to Phyllis as her share of his estate after she married Reginald Brooks; then he moved across the road to a farm called Misfit. He used to check on his old house with a telescope from Misfit's porch "and create angry scenes if Phyllis made any alterations of which he did not approve, which meant all of them" (Nancy Astor quoted in Sykes, p. 171).

were to have a house party and invite a dull relative or friend to stay along with someone else who was brilliant, I can't think of a better person to invite also, to make it a successful mix, than Bob Brand. He was like a clever common denominator. He would be perfect for your most clever and your most dull friends . . . no matter who was there, he'd make them both happy. Bobberty Salisbury was another like that.

I liked Phyllis very much and got on well with her after I moved to England, because we both hunted and we both shot and we had a lot of friends in common. Aunt Phyllis really was a beautiful rider, probably the finest horsewoman in England in her day. And she told me everything about my hunting when I first moved to England . . . how to put my hat on, what lipstick to use—it wasn't salve, it was liquid lipstick—and how my veil ought to look. Phyllis hunted right up until she died; in fact, it was a day out that killed her. She rode one day with the flu and caught pneumonia.

The baby of the family, as Nora Langhorne was thought of all her life by her sisters, was not at all "made in the minor key." She was the "madcap of the Langhorne family,"[21] a free spirit who never really grew up. Nora was born twenty years after her eldest sister, Lizzie, at about the same time Lizzie gave birth to her first child. If the eldest Langhorne daughter was a postwar baby, born into austerity and imbued with the last vestiges of antebellum tradition, Nora was born into the increasingly adventurous age of the Gibson Girl, the Gay Nineties and the prosperous latter years of Mr. Langhorne's railroading career. It was Nora's footprints in the pavement at Mirador.

Nora learned very quickly how to stand out in a family of standouts. Of all the entertainers in Mr. Langhorne's Circus, Nora was perhaps the most gifted. She could play the guitar and the piano and sang beautifully with perfect pitch. She sang to amuse her audience and rarely made it through a verse without giggling infectiously. And she was a natural mimic, carrying around a full repertoire of characters wherever she went. One of the favorites was an imitation of a rural "colored man" like those who worked at Mirador. Using a rough, drawling accent and awkward, stumbling gestures, the character told the audience the Uncle Remus stories all Virginian children grew up with. Nora could easily have gone on stage professionally and maybe become as big a celebrity as Irene and Nancy, but that was not done in her day by a lady of her upbringing. To her, the laughter of her family and friends was enough. Her daughter Joyce Grenfell, however, inherited Nora's charm and talent and did make a career for herself on stage and in films. **If you had an hour to spend with anyone in the world, you'd spend it with Nora.**

Nora had a heart like a hotel. She couldn't see a man without making him fall in love with her. It was sort of a disease. She survived on admiration. She was engaged to three men at the same time once, had each convinced he was the only one until the fiancés all sat down to tell each other the good news about being engaged to Nora Langhorne. One of Nora's beaux was a Spaniard named Soriano, who dressed very smartly and brought a dozen or so pairs of shoes with him when he came to stay at Mirador. Grandfather asked him if he planned to walk back to Spain. Another time Grandfather was

having his bath and a young man came in and said, "Mr. Langhorne, I want to ask you, can I marry Nora?" Grandfather said, "You're the fifth young man who's asked me that this month. If she still loves you two months from now, you can have her."

Nora was only eleven when her mother died, and she was always fawned over by her father and older brothers and bossed by her sisters. Grandfather took her from school to school because she was always unhappy. She was not beautiful like Irene and Nancy, yet there was something entrancing about her. She could make anyone she talked to feel like they were the only person in the world. She was engaging and so interested in whomever she was with at the time. But the minute she turned away, you were forgotten. She very much lived for the moment.

Nora eventually married Paul Phipps, who was a friend of Waldorf Astor's and the same age. He was *the* young man in London and was most attractive and a great gentleman. Very erudite, a very funny sense of humor. His grandfather used to say, "He's a great gentleman but he won't make any money." But Paul turned out to be a very good architect and worked in the Lutyens office with Lutyens, who taught him a great deal.

The Phippses were English, but Paul's mother was a Butler-Duncan from New York, whose family address was One Fifth Avenue when it was a house instead of a block of flats. Paul's mother was very beautiful in her day, and Sargent painted her portrait. When they had the big Sargent exhibition in London, Sargent thought her portrait was the best he ever did, so it was put on the cover of the catalogue. Paul's sister married Miles Lampson, who became Lord Killearn and was the Ambassador to Egypt during the war.

Paul adored Aunt Nora, but Aunt Nora ran off with a Yale football player named Lefty Flynn, who looked like a housemaid's idea of God. Eventually Uncle Dana tracked them down to a bar somewhere in the west, where they were singing together for their supper and living in impoverished bliss, and only got Nora to come home when he told her they were about to be arrested for bigamy, the police just a few steps behind. I don't think either of them knew what "bigamy" meant, though. Years later, at her daughter Joyce's wedding to Reggie Grenfell, Nora heard wedding bells and up and ran away to Lefty a second time and married him.

"But Oh! for a good hot summer at Mirador," wrote Irene Gibson in a letter to her niece Nancy in the late 1930s:

Nora Langhorne was "the gentlest, the most romantically inclined and least premeditating of all the sisters," wrote her nephew Michael Astor. Her "weakness was for falling in love in a somewhat haphazard fashion" (Astor, p. 29).

Lightning Bugs, Frogs singing and a guitar and just that delicious time. We did have so much fun. I was telling Dana about old Mr. Woodward, and Nannie forcing him to sleep on the lawn and he, Mr. Woodward, telling Father how to keep young and agile, gave him an illustration picking up a handkerchief and Father calling him "Damned Old Fool." And Ned Craven lending me the smelly riding gloves to drive old Mr. Woodward in the Kentucky brake cart in case he tried to hold my hand! He did not do that but came out bluntly and asked which I would like, a cottage in Newport or a yacht. . . . He would go to the Bank and return by 11 o'clock and we would be together from then on. How nice! I came home and had hysterics. He put in my hand at breakfast under the table a little note which said, "The dew is on the flowers, etc. etc. Oh! come my love with me." Nora was "Dora," Nannie "Annie," Phyllis "Priscilla."[22]

On the porch at Mirador, Genevieve, Chiswell and Phyllis Langhorne and Buck Langhorne's fiancée Annabel Latimer stand behind Nora Langhorne and her beau Señor Soriano.

Nancy Perkins at her aunt Nora's wedding to Paul Phipps in 1909

What strikes me even now are certain details of Mirador: The contrast between the bright, sunny light on the lawn and the dark shade underneath the hemlock tree. Or when I walked over the pointed gravel in the circle in front of the house in bare feet, trying desperately not to put all my weight on the sharp stones, it was such a relief to reach the grass in the middle. Then there was the catalpa tree. It was one thing to avoid at Mirador because it always had huge furry caterpillars feeding in its leaves. There was the great stone arch and its gate, covered in ivy and the bright red flowers of the trumpet vine. They were so impressive and monumental to me as a child.

I remember once standing on the inside of the gate when two strangers, a man and a woman in linen dusters, pulled up outside in their motorcar. They pulled out a Kodak and took pictures of the house and spoke admiringly of it to me. I felt like the heroine in *The Little Colonel.* I stood stock still and answered their questions with an absolute straight face while waves of pride washed over me. I was on the inside and they were out. I savored every inch of the chasm between us. After a few minutes the two of them drove off again down the red clay road outside our driveway.

When I told Grandfather of the strangers, he gave me a firm berating and a long lecture about Virginian hospitality. He was angry I hadn't invited them in for a cool refreshment on such a hot day, a chance to come into the house and rest. Because that's what Mirador really was—it's what the word *mirador* means—a resting place on the side of the mountain.[23]

"ALWAYS A VIRGINIAN"

I've never stayed in a seat once in my life when the band played "Dixie."

PART ONE

IN THE BEGINNING of the seventeenth century, after Captain John Smith first saw the area where Richmond would one day grow, he wrote, "Heaven and Earth never agreed better to frame a place for man's habitation."[1] Charles Dickens visited Richmond in 1842, and though deeply disturbed by slavery, he too was intoxicated by the landscape's natural beauty. Richmond was "delightfully situated on eight hills, overhanging the James River; a sparkling stream, studded here and there with bright islands, or bowling over broken rocks."[2] During his stay there in early springtime, Dickens was the guest of a local planter. "The day was very warm," he wrote, "but the blinds being all closed, and the windows and doors set wide open, a shady coolness rustled through the rooms, which was exquisitely refreshing after the glare and heat without. Before the windows was an open piazza, where, in what they call the hot weather—whatever that may be—they sling hammocks, and drink and doze luxuriously. . . . The mounds of ices and bowls of mint-julep and cherry cobbler they make in these latitudes, are refreshments never to be thought of afterwards, in summer, by those who would preserve contented minds."[3] Thackeray simply wrote after his trip there that Richmond was a "friendly, cheery little town—the most picturesque I have seen in America."[4]

In 1900, when Nancy Perkins turned three years old, Richmond sat comfortably balanced on the fence between what was and what was about to be. On the one hand, the gentle pace of the nineteenth century lingered into the turn

48

of the twentieth. Its avenues, dotted with grand manors and lined in upright, stiff-backed row houses—some "passing into decay, half-hidden by Mycrophylla roses . . . [with] brick pathways through clumps of daylilies, calycanthus shrubs, poppies, larkspur and violets"[5]—Richmond was framed by classical exactness rubbed smooth by history and softened by every possible hue of green. Horses still drew the town, for the most part; tether posts, mounts and boot-scrapes were standard near every stoop, and streets echoed with metal shoe against cobble and hard dirt. Cocks crowed at dawn from back gardens. Water, piped to many Richmond houses directly from the James, gushed from faucets a light, muddy brown. And neighbors, who treated one another formally with all of the "sirs" and "madams" of proper Virginian etiquette, nevertheless knew each other and each other's goings-on intimately, as their parents, grandparents and more distant Richmond ancestors had.

The gait was quickening, though. Electric trolleys operated as early as 1890 in Richmond—the first in the United States—and telephone lines by 1900. The city had a "skyscraper," the American National Bank Building, on Main Street; a flourishing shipyard on the James, and the largest ironworks in the South. The population was increasing and, at the same time, growing less distinct, the middle class having methodically replaced the old planter class as the town's guiding voice. Richmond had mostly pulled itself out of the ashes of the war of thirty-five years before and had become a gem of that despised Northern dictate Reconstruction. Big business, considered a Yankee aberration in antebellum Virginia, evolved into the cornerstone of the Confederate capital, leaving Richmond with the best of both worlds. The prosperity of industry—newfangled inventions and exhilarating technology—came elegantly clothed in the refinement and gentility of a past era.

One of Richmond's central boulevards and a "preferred residential area" at the turn of the century was Franklin Street, where Lizzie Langhorne Perkins lived with her children, Chiswell, Nancy and Alice. It was a wide, cambered dirt road through a quiet neighborhood: dry and dusty in hot weather, muddy in the winter, and bordered on either side by hundred-year-old linden trees. In the spring the linden flowers painted a vista, east to west, white and yellow, and in the summer branches met from tree to tree, forming huge parasols, a sheltering path like the avenues of Provence. There was sidewalk pavement on either side of Franklin perfect for ambling and strolling, stone crosswalks at each intersection and stone drainage troughs near the curbs just wide enough for children to ride their bicycles in.

The smart area of Franklin Street began at Capitol Square, where Thomas Jefferson's state capitol, a copy of the first-century Roman temple Maison Carrée at Nîmes, had stood since the end of the eighteenth century. In 1900 it still appeared as Jefferson planned it, the wings yet to be added.

Next to the capitol was St. Paul's, the cathedral-sized Episcopal church where Irene Langhorne was married, which was surrounded, like the capitol, with columns, and topped with a Wren-esque spire. Traveling west toward the outskirts of the city, where Franklin eventually faded into a rutted farm track through woods and tobacco fields, the boulevard was crowded with houses and buildings reflecting the Richmond citizenry's traditional preoccupation with articulate and sophisticated architecture and craftsmanship. Set behind Richmond-made wrought- and cast-iron fences, manicured flower gardens and front lawns, stood Georgian, Greek Revival, Federal and Italianate structures, some large, noble and dramatically adorned, others modestly conceived and discreet.

Twelve East Franklin and 110 West Franklin could have been transplanted stone by stone, timber by timber, from plantation estates. Both were huge neoclassical houses with two-storey, column-supported porticoes dominating thin street facades. The Haxall House, at 211 East Franklin, was built two years before the outbreak of the Civil War by the owners of the largest flour mills in the South, relatives of Moncure Perkins, Nancy's father. It was Italianate and gaudy, a style then in vogue, and had only a small, single-storey portico. Georgian and Federal row houses filled the spaces between mansions, like Linden Row on the 100 block of East Franklin. The spartan-looking town house at 707 East Franklin—its only superficial decoration shutters and a shallow porch—contrasted sharply with its grand neighbors, but every Richmond schoolchild knew that it was the house where Mrs. Robert E. Lee lived during the Civil War and the house the general came home to after Appomattox.

The interiors of these and other Richmond houses paralleled the variety of architecture. The newer houses, built or bought as a result of recent success, could be heavy and opulent, full of dark woods, plush overstuffing, busy wallpaper and fashionable but useless objects, all trimmed in velvet; the rooms were claustrophobic, the way the Victorians liked them. A "French boudoir" influence found its way to some of these Richmond houses as well. Because their owners could afford it, many such houses were fitted with central heating and electricity. The scattered survivors of the Old Dominion, however, barely hanging on in houses their forebears built, lived among an earlier generation's finery: plain painted walls, family portraits, fruitwood furniture, clean, spare and elegant, charged with history and tall tales. These homes often relied on a fireplace—carved to resemble one by Adam—for heat and were still lighted by oil, gas and candlesticks. Their steps were sloped with use. Magnolia trees grew higher than their roofs, filling the second-floor bedrooms with the languid scent of their blossoms in the spring. Wisteria and honeysuckle draped columns and ironwork; foxglove and roses overran the gardens.

Our house on Franklin Street was of little distinction outside—
in fact, it was hideous—but inside it was very comfortable and very
chic for the day. Instead of the then fashionable heavy Victorian furniture, my mother had a collection of antiques. She was mad about
what you call Colonial furniture, which is really mahogany and Virginian walnut furniture made for houses in the deep South. Furniture was her root and passion. My father would say, "Why must we
have all this furniture in the house?" She would reply, "I'm getting
ready for my house in the country." She always wanted a house in
the country. It was going to be pink or blue.

My mother was before her time in all her tastes. She painted or
papered her rooms in tones of off-gray. One range of color throughout the house made it seem larger than if the rooms were all different colors. And all the doors were painted in two tones of the same
color—an innovation at that time. Instead of lace curtains, which
were fashionable then, she was one of the earliest people to use flowered cretonne as curtains. One of my first recollections was seeing
her seated on the floor inventing brown paper patterns for pelmets
and fearlessly tackling yards of material with a large pair of scissors.
The fact that she had never sewn a thing until after she was married
didn't slow her down at all. She was also adamant about not having
ceiling or wall light fixtures. Electricity was new in Richmond then.
The street lamps were still gas, and a man had to come around at
dusk with a ladder and light them, and most houses were still lit
with gas. Mother had electricity put in on the ground floor of our
house but would only light the room with table lamps. That was
ahead of its time.

Mother was able to do all these things despite the fact that she
and Father had no money at all. They had only £2,000 to bring us
up with, yet the house was beautiful and I went to school in France
and had the chicest clothes of anybody in Richmond. The clothes I
wore didn't come out of the budget; they were all sent down by my
aunts and their friends to give to the mountain people around
Mirador, but they never got further than me. I was extremely well-
dressed. I became engaged to Henry Field in a dress belonging to
Mrs. Rafe Thomas, who was later Mrs. Cole Porter. We also had
three excellent colored maids despite having no money. We had a
nurse, a housemaid and a cook. Beds were turned down, clothes were
put out and all the meals were cooked. Everything was done for us.

Our first cook was Maria Woods, who was with us as long as I
can remember. Louise Dense was our cook after her. Louise and her

sister were also with us for years. Louise used to have to go to my mother for the key to the stockroom if she needed anything. Like Nanere, Mother kept the keys on a long chain. It was rather a throwback to the days when house stores were kept locked away because they were so hard to come by. All the flour, butter, lard, bacon, sausages, meat and sugar. But unlike Nanere at Mirador, Mother didn't always escort Louise to the storeroom; she often gave her the key and let her go on her own. I've often wondered why she even bothered with the key. I imagine it was because it was the way things had been done in Virginia for generations.

During the Civil War men and matériel headed toward the front along Franklin Street. General Longstreet's "walking cavalry" passed down the avenue, and Jeb Stuart and his cavaliers rode out Franklin to defend the Confederate capital from McClellan. Later in the war Stonewall Jackson's casket was borne up Franklin, and after the surrender and burning of the city, "vagabond processions of . . . scalawags celebrated the capture" of Richmond up *and* down Franklin.[6] Four decades after the war, however, the avenue was again firmly in Virginian hands, with most of the same sweltering, sweet-smelling aura of the antebellum town restored for at least one more generation. On an average day only a smattering of traffic broke the silence underneath the linden avenue. Purveyors and farmers in covered wagons called on residents with eggs, watermelons, quail and wild duck, or oysters from the bay. Horses stood tethered to their posts, swatting flies with their tails. Housemaids in aprons and caps swept the steps and the pavement in front of houses.

On holidays and special occasions Franklin Street came alive. Running through the city as it did, it continued as Richmond's parade route. When Barnum and Bailey's Circus arrived in town, Alice, Nancy's younger sister, remembered the

> usually quiet street suddenly became noisy and crowded, as in the distance the band could just be heard. . . . Excitement rose as the brassy music got louder and louder, and at last the bandsmen appeared, stepping out proudly . . . , blowing their horns and beating their drums. Next came the wild animals in their cages . . . followed by the beautiful ladies in spangled dresses riding broad-backed palfreys.[7]

There were political rallies and memorial processions on Franklin. Teddy Roosevelt rode up the street floating on a sea of top hats and frock coats in 1905; every few years, armies of Confederate veterans marched in their tattered dress grays during emotional Civil War reunions.

We had the best view of all the parades from our house on Franklin Street. I remember especially the parades for the soldiers' reunions. I was seven or eight the year they dedicated the statues of Jefferson Davis and Jeb Stuart. Fifteen thousand veteran soldiers and fifty Confederate generals marched through Richmond that year. The parade took more than two hours to pass. All of the children of Richmond helped pull on the ropes to raise up the statues on Monument Avenue at the end of Franklin Street. I pulled up Jeb Stuart. Aunt Nannie helped pull up General Lee when she was a girl. We always used to see soldiers who had survived Pickett's charge at Gettysburg in the parade. They were heroes to us.

My Gibson cousins from up North didn't know a thing about the Civil War, but we were fed on it like mother's milk. To us that war seemed just around the corner. My Grandmother Perkins used to tell me stories. She was still extremely bitter. She said the real slaves during the war were not the Negroes but the women who had to look after the plantations and the farms while the men were off fighting. Her husband had a plantation in Buckingham County. She said as a plantation wife you had to be a doctor, a teacher and a provider when there was very little left behind by the army to provide from. They had to feed, clothe and house everyone on the plantation. She hated slavery, but as some of us felt about the British in India, she thought that emancipation should have been carried out gradually. She thought it a horrible thing to turn thousands of people out on their own with no jobs or education when they were used to always being looked after.

We also had the best view of the Sunday parade on Franklin Street, either from our front parlor window or from Grandmother Perkins's front porch across the street. Every Sunday when the services finished at All Saints Church on the next block the congregation emptied out and everybody visited with everybody else. Ladies wore dresses with pinched waists and long skirts that touched the ground, and had "rats" in their hair. They carried parasols and wore bonnets. If a lady was particularly admired, she was bunched with violets and wore them pinned to her waist, not on her shoulder. The men wore tailcoats and top hats and carried walking sticks. Richmond was very small and everybody knew everything about everybody else. If someone bought a new dress at Hollander's, the big shop in town, everybody in Richmond knew.

I remember seeing Miss May Handy walking up Franklin Street after church with her parasol. She was a great beauty in her day in

Nancy Perkins, right, with her first cousin Babs, the daughter of Irene and Dana Gibson, in 1900

Richmond . . . Aunt Irene's only rival. By the time I was a little girl she was married to a very rich Mr. Potter and lived somewhere else. She was so beautiful, they even named a kind of violet for her . . . but she never smiled. Whenever she came back to Richmond, the children sang, "Five cents for cake, Ten cents for candy, Fifteen cents to kiss Miss Ma'Handy."

There was a New Year's Day parade up Franklin Street as well. Everybody kept an open house and served delicious eggnog. I have my great-grandmother's receipt, which calls for one glass of whiskey and one glass of brandy for every one egg. You can imagine.

But most of the time where we lived in Richmond was very quiet. We could run back and forth across the street because there was no traffic at all, and we could play in our garden or our neighbors' gardens, or we could use the yard of the Commonwealth Club on the corner to play hide and seek and prisoner's base. It was an intimate and friendly neighborhood. If someone was having a delicious dessert at lunch in Franklin Street, you'd see a maid carrying the leftovers on a tray with a cover to a neighbor down the street. Miss Davis lived on the corner opposite the Club, and Mr. and Mrs. Sutton lived one house away, at 404 West Franklin. The Parrishes were next to the Suttons, and Mr. and Mrs. Palmer lived next to the Parrishes. The Palmers had drawing and watercolor classes once a week in their back garden if the weather was good. Grandmother Perkins lived across the street from us, and the Christians, who had a beautiful garden, lived on the corner next to us.

As children in Richmond most of our world was on or near Franklin Street. Sometimes we would walk west to the Old Soldiers Home to wave at the last remaining veterans who sat on the porch during the day. You could still see what was left of Confederate trenches bordering the empty fields along the way. Our school was just a block east of our house in Linden Row. It was Miss Phroni—short for Saphronia—Pegram's school. She had boys and girls there, and her schoolroom, which had been a cook's bedroom, was in her mother's house. To get to the schoolroom, we had to go up the alley in back of the house, through the back door and up the stairs, where she sat in an enormous starched white dress. I remember she always used to say to us, "Ye gods and little fishes, children, you'll drive me to drink." She used to make us recite poetry every Monday morning. I would recite, "I remember, I remember, the house where I was born. . . ." She didn't catch on for a year that I said the same poem every Monday morning.

We had to go up to Miss Young's room for arithmetic, which was on the third floor of the house and must have been a dressing room . . . one of those narrow rooms at the end of a hall. We always had to tiptoe up so that we wouldn't disturb Mrs. Pegram, Miss Phroni's mother. She must have been very old by then, and she still dressed in mourning for her husband, who had been killed in the Battle of the Crater.

Miss Jennie Ellett was our history teacher. She was a marvelous teacher and had taught my aunt Nancy Astor, who was very fond of her. I never did like Miss Jennie much because she made us write very difficult compositions. She did teach us an awful lot, though. We started with Greek history, then Roman, then English, and then American. When we got up to Abraham Lincoln, Miss Jennie said, "We'll skip that."

We spent a lot of time when we were little across the street at Grandmother Perkins's house. We were welcome at all hours of the day and used to love running up the steps to the porch—which had an enormous wisteria bush growing over it—and through the front door with the silver handles. I can see her house now. In the hall where you walked in were two framed pictures of coats of arms. One was the Harden-Perkins crest; the other was Moncure. She was very proud of those. The front parlor was next to the hall and was papered in a pink damask design of a large bold pattern. On either side of the Victorian marble fireplace Grandmother had two St. Meminses of her mother's great-aunt, who was a Walker. St. Memins was a French artist who came to Richmond in the early eighteenth century and made portraits on pink paper. Every prominent house in Virginia had them at the time. She left them to me when she died, and I gave them to my niece. She also had two enormous pictures of Virgins and Marys in that parlor in thick carved frames that looked like hundreds of gold teeth. My grandmother would say, "Those frames are very valuable. They're worth at least a hundred dollars each." A hundred dollars was like a million then, but you would have paid a million not to have them.

To this day I can smell the damp earth of her back garden near the run-down wooden fence. Violets grew there. We buried rows and rows of puppies in that corner. Grandmother Perkins used to let me have a funeral for my puppies, who always died of distemper. They were all called Coco or Dixie. I must have had twenty Cocos and twenty Dixies. I used to take them across the street from our house in a procession, wrapped in a shoe box. I was always the widow, dressed in the deepest black, and my grandmother's cook, Aunt Mary, would come out back and sing a song.

I was very fond of Grandmother Perkins. My mother was, too; she called her "Mother Perkins." She died at seventy-three and we thought she was as old as the hills. She was extremely witty, intelligent and very old-fashioned. I remember after lunch when everybody had coffee, it was tea for Mrs. Perkins. She always dressed in black and wore a cameo brooch pinned to the high collar of her dresses. She wore her diamond engagement ring and wide gold wedding band on her finger. Whenever she went outdoors, often to cross the street and bring us Aunt Mary's thin biscuits if we were ill, she covered her yellow-streaked white hair with a bonnet that tied underneath her chin.

Her maiden name was Alice Lee Moncure. Her father was a Moncure from Stafford County, and her mother was a Haxall from Richmond. The Moncures were very distinguished—all judges and bishops—and lived on plantations. She was named Alice Lee because their blood was all mixed up with Lee blood. After the surrender, when Robert E. Lee was riding away from Appomattox near Merrywood, the Perkins's plantation, he rode by and stopped to say hello to my grandmother. He called her "Cousin Alice." We're related through the Gascoignes. Through the Perkinses I'm also related to Charles Lee and Hancock Lee, who were both R. E. Lee's ancestors.

She really was a remarkable old girl. She was very amusing and at the same time quite a saint. She held that family together pretty much entirely on her own from the day her husband went off to war. And right up until the day she died she had a full house and never slowed down. She had Aunt Bell, who never married, living with her, and Uncle Willy and his daughter Grace after his wife died. Uncle Willy was never much of a working man. After my parents separated, my father moved across the street into her house, too. She must have had a hell of a time, but she never tired and was always amusing. She loved people. That house was always full of people. I used to love going there for supper. She would say, "You must have two waffles, one to keep the other one warm." The waffles were made by Aunt Mary, who also lived in the house. Aunt Mary came to Richmond from Buckingham County, where she had been a slave at Merrywood. She never left Grandmother, though, despite being freed.

Polite Richmond society congregated at "Germans" and at "at homes" in the early part of the century. The first Richmond German, which became the annual debutante ball, took place in 1870 in the drawing room of a Mr. and Mrs. Montague on West Franklin Street: "The gentlemen came in their 'Prince Alberts' which had been laid away during the war years. . . . Ladies wore gowns ingeniously renovated from pre-war finery. White gloves were obligatory, for no gentleman would have dreamed of taking a lady's hand or enclosing her eighteen-inch waist with bare hands. At least a foot of daylight must come between partners as they whirled, swooped, reversed and stepped to a polka, a schottische or a Strauss waltz."[8] Germans were named for the dancing—quadrille or cotillionlike choreographed figures—and were so popular that small weekly gatherings called Monday, Tuesday and Friday Germans were held throughout the year.

There were Morning Germans every day at the White Sulphur Springs in the mountains of West Virginia, the Newport of Richmond society. Mr. Langhorne took a cottage there for his family in the hot summer months when they still lived in Richmond, before he bought Mirador. In the 1890s guests at "the White" would either drink or bathe in the gaseous waters, as Stonewall Jackson did in 1859 to cure a liver ailment, or meet in the ballroom of the hotel for dancing and conversation. Cotillions included "the National Figure, in which ladies carried drums suspended from their shoulders and beat a tattoo while their partners waved flags; the Butterfly Figure, in which the ladies fluttered about waving great wings of chiffon as gentlemen pursued them with nets; the Slipper Figure, in which favors were tiny silver slippers filled with candy; the Coach-in-Four Figure, with gentlemen driving the ladies harnessed four abreast and covered with jingle bells around the ball-room."[9] These figures and favors were dreamed up by Jo Lane Stern, boy telegrapher during the Civil War and student of R. E. Lee's at Washington College. He was to the White and later the Richmond German what Ward McAllister was to the Patriarch's Ball in New York. (Stern chose Irene Lang-horne to lead the Richmond German at which McAllister discovered her.) At the White's Morning Germans, large orchestras provided accompaniment and liveried waiters carried breakfast trays to and from the tables.

At homes in Richmond were more staid affairs. At these weekly formal open houses, ladies of prominent households received visitors and served tea and cakes, drinks such as a julep or cherry bounce. The entertainment might include a daughter or guest playing the piano or singing. Conversation was charming and witty, although Ellen Glasgow, the Richmond-born novelist, recalled that "my friends . . . still read as lightly as they speculate."[10]

At-home days were listed in the *Blue Book*. The 1906 edition of the Rich-mond and Norfolk *Blue Book* was subtitled "Elite Family Directory/Club Membership." (The publisher insisted in its preface that "the title 'Blue Book' is given the work because of its blue cover. It does not refer to blue blood as many people suppose.") In addition to names, addresses and at-home days, the directory provided a family's history. For instance, "Perkins, Mrs. William H.: 414 West Franklin Street; . . . Mrs., nee Moncure, seventh in descent from Colonel Gerhard Folke, member of the House of Burgesses 1663." Or, "Perkins, Mr. and Mrs. Thos. Moncure; 409 West Franklin Street; Mrs., nee Langhorne; sixth in descent from John Langhorne, member of the House of Burgesses 1748."

My mother always said that we had "a position." Grandmother Perkins used to say, "Don't ever forget, you're related to five presi-dents." I've forgotten how now. Virginians were frightfully interested in that sort of thing because they had nothing else to be interested in. We were all related to each other one way or another. If your family had been there since around 1660 like ours, because there were so few people in the colony, everybody ended up being cousins more than once. If you'd been there that long, you were obliged to be connected in some way. You look back now at your family tree and wonder why *do* you have any good sense: the same names over and over. We didn't have the influx of immigrants they had in the North, where there were big cities and jobs. In Virginia it was all living on your land and grow-ing tobacco. They scratched along.

I had a cousin named John Abbott who wanted to marry me when we were young. He was frightfully good looking, but my mother said, "You simply can't marry a cousin." His mother and my mother were first cousins. "You'll have children like May Jones." May Jones was my mother's double first cousin. She looked like a bun you had put in the oven but hadn't been completely cooked. I used to tell John that if I could possibly fall in love with someone else I would. I wouldn't have children that looked like May Jones.

A constant pastime in Virginia was to sit around under the trees and talk about who we were descended from and who we were related to. Who begat whom, as in the Old Testament. On my Langhorne side there were Randolphs, Beverleys, Steptoes, Wyatts, Dabneys, Keenes and a half-dozen others. Jeb Stuart was a cousin through the Dabneys. He stayed with my mother's grandfather during part of the war; her great-aunt remembered coming into his room as a child and finding him so exhausted he was asleep on the bed with his boots on. After the war Jeb's widow Flora opened a school called Stuart Hall in Staunton. My mother went there and had to share a room with Jeb's daughter. Mother was expelled for kicking a ball back to some boys who were playing football. She hated cousin Flora. On my Perkins side there were Fowkes, Gascoignes, Browns, Walkers, Lees, Haxalls and Moncures. We had a lot to talk about. We'd say things like, "We must have Cousin Mary to stay because we've always had Cousin Mary. We know she doesn't wash and she's a kleptomaniac, but we've had Mary to stay for generations." I was brought up on that. Kin were very important to us—it was all Virginians had left by then.

Even my parents were related before they married, through Nanere's side. They met in Richmond just after Grandfather moved the family there from Danville and were married in 1884 when Mother was seventeen and Father was nineteen. Father had spent his early childhood at Merrywood, where he was born in the last year of the Civil War. He must not have had idyllic memories of his rural upbringing because he rarely came with us to Mirador when we went. In fact, he loathed the country and much preferred the company of other Richmond men at the Commonwealth Club. When he was in his youth, Virginia was called "Military District Number One" by the Yankees, and all of the countryside around Merrywood was destitute from being a battlefield for four years. He was an old-fashioned Virginian. I remember he told me when I was a young girl, "I'd rather see you dead than marry a Yankee." I married two.

Despite his plantation background, Father became a business-man in Richmond. There wasn't much else for him to do. He was chief clerk at W. S. Forbes when I was born, then he had his own provisioning and meat-packing business on East Canal Street called T. M. Perkins and Co. I remember when he went out to Chicago on business in 1910 we prayed for him because to us Chicago was the wild and woolly west. He was very tall, held himself very straight and was frightfully good looking. He had a thick moustache, always wore suits with four-button jackets and short lapels, and white shirts with long, stiff collars that virtually covered his neck. He fit in well with the Langhorne family because he was as good a tease as most of them and it was always said that he was the only man around who could better Grandfather in repartee. He was a very amusing and popular man. My brother, Chillie, my sister, Alice, and I all called him "Sir."

When my mother and father were married, Mother must have been very beautiful. I never knew her as thin and as lovely as my Langhorne aunts, but Bessie, Cousin Lucy Abbott and Nancy Craighill all said that when she was younger she was prettier than any of them. She weighed only ninety-eight pounds when she was married. She had lovely legs and feet, a lovely mouth and skin, bright green-blue eyes. And Mother put her clothes on impeccably. Lucy swore that my mother was the prettiest and chicest of all the women she ever saw in the family, and that Mother had the most elegant way of dealing with an umbrella or parasol . . . she never explained to me what she meant by that.

Mother's brothers and sisters considered her more a member of Grandfather and Nanere's generation than their own. She was only seventeen years younger than Nanere and in life became Nanere's support and standby, perhaps the cardinal reason why Mother and Grandfather fought so. She was close to her brother Keene—he worshiped her—but the others regarded her as a severe second mother, one without Nanere's tenderness. Nannie told me Mother once washed her mouth out with lye for using a bad word. I remember, though, what Grandfather told me when Mother died. He said he couldn't remember a time without my mother, when she wasn't there, and he always looked on Mother as being a trouble-some older sister. She had known all of the harder times and the difficult years that he and Nanere had gone through, trying to raise a family with very little. I've always been sure that was why he was so good to me.[11]

Lizzie Langhorne, the eldest of the five beautiful Langhorne sisters, was the only one to marry a fellow Virginian and remain close to home. Nancy wrote of her mother to Robert Brand, Phyllis Langhorne's second husband: "Her life was in a pond and Nannie's in a sea but she was the king fish in that pond."

Mother was very strict and old-fashioned in raising me. She would say things like, "Don't lose your dignity." That's a terrible thing to tell a child. "Don't try to be like other people. You must be dignified." I remember all the other girls who lived on Franklin Street were allowed to run into each other's houses without ringing the doorbell, but my mother wouldn't hear of it. "I'll not have frisky little girls running in and out of my house. They can ring the door-bell and the housemaid will let them in." I always cried, "But I won't be popular."

I remember my mother most with a round frame of fancywork in her lap and her long, thick, dark brown hair done up in the style

On the front lawn at Mirador, Thomas Moncure Perkins, Elizabeth Langhorne Perkins and two of their three children, Nancy and Chiswell

of a Gibson Girl. In many ways I feel I've lived her life. I've had all the things she wanted, and I've done all the things she wanted to do. She was amusing and witty and strong. She was always frightfully chic; she looked extremely rich, though she wasn't at all, and always had real lace. I had a patchwork bedspread made of her lace. My boys were born in a bed with that bedspread on it. It was the whole history of my life and hers in that real lace.

PART TWO

Antebellum Virginian landowners were insatiable builders, partly by necessity: they started from scratch in the primeval forest of the New World; and partly by inherited inclination: they were stepchildren of the British rural gentry and aristocracy, themselves energetic builders. The first settlers assembled plantations and small communities along the rivers and bays; their sons added acres to the holdings, and society and culture to the province; their grandsons, Virginia's "Great Generation," helped create a political institution and an entire nation. Working from the ground up with whatever the Lord and the land provided and the few ideas and materials that could cross the Atlantic by ship, this brotherhood of landowners carved its own Utopia, an Anglo-Saxon paradise dedicated to life, liberty and the pursuit of happiness.

Houses stood at the center of the Virginian system. In the vast and lonely countryside there was little social contact, with villages few and very far between. Most of the sparse European and African population either lived in the plantation houses or worked for them and never left their grounds. The earliest houses were little more than vernacular roofs over the immigrants' heads; but as soon as fields were cleared and profits from tobacco secured, the landowning barons built for themselves true feudal manor houses—splendid exaggerations to fortify themselves, strong doses of European civility poised against the elements and the isolation. Hogsheads of tobacco traveled down the James on flat barges, river sloops and catamaranlike tandem canoes, bound for ships bound for England. Carved Portland stone, window glass, china, musical instruments, silk and books returned upriver.

Like daubs of brilliant Georgian radiance on the huge green landscape, in rough, sometimes hostile but always breathtaking locations, these English-style mansions thinly dotted the Crown territory, popping out from a bluff, nestled in a dip in the land or settled regally under a magnificent grove of ancient oak trees. They were called Hundred, Flower de Hundred, Shelly, Shirley, Clover Hill, Cloverfields, Poplar Grove, Poplar Forest, Sherwood Forest, Midlothian, Chelsea, Berkeley, Hampstead, Level Green, Bowling Green, Otter Burn, Horn Quarter, Hickory Hill, Criss Cross, and they were the physical embodiment of all things Virginian and all attributes Virginians admired: both refined and rugged, inspired yet languid in the tropical heat, formal but comfortable and at ease. They were the concrete expressions of educated, genteel men of the soil. Through the years the houses became clapboard-and-beam memoirs of their families and their epoch, some surviving into the twentieth century—though slipping inexorably into dereliction—

when a young Nancy Perkins fell in love with their romantic aura and "dignity."

The stories and the houses have gripped me since I was a child; and they influenced my idea of beauty, and what is beautiful in a house, more than anything else ever has. Mother used to take us to see the old houses in Virginia when we were children, or take us to stay with friends who lived in them. We made great treks in the springtime. They weren't museums then, and they didn't look as though they were polished up for an article in a decorating magazine, as they do now. When I was a child, Virginian houses were still occupied by the descendants of the people who had built them in the eighteenth century. Many of them were ramshackle and their gardens were completely overgrown; that was their beauty, that was their charm. They had once been very grand, but the war and agricultural depression changed all that. Things were shabby, not shabby from poverty, shabby from use . . . you know, chairs had been sat in until the springs broke, but they did have springs. You get the same sense in some English houses, the sense of survival of the fittest, of hanging on against everything . . . time, circumstances, progress. It was the most romantic thing in the world to me.

The drawing room at Warner Hall was so large that during parties there was space enough for the children to hold their own cotillions in one corner. A tunnel from the main house at Berkeley led to a circular, sixteen-foot-diameter underground Indian shelter. Wilton had four twenty-six-foot chimneys. Robert "King" Carter—who owned 300,000 acres in the early eighteenth century—and his immediate family built or owned more than a dozen plantation houses, including his own, called Carotoman. Of his sons, Charles owned Cleve, John owned Shirley, Robert owned Nomini and Landon owned Sabine Hall. Carter's Grove cost £500 to build. **I saw Carter's Grove as a child. Later it was for sale for only $3,000. You can see how poor they were by then. I tried to get Nancy Astor to buy it.** Point of Honor in Lynchburg was built on the site of a duel. Bowling Green was named for a natural, perfect clearing nearby sometimes used for horse racing. The Lee house, Stratford, had a wooden roof deck suspended between its chimneys for dancing, promenading and viewing the Potomac. At Mount Airy, Colonel Tayloe built an orangery to house his collection of rare plants and trees.

General Cocke, a teetotaler, installed a huge cast-iron, pitcher-shaped fountain at one end of the pond at Bremo. It was his "temperance memorial" and was designed to overflow rather than spout. He also built a Palladian barn with a pedimented portico supported by columns of rough-hewn stone and timbers. There he kept his carriages and, in the cupola, a bell that the Marquis de Lafayette sent him in return for a flock of American turkeys the general had shipped to France for the marquis's park. **Bremo was still untouched in my youth. It was one of Jefferson's best Palladian interpretations. It was the only house I knew of in Virginia with a ha-ha to keep the cattle from the lawn, and its library on the ground level had wooden sliding panels that pulled out to cover the books. It also had Jefferson's lazy Susan cupboard in the dining room and triple-sash windows that disappeared up into the wall and opened tall enough to use as a door.** Lafayette, George Washington, Thomas Jefferson, Dolley and James Madison, Andrew Jackson, Martin Van Buren and John Tyler all slept in the best guest room at Castle Hill at one time or another. A ghost resided there as well, and was known to shout at visitors to "Go home." Future President Jefferson played his fiddle in the parlor at Castle Hill so future President Madison could dance. Washington proposed to Mary Cary in the drawing room at Carter's Grove. She refused him. Jefferson proposed to Rebecca Burwell in the same drawing room. She too refused.

My Grandmother Perkins told me stories about living at Merrywood, her husband's family's plantation house. She moved to Merrywood after marrying my grandfather. The thought of moving away from relatively lively Richmond to the countryside worried her . . . like most of rural Virginia, Buckingham County was then completely isolated. But her husband's family had plenty of cousins nearby called Ellis, who were Perkinses through their mother's side. They all had plantations, so there was plenty to do. My grandparents' social life consisted of bringing out the coaches and riding-horses—Grandmother rode sidesaddle—and visiting, with the whole family in tow. They would drive over to Afton, one of the Ellis houses, with no warning, arriving with children, slaves and animals. In good weather they would play cards on the porch and the men would drink juleps; in the winter they would dance and sing after supper to a fiddler. They had tremendous amusements among themselves with these great entourages. For days on end the visitors would eat the host out of house and home, and when the food was gone they would all get back into their carriages and onto their horses and would move on to stay with the Eldridges, more cousins, who had a lovely place, and eat *them* out of house and home. That's the way they visited before the war.

After the war, life at Merrywood was exactly like *Gone With the Wind*. The same poverty, the same struggle, the carpetbaggers, Yankee Reconstruction. Grandmother said Merrywood was impossible to keep up with a family to look after, a husband crippled in the war and no help. She tried for a few years before deciding to move her family to Richmond to be near her mother's family. Growing up on a plantation, none of her children had ever seen a train, so when they got to the station on the James River and the steam engine came up the track toward them, Uncle Willy, who was about ten, ran like a jackrabbit. He was scared half to death. They didn't leave for Richmond that day because they couldn't find Uncle Willy.

She also told me about other houses she visited before the war. She stayed at Rosewell on a number of occasions, where she said the staircase inside was so wide you could drive a four-in-hand up the steps. She also said there was a pond on the roof where Thomas Jefferson and Governor Page used to fish. When she was staying at Brandon with the Harrisons as a girl, they went to paper one of the wings and came across a secret closet. They found a human skeleton inside. It must have been someone hiding from the Indians. Those things thrilled me.

Rosewell was considered the grandest of houses in eighteenth-century Virginia, "the lordliest mansion of a time when Colonial Virginia was baronial Virginia."[12] Begun in 1721 by planter Mann Page, a son-in-law of King Carter, the brick house was so large, the plans so ambitious, that it took almost twenty years to build; it was finished only after Page's death, by his son Mann Page II. The construction nearly bankrupted the family: Mann Page II sold land to pay his bills—a drastic recourse in Virginia, where acreage was valued above all else. But Rosewell was a stroke of majesty and enchantment, rising up in the middle of nowhere after miles of nothing but forest, field and river, a fairy-tale castle, its two glass-and-wood cupolas towering well above the treetops on the bank of the York. All of the Virginia Tidewater houses, imposing and very much alone, dazzled any upriver traveler as they hovered into view.

The Page family and a steady stream of guests used Rosewell's vast roof as an open-air parlor to escape the still heat below. The cupolas were sheltering summerhouses; a seat in one offered a bird's-eye view of half the county and of Rosewell's English-style formal gardens that at one axis culminated in a ha-ha. Thomas Jefferson is supposed to have written a draft of the Declaration of Independence in one of the cupolas, and read it to his lifelong friend and confidant John Page, another hereditary master of Rosewell.

Rosewell was barely holding on when I was a little girl. Windows were broken, shutters were dangling by a thread, the stone steps up to the house had been stolen or sold and replaced by wooden ones. The outbuildings had been torn down years before. The man who bought it from the Pages cut down the cedar avenue and sold the wood to make tubs. He also tore the wainscoting off the walls and the lead off the roof. Then, when I was about ten, Rosewell, once the finest house in Virginia, burned to the ground; all that was left standing were some outside walls. Years later I went back to find the walls still standing, now covered in ivy and vines in the middle of a field of cattle grass.

Westover was owned successively by William Byrd I, II and III. The first William amassed the estates and the fortune; the second designed and built the house; the third embellished the property before losing it to gambling debts. Westover rested high above the river; a lawn swept 150 feet from the house to the landing. Completed in 1730, constructed of red bricks fired on the plantation and paneling cut and carved from indigenous trees, the Georgian mansion rose three storeys, with a dozen dormer windows and four mammoth chimneys breaking through its slate roof. Inside, fine paintings and portraits adorned the paneling. Imported furniture sat atop imported rugs around an imported marble mantel, beneath rocaille ceilings rich with medallions and garlands. In one room William Byrd II assembled the largest library in Virginia, second only in the Colonies to the Reverend Cotton Mather's library in Massachusetts: 3,625 leather-bound volumes, including the architectural portfolios from which he drew his plan for the house. Outside, Westover was surrounded, like a Parisian town house, by a wrought-iron *clairvoyée*, its stone piers supporting stone pineapples—an ancient symbol of hospitality—vases and ball finials. Tulip poplars, elms and sycamores grew to enormous sizes in the rich Tidewater soil, shading the house, the walks and the pleasure gardens.

William II's daughter Evelyn was supposed to have been the loveliest belle of her day in Virginia. When she was presented at court in London, King George II commented aloud how pleased he was that his colonies were producing such "beautiful Byrds." While in London Evelyn fell in love with the Earl of Peterborough, but her father refused to allow a marriage. Back at Westover, she died a spinster at twenty-one, a rarity in a society so small and insular that eligible girls were snapped up barely clear of adolescence. She died of a "broken heart." Her ghost, in hoopskirts and high-heeled slippers, haunted Westover for years, to be joined later by the specter of her sister-in-law, the former Elizabeth Carter of Shirley, who died when a bookcase fell on top of her, and that of her brother, William III, who shot himself.

I remember being shown what they called a "johnny house" at Westover. "Johnny house" was Virginian slang for loo. At Westover they had the most fantastic eighteenth-century paneled johnny house, which had eight seats around it. It was where the girls would go and read their love letters while they relieved their bowels after breakfast. That was what most country houses had in Virginia. The men had their own special johnny house on the other side of the house; I don't know if they had an eight- or six-seater. Thomas Jefferson had the first indoor loo at Monticello, but a lot of people still felt it was unhealthy to have plumbing in the house even in my childhood.

Many of the Byrd family portraits painted by Lely and Kneller and other European court painters ended up on the walls of Brandon. Evelyn Taylor Byrd, the daughter of William III and niece of the unfortunate "beautiful Byrd," took the portraits with her when she married Nathaniel Harrison III, the son of Brandon's builder, Nathaniel Harrison II. Virginia's leading families were all related, or at least acquainted: Nathaniel Harrison II married Lucy Carter, daughter of King Carter of Carotoman, and was a classmate of Thomas Jefferson's at the College of William and Mary. It was thought that perhaps Jefferson helped Harrison design Brandon. The house bore Jefferson's signature, as it had one of Virginia's first unified designs: The traditional dependencies on either side of the house were instead built into Brandon, becoming wings of a single structure.

Brandon sheltered generations of Harrisons; the family held on tightly to the house and the land. George Evelyn Harrison inherited Brandon from his father, Nathaniel Harrison III, while George's wife survived him by nearly sixty years. She was called "Old Miss" and she kept the house through the Civil War, when its barns and stables were burned by the Union Army, its paneling ripped out in search of treasure. Brandon's brick facade was pocked by enemy target practice: Harrison's Landing—Brandon's James River wharf—was where the Union Navy was stationed during the Peninsular campaign against Richmond. At the death of Mrs. Harrison in 1898, her daughter-in-law, Mrs. George Evelyn Harrison II, became chatelaine of Brandon and the keeper of Evelyn Byrd's pink brocade ball gown.

Brandon made the biggest impression on me. I went with my mother on a tour with the Colonial Dames. The Harrisons still owned it and were still living there after 250 years. It had survived despite four years of war at its gates and the total destruction of Virginia's way of life. But the dignity of its beauty surpassed the difficulties.

I went back with Alice Hay after I was married, when the Harrisons still owned it. There was a rickety sign on the gate saying $1
TO COME INSIDE. I said to Alice I thought it was marvelous, and she
said to me, "Nancy, you like everything so run-down; I don't know
why you don't like the houses on Long Island." I told her I couldn't
stand Long Island and that this was really romantic to me. There
was this muddy, muddy river and this family barely holding on.

The next time I went back, the Harrisons had sold the house to
send their children to school. They had been there for three hundred
years. Now it had a garden with irises married to peonies and a
swimming pool with perfect pale blue water. We vulgarize everything we touch.

Tuckahoe was further upriver from Brandon and another plantation
house connected with the ubiquitous Thomas Jefferson. The Jefferson family lived there for seven years when he was a boy; his earliest memory was
being borne on a pillow by a slave on horseback from his father's estate in
Albemarle County to Tuckahoe.[13] His mother, Jane Randolph of Dungeness,
was the first cousin of William Randolph of Tuckahoe; both were grandchildren of William and Mary Randolph of Turkey Island, who were known as
the Adam and Eve of Virginia, their innumerable descendants including
Robert E. Lee and John Marshall. Thomas Jefferson began his prodigious
education at Tuckahoe, in the tiny wooden schoolhouse near the rose garden
and the Randolph family cemetery, and he learned to ride and shoot on the
grounds. Tuckahoe was the first large house that Jefferson, architect to the
nation, saw firsthand and lived in.

The Tuckahoe Jefferson saw was the result of changes and enlargements
over time, inside and out. The original building was a simple, gable-roofed
frame structure. Thomas Randolph then built a second house, a copy of the
first, and connected the two with a long, wide hall so his new Tuckahoe
formed a perfect H. In 1779 a guest wrote, "It seems to be built solely for the
purposes of hospitality . . . the family lives in one wing while the other is
reserved . . . for visitors."[14] While the Jeffersons lived there, they took over
one side and the Randolphs stayed in the other.

The interior of Tuckahoe was as fine as any house's in Virginia, with
carved walnut paneling and a walnut staircase with carved daisies, acanthus
leaves and spiral balusters, though it could never have been considered
pompous or luxurious. The exterior of both wings and the hall was wrapped
in modest, whitewashed clapboard embellished with few decorative trifles,
other than understated pediments over the four entrances—a polite nod to

fashion. Tuckahoe's scale was intimate, and the grounds were without formal landscaping. The farm reached right up to the front steps. There were certain twists as well, certain knots of charm that gave it warmth. Mixed in with real Hepplewhite, for example, were copies cut and upholstered in the plantation's workshop by slaves or journeymen carpenters; one settee might have passed for an original had large brackets not been needed to secure the sculpted legs. In the White Parlor—the most formal reception room, with a fireplace framed in marble and an Adam-esque wooden mantel—the workmen used new wood for the paneling so that in time the planks separated and warped. Gilt Chippendale mirrors hung on waxed Virginia pine walls; a Van Dyck hung beside a spitoon. This contrast between the old world and the Colonial let in a breeze of informality and ease typical of Virginia, perfectly suiting this family that over the generations scratched initials in the dining room windows with their diamond rings.

We went and stayed at Tuckahoe, the Randolph house. It was higher up the James, further inland. The romance of the place made its past alive. An unclipped box garden led to the wooden school-house where Thomas Jefferson spent his youth. The lawn was shaded by trees that he probably knew. I remember the fat double-daffodils that had seeded themselves in large numbers in the grass.

Monticello, the house Jefferson would grow up to build for himself, was in Albemarle County, not far from Mirador. Of all the achievements of his life—political, academic, horticultural, musical, philosophical and architectural—none was closer to his heart than this haven atop his "little mountain" that took him fifty years to realize. He dreamed of it throughout college, where work toward his law degree was supplemented by study of the drawings of Andrea Palladio and James Gibbs that he found in books in the William and Mary library. Actual construction began when he was twenty-five with the clearing and leveling of the mountain, but four years later all that was there for him and his new wife to move into was the small, square, single-room "honeymoon cottage" that would eventually become a dependency of his mansion. While his vision became grander and more ambitious as time passed, the completion of the house was delayed year after year by lack of funds or proper materials, by the seasons, the weather, by his own political career and his responsibilities to the nation, but most of all by his excruciating perfectionism.

Thomas Jefferson is one of the people I'm most looking forward to meeting in heaven. He was an extraordinary man with so many facets. I've always been interested in the same things he was. And on his tombstone he doesn't say anything about being president for

eight years. He only mentions writing the Declaration of Independence and founding the University of Virginia. I admire that. If anyone else had written the epitaph there wouldn't be a headstone big enough. I think Robert E. Lee was a great man as well, but I don't particularly want to meet him in heaven. He was too much of a saint.

Monticello was nearly completed just after the War of Independence, with Jefferson's family living in the finished parts. The walls of the main block were up and the two-storey columns in place; the roof was on. Jefferson was sent to France as ambassador, however, and while there he saw in stone the antiquities he until then had seen only on paper. He sat and stared at the Maison Carrée at Nîmes "like a lover at his mistress"[15] for an entire day; he soaked in villas by Palladio in northern Italy and contemporary French interpretations of classicism like the Hôtel de Salm in Paris. Returning to Virginia with a head full of ideas and shipping containers spilling over with French furniture and wine, he immediately had his workmen tear apart much of Monticello, dissatisfied now with his initial effort and ensuring for his family another quarter-century of "disruption, discomfort and change."[16]

His guests suffered as well; those enamored of his company paid a price. Jefferson went on having friends to stay at Monticello, although "new rooms were not yet plastered and nothing was painted . . . and even though windows were probably installed, there were few doors and hence little privacy."[17] One guest "found the president living in a state of romantic squalor."[18] The house was "in a state of commencement and decay, Virginia being the only country as far as I know where inhabitants contrive to bring these two extremes as near to each other as possible by inhabiting an unfinished house till it is falling about their ears."[19] Another guest mused, "The ground plan is a good one, and the elevation may look well if ever completed, but Mr. Jefferson has so frequently changed his plan, & pulled down and rebuilt so often that it has generally more the appearance of a house going to decay . . . than an unfinished building."[20]

Jefferson's contemporaries never thought he would see the fruit of his labors, yet he lived to the age of eighty-three and even built for himself a second house, Poplar Forest, where he could escape Monticello and the side effects of his own hospitality. Meanwhile, Monticello became an acclaimed masterpiece of architecture, both practically and aesthetically. The hexagon he manipulated throughout allowed for more light and wall space. His insistence that the house appear to be a single storey when it was actually three—in deference to Roman design—and the manner in which he achieved this illusion gave the exterior a sense of immovable stature. His unerring eye for detail in the rooms—the perfectly proportioned doors and fanlights, wall molding and ceiling decoration—and all of the contraptions he invented for pleasure and "convenience" graced the house with the highest of architectural standards, visual unity and charm. His grounds and gardens were no less extraordinary, no less imaginative. A dome sat upon Monticello like a crown on a king.

When I was born, Monticello had been left to dereliction for a generation or more. There is a photograph of it, taken about the time I was a child, that illustrates what I'm talking about, that illustrates what moved me about all the houses in Virginia when I was young. It shows the house missing windows and shutters and with a broken and patched fence and tree stumps in the yard. It's a grainy, black-and-white picture, and it shows the devastation of disuse. But it shows its dignity as well. There is more to the house in that picture than anything any amount of money can buy. That's the way it was when I was a child: All of these houses were like enormous Sleeping Beauties, undisturbed by wealth or fashion.

1910 TO 1920

"Nancy was thrilling when she was young," remembered her sister, Alice. "Always very thin, always very pretty, with red hair like our father and Aunt Bell. All the time I was a tough little girl and kicking around, she was dressing up and trying to attract beaux.

"Nancy always laughed very easily . . . but she was very shy as a girl. It was quite extraordinary. She had no self-confidence at all. I think she got over it when she married Ronnie Tree, but she was madly shy as a child."

It really was an extraordinary thing. I was catapulted, because of the times and because of my family, into a very interesting period . . . catapulted into two continents. I remember as a very young girl going to the Astors' town house in St. James's Square when A. J. Balfour, the Foreign Secretary, was there having lunch. You didn't have enough sense to come in out of the rain, but you still found yourself sitting next to a prime minister or a cabinet minister at lunch or dinner. It had nothing to do with me; I was catapulted there by my family. Nannie in politics, Aunt Irene in the artistic world and New York society, Aunt Phyllis and her second husband, Bob Brand, in the banking and business world. One had the top of everything.

I saw Europe for the first time in 1910, when my mother and father took Alice and me abroad to live. My brother, Chillie, was old enough to stay home. Father went to Nurheim as a cure for his weak heart, I was sent to school in a convent in Territet in Switzerland, while Mother and Alice stayed in Paris and Caux; we then moved to

Nancy Perkins during
her engagement to
Henry Field

Tours the next year and Alice and I attended the *lycée de jeunes filles*.
Mother was determined that I should speak perfect French. She
could understand it and adored reading memoirs and was quite
interested in French history, but she couldn't pronounce a word of
it. I think she would have liked me to marry someone in the diplo-
matic service . . . you couldn't have found somebody who would
have hated it more or who was less suited than I.

On the weekends that year we visited the chateaux in the countryside around Tours as Mother loved seeing old houses; Mother
got in very much with high society in Tours. I remember spending
the weekend with Madame Thierry, a friend of Mother's, at Chenonceaux, the château that had been owned by Diane de Poitiers.
Diane was Henry II's favorite and was given the house by him. The
River Cher passed under the main rooms of the house, and you had
to walk over a drawbridge to get to it. On the bank there were two
formal gardens, one built by Diane the royal mistress and the other
to rival it by Queen Catherine de' Medici, who took the house back
from Diane after Henry died. There were flower borders, a box-

wood maze, a *potager* and an orchard. I loved the walled garden. I was about twelve when we stayed there, and it affected me the way Brandon had. Here was living history. Here was where Diane de Poitiers used to bathe in the Cher right from her chamber and where Catherine de' Medici gave the huge fete in honor of the wedding between her son François II and Mary Stuart. We also went to see Amboise, Plessis-les-Tours and Villandry.[1]

Nancy was taken to England for the first time in the spring of 1910. She and Lizzie and Alice went to visit the Langhorne aunts living there and to attend the funeral of King Edward VII, an event as lavish as his reign—England's Edwardian epoch—had been. Twelve-year-old Nancy wrote in a letter to her father, who had returned by himself to Richmond:

I saw eight Kings . . . and the different way they salouted the flag was very pretty, you can't imagine how wonderful it was, and everyone said there has never before been a sight like that. . . . The Kaiser looked the best on his horse I think. The Queen Mother rode in a carraige with her sister the Empress and King George walked behind his father's coffin, and the coffin was pulled by the sailors, and it just had a crown on it, the two Princes George and Edward (or should I say Edward and George) also walked. . . . I saw the Archbishop of Canterbury, as he had to receive the procession on the steps in the sun without a hat and held a purple book in his hand, and it dropped in the funniest moment, he had a little boy to hold his train. Poor man he had a bald head, and I certainly did pity him.[2]

While in England, Mrs. Perkins and her two daughters stayed at the Astor town house in London and at Cliveden in Buckinghamshire.

Cliveden was on a much bigger scale than any house I'd ever known before, but it was a center for the family, the doors were always opened wide, and from the first time I went there it was a second home. What I remember best from my first visit is my fury at having to play paper dolls under the billiard table with my little sister, Alice, and being put to bed at the same time as she even though I was five years older. I was so ashamed. Aunt Nancy's son Bobbie Shaw and I were bathed together in front of a fireplace in the nursery in a tin tub placed on top of a blanket. Before we were put to bed we were fed porridge and a digestive biscuit by the housemaid. I thought that was wonderful. At home we only had a glass of milk or cocoa, bread and butter and damson jam for supper. Sometimes a

soft-boiled egg. We had our supper at six at Cliveden, and before we went to bed at seven-thirty we were allowed to see our aunts in their evening dresses before they went downstairs to dine. Nanny Gibbons held sway in the nursery. I made the mistake once of calling her "Gibbons" because I had heard my aunt call her that. I was quickly and firmly told that she was to be called Nanny or Mrs. Gibbons.

By the time Nancy Perkins saw Cliveden, her aunt Nancy Astor had already undertaken the task of redecorating the house. As chatelaine her job was to eradicate the "splendid gloom," as she called her father-in-law's taste; to bring the old palazzo on the Thames some of Mirador's gaiety. William Waldorf Astor had turned an already cheerless building into a museum for his vast collection of antiquities and Victorian proclivities, a style disparagingly called Fifth Avenue/Long Island Eclectic. It included gilded samplings from revival movements of the Italian Renaissance, French Gothic and Adam periods in decoration. W. W. Astor thought of Cliveden principally as a backdrop for his sculptural fragments, Roman sarcophagi and objects like the great hall's sixteenth-century stone fireplace, which he had extricated from a French château, rather than as a home for a young couple and their family.

There was not a great deal Nancy Astor could do to make the place more suitable to her taste. Much of the sullen nature of the interior was inherent in Cliveden, it being after all a nineteenth-century version of a sixteenth-century Italian villa, built in the middle of Buckinghamshire. But she went ahead once Mr. Astor, now installed behind a mechanical drawbridge at Hever Castle, promised never to return. His beloved antiquities went first, then the Renaissance mosaic in the floor of the great hall and then the columns and the ceiling in the drawing room, the painting of which he had supervised himself. "The place looked better," Nancy said, "when I had put in books and chintz curtains and covers, and flowers."[3] Her choices of antique Georgian furniture made the interior lighter and fresher. Arrangements of cut flowers and forced potted plants were brought up from the estate's greenhouses at dawn every morning all year round whenever the Astors were in residence, and placed in corners and on tables in every room.

All her houses—Sandwich, Glendoe, London, Plymouth or Cliveden, wherever she was—were very cleanly decorated with light and air and were very cheerful. But Cliveden had the best smell of any house I've ever known, because in the vestibule there were great banks of a plant from New Zealand called humea that has a delicious, grassy smell. And the staircase old Lord Astor had built was made of sandalwood, which smelled delicious. We used to love that staircase as children. On the stairs he had had carved on the newels

The entrance facade and forecourt of Cliveden, the Astors' country home, which before the Second World War was one of the last of the great British "power houses"

the people who were connected with Cliveden's history, like the highwayman Jack Sheppard, holding a pistol in his hand, and Lady Shrewsbury, who was the Duke of Buckingham's mistress.

At tea in the hall of Cliveden you would always find the five small Astor children and all the cousins their age playing games of hide and seek among themselves in and out of the guests' legs. The legs might have belonged to a prime minister or a distinguished foreign ambassador. Tea—really a tea party—was at five o'clock. Guests would go to their rooms and change from their tennis clothes, or the tweeds they were wearing for walking or riding, into afternoon dress. When I was a girl I had several afternoon dresses; they were

William Waldorf Astor, working with the architect J. L. Pearson and the
artist W. S. Frith, installed the sandalwood staircase at Cliveden after he
bought the house in 1893.

usually silk and weren't the sort of thing you'd wear on the street. The tea itself was a tremendous meal. All kinds of cakes and scones and delicious fresh loaves of crisp bread, which you would cut for yourself on a wooden cutting board and spread with the jams that were laid out. Tea was in the hall in the colder months or a tent pavillion on the terrace in the summer.

Dinner was always prompt because of the chef. It was at eight or half past. There was a gong that would be rung by Mr. Lee the butler at half past seven, which was dressing time. At Cliveden you always dressed in full evening clothes for dinner, and there was always a bouquet of flowers for every lady.

It was at the dining room table that this mixture of people my aunt invited down would finally congregate. The cousins from Virginia, local constituents, important national and international politicians, painters, healers. It was the most extraordinary thing, and she was the lynchpin. Nannie was at the center of it all. She made it go and helped them mix. It was her personality and her charm that held such a diverse group together under one roof. She was a magnet and a catalyst and very amusing. Her curiosity and her humor enchanted everybody and terrified some.

For evening amusements at Cliveden there were charades and skits; there was no television or radio. All the aunts were excellent mimics, and there was a dress-up box in the upstairs hall. Aunt Nannie did a very good hunting lady with the aid of false teeth, or a superb Charlie Chaplin. And she was completely convincing as Margot Asquith. When we were all older, Bobbie Shaw had everyone roaring with laughter as a clergyman making his sermon points with all sorts of facial gymnastics. When Aunt Nora visited, she would charm everybody with her singing and guitar playing.

Cliveden's exterior was impressive but busy; its cosmetic makeup left no breathing room, no resting place to pause and reflect. Pilasters streaked up all four fronts and didn't hesitate until they vanished into deep cornices and massive crowning urns. The frieze that wrapped around the top of the house was gouged with Latin inscriptions declaring Cliveden's long history, its various *"insane substructiones."* Windows and doors were obsessively dressed with pediments or quoined arches. Cliveden was hot-blooded and aggressive to the eye and should have been completely incongruous with the cool, unobtrusive Thames-side countryside. But the Astors' Cliveden was the third Cliveden on this same promontory—the first two had been destroyed by fire—and when the Duke of Sutherland commissioned this version, he didn't plan the house

The garden facade of Cliveden overlooked the massive terrace Lord Orkney commissioned and the Borghese balustrade that Waldorf Astor brought to Buckinghamshire from Rome.

for a typical rural English setting. By that time the acres surrounding the site had been completely transformed and no longer even resembled Buckinghamshire; now they were Italian and French, with overtones of the English Landscape Movement. There was a long, flat parterre, romantic garden rooms, wooded paths and miles of avenues: The grandiose house was really subordinate to the glorious gardens that framed it.

In the first half of the twentieth century Cliveden's grounds were at their zenith; the park took 250 years to mature to the stage in which the Astors found it and Nancy Perkins first saw it. Oaks and beeches had grown stately; hedges were tall and full, as impenetrable as stone; and all of the architectural features of the garden, the walls, paths and steps, had taken on the patina of age and now melded with the horticultural features. Throughout its history various owners and tenants of Cliveden contributed something to the gardens. George Villiers, the 2nd Duke of Buckingham and cousin of Barbara Villiers, the Duchess of Cleveland, commissioned the long tongue of a parterre that stuck out along the Thames. George Hamilton, the first Earl of

"Nancy had her father's hospitality," wrote Lady Astor's biographer Christopher Sykes, "and this was one main basis of her social success." Cliveden was "a place of continual merriment and entertainment . . . all with a touch of American informality and her own eccentricity which gave her parties a spice not always to be found in the strongholds of society" (Sykes, pp. 108–9).

Orkney, excavated and constructed the terrace and terrace wall that stretched along the south face of the house—ambitious projects in the seventeenth and eighteenth centuries, requiring pharaoh-sized labor forces to move the tons of earth to flatten the parterre and erect the great step between the parterre and the house. The terrace wall was the same height as the principal storey of the house and mimicked its Palladian character. Orkney also planted many of the beech, oak and yew trees, as well as the flowering cherry and whitebeam, when he bought Cliveden in 1696.[4]

Frederick, Prince of Wales, rented Cliveden after Orkney's death. The son of George II and father of George III, Frederick never was himself king, dying before his ascendancy from a blow to the chest by a cricket ball while playing with his children at Cliveden. The grove of ilex trees was thought to have been one of the prince's contributions during his tenancy. One hundred

The grand parterre at the back of Cliveden enticed the eye along its lawns and beds into a stunning vista of the River Thames.

years after George, the 2nd Duke and Duchess of Sutherland arranged and replanted the beds in the parterre in strict geometric patterns, and made other changes in line with Victorian fashion, though they concentrated mostly on rebuilding the house after the second fire. The Sutherlands, like the Astors fifty years later, entertained royalty and politicians at Cliveden. Queen Victoria was a regular guest and an intimate. To please Her Majesty, the Sutherlands even went to the extreme of having all the beds in the parterre replanted one night so the Queen could wake up to a fresh view from her bedroom window the next morning. Queen Victoria gave the Sutherlands the statue of the Prince Consort that stood in the Ilex Grove. William Gladstone, prime minister under Victoria, often stayed at Cliveden as well; it was he who composed the Latin inscription engraved in the house's frieze.

Lord Astor's passion for antiquities added greatly to Cliveden's opulent gardens. Against Orkney's yew walls in the forecourt he arranged eight of his Roman sarcophagi from the second and third centuries. Heavy, deep, rectangular and decorated with a procession of figures beautifully carved in relief, the white marble pieces jumped out from their evergreen backdrop; the sculpted bushes, kept at knife-sharp right angles by Cliveden gardeners, accented the ancient caskets' shape. Astor also installed the "Fountain of Love" by the American expatriate Thomas Waldo Story. It was fixed at a corner in the drive, so every carriage passed it on its approach to the house and headed toward it when leaving the forecourt. Huge and baroque and as much a folly as a work of art, the fountain depicted in marble three ladies and three Cupids perched on the edge of a giant scallop shell, frolicking in the waters of the mythical source.

Lord Astor's most celebrated addition to Cliveden's grounds, however, was the Borghese balustrade. Almost as long as the length of the house itself, this artifact was so cherished by the Roman people that its exile inspired the Italian government to write laws forbidding the removal of such national art treasures in the future. Like his other prizes from Italy, the sixteenth-century balustrade from the Villa Borghese was disassembled, crated and shipped out the Mediterranean, up the Atlantic and along the Thames to Cliveden. There it was established in the lawn between the parterre and the terrace. Created by the sculptors Giuseppe di Giacomo and Paulo Massoni for Cardinal Scipione Borghese,[5] it was made of a combination of simple brick and carved stone with Borghese eagles and dragons at the corners, fountains at the terminals and graceful balusters interspersed with wall and seat. At Cliveden delicate climbing vines grew up and in between the crumbling 350-year-old bricks.

However old you were, there were plenty of amusements at Cliveden. In the electric, flat-bottomed canoe on the Thames, or in

the punts, or on the practice golf course. There were two grass tennis courts and one hard court at Cliveden, where you always found couples playing mixed doubles. The ladies wore flowered hats and silk morning dresses instead of whites, served with a sweeping underhand and never played at the net. Gentlemen who forgot to bring their tennis shoes down for the weekend had to play in stocking feet. As children we loved driving pony carts and were thrilled by the cave on the estate that Jack Sheppard used as a hideout.

The younger Astors continued the house's opulent tradition before the First World War by employing an outdoor staff of between forty and fifty. This did not include the stable servants. There were more staff looking after the park than attending to the family, guests, laundry and silverware. They had men to cut and roll the lawns behind "motor mowers" and shire horses with leather socks over their hooves, men to trim the topiary and the hedges, others to rake the miles of gravel paths. There were plantsmen who cultivated seeds, raised seedlings and planted thousands of annuals and perennials that the garden—as their mistress determined—required. Nancy Astor was a keen gardener, which meant planning flower beds with the head gardener or getting out with a basket, trowel and secateurs herself on a rare lazy afternoon. She left her mark in the landscape as Orkney and Prince Frederick had, not with any grand architectural stroke, but with a sure eye.

Nannie always used to say whenever she saw someone's garden, "Mr. Shaw said you must always have a touch of red; it brings out all the colors." We used to repeat that line to each other like Polly.

The aura achieved by the planning and labor was much of what made Cliveden such an inviting, seductive place to stay—even if one's politics contrasted with those of Lord and Lady Astor. This was the playground where the Astor children and their cousins rode and played tag, where Langhorne sisters and government ministers savored the trickle of a fountain, the view of Cliveden Reach far below the terrace or the shade of the magnificent ancient tree called Canning's Oak. Songbirds and stained marble, stone grandeur and the sweet scent of viburnum and lilies of the valley in May: This was the twilight of perfection and the realization of a very old, very passionate dream.

We spent two straight years in Europe and returned to Richmond in 1912. My parents were now separated from each other. It was like going to the devil, because we didn't really know what "separation" meant. They were both strong willed, and I remember awful rows. I was brought up in a house where if your mother and father were

fussing you heard it. If houses are big enough, you don't have to fuss. I was devoted to both of them, so I had a hard time understanding it, but I'm sure even after they separated they remained close to each other. Father only lived across the street in Grandmother Perkins's house, so we saw a lot of him. Whenever Mother left the house, Father would call to her, "Lizzie Langhorne, where are you going?" Mother thought it appalling that he would live across the street; she was very conscious of her position. But I'm certain the two of them remained very close.

In 1914 Father took ill with dropsy. He died that spring. It was a shock to everybody, as he was only fifty-five and his mother had always said he had a fine constitution. I was at his bedside when he died, and his body was laid out in our drawing room. Two weeks later Mother went to New York by train to escape her grief and stay with Aunt Irene. Alice and I were left in Richmond. Mother never looked better than she did then. She arrived in New York early in the morning, and a friend of hers came to see her. The two of them were leaving the house to go buy bird of paradise feathers for their hats when Mother said, "Oh, I don't feel well," and she collapsed. I remember going over the mountain by carriage to get the train to New York. There were hardly any good roads back then. By the time we got to Wainsborough, though, there was a message saying that she had died. She had had a stroke. In two weeks' time, Alice and I had become orphans.

After the funeral there was a great meeting between Grandfather and our aunts and uncles where they discussed what to do with Alice and me. My brother, Chillie, was old enough to look after himself, so he wasn't a problem. Aunt Irene offered to take me. Babs Gibson was exactly my age, and we were very close. Alice was awake in the study and overheard them talking about who would take her. Keene offered because he was devoted to Mother, but in the end Phyllis spoke up and Alice went to live with her and her children at Mirador. Grandfather had given Mirador to Phyllis by then and was living across the road in a house he called Misfit because he was the "misfit" of the neighborhood now that so many of our neighbors were Yankees.

I can't tell you how it was to lose Mother and Father; I was close to them both and was devastated when all of a sudden they were gone. But being taken in by Aunt Irene made it much easier to get through the trauma. I knew her the best of any of the aunts. I had spent a good part of every summer at Islesboro in Maine with Uncle Dana and Aunt Irene in their house on Seven Hundred Acre Island.

I was delicate as a child and couldn't take the summer heat in Virginia. I was sent to Islesboro for July and August from the age of about seven, so the Gibsons were like a second family to me.

The Gibsons' house in Maine was lovely. Uncle Dana bought a point of Seven Hundred Acre Island, and as you could only get there by boat it was very private; just a wild island covered in wild blueberries. The Gibsons' house was white clapboard with green awnings, and Aunt Irene had a beautiful flower garden from which she kept the house full of cut flowers. The first thing she did in the morning was to fill the glass bowls on every table in the sitting room with her arrangements. The sitting room was painted green with white woodwork, and all of the furniture was green and white. Irene collected the furniture that you could get up there, very pretty pine and simple things in mahogany. Good furniture with a good line. That's where I learned about painted and pine furniture. French windows opened onto a brick terrace, and there was a large stone fireplace with a model of a ship on the mantelpiece. Aunt Irene had old hooked rugs on the floor; she was one of the first to collect them. Uncle Dana used to sit in a green armchair and tell Babs and me stories as long as we tickled his feet.

When Aunt Nora was staying with us, she invariably attracted an entourage of beaux and friends who lived in Islesboro to come around for tennis during the day or, in the evenings, to come sit on the porch and amuse each other. There seemed to be a lot of young men from Harvard. Ruth Draper was Nora's age and one of Nora's friends. Her family almost invented Islesboro. She was not a very pretty girl, but she had a wonderful sense of humor that she entertained their crowd with. She would do the monologues on the porch at Islesboro for which she eventually became so famous on stage. I remember being seven or eight years old and watching Ruth, who must have been seventeen or eighteen, doing the "Cab Driver." And she did the "Maine Woman" who always spoke the line "smart as a whip, now sick as a cat." I think she started doing monologues because she wasn't a great success with the boys; she never had anyone in love with her until she was much older.

Babs and I had a group of friends our own age that people called the "Grand Army." We all came up every summer and hung around like a gang. Eleanor Spray, Austin Flagg, Henry Kidde, Margot Biddle, Babs and me and a few others. We went to clambakes and tennis tournaments all summer, and on Friday nights we were allowed to dance in the laundry at the Inn on the big island. The Inn had burned down, and all that was left was the laundry. We had to be home at half past nine those nights and would return across Gilky Harbor in one of the Gibsons' two launches, either the *Babs* or the *Boy*.

We used to take a launch to Dark Harbor on Sundays for church. Aunt Irene always got dressed up for it. No matter what the weather did—even if it was storming—she would dilate her nostrils, throw out her bosom and go forth. Everybody admired her; she was the beauty of the place. And she always sang out in the church in Dark Harbor, the way she did in Greenwood, and led all the hymns.

It was the relaxed and intimate life at Gibson Point that I loved the most. Uncle Dana giving lessons in sailboat racing strategy using forks and knives as the boats, or sitting on the porch in the evening discussing the day with the caretaker. Aunt Irene gardening. Spending nights with Babs in the stone house Uncle Dana built for her on one of the two Ensign Islands that you could see from the house.[6] Sparkling, windy Maine summer days. Aunt Irene and Uncle Dana treated me as one of their own children all along, well before my parents died, and Babs was my most beloved cousin.

I turned seventeen in the autumn of 1914. It had been my mother's plan that I "finish" in Rome at the Sacred Heart Convent. She always said convents were good for "girls and half-wits" and that I was both. But the 1914 War was about to begin in Europe, so Aunt Irene and Grandfather had to find an alternative for me. At that time a cousin of my father's from the Haxall side, Charlotte Noland, was opening a school for girls in Middleburg, called Foxcroft, like St. Timothy's in Baltimore. St. Timothy's in the time of my aunts was the best girls' school in America. Phyllis went there. It was run by Miss Polly Carter and her sister, who were from Redlands, the Carter house not far from Mirador. Miss Charlotte was a relation of theirs as well and taught basketball at St. Timothy's.

Miss Charlotte planned her school for young girls, but because of the war there were eight or nine of us older girls who would have gone to Europe but were sent to Foxcroft instead. Flora Whitney was in my year. She was one of the few people I've known in my life with real charm. I remember her with her golfing socks on to keep warm in the open classrooms, and her ballet toe shoes. She had taken ballet lessons and used to practice her toe stands around her chair during classes. And Adelaide Jones from the Pittsburgh steel family was there. We called her "the Queen of Sheba" and "Shebes." She arrived the first day at the train station with seven trunks full of clothes. They

Nancy Perkins, second
from left, in Islesboro,
Maine

only let her keep one trunk, the one with her underclothes, and sent
the rest back to Pittsburgh. She couldn't have possibly gotten it all
into the Pink House, where we lived. There were three girls to each
room, where we dressed and hung our clothes, and we only had two
shelves and three hooks to ourselves. We all slept in a long row on
the sleeping porch on canvas cots in flannel pajamas and sleeping
bags with red blankets and no sheets. I can smell those horrible sleeping bags now. We barely had a roof over our heads and were literally
sleeping outdoors in the middle of winter.

Miss Ida Appleton was our chaperone. She used to sing, "It's
hard to love, it's mighty hard to love, it's hard for you to make up
your mind. This gal she's busted a million fellas' hearts, but she ain't

goina bust into mine." Our house was across two fields, which we had to walk over a half-dozen times a day. We'd smoke what you call "rabbit tobacco" in the field, which was a weed you could pull up. We thought that frightfully naughty. The house across the road from the Pink House, called the Pot House, was where all the local drunks went at night. We could hear them leaving very late and saying, "We mustn't wake up the young ladies." The young ladies were listening to every word they said. There was another house nearer to the classrooms and main building where the younger girls lived. Alice lived there with Polly Lee, Robert E. Lee's granddaughter.

Miss Lowe taught us mathematics and German. She wore a Tyrolean hat with a feather in it all through class. Mademoiselle Millet taught us French. She was very small and wore her hair in a very stylish French roll. She read us French poetry, had us memorize verbs and told me, "A woman should always use the same perfume." Miss Rosalie taught us literature and English, and Miss Elizabeth Lemmon came in from Welbourne to teach us dancing, how to sit and get up from a chair properly and how to curtsy. The classrooms were shacks in the orchard that in the wintertime were so cold we wrapped ourselves in steamer blankets to keep warm. Miss Charlotte coached basketball and riding, gave Sunday sermons and led morning prayers. Most of the time she would get up in front of us fully clad for the hunt except for her bowler hat.

The summer after my year at Foxcroft, in 1915, Alice and I accompanied Aunt Phyllis on a steamship to stay with Aunt Nannie in England and Scotland. We prayed thoughout the entire voyage, because German U-boats were sinking passenger ships. It was a long journey, and Alice was seasick most of the time. We stayed at Cliveden, and in Scotland we stayed at Glendoe Lodge, the Astors' house there. All of the Brooks cousins, the Phipps cousins and the Astor cousins were there that summer. I was a plump little girl of seventeen. Bill Phipps was in the Navy, so they took me to see all the ships coming in from the Battle of Jutland. Uncle Paul Phipps, Nora's husband, was in the Sherwood Foresters, so we went to Sunderland to visit him.

I met the most handsome man I'd ever seen in Sunderland that afternoon. John Webster. He was a friend of Paul's and in his regiment. Evidently he took a shine to me, because by the time we got back to the house he was there. He must have been about twenty-eight. There were croquet parties that summer, and he was always there. When we played blindman's bluff I always seemed to catch him. I knew who he was because his hair felt like a whisk broom. I fell so in love with that man . . . I thought he was wonderful. But that was all. I woke up one day and his regiment was gone. He wrote to me for some time after we met, and he signed his letters "J. R. Webster." That autumn, when I went back to America, he wrote to me from the trenches in France and invited me to stay with him in India after the war. We kept up the correspondence for a year, but eventually I had to write him and tell him I was engaged to Henry Field. The next thing I knew of him, I opened a newspaper and there was his picture. He had been killed in action in France.*

Despite the war, as I was to be brought out in the winter of 1915-16 in New York with Babs Gibson and in Richmond, Aunt Nannie fitted me out with a debutante's trousseau. I was given six sets of underwear, six nightgowns, five evening dresses, two smart suits and one country suit, a silk house dress and a gorgeous beaver coat that was edged with fur. My evening dresses were all pale, *jeune fille* colors and came from Jay's, the best debutante dress designer, but I still ended up looking like a very plump little English school-girl. I stood out completely at the parties with all the slender New York debutantes in sleek scarlet and green chiffons. I remember the dancer Irene Castle's bobbed hair was in fashion my year. Babs had a dress that was low cut in the back. She kept saying to me, "I can't walk down the street; people follow me." Well, nobody followed me at all. The girls in New York were much more sophisticated, much more forward, than the English debutantes. I remember someone saying, "Oh, someone kissed her so hard he almost broke her tooth." "Kissed her!" I said. I thought you didn't kiss anybody until you became engaged.

In New York the Gibsons didn't give Babs and me a ball, but we spent the season going to all the debutante parties. Babs was really the debutante, and I was kindly included at whatever she was invited

---

*Lt. Col. John Webster, MC, DSO, wrote in his diary on December 1, 1916: "Shaw-cross and I again went shooting this morning, we got 1 hare, 2 snipe and a partridge. Shawcross hit two other partridges, but unfortunately they got away.

"In the morning I got a letter from Nancy Perkins saying she was engaged to a man named Henry Field from Chicago. This was a very hard knock. In the afternoon I got orders to proceed to France—blow no. 2. So, to help clear away my sorrow, Shawcross, Binney and I went and dined very wisely and very well at the Club, and went on to the Empire afterwards." (From the Papers of Lt. Col. John Webster held in the Department of Documents at the Imperial War Museum, London.)

to. The parties were mostly in people's houses, although the big charity balls were still at the Brevoort. The Brevoort was a hotel and restaurant in Aunt Irene and Uncle Dana's day. It was like the Ritz; everybody went. And people had dinners at their houses before the parties. I remember getting very tired, not being used to going out so late, and having to splash cold water on my face to stay awake. And I remember the boys always cut in while you were dancing. You'd be terrified that the young man you were dancing with was holding out a dollar bill behind your back.

Stanford White was at the peak of his abilities and fame in 1902 when he designed for his friend Charles Dana Gibson the town house where Nancy stayed. Part of the same New York society as the Gibsons, the buoyant, flamboyant third partner of McKim, Mead and White had by then been the principal architect on dozens of projects, including houses for the writer Thomas Nelson Page and Charles Tiffany in Washington and for the railroad executive Stuyvesant Fish in New York, the Century Club and the renovation of Thomas Jefferson's Rotunda at the University of Virginia. He designed and oversaw the building of the Gibsons' house in only twenty months. I never met Stanford White; I was only seven when he died. But I remember learning to read with the newspaper accounts of the trial of his murderer, Harry Kendall Thaw of Pittsburgh.

Five narrow storeys tall, with a splayed entrance step and a portico supported by columns and pilasters, 127 East Seventy-third Street was a variation on a standard being built all over the newest fashionable neighborhood of New York City, Manhattan's Upper East Side. The Gibsons' house, however, was thought to be "more geometrically severe" than the work of most architects of the day, including White himself; it was "simple yet well proportioned and only modestly embellished internally as well as in the austere facade."[7] It instead reflected a new turn for American taste and American architecture, a return to the less flounced plans of the American colonies, neoclassicism as seen through the eyes of English Georgians and a style heralding an end to robber-baron vulgarity. Its redbrick face must have reminded Irene of the genteel row houses of her native Richmond.

You walked through a pillared entrance into a great stone hall. Uncle Dana had studied in Spain and bought an enormous stone fireplace there and a whole lot of Spanish furniture. Then you walked through to the stair hall that was two storeys tall and also made of stone. At the back of it was a door to the kitchen and the laundry. Think of that: They had laundries in New York houses then. Then you went upstairs and there was a lovely parlor facing the street, which had very pretty spindly, sort of Adamy, eighteenth-century furniture, a piano and a lovely rug. It was wood paneled and decorated in pale colors. On the other side of the square hall was the dining room. It was also paneled and had heavy Spanish furniture and a wonderful Spanish screen.

When you went up another flight, there was a library on the street side above the drawing room with another stone fireplace, and in the back over the dining room was Aunt Irene's room. It had beautiful painted furniture and a four-poster bed. Her bath was behind it. Half of the stair hall on that floor was taken up by Aunt Irene's wardrobe and dressing room. On the floor above that, over the library, was the room I had when I was there, and Uncle Dana's room was in the back above Aunt Irene's. We had a bath between us. Then on the top floor was Babs's room and a bath, and above Uncle Dana's room was Aunt Irene's maid's room. We had a French maid who looked after all our clothes.

Uncle Dana didn't work at home; he drew his cartoons and painted at a studio at Fifty-ninth Street and Sixth Avenue, near Carnegie Hall. He went there every morning. I never went to his studio, he didn't like us to do that, but I did sit for him a number of times in Islesboro. We were always bored to death of posing for him. In New York he was home by three in the afternoon because painting and drawing strained his eyes. He napped until teatime. He had bought *Life* magazine by then, because he wanted to have something his son could go into when he died. He had been a cartoonist for *Life* for years, and when it came up for sale, the others persuaded him to buy it. But he knew nothing about journalism and lost a great deal of money before he gave up and sold it to Luce.

I was reading a biography of Dorothy Parker recently, and what struck me was that this was the time when I was a girl and living in New York with the Gibsons, and those were the people I saw coming in and out of their house. I don't mean to say that I was part of it, they wouldn't know me from Adam; but they were the world of that side of my family, they were the people Uncle Dana and Aunt Irene were in contact with. A few names came back to me, names I heard every day, like Heywood Broun, Robert Sherwood and Richard Harding Davis, all those people who in those days were working for *Life*. They had the world by the neck . . . and they all went to the Algonquin for lunch.

I went to Newport that season for Flora Whitney's ball. I stayed at the Breakers, her family's house there. Grandfather took a flat in

Richmond in the winter, so I came out at the Richmond German and attended all the Richmond parties. The Richmond German was like the Charleston St. Cecilia. It was *the* event. Long gloves were worn; young men dressed in their first white tie and tails; all the town matriarchs attended. It was ruled by a strict committee, who decided who could be invited. Mr. Joe Lane Stern led the debutantes in their parade and all of the quadrilles.

That year I spent time with Aunt Phyllis at Mirador and Grand-father at Misfit while I was in Virginia. The only time Grandfather would let me go to Charlottesville was to go to the dentist. I liked so many different boys at the University that I was willing to let that dentist drill a hole in any tooth he wanted. I also had beaux in Isles-boro who went to St. Mark's and Groton. But I'll never know how many people wanted to marry me, because I fell madly in love with Henry Field when I was still very young. I met him in Islesboro in the summer of 1916. I was playing golf with Margot Scull, who later married Alexander Biddle; Henry was with his older brother Marshall Field III. One was tall and one was short and both were wearing what we called correspondents' shoes. When I saw them I turned to Margot and said, "I'll bet it's the short one who's going to be left for us to go dancing with."

Henry was the tall one. I remember telling him I couldn't pos-sibly marry him because I didn't know how to order lunch. We were married anyway in February 1917 when I was nineteen years old. He must have really loved me because he said he thought I had a pretty nose, even though I have the nose of an elephant.

Henry was American by birth but had been brought up in Eng-land from about the age of five, when his mother married Maldwin Drummond of Drummonds Bank. They lived at Cadland on the Solent. They owned the whole coastline; the estate stretched all the way to Southampton without a building on it except for a charming house on the beach which Marconi rented from them. At Cadland they put the names of houseguests on the doors of the rooms they were staying in. Henry went to Eton as a young man, then joined a British regiment during the First War after the government allowed foreigners in.

The rest of Henry's family was in Chicago, and when I first went out to see him there, before we were married, I remember how nice they all were to me. Everybody gave me dinners and parties. I went out by train from Mirador. My aunt wouldn't let me go without a maid to look after me and make sure I was well dressed. As I didn't

Nancy Perkins and Henry
Field in front of the Gibsons'
house on Seven Hundred
Acre Island in Maine in 1916,
during the summer they
became engaged

have a maid then, she gave me hers, who was called Atkins. She was
an English lady's maid. Atkins and I arrived in Chicago in terrible
weather—a dark, dark train station in that dark, dark city. The train
was late. While Henry was waiting for me he was walking around
looking in shop windows and spotted a car that he liked. He bought
it for me. He said he thought I should have a car so I wouldn't be
dependent on his brother Marshall and Marshall's wife, Evie. With
the car came a chauffeur with a coonskin coat and a coonskin hat. I
went out from the station that day in my own car. It had blue
enamel handles and blue enamel boxes in front, and the chauffeur
sat outside in the open with nothing over him. A very chic little car.
I remember thinking at the time how funny it all was.

Because Henry was Catholic we were married by the head of the Catholic Church in New York at the Gibsons' house. Cole Porter was an usher. He had just graduated from Yale, where he was a classmate of Henry's brother-in-law Buddy Marshall. Neither Henry nor his brother knew many people in America because they were brought up in England, so Buddy got his own classmates from Yale to usher at our wedding. Cole looked like a frog and was very amusing. In those days he played the piano for everyone and sang his songs. I've always thought his humor very subtle, almost too good; he was too subtle for the hoi polloi. After Ronnie Tree and I were married, I used to see Cole and his wife, Linda, in Paris. She was the most beautiful woman that's ever been; she really was the acme of chic.

Henry and I were going to live in Chicago and in Virginia. I insisted on Virginia before we were married, and it was Henry's grandfather Marshall Field's wishes that he live in Chicago after Henry turned twenty-one. We couldn't have Mirador, so we were going to buy a house called Morgan, which was nearby. In Chicago we were going to live in a duplex apartment on the lakeshore. I'd never heard of such a thing as a duplex, but it was supposed to be frightfully modern to have one. I remember the wind off the lake always blew something in your eyes.

I was told that our apartment would be done up by Marshall Field's, Henry's grandfather's store, and that I should choose what I wanted. It was my first decorating job. I chose blue silk curtains with headings for my bedroom. No pelmets. And for the sitting room I chose blue taffeta curtains and chinoiserie chintz on a yellow background for the sofa and chairs. On each side of the fireplace we had bookshelves with Japanese vases with white cherry blossoms on them. What I was most proud of in that room were the two mirrors I bought to hang opposite the windows on the lake. I hung them there so that when the curtains were closed the mirrors would reflect the blue taffeta.

We never lived in our duplex. I had all the patterns to show my friends, but we never moved in. After we were married, we took a long honeymoon along the California coast in a motorcar. It was blissful, and we were deeply in love. By the time we got back, America had entered the 1914 War, and Henry wanted to sign on. Before enlisting, he decided he ought to have his tonsils removed, as they had given him trouble from time to time. While he was having this simple operation, I took Alice to Lake Saranac because she had developed something in her lungs at Foxcroft, and because there was a history of TB in the family Grandfather thought she ought to be careful. Henry's operation should have been routine, and he should have been out of the hospital in a few days. But the doctor didn't tell him not to eat before the operation, and he somehow developed an infection and then an abscess behind his heart. He was so sick. When they went to drain the abscess, he was so weak that it killed him. We were married for only five months when he died, and three of those he spent in Bellevue Hospital in New York. He had been so alive, so handsome and so gay, and he was dead ten days short of his twenty-second birthday.

Henry was buried in the yard of the Emmanuel Church in Greenwood, the church Aunt Nannie built in memory of Nanere near Mirador. I couldn't even bear to leave my carriage to attend the service.

I was in mourning again. I was dressed in black at Foxcroft after my parents died and now for another two years because of Henry. It was the way things were done before the First War. There were still ladies in Richmond, when I was a little girl, mourning for husbands lost in the Civil War. It was for respect, but you really wore black as a protection against people asking you out. To let them know. First you wore deep black, then you went into black and white, and then in the third year you would wear gray and mauve. There was an etiquette to it. I remember Mother being very upset with Phyllis and Nannie for wearing brown shoes at Mirador when they were in mourning for Nanere. Mother was in mourning for three years for her mother, then two more for her brother. But the First War changed that. Especially in England, where an entire generation was wiped out. No one needed to dress in black because everyone lost someone. Nobody paid attention to mourning after that.

The first year after Henry died I lived in Richmond. Grandfather was getting very old by then, but we got on very well together and he was the great support he had always been.[8] The rest of the family rallied round me as best they could. I rented a flat for myself and stayed pretty close to home. I didn't know how to run a flat, I was only nineteen, but Richmond was still very small, and old Wash found me servants. I had a cook called Roxy, who got so excited when I had a guest for lunch she served the sweet first and then the omelette; and a maid named Annie, who had a pair of shoes that creaked so much I finally had to speak to her about them. She said to me, "Yes, ma'am, they cried so much this morning I nearly left them at home." I still had Atkins with me, and I had a chauffeur named Melvin for a while to drive the car Henry gave me. He wore the same coonskin coat and the same coonskin hat as the chauffeur in Chicago, but had to stuff the hat with newspaper as it was far too big for him. I remember the neighborhood dogs used to go crazy whenever Melvin arrived all got up in his coat and hat. He would tell me, "They takes me for a possum, Miss Nancy."

To keep me busy that first year, cousin Lucy Abbot sent her nine-year-old son, Brookie, for me to look after. Actually, it was he who looked after me. He certainly seemed more grown-up, and he was horrified by my behavior. He used to say, "You're so undignified." To entertain him once, I donned a pair of roller skates and skated around Monroe Park, my crepe widow's weeds and veil flying from side to side. He promised never to go outdoors with me again as I "hurt his dignity."

The following autumn I moved up to New York and took a nursing course, then worked at what was called the Flower Hospital. I decided to work there because I thought the name sounded nice. It was anything but nice. Some of the war wounded were there. The Flower Hospital was on the East River, and I used to wash up at the Officer's Club in the evening. I met Alexandra Emery there one day when I was washing my hands after work. I had hardly said hello to her when she invited me along on a trip she wanted to take to the Far East. I was to be her chaperone at the grand old age of twenty, as I was a widow. She said it would be easy. All we had to do was walk down Fifth Avenue to the Cook's office and buy a ticket to China. I said I'd have to go to Virginia and ask Grandfather, because it was a very long trip and the First War had only just ended. Grandfather said, "Go." He thought it would be the best thing in the world for me. The next thing I knew, I was crossing Canada, sharing a drawing room on a train with a perfectly strange woman and a basket of oranges—the perfectly strange woman's feet in my face—thinking, "What in the world am I doing here?"

It was a very long trip to Japan back then, it took ten days by ship, but we met three young Mexican grandees who were doing the Grand Tour, one named Yturbe and two brothers called Beistegui, whom we befriended. The elder Beistegui brother, Jack, had his head shaven—something had happened to him—he looked like a

A sketch by Scaisbrooke "Brookie" Abbott, Nancy's cousin and lifelong friend, of Nancy roller skating in Monroe Park, Richmond, dressed in her widow's weeds

very ugly convict. We called him "Big Brother." The other was Charlie Beistegui, we called him "Little Brother." Little Brother looked like a tall, thin mouse with a very long tail. He was very elegant even then. Little Yturbe spat when he talked in his high-pitched voice, but was very sweet. Charlie had gone to Eton with Henry, so we all became friendly crossing the Pacific and ended up traveling together when we reached Asia. I've always said I knew Charles de Beistegui before he was so stylish and smart.

It turned out to be a marvelous trip. We went from Japan to China and Korea and then back through Japan. In Japan we went cormorant fishing, fishing with birds—Charlie, Alexandra and me—with our Japanese guide in sailing canoes. We got becalmed coming

Nancy Field, in veil, and Alexandra Emery near the Great Wall of China, 1919.
Between them is Charles de Beistegui; his cousin Señor Yturbe is at right.

back and had to spend the night in the water because of the mos-
quitoes. And we shot rapids in Japan. I was still in widow's weeds.

They were terribly good to us in China at the American and
British consulates. They had been stuck out there all alone since the
war had started and hadn't seen anyone. Miles Lampson was the
First Secretary in the British embassy in Peking. His wife was
Rachel Phipps, my uncle Paul Phipps's sister. I particularly remember the wall around Peking. You knocked on a door, like the door
of a barn, to get in. There was still an Emperor in China then, a little boy. I knew his tutor, who was an Englishman named Johnson.
Johnson gave me a piece of paper the young Emperor had been practicing the signatures of King George and Woodrow Wilson on, and
in tiny handwriting, "In the spring they played baseball." I still have
it. And Mrs. Willard Straight gave me a letter of introduction to a
Manchu princess. All we wanted to ask her was if she wore corsets
and what were her underclothes like.

When we returned to America, as our trip to China and Japan
was such a success, Alexandra and I planned another, this time to
India. I was to spend Christmas that year at Cliveden and would

stay in a flat rented for me on Mount Street in London. Then in January we would leave for India. Alice and Alexandra and I sailed for England from New York on the *Mauretania*.

In London I should think I had quite a gay time and did nothing but sleep late, eat lunch every day at the Ritz, Claridges or the Berkeley, shop, have tea, see picture exhibitions, dine, go to the theater and dance. I saw Aunt Nora and her little boy Tommy, Aunt Phyllis and Nannie. And I saw a great deal of Ronnie Tree, who came around to see me at the flat on Mount Street to discuss my future. Ronnie had been on the *Mauretania;* he was Henry's first cousin, the son of Marshall Field's daughter Ethel, who was by then married to David Beatty, the dashing Admiral of the Fleet and hero of the Battle of Jutland. The Beattys lived at Brooksby Hall in Leicester, where they hunted with the Quorn. I went and stayed with them while I was in England before our trip. I remember meeting Grand Duke Dmitri of Russia—who Alexandra's sister Audrey eventually married—at dinner at Mrs. Lowenstein's in Leicester. He told us all about how he killed Rasputin.

It turned out a trip to India was impossible. Because of the war we couldn't book passage; the government wouldn't let us. So Alexandra and I agreed to go through France and North Africa in January with Ronnie and Jerry Preston. In Paris Yturbe saw us off with bunches of roses, violets and chocolates. People crowded around our car because they thought we were Douglas Fairbanks and Mary Pickford. The countryside was still devastated from the war. We visited the battlefields, and I remember how difficult it was to get petrol for the car. The roads in France were so bad in many parts we seemed to puncture our tires every day.

The car was then shipped from Marseilles to Tunis, and the four of us for three weeks had a very funny time dressed as Arabs traveling through the desert on camels and mules. We had fifty porters and armed guards with us, a small orchestra and enormous tents. After Africa Jerry went back to the south of France and Ronnie, Alexandra and I went to Rome and Paris, where we joined the Dana Gibsons and the Roger Winthrops, who were returning from a cruise with Clarence Dillon.

Ronnie and I were married at St. James, Piccadilly, on May 5, 1920; I was given away by Uncle Waldorf. Ronnie was American but had been brought up and went to school in England and never wanted to live anywhere else. He really felt more at home in England and with his English friends. One of his grandfathers was a dis-

Jerome Preston, Nancy Field, Ronald Tree and Alexandra Emery during their trip to North Africa in 1920. "From then on I began to see a great deal of Nancy," wrote Tree in his memoir, "and I fell in love with her. . . . She was beautiful, charming, elegant, but also possessed the unique wit which she inherited from her relations" (Tree, p. 29).

Nancy riding astride in the North African desert in 1920

Following the First World War, Ronald Tree was invited to join his great-uncle Thomas Nelson Page's delegation in Rome. Standing behind Ambassador and Mrs. Page were Marshall Field III, James Bruce, Thomas Lindsay and Tree.

tinguished judge in Chicago named Lambert Tree, who eventually became Ambassador to Belgium and then Russia. His Tree grandmother was a Miss Magie; her father owned the half of Chicago the Fields didn't, and if the Chicago fire had gone the other way the Magies would have become as rich as the Fields became. Arthur Tree, Ronnie's father, married Ethel, the daughter of Marshall Field, and the two of them went to live in England and Europe. Ronnie was their only child. She then married David Beatty, whom she met out hunting shortly after Ronnie was born. Ronnie was raised by his father at Ashorne Hill in Warwickshire.

Ronnie was the most intense, conscientious and thoughtful man I've ever known. He always felt very strongly about whatever he was doing . . . really the most commendable person. He joined the American Naval Air Service during the First War and was one of a handful of people who learned to fly. He worked for Thomas Nelson Page, the American ambassador in Rome, as an honorary attaché after the war. Mrs. Page had been married to Ronnie's great-uncle Henry Field, who my Henry was named for, then married

Mrs. Henry Field on her wedding day, February 1917

Thomas Nelson Page after he died. Page was from Virginia and had written *Two Little Confederates* and a biography of General Lee. Ronnie learned a great deal about art and houses and antique furniture during his time in Rome. He was extremely good looking, and the most soigné man I've ever known.

Just after I married Ronnie I went into a shop to change my address and said, "I used to be Mrs. Field, now I'm Mrs. Tree." All the man said to me was "You're very rural."

A HOUSE OF HER OWN: MIRADOR REVISITED

AN ARTICLE FROM the front page of *The New York Times* on June 8, 1929, read,

COUPLE MISS LINER, THEIR TWO CHILDREN SAIL;
OLYMPIC WAITS IN BAY TILL TUG BRINGS PARENTS

The White Star liner Olympic, outbound from New York, left its pier at 11 o'clock last night, then paid the unusual courtesy to two trans-Atlantic passengers of anchoring in Quarantine an hour later and waiting for them to overtake her in a fast tug.

The passengers were Mr. and Mrs. A. Ronald Tree of New York, Virginia, London and Northampton, England, the former a nephew [sic] of Lady Beatty, the latter the niece of Lady Astor and formerly the wife of Marshall Field Jr. [sic] in Chicago. They had been to the theater and missed the boat, but their two children, Michael, seven years old, and Jeremy, three, had sailed on the liner with their nurse.

Mr. and Mrs. Tree, who have an estate, Mirador, in Virginia, had booked passage on the Olympic for themselves, their children, the children's nurse, a valet and maid servant. They were returning to their Northampton, England, home Kelmarsh Hall.

Michael, Jeremy, the servants and the Trees' baggage were safely stored on board, and the children put to sleep. Michael is just recovering, Mrs. Tree said later, from a serious illness. Through misunderstanding of the time of sailing, the parents went to the theater, confident they had time to get to the pier, where they thought the Olympic would sail at midnight.

The valet, the maid servant and the nurse were in a quandary as time passed and the Trees did not arrive. They removed the baggage to the pier whence it could be transferred to the Arabic, a White Star cabin liner which sailed two hours later, and which took a few days longer to cross the Atlantic than the Olympic. The valet and maid waited with the baggage.

But the arrangement did not suit Mrs. Tree at all. She almost collapsed on learning the news because of her fear for Michael. The White Star marine superintendent, told of the case, wired Captain William T. Parker to hold the vessel at Quarantine. At midnight the Trees departed to catch the boat, taking a swift New York Central tug from pier 60, at the foot of West Nineteenth Street.

When we arrived at the pier and found the ship had left, I told the man there I was nursing a child and he would starve if they didn't stop for us. Michael was seven and Jeremy three. He asked me if we knew anybody on the board of White Star and I asked him who's on the board? He said so-and-so Vanderbilt, whom I'd never heard of but told the man that we were "intimate friends." When we got to the ship and climbed up the steps and on board, I went straight to my room and stayed in bed for three days. The captain was furious. He was furious that he had just turned this great ship around and was headed out to sea when he had to drop anchor for us. The captain told me once I had emerged from our suite that it was a good thing I had stayed there, because he wasn't sure what he would have said.

PART ONE

During their first three years of marriage, Ronald and Nancy Tree lived in more than half a dozen houses. Like a royal progress, they moved from Virginia to New York and back to Virginia, to Massachusetts or Long Island in the summer, to Melton Mowbray in England to foxhunt, to London, then back to New York and Virginia. The first autumn they were married, they rented Mirador from Phyllis Brand; then in the winter they moved to New York City, where Ronald Tree enrolled in the Columbia University School of Journalism and Nancy took an economics course at Hunter College. Tree wanted a career in politics and public service, following in the footsteps of his Tree grandfather, who was by turns an ambassador and a judge. In England, where Ronald was raised, politics remained a gentleman's career, civic leadership still a responsibility and an acceptable profession. **I wanted Ronnie to go into politics in Virginia; I had it all worked out. I said to him,**

"We've got a running start. We're young and we've got money." First we would buy the Charlottesville *Progress*, then we would buy the Lynchburg paper that controlled the tobacco vote. That was my fantasy. Tree believed that college, and an education in journalism, was the ideal way to meet Americans, learn their curious idiosyncrasies and study their entirely foreign sensibilities. He later wrote, "I was conscious of two obstacles. First, I had an English accent which, try as I would to exorcise it, remained stubbornly with me. . . . Secondly, I was conscious of the gulf between me and the people whom I liked and admired, but with whom I felt no rapport—a gulf as much due to my upbringing in another country as to my personality: I was shy."[1]

That spring Nancy returned to Mirador and Ronald commuted from New York on weekends. He would always arrive exhausted, because back then it was an overnight trip by train and it was always difficult to find a berth. In the summer they rented a house in Beverly Farms near the shore in Massachusetts. Nancy was pregnant with her first child and spent the summer touring New England and especially New English houses. There there were lovely town houses built for clipper ship captains. They would buy a ship, make a couple of trips to the Orient, bringing back china and Chinese paper and slaves, and be rich enough to build a big house and retire before they were twenty-five. Ronald Tree played polo that summer.

The Trees moved back to Mirador in the autumn, then that winter they again rented in New York, this time a house on East Ninety-sixth Street. Their first son, Michael, was born in that house. It belonged to Ogden Codman, and it was perhaps a stroke of fate for Nancy Tree to live there, for Codman was one of the period's most celebrated decorators and architects. His work, mostly domestic and nearly always for patrician clients, included houses, additions, interiors and gardens for his family's friends in Boston (Thayers, Ameses and Crowninshields), his cousins in Newport and his New York society acquaintances (Burdens, Clewses, Vanderbilts, Frelinghuysens and Emerys). He worked as well in four different houses owned by Elsie de Wolfe, whom he strongly influenced.

Codman himself would have preferred to be remembered as an architect, but it was partly because of Codman that interior design has risen to the rank of respected artistic discipline. *The Decoration of Houses* (1897), a book he wrote in collaboration with Edith Wharton, was the first widely published dissertation on and guide to decorating. In it the two argued that the proper arrangement of the inside of a house was nearly as difficult, sophisticated and learned a task as sketching elevations. It was a precise science, they suggested, a combination of mathematics, psychology, social anthropology and

Mr. and Mrs. Arthur Ronald Lambert Field Tree on their wedding day in 1920

history; it required a knowledge of architectural proportion as it did an intimacy with the lifestyle of the occupants. Such proclamations were a revela-
tion in their day, but Codman, the dandy from Old New England, and
Wharton, the indefatigable observer of Old New York, were singularly qual-
ified to pass such advice on to those in whose houses they regularly dined.
Their book was a big step toward the advent of the professional decorating
ladies of the coming century.*

In his own designs Codman was the master of the genteel, refined yet
opulent interior. For his clients he executed sumptuous wall treatments,
mostly Louis XV and XVI, and was adept at utilizing building materials the
French used, such as the gray stone of Parisian town houses. In furnishing a
room, he preferred period originals, but if he couldn't find the piece he
wanted in antiques shops, Codman wouldn't hesitate to have a copy made,
often just as beautiful and doubtless more sturdy. The house the Trees
rented, 7 East Ninety-sixth Street, he considered one of his favorite and
most successful projects. He built it for himself, and was both its architect
and decorator.

> It really was the most beautiful house in New York. You drove
> in, as you do in France, through two great storm doors in the facade
> into a cobbled courtyard. The front door, which was wrought iron
> and plate glass, was on the side under the porte cochere. Inside there
> was a stone entrance hall and the most lovely staircase going up to
> the main floor, where there was a long library/drawing room that
> stretched across the entire front of the house. It went over the porte
> cochere. The drawing room was paneled, with a fireplace and inset
> bookshelves at both ends. We took the house from Ogden Codman
> furnished, and the drawing room was filled with lovely French fur-
> niture. Very, very good furniture. Codman had perfect taste. I
> remember the curtains were made of unbleached sailcloth or muslin.
> It was all very smart.

One question Ogden Codman began to answer at 7 East Ninety-sixth
Street was how to make a house more livable while retaining the elements
of grandeur and order necessary to his and his clients' social positions. The
architectural and interior design of his house was, in most details, meticu-
lously neoclassical. The undemonstrative exterior was based on a Bordeaux
town house, with stone swags, a second-floor balcony and tall French windows. He superimposed balance onto the interior by repeating certain

---

*Codman's client Elsie de Wolfe later published her own book, *The House in Good
Taste* (1913).

The porte cochere of Ogden Codman's town house on East Ninety-sixth Street in New York. Codman bought the land from Andrew Carnegie in 1908 and was a pioneer of sorts in developing a mansion so far uptown in Manhattan (Metcalf, p. 28).

architectural forms, such as paired double doors with rounded transoms, which mimicked the shape of the French windows and rhymed with the arches and sculpture niches throughout the house's rooms and passages. The same reverence for symmetry carried over into his arrangement of a room's furniture. A looking glass on one wall mirrored a looking glass on a far wall; a bookcase stood opposite another bookcase. For every one chair there was a partner, and side chairs were kept in "couples." It was this studied and unrelenting rhythm that allowed him to let go a bit when choosing the furniture he used.

Society in New York, Newport and Long Island remained obstinately formal, especially in entertaining, right up through the First World War toward the Second. Attire was strict—Codman himself dressed as he decorated, with not a hair out of place—as were etiquette and manners. Houses conformed to and reflected the same rules and rigidity. To the generation of decorators preceding Codman, generally no more than glorified upholsterers, "formality" meant uniformity; room after room in Gilded Age houses similarly caricatured Versailles or resembled period displays in museums. Few showed any originality. But Codman was a great connoisseur of many

Mirador in 1909, painted by Hoffbaur. Nancy Perkins was born in the cottage at the
left of the house, which was originally the kitchen.

Nancy's rounded hallway and spiraling staircase were decidedly grander than the straight passage and steps of Mirador in her grandparents' day but were in keeping with other houses in Virginia built in the same period.

A Mirador guest room as rendered by Scaisbrooke Langhorne Abbott

"Such a time as I have had moving things," wrote Nancy to her sister, Alice, from Mirador in 1922. "I begin doing it early in the morning [and continue] until late at night. We are living upstairs and very gradually getting straight. I have a man repairing furniture and two making curtains and covers, etc. It is all so lovely."

different periods in the decorative arts, moving about easily in the various genres of eighteenth-century England, France, Italy and Colonial America. A collector as well, he owned the finest examples of the furniture he admired. The rooms in the house Nancy and Ronald Tree rented were indeed formally arranged, but instead of being locked into one period, they displayed the best examples of different but related styles. Codman thus overcame the standard monotony and contributed to a subtle fluidity in his designs.

Owning good furniture—among his treasures were a real Chippendale breakfront cabinet, a Louis XV marble-and-gilt console table, rare Sèvres urns and soup terrines—along with his exacting arrangements, allowed Codman the addition of furniture that wasn't rare or swank but *was* comfortable. That was new in this setting and in the society to which he belonged. At one end of his living room, Codman's matched bookcases were real Chippendale, the sofa was Queen Anne and one of the two pairs of side chairs was original Louis XVI. But the other pair, placed between the museum pieces, were common French country *bergères*. All of the pieces were regimented and covered in patterned cotton upholstery so they visually conformed, but it was now a room in which to sit back, rather than pose bolt upright on the edge of a priceless two-hundred-year-old seat or a copy thereof. Codman's layering of different periods and this inclusion of comfortable furniture in his rooms left a lasting impression on Nancy Tree.

No room of Codman's, perhaps no room in all of New York, compared with his dining room at Ninety-sixth Street. It began with the perfect shape, perfectly round, and perfectly proportioned from ceiling to floor. He divided the room like a pie eight ways, using three French windows—opened onto the park on warm nights—two sculpture niches, a niche for serving, and two doors, one for the guests and one for the staff. Each aperture was matched in size and design, and each was equidistant, like cogs on a wheel. Codman then gave the room a round carpet and a round table and surrounded the table with cane-backed chairs. Crowning it was a chandelier with real candles. It was all very neat, tidy and elegant, all achieved with a minimum of distractions. This was Codman's other great lesson to the *beau monde:* Brilliant simplicity was far more pleasing than overcrowded opulence. It was the lesson of the age to come: Reduce, reduce, reduce.

I used to have dinner parties of twenty-five or thirty people there, dinner parties of rather distinguished people of all ages whom my aunts knew. I had a French cook in those days who made delicious food, whose name was Elise Dufour. And I had a ridiculous lunch party for the English actresses Gertrude Lawrence and Beatrice Lillie at Ninety-sixth Street. They were friends of Nora

Codman decorated rooms at Kykuit for John D. Rockefeller, Jr., at Hyde Park for Frederick W. Vanderbilt and at the Mount for Edith Wharton. Few, though, were as striking and graceful as his own dining room, shown here.

Phipps's, and when they came over to New York they brought a letter to me from Nora. So I invited Mrs. Henry Clews and Mrs. Griswold, all these New York *grande dames* who were Aunt Irene's friends, to meet these two slap-and-tickle actresses. There we all were, waiting for Bea and Gertrude in this beautiful drawing room with fresh spring flowers and lovely books and French furniture, in the most wonderful house in New York, all these ladies like old Mrs. Clews, sitting there in her dainty little face veils, her hair done up on top of her head in the most stylish way, her wonderful little shoes—when in walk these two actresses in filthy riding costumes and boots that they had rented for a ride in Central Park before lunch, both of them looking very sweaty and like hooligans. Bea Lillie, the funniest woman I've ever met, took one look at this party, one look at the ladies I'd assembled, and said, "Oh, I feel faint," and had to be carried downstairs, where a cab was called for her. Gertrude Lawrence wasn't as quick and had to stay for the afternoon in her ridiculous

The library at 7 East Ninety-sixth Street. Codman "resented the loss of refinement to life in New York" after the First World War (Metcalf, p. 30). Moving to France in 1920, he left his town house available for the Trees to rent.

riding costume, chatting with the *grande dames*. I was about twenty years old and didn't know any better, but I learned not to mix my drinks after that.

People still lived in New York back then. The city was home, not just a Grand Central Station for commuters. And there was a great deal of social life amongst these families whose parents and grand-parents had been friends. The Roosevelts, the Delanos, the Hayeses, the Lawrences. Lots of friends lived in the Murray Hill district, which had brownstone family houses, and Washington Square and lower Fifth Avenue still had people living there. One Fifth Avenue was a house where the Butler-Duncans lived. They were Paul Phipps's grandparents. Across the street in 2 Fifth Avenue the Wiborgs of Cincinnati lived in an old-fashioned double-fronted house. He made his fortune in ink in Ohio. There were three very beautiful Wiborg sisters. One married Stuyvesant Fish, and one married a man called Gerald Murphy, who was a friend of Zelda

Fitzgerald's and lived in Cap d'Antibes.[2] The third daughter, Hoytie, never married. They were all very beautiful, they all played the guitar and sang, and they all came to England and were a great success. They had tremendous parties at their house near Washington Square. A lot of Englishmen used to come to Hoytie's parties. . . . They were the first of what they called the "free and easy parties." Edith Deacon used to be there. She became Mrs. Harry Gray, and her sister became the Duchess of Marlborough. She would come to those parties with a great bunch of orchids pinned on her shoulder. And I remember a wonderful party for the artist Sert, who had come over to New York. Hoytie always had artists to her parties to mix with everybody else. When Sert came over, they hung a room in the house with his pictures of all different kinds of red. No one had ever seen these clashing reds on a wall like that. Ogden Phipps bought them all.

There still used to be tremendous balls at Mrs. William K. Vanderbilt, Jr.'s, house at Fifth Avenue and about Fifty-third Street in the early twenties. There were two big Vanderbilt houses next to each other there. I suppose they're gone now, but that was all still going on when I lived in New York. I remember another ball at Old Mrs. Willie K. Vanderbilt's—her mother-in-law's—when I lived in New York. Old Mrs. Willie K. started Sutton Place; she was supposed to have great taste. My Aunt Irene took me to see her house, and Old Mrs. Willie K. showed me around. I imagine Elsie de Wolfe decorated it. The only thing that I remember is that on the lavatory seat she had a cushion, a chintz cushion with a frill. I remember thinking to myself that if you really had to use it in an emergency, it would have been very difficult to uncover the seat, and the cushion might drop in the bowl.

I was also invited to lunch at Elsie de Wolfe's house a number of times. I was never an intimate friend of hers, but there was no question of meeting her and being acquainted. New York was very small, and everyone seemed to know each other. I imagine she knew the Gibsons, but I think Aunt Irene rather looked down on her. She was a lesbian or something. But she was very chic. She must have been about fifty or sixty when I first knew her. When her hair went gray, she had it dyed mauve or blue to match her eyes; she was the very first to have blue hair. When I went to have lunch with her, she showed me around her house, and I remember she had an orchid in her bathroom. Nobody ever had flowers in any bathroom I had ever been in. But she had this orchid on a very pretty old glass thing, and as I was looking around the rest of the bathroom I backed into the very pretty old glass thing and broke it. I've never felt so ashamed.

A few years later I would see her—by then she was Lady Mendl—in Paris at Chanel when we were both buying our clothes. She really was frightfully chic. She had bought the Villa Trianon at Versailles and restored and decorated it. She had a tremendous amount of money from buying furniture for some very rich man, I've forgotten who, and had great business ability. I suppose she had good taste. She was considered the last word in decorating. She had a way of getting a pink flush in a room: You painted the room pink, then painted white over it. That was supposed to be very chic. But I wasn't impressed by her in the end. When I went to see her house at Versailles, she took me to see the bathroom: There was that orchid in a vase again. I thought it absurd. By that time I had got places. She had it because nobody else had it. Everybody was questing for something new, that was the most important thing to them; they seemed to always want to break ground.

There were a few ladies in New York who really did make an impression on me though. I remember Mrs. Freddy Beach had a wonderful way of arranging furniture. She went abroad a great deal and collected very good old china, and when you went into her drawing room—it sounds perfectly silly now—there were two of her best soup terrines, displayed on top of old mahogany washstands. Everyone thought that very stylish. The first time I saw a sulphur yellow room was at Edith Baker's. Another was Mrs. Burden, who had a big house on Long Island, where she had installed the old gates from Devonshire House that she bought when they tore it down. Hers was a lovely house with a lovely garden that Billy Delano designed. Mrs. Burden was the first person in America to use old Portuguese table covers—old flowered-cotton tablecloths—as upholstery on furniture. They didn't match, and they were old and faded. It was the first time one saw old chintz used like that. Now it's been run into the ground by a few New York decorators who have twenty-nine different modern chintzes all over every room.

I never wanted to start something, as those New York ladies did. I always had a nostalgia for the past. That was the strongest drive in me.

FOR THE NEXT two years Ronald and Nancy continued to travel between New York, Virginia and the shore. We always took very nice houses on the

North Shore—one year we rented the Spelmans' house: We moved all the servants there from New York. Ronnie played polo every day, and I saw a great deal of the Appletons, who had been there forever, and Alice Hay, who was a great friend of mine. Nancy was pregnant with her second child. The baby, a daughter, was born prematurely at Mirador that autumn and died six hours later, isolated from medical attention. She was buried next to Henry Field in the Emmanuel Episcopal Church graveyard in Greenwood, in a small lot surrounded by a brick wall with a wrought-iron gate inscribed N.T.

The Trees spent another winter in Codman's house in New York, then the next spring at Mirador, then rented the Rumsey house in Westbury, Long Island, for the early summer. The Prince of Wales, the future King Edward VIII of England, arrived on Long Island to play polo, and a string of dinners, dances and balls were given in his honor. A lot of English people came to Long Island that summer. There was Violet Westminster, Nada Milford Haven, the Airlies. They all came over. Fruity Metcalfe was with the Prince and old Lord Wimbourne brought over a team. He was a terrible cad. That ambassador was there who, it was said, had a brain that was always shut and a fly that was always open. His wife looked like a lamb chop. There were a lot of balls that summer, a lot of entertainments for the Prince. I gave a dance at Pat Rumsey's house and the Prince came. That August Nancy rented a house in Southampton, Long Island, with her friend Alexandra Moore, who had a son the same age as Michael Tree.

After Christmas, for what was left of the foxhunting season, they rented a hunting box in Langham, Leicestershire, where they spent January, February and March following the Cottesmore Hunt. Langham was just down the road from Melton Mowbray, the town where Chiswell Langhorne rented houses for his daughters Phyllis and Nancy when the two traveled to England to hunt at the end of the nineteenth century. In the 1920s, when the Trees stayed there, Melton was the undisputed capital city of international hunt society. Melton was "Where the business of life is to hunt every day/And the nights must take care of themselves as they may," wrote George Whyte-Melville, a "hunting poet." Ronald Tree's stepfather, the first Earl Beatty,* lived near Melton at Brooksby Hall, while Ronald's cousin by marriage Major Algie Burnaby was Master of the Foxhounds for the Quorn, one of the packs that attracted the swells to Melton. The Prince of Wales kept a suite of rooms at Craven Lodge for the season, the Lodge being a sort of aristocratic boarding house that provided stabling for horses and lavish entertainments for hunt followers. And the Embassy Club of

*His full title was Earl Beatty, Viscount Borodale of Wexford, Baron Beatty of the North Sea and of Brooksby, GCB, OM, GCVO, DSO, PC.

London opened a satellite at Melton in the 1920s; so between nightclubs, Craven Lodge, the manor houses and hunting boxes, the formal yet ecstatic atmosphere in this somewhat quaint English village produced its own version of a Scott Fitzgerald–style Roaring Twenties. In Melton a colorful mixture of the era's fast opulence—top hats and pink coats during the day, white tie and tails or ball gowns at night—resided alongside rural England's earthiness.

> We sent two grooms over to England with our horses two weeks ahead of us to acclimatize the horses to the country. The grooms took over ten or twelve horses, four or five for me and five or six for Ronnie: You could really only ride a horse once a week, and you needed two horses a day. When we traveled two weeks later, we took with us on the ship Michael and his nanny, Nanny Weir, who was with my children from the day they were born; a nursery maid; Ronnie's servant; my maid; all of our linens, in an enormous container that looked like a coffin; a cook; the car; a chauffeur; and our personal belongings. Everything went first by rail, then by ship, then by rail again when we got to England. The ship passage took a week. It seems quite extraordinary how one lived then. After we moved to England, we used to do the whole thing in reverse, send the horses and cars and children to Virginia.

In the summer of 1925, with Nancy pregnant with her second son, the family rented another house in Southampton, then moved back to Mirador that autumn. She took a steamship to England after Christmas and rented a house on Charles Street near Berkeley Square, where Jeremy was born. Ronald Tree stayed on at Mirador, acting as host to Lord and Lady Astor, who were visiting Virginia. That spring, after Jeremy's birth, the Trees hunted in Northamptonshire with the Pytchley—the more physically demanding, though less glamorous, hunt country not far from Melton—and stayed at the dower house at Kelmarsh Hall, renting it from Captain "Jubie" Lancaster.

PART TWO

I'm a land snob. The first land I bought in Virginia was Misfit, a few years after Grandfather died, when Ronnie and I were renting Mirador from Phyllis and living between New York and Virginia. Then Phyllis sold Mirador to me in about 1922: She had married Bob Brand and moved to England, so she was rarely there. Over the next years I bought all the land going up from Mirador to Greenwood. Then there was the land up on top of the Blue Ridge where, when I was a child, my grandfather and his neighbors used to send their cattle in the summer because it was cooler and bluegrass grew there. I remember my brother, Chillie, would drive the cattle up there for Grandfather. I owned that land, too. I owned about one thousand acres. I could ride on my own land, up the mountain, to the station or the post office, or I could cross over the macadam road to the other side of the county. I simply love the soil. I haven't got any left now, but I've always loved the land.

Mirador was Nancy's first full-scale decorating project. Phyllis and Reginald Brooks had made only minor alterations to the house, so when it became Nancy's, Mirador was much as her grandmother had left it more than twenty years before, still resonating in Mrs. Langhorne's own rendition of Gay Nineties fashion: the same furniture, upholstery and pictures. It completely lacked modern conveniences. **Until I bought Mirador the house was only lit by oil lamps and candles; there was no electricity. At night you read by lamps; there were also candles by all the beds. I had Mirador wired when I bought it.** Only twenty-four years old, Nancy was nonetheless well-equipped to bring Mirador into the twentieth century.

She had been weaned on style; good taste came without effort. The fashionable world saw the Langhorne way as attractive and alluring—all who came in contact with their family over the years beheld it—but to Nancy it was the ordinary language spoken at the breakfast table. In the boys it was evident in their crumpled woolen suits and worn-but-well-shined leather riding boots, their heavy Virginia drawls, their loose posture. It was apparent in Mr. Langhorne's walrus mustache, his ever-present cigar, his "delicacies" and matchless self-assurance. The sisters had their interested eyes, pinched waists and perfect seats on horseback, as well as the spontaneous charm that was always punctuated with a pause and a raised brow. And Mrs. Langhorne seemed to possess all the grace, all the manners and all the patience of the Old Dominion itself. This unaffected Langhorne way was second nature to Nancy Tree, her natural form of expression.

Decorating was just another manifestation of the Langhorne legacy. Mirador was both a repository and a backdrop for the family's élan.

My family was full of decorators. My mother and every one of my aunts had good taste, and every one of them loved things that were unique to them. I remember some little ideas, like Aunt Irene's curtains made out of sailcloth. I thought that a very clever trick; you

didn't have to line them. Aunt Nora had tremendous flair, tremendous originality. She used to say, "I want plain walls, then I want all the color around the room like the color you see in a herbaceous border." Phyllis had a marvelous taste for getting furniture, as my mother did. But Phyllis's houses were extremely sad, where Nancy Astor's and Nora's were frightfully gay. It's very curious; my mother had it, Nora had it, all these Langhornes seemed to have it.

While Nancy was still a little girl, her mother, Elizabeth, bequeathed to her some of the more tangible rituals of decoration with scissors and pelmet patterns on the sitting-room floor. Her Aunt Irene confirmed the inheritance at the cottage and garden in Maine and the Stanford White house on East Seventy-third Street with her knowledge of antique furniture. Nancy Astor, always larger than life, showed Nancy Perkins something about thinking big and taking bold steps. By the time Nancy Tree became mistress of Mirador, what she had absorbed from her family had been refined by trips to historic houses all over Virginia and Europe.

I was always searching for beauty. I wasn't as interested in the houses as I was in their ambience. In the furniture, in the history, in the garden. You never really could put your finger specifically on whatever created beauty, it was too illusive, but houses were where I found it the most.

I remember visiting an old lady's house in Bristol, Rhode Island, with my mother. The woman had some very fine china . . . the family evidently had had clipper ships in their past. She kept the china in a cupboard, and around the handle on one soup terrine she had tied a pink ribbon. That's what I loved. This lady thought that very beautiful, decorating her greatest prize with a pink taffeta ribbon.

There was no lack of references and ideas when Nancy set out to decorate Mirador, no lack of confidence or of resources. There was, however, a dilemma. To make it her own and to bring into the present a house that was built in 1825 and last spruced up thirty years before, Nancy needed to make drastic changes. This meant altering the very house that had inspired her love of houses, the place closest to her heart and at the center of the family clan. Change was inevitable, but it couldn't be to the total banishment of the spirit of Nancy's rich childhood, or of Mrs. Bowen's ghost.

The Trees started with architectural alterations to the old house, to give their family more room inside, and to visually alter the overall design of the house somewhat as well.

When Phyllis owned Mirador she made the back drawing room longer by filling in that part of the back porch. It faced the garden and the Blue Ridge. As I intended to spend the rest of my life at Mirador and needed more space, I filled in the rest of the porch, straight across and right up to the roof, making it part of the house. I made brick arches underneath where there had been pillars. This gave me inside space for bathrooms. I'm not talking about little bathrooms. Mine were big bathrooms with cupboards and cork floors. They were more like proper rooms, with a window in each of them and prints on the walls. That was something new. In Grandfather's day there were only two bathrooms and there was always a shortage of water. His bathrooms had tiny taps. I was always bathed in about four inches of water. Reggie Brooks built an artesian well, but the taps were still small, and even then the water only trickled. I said, if I ever get this place I'm going to have real water pressure. So I put laundry taps in the bathrooms, and the water gushed out.

Behind where I filled in the old porch I made a new one from stone, where we could sit. I left it uncovered. I had steps coming down to the back garden from either side of the new porch so the back of the house remained balanced. My bedroom, which was in the wing downstairs, opened onto the porch. I slept downstairs on the ground floor as Grandfather did; it was much cooler. Ronnie's room also opened onto the porch. We had separate bedrooms because Ronnie had a white servant and I preferred colored servants. I made Grandfather's "spare room" into another sitting room and put in it the old mantelpiece from the Cabell house on the James called Soldiers Joy. I never really enlarged the shape of the house, never hurt the original square proportions . . . we got more space by altering the inside and filling in the back porch, but I didn't get any more rooms than it already had. I returned the front porch to the size it had been before, and I took the attic window off the front of the house.

The one problem we did have with our plans at Mirador, as I saw it, was with the hall. It would have been too long and too narrow now that we had extended the back of the house. I said to Billy Delano, a friend of ours from New York who was our architect at Mirador, "Couldn't you hollow out the middle of the hall, make it round and two storeys tall and put a skylight at the top?" Which is exactly what he did. It turned out to be perfectly beautiful. It gave a

Nancy restored the box hedges leading up to the front steps of Mirador that her grandfather had pulled up twenty years before, but she left the walk—worn, cracked and pitted—just as it was.

great deal of light to the stair and to the hall. The new staircase swept up the round walls to the second floor, where a gallery completed the spiral. This was very much in keeping with other houses in Virginia built at the same time. And we were able to retain the straight path between the front and back doors for the cool breezes. We inlaid the floor with black and white tiles as in the Codman house, a pattern you see in a lot of old houses, and we added an inlaid compass at the hall's center. We painted the walls a kind of light sandy yellow, and we hung them with the Napoleonic prints that had belonged to my great-grandfather. I found a rounded bookcase in England that fit the rounded wall of the hall, and filled it with orange Chamberlain Worcester china. Under the stairs I had an old red-leather trunk, which held fire logs.

Nancy kept most of the furniture that had been in the house since her grandparents' day, and with it, despite the architectural alterations, saved the sense of a continuum, of stability, of established ease, that characterized Mirador. I had all the mahogany four-poster beds in the bedrooms and a lot of the same tables and chairs. What I did do at Mirador was have new upholstery and curtains made of different patterns and colors of chintz, which was

The new garden facade of Mirador with the flagstone porch William Delano and Nancy designed for it. (Nancy's bedroom was in the wing to the right.)

quite a step in the twenties. But only old chintz. Old chintz fit the mood of the house; I wanted the feeling that it hadn't been decorated at all, just lived in.

The familiar furniture was rearranged "à la Codman," as Nancy wrote in a letter to her sister Alice: "the old wing chairs and two comfy ones . . . with tables and the bench in front of the fire." Mixed among the heirlooms were "Leach prints and the needlework rug [and] spinet I bought. . . . It is all too lovely. The living room is exquisite . . . the library is beautiful."[3]

Billy Delano worked with the Trees in landscaping Mirador as well. I remember sitting on the porch with Billy, looking out over the back garden to the mountains behind the house and discussing how we could bring the mountains into the garden, how we could make them part of the garden. Delano was a modern successor of Georgian England's architects, equally adept with overdoors and quadrant passages as with the length and breadth of avenues, axes and sunk lawns around the house. Versed in the wedding of building to surroundings, Delano saw that "the land about the house seem[ed] neither a preparation for it nor an extention of its character, but an indispensable member of a carefully pondered scheme."[4] **Billy's knowledge of classical architecture greatly influenced me.**

William Adams Delano specialized in country houses, still a thriving business between the wars, and "epitomized the elegant, witty, well-educated society architect."[5] Descended from the Boston Adamses on one side of his family, he was born in New York, raised in Philadelphia and educated at Lawrenceville, Yale and the École des Beaux-Arts in Paris. He apprenticed with Carrère and Hastings, the leading country house designers of their day, and worked directly under Thomas Hastings. Hastings had himself apprenticed with Charles McKim of McKim, Mead and White, who had in his turn worked in the studio of Richard Morris Hunt. The torch of influence and fashion passed from one to the next, with Delano becoming the most sought-after domestic architect in America in the first two decades of the century. In his fifty-year practice in Manhattan, Delano built only one skyscraper in a period when they sprouted out of the ground like weeds, but he designed over a hundred country houses in his career for friends and friends of friends like Henry Walters in Baltimore, John D. Rockefeller, Jr., Gertrude Vanderbilt Whitney (he was an original board member of the Whitney Museum), Adele Burden on Long Island and Paul Mellon in Virginia. With Delano, Nancy was again associated with one of the era's most influential neoclassical architects: architects who have been relegated to relative historical obscurity by the advent of the Modernists, yet who received the bulk of the actual building commissions of the day.[6]

While we sat there and talked, Billy sketched our thoughts so I could see how they might or might not work. He could do charming watercolors and little drawings. He was very patient, and it was he who taught me that the garden should relate to the house and that there was great value in long, framed vistas to distant points. They kept one's eye from sliding sideways.

We brought the Blue Ridge into the garden by changing the horizon line at the back of the house. I made a wide lawn down the center of the garden, straight out the back porch, bordered by a brick wall on either side and tree boxwood. I wanted the box to grow tall and thin and hang over so that sunlight could shine through it like at the Villa Frascati. I planted a row of willow trees to the left behind the box so there was something there while the box grew, and to the left I kept Nanere's square rose garden.

The back lawn was divided into two sections; the first, a sunk lawn, stopped where the old smokehouse was off to one side. We still hung hams in it, and the hummingbirds loved the trumpet vines growing outside. To balance the smokehouse, I built a garden room of the same design opposite it. I connected the two buildings, across the lawn, with an arched passageway like the ones between the main house and the wings at Mount Vernon. The arches were the same shape as the new arches under the porch in the back of the house; we covered them in wisteria.

Immediately behind the arched passageway was another section of lawn, bordered by apple trees and a double row of flowering pyrus trees. It ended in a round, brick double-stair with a small *jet d'eau* in the middle. There were a few old pear trees around it that we left, and the lawn and the trees provided us with a lovely shaded spot to sit. Up the round steps was a path, skewed to the right, that led along the length of the tennis court. The court had been built originally with the sun in mind instead of symmetry but was thankfully hidden by thick honeysuckle. To hide the cockeyed angle of the path, and to balance out the court, we raised a tall wire net to the left of it, as though there was another court, and let honeysuckle drape over it. From below, the arch framed the rounded steps and the fountain. The new honeysuckle wall blocked out the valley that had dragged the vista down with it, so now, from the porch or my bedroom windows, your eye went up the lawn, over the wooden arches and the honeysuckle, straight up the face of the Blue Ridge. It was as though we had moved the mountain to the base of Mirador's back garden. It was a great success.

There was more garden off to the left and to the right of the central lawn, and in organizing it Billy suggested we look for balance as in Italian and French gardens. This gave order and complemented the lines of the house. Where the vegetable garden had been in Nanere's day, we made a grass opening in the shape of a lady's slipper. I used dogwood and mock-orange for the back and the heel of the shoe near the brick path, and for the sole I planted a hedge of bridal wreath. At its instep, we made a path across to the other side of the garden, a cross axis, that ended in a small, round pool surrounded by willow trees. On that side of the back lawn we had the new vegetable garden and greenhouse. The vegetable garden had a path of flowers that ended in a sandpile for the children to play in, with a pretty lattice entrance. The lattice looked like a summerhouse from the distance; Nanny Weir used to sit on the bench near it while the children played in the sand and rode their bicycles up and down the paths.

A few years later I copied at Mirador Thomas Jefferson's serpentine walls from the University of Virginia. He used the serpentine shape because if a wall curved back and forth like a snake it could stand up even if it was only a single brick thick. You saved bricks, which were rather precious when you had to make them yourself. We

Mirador's twinned serpentine walls draped in climbing roses and flanked by magnolias

were raised to think Jefferson invented them, but actually they're all over Essex. But what he did do was pair them. I think that's marvelous; there must be two at a time. At Mirador I bought some old bricks and put a pair of serpentine walls to the right of the house; I planted magnolias up and down both walls. Out the back of the serpentine path, a hill dropped down sharply to a lake that I made by stopping a small stream where they used to grow watermelons.

Serpentine walls and wooded walks, crisscrossing paths, vistas, the water jet, all of the garden seats and resting spots that stretched out from the old house—the architecture acted as a superstructure on which nature could flourish, as a trellis does for sweet peas or a climbing rose. But the garden's newness was fast buried by "quantities of old favorites," a very long list of flowering shrubs and plants. It was very important to me that all of the hard lines of the house and the garden be softened, that they be tempered by overgrown, dripping plants and vines like the trumpet vine that buried Grandfather's stone arch. Huge shade trees grew all around the house, saving it from looking like a bald-headed man sitting in a red clay field. The trees made the house and lawns shimmer with dappled shade and sunlight. Spilling flower beds and shrubs kept paths and walls from looking too perfect, too new or too stiff.

The view from the back of Mirador, over the garden buildings, into the Blue Ridge
Mountains

Propagation of annuals and perennials began in the winter of 1923. Anything that could be raised from seed was grown at Mirador by Mirador gardeners. The trees and bushes were ordered from nurseries all over the East
Coast. An extravagant list of perennials included *Campanula persicifolia* (peach,
bells, blue and white), *Coreopsis lanceolata grandiflora*, delphinium (blue and
white Chinese, sky-blue *D. belladonna*, deep blue *D. bellamosum*, lilac Queen
Wilhelmena and mixed Gold Medal Hybrids), sweet rocket (lilac and white),
foxglove, *Lupinus polyphyllus*, *Aquilegia* and *Anemone* St. Brigids. A few of the
annuals Nancy used that first year for bedding were ageratum, sweet alyssum,
candytuft, petunia, *Phlox drummondii*. Others were planted among the perennials in herbaceous borders or planted in lines in a cutting garden. Each subsequent year the list grew, always with an emphasis on "old favorites": plants
and flowers that were traditionally Virginian, simple, never ostentatious.[7]

Irene Gibson and Phyllis Brand should have been the harshest critics of
what Nancy was doing to their old home, yet Aunt Irene wrote to Nancy that
"everything you have done here has responded to you—every old thing
blooms for you, and you are just the big part of it all."[8] Later she wrote,
"Mirador has never looked lovelier. It is a sweet place, and I think that lawn

coming up to the front is one of the loveliest things in the world—the peri-winkle is like big dark waves and, as Marion Cran says, is 'The joy of the ground.' It is what people feel in a garden and in a place . . . loved and made with affection and flowers with delicious scents that really score. . . . Your willow and magnolia trees are doing well by the wall."[9]

Aunt Phyllis wrote, "Mirador looking lovely. I always feel she is so glad to see me. I could never really feel anywhere else is really home but here, and [it's] as if I had never left it. In spite of the dryness Dowsett has kept the garden looking lovely and green. Those cedar trees by Callie's cottage have grown so much even since last year and look lovely, and the gate at the end is a great improvement, and the vines on your serpentine wall are looking very fat and well grown now. It is all perfect."[10]

AFTER THE TREES bought Mirador, a large cast of supporting characters continued to take care of the house, the garden and the farm, both when the Trees were in residence and when they were away. The gardens especially needed attention all year round and required a sizable staff, as did the home farm, with its cattle, pigs, chickens and other livestock. Mirador remained pretty much self-sufficient. Some of the staff traveled with the family: Ronald Tree's valet, Nancy's lady's maid, Nanny Weir and sometimes the grooms; most of the others were attached permanently to Mirador. The housekeeper, Miss Jenny White, who came to Mirador from New York when Phyllis owned it, and a housemaid from Scotland named Helen were exceptions, as they had come to Mirador from other parts. The rest—the garden workers, the farmhands, the odd man, as well as Callie Brown, a maid there for over forty years, and Nancy's cherished butler, Stewart Wood—lived their entire lives in the vicinity of Mirador. In many cases their parents had worked for Mr. Langhorne and for Phyllis.

> I've always said this: I'm most grateful for having grown up in the South because of the servants I was brought up by and with. We lived very close together at Mirador. They were as much a part of the place and the day-to-day life as the family. We really had the strongest attachment. An old butler at a friend's house in Richmond said to me a few years ago, "You know, Miss Nancy, nobody remembers the good relationship we had between our races, and it ain't never going to be the same." It wasn't familiarity; it was a very strong understanding. We felt very dependent on each other, something irreplaceable that comes from having lived together side by side, generation after generation. They stayed with the family for years and years, fathers to sons, mothers to daughters. Several of them had known slavery. You feel something with them you don't

feel about foreign servants that have come from a different part of the world. I never would have had what I've had if I'd been brought up by Irish maids who knew how to turn beds down but were distant. We shared a common heritage, a common past. They had known the old ways, knew the way things were done, as much as we did. It's something that makes me very much more close to Southern women than to Northern or English women.

At Mirador there was Aunt Veeny Barbour, Emily Pate the housemaid, Fountain Winston, Aunt Anne Brody, who was the cook in my grandfather's day; Aunt Liza Pie, our mammie; Aunt Margaret, Aunt Lucy Crapp, Callie Pearl, who was Mrs. Virgil Homer Brown, and the whole Washington brood. Estelle was my cook. Richard Wood was the butler in Grandfather's day, and his son Stewart Wood was Phyllis's then my butler. They all lived at or near Mirador, some in cabins behind the house that had been slave quarters before the war, others in the woods around the place and around Greenwood. Aunt Veeny Barbour was very old when I was a little girl. She used to come down to see Grandfather and get a dram of whiskey and sit and talk to us. She had been a slave and was twelve years old when Sheridan and his army came over from the valley at Afton right down in front of Mirador. When she heard the Yankees were coming, she got so scared she climbed into a hollow tree. A Yankee pulled her out by the feet. They were perfectly terrified of the Yankees, but there was no fighting near Mirador; the troops were marching through to take Charlottesville. I remember when Grandfather asked Aunt Veeny Barbour who the father of one of her children was, she said, "If a jigsaw hit you, would you know which tooth it was?"

Fountain Winston was a fascinating old boy. I don't think he was old enough to have been a slave, but Aunt Lucy Crapp, who lived next door to him, had been. I remember one Christmas Eve we went out into the woods where Aunt Lucy Crapp and Fountain Winston lived to collect holly . . . when we got near to their houses we could smell their coffee. It was the most delicious smell I think I've ever smelled. So we went in and shared a pot of coffee with them. They were preparing their "fixin's" for Christmas, too. When I owned Mirador, we celebrated Christmas Eve with the white workers on the place and Christmas Day with the colored workers. We had a huge Christmas tree in the squash court, lit by real candles, and Stewart stood by like a sentinel with a sponge on a pole and a bucket of water watching for fire. Each child got a present, an orange or a bag of candy, done up in a green or a pink bag.

Aunt Veeny Barbour on
the steps at Mirador at
the turn of the century

Aunt Ann Brody was as old as I am now and lived eight miles
away after she retired from cooking at Mirador, but she came down
the road regularly to spend the day and get her dram. They liked
their whiskey straight . . . two fingers full absolutely straight. When
she retired, Grandfather offered her a house to live in, but she said,
"I'd rather have my own store, so I can get whatever I want when I
want it."

Colored servants did most of the work around the house at
Mirador, cooking, cleaning, serving at the table. The aunts' maids
when they were girls were colored. A colored odd man brought in
the wood in the wintertime, and Callie Pearl cleaned the grates for
the fireplaces and lit fires every morning in our rooms before we
got up. John Pate, Emily the housemaid's husband, was Grandfather's coachman. The Pates were born slaves. Reuben used to cut
the lawns around the house with a yellow mule called Jack. They
would drive up and down the hills together. It was a very special,
close relationship we had in Virginia. Not like employee and
employer. The feeling was very good and easy. I think I owe any
sense of the ridiculous I have, any sense of fun, to having been

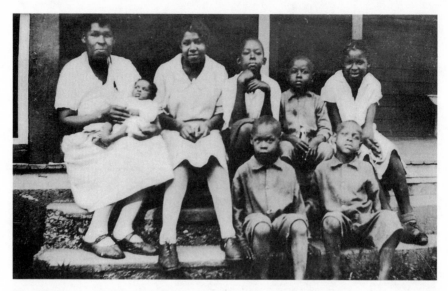

The Washington family in the 1920s

raised by colored servants. A sense that life needn't always be taken so seriously.

In those early years we lived at Mirador from April until the end of June, when it got too hot to be there, and from September until Christmas. After Christmas, when the roads were too muddy to pass and the red clay became so thick and heavy from the rain, you could only get through on a mule. But we were there for the ideal months, in the spring and early summer, when the gardens and woods came to life, the air was laced with honeysuckle and the nights were cool enough to sleep comfortably. And we came back in the autumn, as the weather became bearable again and when the hunting season started. Ron was the Master of the Greenwood hounds; he took them over from Algy Craven.

We had the Mirador farm to run. Funnily enough, before the Civil War they grew grapes at Mirador; it was a wonderful place for growing grapes. In Grandfather's day we grew apples. We had the most marvelous apples, called Albemarle pippins. Albemarle pippins were so good that they were the only apples from America that could be exported to England free of duty. One of the Carters from Redlands had taken a silver basket of them to Queen Victoria, who liked them so much she allowed their import without taxes. She never did return the silver basket that had been in the Carter family for gen-

Mirador neighbor Fountain Winston

erations. When I bought Mirador I had seven thousand apple trees. And we had one tree for lady apples that didn't bear fruit until it was twenty-five years old. We kept a basket of lady apples on the hall table in the house, just as my grandparents had.

In my day our apple crops somehow coincided with a much larger crop of apples in New York State, so there was no money in it. We had to get out of apples. We cut down our orchards and went into cattle. Dairy cows, guernseys. Because of the cattle we turned a lot of Mirador to grass and had to contour much of the land. Mirador is very hilly, and in Virginia we had terrible rains. It would rain and rain for three days and wash all the topsoil down into the rivers. So we contoured, which is a very old practice over here in England, to keep the soil in place. We had the most wonderful cream from our guernseys, and we were paid very well for it.

I remember we held the annual meeting of the Guernsey Breeders Association at Mirador. We set up the chairs and a lunch under some trees in a field, and everyone talked about their cows. We also hosted the Albemarle County Horse Show, when people from all over Virginia came out to compete and watch. That was a great success. And we had barbecues at Mirador for the people who worked on the place and for the farmers and neighbors around us who were

Stewart Wood, the Trees'
butler, was the son of
Richard Wood, Mirador's
butler when Chiswell
Langhorne lived there.

**friends and whose land we hunted over. We would barbecue a whole
cow. They dug a deep pit in the field, and the men sat up all night
cooking. They were like fairs. We had a sort of point-to-point race
that all the farmers rode in. We made jumps in the fields where the
spectators stood and watched. And we greased a pig. The boys and
young men would run after it and try and catch it. Everyone was
thrilled with the barbecues, and several hundred people would come.**

Mirador continued as a center for the extended Langhorne family for the
next thirty-five years. The joy of the place remained, beyond the beauty of the
house and the land—voices resounding in the halls and at table, in the fields
and on the porches. All of Nancy's aunts, none of whom lived in Virginia anymore, spent holidays from time to time at Mirador, often bringing their children and grandchildren with them. The Langhorne sisters' returning attests
more than anything else to the spirit of their father still being in residence.
"Nance, I have bowls of honeysuckle in my room and the night breezes waft
it over this old face of mine," wrote Irene Gibson from Mirador to her niece
who was in England. "We are having waffles and turkey hash for supper.
Wouldn't you love some."[11]

THE TRADITION OF hospitality begun by the patriarch continued with
his granddaughter, even in the most difficult years during the Second World
War. The Trees, then living in England, put Mirador at the disposal of the

Ronald and Nancy Tree at Mirador in 1925. "I get up in the morning to go and school my roan for the Richmond show," wrote Nancy to Alice Perkins Winn in a letter circa 1928. "And then I hunt for shade and avoid caterpillars and stroll about the garden and chat and come and sit down and cuss you for not sending me some fancy-work. . . . A bob-white is whistling now."

British embassy in Washington for the length of the war as a weekend or holiday retreat for the ambassador. Lord Halifax was Britain's wartime representative to the United States, and he and his wife took full advantage of the generosity offered them. Halifax was a political ally and friend of Lady Astor's and a regular guest at Cliveden. He thought Mirador had "the atmosphere . . . of England in the 1860s," and he reveled in the gardens he considered "exquisite, and redolent of the Southern past with its slave quarters and white pavilions, its judas trees and dogwood, its hedges covered in honeysuckle in May, filling the garden with scent, and in September orchards bright red with apples and smelling of cider."[12]

Halifax was the Viceroy of India between 1925 and 1931, and was at one point touted to be a prime minister of England. But his star dimmed irrevocably during the Munich crisis, when Neville Chamberlain, the prime minister Halifax served under as foreign secretary, signed the infamous Munich Pact with Adolf Hitler. The embassy in Washington was a considerable

Preparations for a Mirador barbecue

climb down for Halifax, who felt it was he, not Winston Churchill, who should lead the British people through the war. But judging from his memoirs, Mirador was at least a small consolation for exile. He wrote: "Trees, shrubs, flowers, everything seemed to do well in that most welcoming of gardens, in which we spent many of the summer week-ends, while inside the house our comfort was constantly ensured by the British housekeeper Helen, and the devoted servant Stewart, who looked after us as if we had belonged to each other all our lives."[13]

I never expected to own Mirador. From my earliest youth it was the house of my dreams. And no matter where I've lived, I've always tried to get back there. It was a salve to me and seemed more of a friend than just a house.

After we moved to England, I often went to Mirador by myself in the spring after the hunting season and before my sons were out of school. I remember the joy of sitting out on the back porch with a mint julep in my hand and looking out at all my land. Once I was sitting there when I heard my brother, Chillie, coming up the walk to see me. I quickly took the mint julep and hid it behind the blinds

A house party in 1924: from left, Mrs. George (Edith) Baker, Irene Gibson, Nancy Tree, Mrs. (Bessie) Hobson and Mrs. Chief Lawrence

The fourth generation of Langhornes at Mirador, Michael Tree and his cousins fish in the pond there.

in my bedroom because I didn't want to share it with him. It was Prohibition and almost impossible to get good whiskey. When he came up to me, I was roaring with laughter. "What are you laughing about, Nancy?" "I've got something special, and I'm not going to share it with you." There is nothing in this world like sitting down, drinking a mint julep and looking out over your own land.

On owning Mirador Nancy said: "Once an aunt told me, 'If you have a wish all your life and never vary you will get that wish.' I had it and I got it."

KELMARSH HALL

"My cousin Nancy only paid us visits, but these I looked forward to," wrote Michael Astor. "I loved her appearance, and the way she dressed, and the lack of importance she seemed to attach to age. . . . She brought into a room a flavour of another, more exciting world, of what I thought of as 'fast' women and 'worldly' men, who lived uninhibited lives and were not forever concerned with ethics, and whom I felt I would get along with."[1]

PART ONE

We were in London in the early spring of either 1925 or '26. It was after the hunting season, and we had a little time before our ship sailed for America. That was my favorite time of year in London. They called it the Little Season, as opposed to the Season. During the Little Season there were always small dinner parties and clubs to go to, like the Embassy Club or Café de Paris. The people that you hunted with would be there, and the army officers who had their regimental dinners that time of year would be there with their girl-friends. It was much more intimate and gay than the Season, in June, with all its grand balls.

One night after dinner we went to a nightclub in an alleyway off Berkeley Square with some friends of ours, and on the way out this little man approached us and offered to tell our fortunes. Everybody put out their hands and had them read but me; I didn't want it done. But they all pushed me and said, "Go on, do it," and when I finally did, the man looked at my hand and said, "I don't understand this; you don't die, but your life stops."

The Duchess of York (now the Queen Mother) and her daughter Princess Elizabeth (now Queen Elizabeth II) with Nancy and Ronald Tree and a Pytchley hound couple in front of Kelmarsh Hall, c. 1930

We were settled back at Mirador a few weeks later. One morning Ronnie and I and the house guests staying with us went riding after breakfast. It was a very rainy, muddy springtime as always, and the dead leaves on the forest floor were slippery under our horses' hooves. I was riding a young hunter I had been schooling that morning. At a fence we came to I held him back and let the others jump it ahead of me. As I pulled back on the reins this young horse reared once, then twice, then slipped on the wet ground and fell over backwards. I was riding sidesaddle and couldn't get out of the way. He literally sat in my lap. I didn't feel any pain at all, but I couldn't move either. It took them almost five hours to get an ambulance to me from Charlottesville because we were so isolated and the roads were so bad. For five hours I lay there, not able to move, thinking about what the little man in Berkeley Square had said only two weeks before. I was certain I would spend the rest of my life lying on my back.

I was in the hospital for six months after the accident. I broke my pelvis in five places and broke my back at the base of the spine, but my spinal cord wasn't cut, so I wasn't paralyzed. All they could do was cover me in plaster and keep me in traction. Ronnie stayed by me the whole time, visiting me in the hospital in Charlottesville every day, making the long drive to and from Mirador on the dirt roads and spending the spring and much of the summer in Virginia when we would normally have gone north to escape the heat. It was particularly hot that year, and there was no such thing as air conditioning. When I left the hospital, we took a house in Islesboro, where it was cooler. They took me up in a private railcar, and I had to have a nurse. When it cooled down, we returned to Mirador.

That accident, although I recovered and was riding and hunting again not long afterwards, that accident completely changed our lives and our plans for the future. While I lay there in that hospital half-dead and in traction, Ronnie decided that if I *had* died he would have moved back to England. He told me he never really liked living in America, that he was really an Englishman. Ronnie had an English accent and English mannerisms, and it was made plain to him in the last few years of living in New York and at Mirador that he could never enter politics, which was his ambition, in America. So while I lay there, he asked me if I would move to England with him when I was better.

I loved my early married days in Virginia. I used to have such fun then. I didn't like coming to England; it was a very different place, and we led a very different life. But Ronnie had valiantly tried to live the life I wanted for three years, so I now agreed to try his; that was, provided I could always keep Mirador and return to it for a time each year.

We were very young, but Ronnie thought he had wasted three years in Virginia. I understood, and I felt quite guilty that I had delayed and perhaps jeopardized Ronnie's career by insisting we live in America. Fortunately, we had a lot of family in England, so in many ways our life was made for us there as well. All of the aunts but Irene lived in England and knew a great many people. Nannie had been elected to Parliament in 1919 and was well into her extraordinary career. She made Cliveden an open house for all of us, and it was certainly an ideal place for a young man whose ambitions were in politics, as Ronnie's were, to meet the sort of people one ought to. We're a very clannish family. We were very lucky in that way. We were helped enormously in England when we moved there by at once getting into a sort of family entourage.

When we first came over, we went to Ireland on a "Sponge Tour," where we went from hunt country to hunt country riding with all the different packs, seeing the marvelous countryside from our mounts. We had wanted to take a house, but there had been the terrible "Troubles" after the war and a lot of the big houses had been set alight. While we were in Ireland Ronnie received a wire offering him the position of Joint Master of the Pytchley Hunt in Northamptonshire. They were looking for someone to come in and liven it up . . . to attract some of the young bloods hunting at Melton Mowbray. This is exactly what he was looking for; Master of the Foxhounds was the ideal training ground for politicians. So we went to live in Northamptonshire in the spring of 1926.

RONALD TREE was appointed Joint Master of the Pytchley during the last great era of British foxhunting. It was a time when an "MFH" after a name still meant that the bearer held an important position in the community, and when Master of the Pytchley was "probably the most famous among hunting titles."

Foxhunting was a monument left behind by the eighteenth-century English Whigs, the same Georgian landowning class emulated by Virginian planters. Whig "treasure houses," their other legacy, survived as huge testaments to the superb architecture and decoration created during their epoch, while their favored pastime, hunting to hounds, complemented this ruling class's indomitable *joie de vivre*. Neither changed much in their first 150 years, despite the swirl of social and economic evolution around them. Many of the big houses still standing in the 1920s were managed along similar lines to those the Georgians had refined, and the techniques and etiquette of the original "sport of kings" had been altered little beyond the cut of lady followers' habits. Perhaps it was the inherent beauty and seductiveness of the country house milieu that allowed the trappings of a past age to outlive the inventors. Maybe the heirs of Whig property and tradition learned to adapt with the times—to open their heavy oaken doors and invite outsiders to join the club whenever it became propitious. Either way, the country house and its kennel full of hounds maintained their overwhelming allure well into the twentieth century, however anachronistic they may have become.

It was immensely popular in Britain between the world wars, when Ronald Tree was with the Pytchley. As a sport, hunting became an outlet for the euphoric celebration of life after five years of war on the Continent; as social ritual, hunting remained a comforting bastion of the past in the face of dizzying changes and insecurities. The period's prosperity made it possible on a very grand scale. In the 1920s the British "leisure class"—what part of it survived—supported dozens of packs and met to hunt between two and six days a week for nearly six months every year.

> **There's nothing like it. There's nothing like a good day when you fly your fences. You have a good horse, a big fence or hedge with a ditch on one side—in Pytchley country they were often eight feet high—you have soft grass to take off from and land on. You ride at it hell for leather, then you *whooosh* over it like that. It's a marvelous sensation.**

The Pytchley was historically one of the richest hunts in England, physically one of the most challenging and, in 1927, a fantastic spectacle to observe, a bright interlude in the Midlands winter's monotonous landscape. The field of followers could be three hundred or more strong of a morning, a great army whose soldiers were dressed impeccably and mounted incomparably. When they gathered—a mass of animals and humanity, like a billowing cloud on a windy day, swirling in and around a backdrop of architecture and farmland—Pytchley hunting squires sat buttoned up exquisitely astride towering thoroughbreds. Full of fresh air, boundless charm and self-assuredness, these glorious "thrusters" instinctively snapped the hats from their heads in salute to the Master's wife or a neighbor's daughter as they waited to risk their lives for a day's amusement. The women next to them were no less larger than life, and it was widely held throughout the hunting world that "the Pytchley ladies are the greatest thrusters in the Shires."[2]

Ronald Tree rode at the head of this army, alongside the other Joint Master, Captain Jack Lowther, and behind the huntsman Frank Freeman, the

The Joint Master and his wife, 1928. "Nancy and Ronnie brought with them exceptional extravagance and dash," said one hunt follower of the day. "The Pytchley was an old-fashioned country and some of us had never seen anything like it."

whippers-in and the eighteen and a half couples of foxhounds with names like Stateman, Velvet and President. "Ronnie went well but was rather heavy in the saddle," said another Pytchley follower. One of Tree's gentleman's gentlemen, his valet or a footman, had arisen before dawn to make sure that his velvet cap was brushed spotless, that every vestige of the previous day's mud had been beaten from his tightly woven "pink" coat,[3] that his leather breeches were an immaculate and luminous white and that his tan-cuffed black calf-boots had been "boned" to a patent sheen. Blind bravery was important when hunting to hounds, but the proper costume was essential.

Nancy Tree made an immediate impression among Pytchley followers with a strong, graceful sidesaddle seat atop her hunters, the cut of her black Melton coats and Busvine habits, the jaunty tilt of her top hat and veil. **You had to be very particular with your veil. The veil had to roll up underneath, and you couldn't show a pin. I used to sit in front of my mirror for an hour stark-stripped naked fixing my hat and veil until I got it right. I also used to wear a white linen waistcoat which was very smart. Aunt Phyllis wore one, too.** She gave chase almost every day the Pytchley met, four days a week, rain, sleet or shine, October through March, from 10:45 in the morning, when the hounds met, until four or five in the afternoon, when it became too dark to

After meeting at Cottesbrooke Hall in 1927, Pytchley followers are led away by their Joint Masters, Ronald Tree (second from left) and Colonel Jack Lowther (center). To the right of Lowther is his wife, Lila.

see, across hundred-acre pastures of hundred-year-old turf, through thickly wooded spinneys and forested woods, over hard log fences, rushing streams and the Pytchley's trademark eight-foot-high "double-oxer" hedges, with only short breaks to rest when the Masters kept the field in check while the hounds "feathered" for a fox, or around two o'clock, when everyone changed to their second horses. "Nancy was a very elegant rider, though perhaps not quite as elegant as Phyllis, who was the best in England," thought a fellow Pytchley follower.

When I first hunted with the Pytchley in the early 1920s, if the fences were big that day and I got worried, I only had to look around at the rest of the field. There were so many old men with long beards out hunting, and so many old ladies, I mean really *old* ladies, going very well and riding frightfully short. I used to think, "It can't be all that bad if they've all lived this long." All that gray hair going like the devil over the country.

One charming old lady was Mrs. Cazenove; out hunting she always had a drip on the end of her nose. She broke her leg one day and just said, "Put me back on my horse," and she rode home. Another was Mrs. Violet Borwick, the daughter of Bay Middleton, the greatest English horseman of the nineteenth century. Lady

Lowther, Sir Charles Lowther's wife, was a Master of the Pytchley during the First War, when most of the men were in the army, and her sister-in-law Lila Lowther, Jack's wife, was a marvelous rider and always looked beautiful in the saddle. She could be very tough, though, and would tell people off if they weren't dressed right. As wife of the other Joint Master I had to smooth some feathers she ruffled. But Lila was very much a person, and I was devoted to her. To this day I can hear her yelling, "Biscuit!" the name of her horse. She had an appalling voice that you could hear for miles around. Jack was a huge man and one of the best heavyweight riders across country.

You see, you admired people if they went well in the hunting field: if they were brave and they jumped enormous fences. It made a great impression on you. When Aunt Phyllis rode with us, she would ask me, "Is there anyone here of interest?" I remember pointing out Jack Elliot. He was the best rider in the field. I said, "Wait 'til you see him ride; it's the most marvelous sight." Phyllis turned to me and replied, "You *would* like him; he looks like an old soup bone." But Jack Elliot rode like nobody else. He slipped through the countryside.

Jock Campbell hunted with us. He was very good to hounds. One day I remember seeing him go off in one direction while the hounds and the field went off in another. I followed him, thinking he knew where the fox was going and we'd end up there first. The more he galloped, the more I went, positive I was being very clever. My dear, he was looking for a haystack to relieve nature behind. It was terribly funny; he couldn't get rid of me. Most of the time he was followed by his wife, Dorothy, and her sisters Sis and Nora. They were the charming Rhodes sisters. Jock was eventually put in charge of the 8th Army at the beginning of the war but was killed when his jeep overturned on the way to his new command.

The three Nichols sisters, all in their teens, rode with the Pytchley then. Mary, the eldest, married "Chicken" Walford, who was in the Scots Greys with their cousin Desmond Miller. Both these officers hunted regularly with the Pytchley. It seems to me they were all called "Chicken" or "Mud" or "Flash" in those days, like Jubie Lancaster's de Crespigny uncles were called "Creepy" and "Crawley" in an earlier era. Chicken Walford was killed in the Second War, leaving Mary a young widow.

The Duke and Duchess of York took a house at Naseby when we were there so he could hunt. Both he and his brother the Prince

The Duke of York (the future King George VI), right, with Colonel Jack Lowther

of Wales were very nice. I wasn't exactly born in the briar patch with either of them, I don't want to give that impression, but when I used to go to Ascot parties at Cliveden, there was always a ball at Windsor which we could go to, or, when Queen Mary and the Duke and Duchess stayed at Holkham House, I was asked to stay as well. But I was simply amongst those present rather than an intimate.[4]

COMPLETING THE PICTURE of a Pytchley meet in the late 1920s—and the Trees' new neighborhood—were the extraordinary settings around which these gatherings took place. Little changed about the Northamptonshire countryside over the centuries, except perhaps a Victorian addition to a manor or a new rectory in a village. When this generation mustered before the chase, they did so in the same situations, in front of the same magnificent mansions, the same houses and village inns, as where the 1st Earl Spencer oversaw the members of the Old Hunt Club at Pytchley Hall in the eighteenth century, where the Master "Glorious John" Buller met the field with hounds so large they were called "great calves," or from where the "Red Earl" Spencer set off with Empress Elizabeth of Austria, Bay Middleton and a field of hundreds following.

They met the hounds on greens in small villages called Barby, Badby, Kilsby, Naseby and Cransley; Sibbertoft, Yelvertoft, Ulvertoft, Bragborough,

Arthingworth, Swinford, Harrington, Orton, Norton, Everdon, Creaton, Ecton and Staverton; Stow-Nine-Churches, Little Harrowden, Little Brington, Great Billing; and at Long Buckby, where they met by the village's maypole. They also met at Mear's Ashby, which was nearby Ashby St. Ledgers, Cold Ashby and Castle Ashby and south of Ashby-de-la-Zouche Castle. At Brixworth, where the hounds were kenneled and the Hunt had its opening meet every year, they gathered in front of Brixworth Hall if Captain Paget, Lord Annaly or someone else had rented it from Vere Wood for the season. In 1928, when the Duke of York attended the meet, the house was empty, so hounds met on the main street of the village, just down the slope from the seventh-century Saxon church.

Dozens of country houses were the sites of Pytchley meets; Northamptonshire boasted an abundance of noblemen's and gentlemen's houses, more than any other county its size in England. Most of these buildings—some stupendous works of architecture, others modest, run-down and lacking any comforts—had been in the same families for generations. A family scion in Pytchley country either hunted to hounds himself or rented his house during the season to sportsmen coming from America or Europe or other parts of the United Kingdom to ride with "the cream of the cream in the shire of the shires."[5]

The Pytchley met at least once a season at Althorp, the seat of the Spencer family since the early 1500s. Althorp had evolved with the fashions over the centuries from a large house of Elizabethan design and character into a Georgian palace. Its imposing appearance in the early twentieth century was the result of a rebuilding around 1790. When the Hunt met there, drinking port and brandy provided by the earl and served by his footmen, it was in the shadow of the huge Corinthian pilasters and the handsome pediment of the facade, with more than a dozen massive chimneys billowing wood smoke into the chilly morning air.[6]

There was Lamport Hall, up the Market Harborough–Northampton Road from Brixworth, an ancient seat belonging to the Isham family. Lamport, too, was originally Elizabethan like Althorp and was converted along classical lines by John Webb, a student and relative of Inigo Jones. The Ishams were one of the oldest families in all of England and counted in their family tree a number of American emigrants and cousins, including Thomas Jefferson. Their motto, engraved in the house's frieze, read: IN ALL THINGS TRANSITORY RESTETH NO GLORY. The Pytchley was always welcome whenever they met in front of the beautiful house, whether it was an Isham in residence or a renter.

Newnham Hall was the site of periodic meets. The whitewashed Regency house belonged to William Romer, a Pytchley Hunt treasurer who was still riding in his mid-eighties. He claimed the secret to his longevity was that every day he drank a bottle of port—"Mind you, the best port." And hounds met at Haselbech Hall, belonging to Captain Bower Ismay of the family that owned the White Star steamship line; he was onboard the *Titanic* but chose not to go down with it. The late-seventeenth-century house had been gutted by fire as recently as 1917, forcing Captain Ismay to completely rebuild it. The Middleton and Borwick family houses were in Haselbech, beyond some fields behind the Ismay house.

Other mornings the Pytchley met at Stanford Hall, just over the Leicestershire border. Tall, square, of ashlar and red brick, with long sash windows and a hipped roof, Stanford could have been a model for Westover or the Governor's Palace in Williamsburg, Virginia. Nancy Tree thought it **the most beautiful house in England.** Stanford was commissioned in the seventeenth century and was continually lived in for almost three hundred years, with most of the same fixtures and furniture. Pytchley country, the Trees' new home, was generously littered with grand architecture, enormous farming estates and old noble families, and in many ways—in its way of life, particularly—bore a resemblance to what they had left behind in Virginia.

ON A BRISK Friday morning in late November 1927, the Pytchley Hunt in all its glory paid a visit to Cottesbrooke Hall, the house Ronald and Nancy Tree had rented for their first season in England. **We took Cottesbrooke from Bobby Brassey, who was staying at the same hotel as us at the Dublin Horse Show that summer. Bobby had a pack in Ireland for the coming season, so he wouldn't be living at Cottesbrooke. I begged him to let us have it. It was the perfect house for us.**

Cottesbrooke Hall was the product of a slow evolution that took two centuries. Thirteen generations of the Langham family had lived there before Captain Robert Brassey purchased the house and the land in 1911. Sir John Langham, 1st Baronet, bought the ten thousand acres in two parcels around 1640. His grandson, Sir John, the 4th Baronet, commissioned the beginnings of the house in 1700. Designed to reflect the status of the family who lived there, Cottesbrooke Hall was a large, powerful sight. Yet because Sir John chose local builders instead of one of the more cosmopolitan architects of the era, its high, handsomely rugged brick walls were slightly unwieldy and self-consciously ornamented in comparison to its neighbors Althorp or Lamport. That was also part of its warmth and beauty. In the 1760s, Sir John Langham, 6th Baronet, contributed the elaborate Rococo papier-mâché decoration in the main stairway of the house that survived into the twentieth century. Sir James, 7th Baronet, added the bows that enlarged each side of the house and laid out the serpentine entrance drive.[7]

The outstretched arms of Cottesbrooke Hall

Not only was Cottesbrooke right in Pytchley country, but it was big enough for us to have family and friends down to stay and hunt. That's after all why Ronnie was asked to become Joint Master . . . so we would liven it up. Aunt Phyllis came, my cousins Wissy Astor and Bill Astor, and friends from England and from America like Mary and Oliver Filley. Once we had the King of Sweden's son to dine. He was staying at Holdenby House. I remember asking a man to the dinner party for him whom I had met out hunting and who looked very well in his hunting clothes. He had wonderful legs for boots. To my amazement, the wife looked rather like I do now—she had a bun in the back of her head—and she had on an evening dress that you could see her flannel shirt showing underneath. She wasn't at all what I thought the wife of this very chic hunting man would be. I was absolutely horrified, because this was a dinner party for the Crown Prince of Sweden.

Ronnie's stepfather, David Beatty, came to hunt with us and stay at Cottesbrooke the season we were there. He was considered the greatest hero of the British Navy since Nelson after he fought on the Nile and then in the Battle of Jutland in the 1914 War. He was the Admiral of the Fleet, then the First Sea Lord of the Admiralty. He loved hunting and excelled across country; he and Ronnie's mother met when they were both out with the Warwickshire.

The admiral was charming, not at all a stiff-backed naval officer. It was because he was Irish and from a family of horse copers. With great conviction he would say to me, "I come from Borodale, where the men all have dash and they wear their hats cocked to one side and . . . ," and he'd give you a perfect description of himself. I used to laugh at that. "They have the eye of an eagle; they wear their hats to one side—these are the brave men of Borodale."

The painter Sir Alfred Munnings stayed at Cottesbrooke twice during the year the Trees lived there: first, when he painted Frank Freeman, the Pytchley's legendary huntsman,[8] and second, when he painted an equestrian portrait of Nancy. Writing his memoirs years later, he said the name Cottesbrooke Hall reminded him of the "large tea table—eggs, fried sausages, toast. A party of men and women back from the chase—Earl Beatty in his shirt sleeves and yellow waistcoat, his coat slung over a chair, attacking sausages."[9] The portrait Munnings painted of Nancy that week included her son Michael, mounted on a pony, and one of the Trees' greyhounds. Munnings wrote:

This was done later in the year . . . using the stone balustrade and yellow autumn colouring as background. Mrs. Tree was riding a rather handsome, dappled grey horse, and the boy, wearing a yellow jersey and black velvet cap, rode a bay pony. The design came well, and this was one of the few occasions when there was no need to invent a background. Mrs. Tree, the grey horse, yellow foliage, balustrade: all were there before me in front of the house, with the October sun casting long shadows, making horizontal lines—so needed in a composition. There was a greyhound in the picture, too; as usual, I was wanting the sun for this.[10]

One of my saddest recollections is of an April morning at Cottesbrooke. At breakfast our host, Ronnie Tree, read out from *The Times* the news of the death of John Sargent. Large headlines were in every paper, as they had been at the time when Kipling died. . . . Sargent's death—a sad loss to the Art World—came as a sudden shock. Realizing this . . . we at Cottesbrooke could talk and think of nothing else but the famous artist.

Sargent drew a wonderful portrait of Ronnie. We had taken a house on Sandwich that summer, and Ronnie was very sunburnt and very good-looking. Sargent said it was too bad he hadn't done the portrait in sepia. He did one of me as well, but I've always hated it. In it I'm absolutely wild-eyed and my hair has no shape at all. I'd just had my hair washed; for some reason I thought that, having your portrait done, you ought to have your hair washed. He must have seen something in me then . . . I wasn't as wild-eyed in those days as he drew me. Sargent evidently saw in me what was going to take place, that I was going to have several nervous breakdowns.

That particular week in November 1927, the Trees filled Cottesbrooke with guests for the first meet Ronald would host as Joint Master. **The Prince of Wales was very kind to us the first year and got it all started by staying with us the night before the Cottesbrooke meet. We had been at a dinner with him when he was hunting at Melton, and he suggested to us that he come and stay with us and hunt a day with the Pytchley. I had the house party for him. I remember I asked Rosemary and Eric Dudley, who were friends of his, to stay, and a few others. The Prince had wanted to marry Rosie at one point, but she preferred Eric Dudley. And I suppose the Prince must have brought along his equerry, Fruity Metcalfe. The Prince was simply charming and his coming was a sort of royal blessing on the Pytchley as far as our generation was concerned.** A correspondent for *The Field* wrote: "All the world and his wife (and sons and daughters too) entered an appearance there on Friday, a beautiful hunting morning. Foremost among the company was the Prince of Wales . . . , and quite a number of visitors from the neighboring Hunts had come to share in the fun." After a preliminary run lasting an hour and twenty-five minutes, the Pytchley hounds "set the seal on the whole performance by killing their fox near the main entrance lodge of Althorp Park."

PART TWO

We very nearly bought Cottesbrooke from Bobby Brassey. The problem, though, to me was that the house sat in a soup bowl. I think it's one of the most beautiful houses in England to look down on in its park, but it wasn't very nice looking out from inside the bowl. I also didn't really like the interior of the house. It still had a

"The cream of the cream in the shire of the shires." Ronald Tree and the Prince of Wales (center) surrounded by a field of Pytchley thrusters (Buxton, p. 78).

lovely little paneled hall with a lovely ceiling and a wonderful stair-case with deep stucco. The hall was early Adam, sort of aquamarine colored with surprisingly strong stucco moulding. But then the other rooms went to ruin and Bobby Brassey had to do them over, sadly it was done in a sort of fake Adam, which I didn't like. I like the early Adam, which is strong, but not the later thin, finicky stuff. So just as we were signing the papers, I said to Ronnie, "Please don't."

About the same time we were offered Kelmarsh Hall, which was only a village over from Cottesbrooke, by Jubie Lancaster. The idea was that we would decorate and modernize the house in lieu of pay-ing him rent. He offered the house to us for ten years. I far preferred Kelmarsh. It had barely been touched, other than someone's adding on a ballroom. The house was still very much as James Gibbs had designed it two hundred years before. The bones were there at Kelmarsh.

Kelmarsh, Northamptonshire, stood at a crossroads. The village consisted of two short hyphens of attached redbrick cottages, one on the
Northampton-to-Market Harborough trunk road, the other by the side of
the Harrington-to-Kelmarsh-to-Clipston farm track—the sort of country
lane forever blocked by herds of sheep or cattle or slow-moving farm machinery. The two rows of cottages met at the intersection, and almost the entire
village was made up of this single right angle of modest dwellings. In 1927 the
cottages were still roofed with thatch; ivy grew up their walls. Kelmarsh, population 120, had been the same for centuries. Like most of rural England, it
remained untouched by the modern world.

The cottages were catercornered to the parish church—built of stone,
with a tall, pointed steeple—in whose lawns Kelmarsh Hall and village
departed were buried and memorialized. There was also a village school; it
had been erected by the 2nd Viscount Bateman in 1850. The church, the
houses and the school all belonged to the landlord, who owned the village
meeting hall and the post and telegraph office as well. There was no public
house or rail terminus in Kelmarsh proper, however. The Kelmarsh Arms Inn
and the Kelmarsh Railway Station were in the village of Arthingworth, a pasture away to the north. But Arthingworth, too, was part of the 2,751-acre Kelmarsh estate.

Kelmarsh Hall was the "house on the hill." It was the home of the landlord, who was also in most cases the villagers' employer. Though the pronounced pediments of the manor could not be seen from the village, its
presence could be felt. The entrance gates bisected a third corner of the village crossroads, their stone and iron a constant reminder of who lived up the
long lime-tree-shaded drive. The village couldn't be seen from the Hall,
either. Milords preferred more picturesque views from their front door or
drawing room windows. In 1825 the 1st Viscount Bateman even dug out the
Northampton Road where it passed Kelmarsh Hall like a great ha-ha. A
clever act of foresight: In his day the only traffic along the road was horse and
carriage, but with the onset of the twentieth century it was used by an ever-
increasing number of motorcars and lorries. Now they, too, passed down the
gut of the ha-ha unseen from even the upper bedrooms of the house. The
view remained pristine.

When Nancy and Ronald Tree rented Kelmarsh Hall for a hunting box,
the house, the village, the Kelmarsh Arms and the four farms that made up the
estate belonged to a young cavalry captain named Claude Granville Lancaster.
Jubie Lancaster was twenty-three years old and a friend of the Trees' through
Bobbie Shaw, Lady Astor's son by her first marriage. Lancaster served in "the
Blues," the Royal Horse Guards, with Shaw and had been a houseguest at
Cliveden a number of times. Lancaster inherited the estate, along with the

family's interest in coal and iron mining in Lancashire, in 1908 at the age of nine; he took charge of it from trustees on his twenty-first birthday, when a great coming-of-age celebration was held for all the tenants, villagers and friends of the family at Kelmarsh. His father, George Lancaster, had bought Kelmarsh from Richard Naylor, a Victorian sportsman-landlord who led the Pytchley for a season; before Naylor the estate belonged to the Hanbury family, of which the Viscounts Bateman were members. In 1618 Sir John Hanbury had bought Kelmarsh from the Osborne family, who had "held the lordship from the days of Edward IV to the end of Queen Elizabeth's reign."

The austere Palladian-style villa Nancy would restore and decorate was commissioned in 1728 by William Hanbury, a member of the fourth generation of that family to live at Kelmarsh. The new house replaced a gabled Stuart manor built by his ancestors. William, like many other young Whigs, was well-educated, well-traveled on the Continent and thoroughly immersed in the philosophical sensibilities that marked the day. He wanted his new house to reflect this, so he turned to one of the two or three foremost architects practicing in the kingdom, James Gibbs. Gibbs was at the top of his profession in 1728. The ecclesiastical masterpiece in London that would bring him immortality, St. Martin-in-the-Fields, had been consecrated in 1726. He had finished one of his finer private commissions by then as well: the house at Ditchley Park, for the Earl of Lichfield.

At Ditchley Gibbs created a Baroque palace suitable for a relative of the royal Stuarts. At Kelmarsh he rendered a dignified, proudly straightforward country seat for a member of England's stalwart landed gentry. Its strength lay in its solidity and balance instead of decorative whims or useless frills imported from Europe; its very girth was set against the sharp winds that whipped the county from the North Sea. The exterior was so concise, so ordered, direct and free of visual elaboration, Kelmarsh Hall might have been the work of one of the Modern architects of Nancy's own generation. Indeed, it was considered "unusually severe for Gibbs,"[11] whose buildings often betrayed "feminine" qualities. Client and architect had eschewed superficial displays of worldliness and taste at Kelmarsh and settled on simplicity. The only concessions made to exterior decoration were the barest of carved-stone ornaments over the windows and on the quadrants, and the great pediments over the entrance and garden facades.

Kelmarsh Hall was the perfect size for the Tree family. They constantly entertained in the seven years they spent there, making Kelmarsh a center for their relatives and for hunting high society from all over England, Europe and America. Not that it was large by English country house standards. Kelmarsh was modest-sized, if not small, in comparison with Cliveden, Cadland or Cottesbrooke. There were no numbers on the doors, no

Kelmarsh Hall, Northamptonshire, England. Nancy wrote on the back of this *Country Life* photograph, "How we apples float!!"

long, dark passages down which to get lost. And though there were six different rooms on the ground floor that the Trees used for entertaining, a guest never had difficulty finding the house party without the help of a footman. Kelmarsh was intimate enough that it could be filled with the same warmth that permeated houses in Virginia, but large enough to offer a certain freedom and privacy.

In many ways it reminded Nancy of Virginia. The red brick the house was constructed of was reminiscent of that in colonial plantation houses. The shape and design of Kelmarsh, a central block with accompanying wings reaching "like great open arms," looked pleasingly similar to Virginian houses, with their matching dependencies.[12] But most importantly, Kelmarsh bore what Nancy called "the stamp of history," the romantic essence she loved so in the houses of Virginia. The same spirits she found so irresistible in her childhood were all conjured up in the lichen-stained steps of Kelmarsh

Hall, the insatiable English ivy burying the house's wings, the skeletal oak and sentinel elm.

The landscape had the same effect. Features in the countryside were at a point of maturity similar to those at Brandon or other Virginian plantation houses. Pytchley country, uninterrupted by signs of humanity, stretched in every direction from the house. Out the back, beyond the lake, pastures sloped and dipped ad infinitum, only spotted here and there with spinneys and single trees of various shapes. Jubie Lancaster's Park White cattle grazed just behind and to the side of the house. In the latter part of the eighteenth century, William Hanbury made the lake and planted many of the trees. He owned landscape paintings by van Ruysdael and Gainsborough and hung his prized Claude Lorrain in the saloon that overlooked these fields; like many Whig landlords, he was influenced by the picturesque when he manipulated his surroundings. From the front door of the Hall, the view jumped the road with the help of a thick hedge of rhododendron, then carried slowly up a hill into a row of cloud-scraping trees at its crest.

Kelmarsh didn't sit in a park like many houses in England. Mereworth, Chiswick and Nuthall Priory in their parks must have looked like gold fillings in teeth when they were new. They're better now, 250 years later, but they're more like palaces than houses in those landscapes. I don't like parks. I like life. I like seeing animals around. I like real country. Only one house in Virginia that I remember had a park, and that was Carter's Grove. I think some Yankee put it in when he bought the place.

To me the charm of Palladio's houses on the Brenta, or houses inspired by Palladio in Virginia, is that you get a sense of the architecture being part of the country it was superimposed on. You get the feeling that the house, no matter how grand, was part of the farm and right in the midst of all the activity. You'd see a simply wonderful building, and it would have a hayloft. A wing attached to the villa would actually be a barn; a barn would be a part of their magnificent house. Farms were all around the houses; they went right up to the front door in Italy or Virginia. In a way, you get the same thing in New England when you see a stable hitched onto a house. I like that, like the whole thing has come up from the ground like a mushroom. Kelmarsh was more like that than any other house I lived in in England.

In the condition in which the Trees rented Kelmarsh, the house lacked any and all reasonable comforts. There was no heat above the ground floor, for instance. The Lancasters relied on coal fires in bedrooms and kept the rest of the house mildly chilly and damp, as was done in most English country houses. The family lived there with minimal plumbing—scattered water closets and a single bath near the master bedrooms—and servants brought around porcelain pitchers of hot water to fill the washbasins throughout the house. Two decades into the twentieth century, there was no electricity, either. Lamps and candles lit the rooms after dark.[13]

The decoration of Kelmarsh was grossly out of date as well. The house, so handsome and straightforward outside, was a jumble of Victorian effusion within, the simplicity of Gibbs's design deadened by the weight of heavy fringing and dark mahogany, of lambrequins, gewgaws and lace doilies. Not only would plumbing, central heating and electricity have to be installed; the Trees would have to redecorate and furnish the entire house.

The first thing I noticed the first time I walked into the hall at Kelmarsh was walls decorated with dozens of crossed pikes. That may have been very chic when they were done, but they made me roar with laughter. The walls were painted a dark, rather sad green then. Sitting in the middle of the room was a plush roundabout with a *jardinière* at the center. The container was made of the foot of an elephant that someone in the family must have shot, and planted with a small palm tree. I thought that very funny.

The rest of the house was just as dark, mostly navy blue and maroon, and stuffed with all sorts of horrible furniture and bric-a-brac. Bedrooms were hung with wallpaper and had brass beds, which I hate. But Kelmarsh was a wonderful structure of a house; it had perfect bones, like the bones in a beautiful face. Underneath the spears and the dark green, the hall was a lovely room. It had excellent proportion. Because it was almost a cube, with the walls as high as the room was wide, there was a very tall ceiling. All the stucco work on the walls and the ceiling was simple and suitable.

In the 1920s the obvious way to approach a job such as this was to hire one of the large London firms like Thornton Smith to execute everything from painting the walls to manufacturing suites of matching furniture. The lady of the house—for it was her responsibility—needed only to approve the fabrics and the carefully drawn furniture arrangements they suggested. Contents would arrive in great vanloads, and the house would be ready. An alternative was to turn to one of the smaller shops owned by a society decorator. Mrs. Guy Bethel of Elden, Mrs. Somerset Maugham, the writer's wife, and later Lady Colefax performed a similar role to that of the larger Edwardian firms, though with a more personalized touch. These women were often acquaintances of their clients, and their names and reputations were spread by word of mouth. They kept Mayfair storefronts and town houses filled with antiques for sale, arranged in the fashion they espoused; they provided samples of fabric for upholstery and curtains; and they had at their disposal the craftsmen necessary for decorating a house. Such modern women were the English equivalents of the American Elsie de Wolfe: friendly, professional ladies of taste who left distinctive signatures that blessed a paying client with a measure of style. They were the forerunners of some of today's *haute* decorators.

Contrary to custom, Nancy chose to tackle Kelmarsh herself. Her impression of what made a house comfortable and attractive was by then firmly established in her mind's eye; she had no intention of allowing any "professional" to leave his or her signature on Kelmarsh. She "did up" the house by assembling a symphony of talents—architects, craftsmen and professional decorators—whom she could orchestrate to execute her own plans. Each she used piecemeal, so no single personality or taste but her own stood out, and from each she gathered resources—carpenters, paperhangers, upholsterers, furniture makers, restorers, carpet layers and the many obscure artisans who performed odd but useful crafts like aging leather or dyeing, bleaching and fading rugs—whom she might call upon in the future. Decorating a house and garden provided focus for Nancy's almost relentless Langhorne drive. Sitting back and watching others work did not at all suit her temperament; there was always an irresistible urge to jump headfirst into any project.

Her uncle Paul Phipps was the chief architect. Once simply **the most dashing young man of his year**, Phipps had developed into an accomplished designer of small country houses. After Oxford he apprenticed with Sir Edwin Lutyens, by then the most celebrated architect in England. It was Lutyens who revolutionized the relationship between English house and garden in a partnership with Gertrude Jekyll and who (with Herbert Baker) designed the British Empire's ultimate statement in pomp: the imperial capital of India, New Delhi. His neoclassical accent strongly influenced his student's own aesthetic. Phipps was asked by Nancy to carve bathrooms out of the existing two-hundred-year-old structure, shoehorning them into what had been dressing rooms or closets or wherever else they might fit. He saw to the installation of plumbing in bedrooms for basins, and the wiring and the central heating. Radiators and hot-air ducts were tucked into the oak floorboards and stashed beneath window seats. This kind of work was a bane to any architect, especially with a client like Nancy, who was a perfectionist and very much aware of architectural integrity.[14]

Phipps brought a Mr. Kick onto the job. Kick was a wage-earning housepainter for the contracting firm Phipps hired for the renovations. In Kick

Nancy met the painter who not only would brighten the depressing Victorian gloom about Kelmarsh, but would infuse the rooms with visual movement that brought the house to life. Nancy worked with Kick for the next thirty years, and her admiration for his abilities was unreserved. **Kick was a true genius. He instinctively understood the effect light and shade have on paint in a given room. He could always figure out how to reproduce any color you showed him, and could reproduce it so it had the *effect* you wanted, which is the point.**

For furniture, like the conveniences, Nancy had to start from scratch; everything the Trees owned remained in Virginia at Mirador. Much of what she bought she found in London shops, scouring the marketplace after lunch for furniture of the right shape or period—a favorite afternoon amusement. **I particularly liked painted furniture. Most people at that time were pickling furniture, but I liked the original paint.** One source was Mrs. Mann, who owned a shop in Mayfair. Another was a man introduced to Nancy by the owner of a hunting box the Trees rented near Melton in the early 1920s. **His name was Bliss, and he was the son, grandson, great-grandson, on back of local shepherds. He lived in the shepherds' cottage in Langham. Mr. Bliss was a lovely man and had a genius for furniture. He was just an ordinary farmer, but he had marvelous taste. I would send him to sales all over England, and he would bid for me. And he always had a lot of the original painted furniture that I loved.**

She worked with Mrs. Guy Bethel at Kelmarsh as well. Mrs. Bethel's fashionable shop in Mayfair, called Elden, sold furniture, but Nancy turned to them mostly for fabrics. Luxurious material from Elden covered many of the easy chairs and sofas around the house, and Elden made all the more lavish curtains for the principal rooms on the ground floor. The elaborately flounced pelmets for the curtains in the drawing room were, twenty years later, the envy of John Fowler and were copied a number of times in houses decorated by Colefax and Fowler. Nancy thought Mrs. Bethel **by far the best decorator I have ever known. She was about seventy when she helped me at Kelmarsh and was perfectly charming. She possessed a great deal of knowledge of decorating and the eighteenth century, but more importantly, she had feeling.**

One dressing room at Kelmarsh was entirely the work and taste of Mrs. Bethel. Nancy saw it in a decorator's exhibition at Olympia in London and thought it so attractive she bought the whole display. The furniture fit the scale of the room and the Georgian mood of the house perfectly, but Nancy was most enthralled by Mrs. Bethel's choice of colors. The addition of color was Nancy's primary concern in decorating Kelmarsh. She noted at the time, on the back of a black-and-white photograph of the room, that "the color of this is pretty. The walls are green, the bed a lovely rose pink, curtains cream with painted Queen Anne valance, a lovely old browny pink bedspread and Chinese pictures painted on glass." The Exhibition Room—most of the rooms at Kelmarsh had a name—was the only room in any house Nancy ever called her own that was completely decorated by someone else.

Miss Margo Brigdon, another fashionable decorator of the day, was hired to make curtains for the bedrooms and guest rooms on the second floor of the house, all of less elaborate and expensive designs than the Elden curtains downstairs. For the third-floor rooms and those in the nursery wing, Nancy hired a seamstress who was the wife of the coal-delivery man from Arthingworth, bought a sewing machine and sat her in a top-floor room to do her work. The seamstress also made curtains for the various servants' quarters at Kelmarsh, which Nancy took an unusual amount of time and care to make as comfortable as some of the guest rooms.

One other bright light worked at Kelmarsh in the late 1920s. For part of the garden, treated and "decorated" as carefully as any room inside the house, Nancy engaged the advice of Norah Lindsay. Mrs. Lindsay wielded quiet yet substantial creative influence in the insular world of English gardening, perhaps second only to Gertrude Jekyll, with whom she had worked. Because Lady Astor and she were friends, the Trees met Mrs. Lindsay at Cliveden; there she had created the magnificent herbaceous borders, planned to explode with color and scent just in time for Ascot race week. **Norah was started on her career by my aunt Nancy . . . and to enlarge her empty purse, Aunt Nancy suggested she be paid something every year to return to a garden and oversee the work she had done there.** Her Cliveden borders, seen by so many visitors, and the garden she and her husband, Colonel Harry Lindsay, kept at their house Sutton Courtney in Berkshire attracted a number of important clients. Lord Lothian hired her for his garden at Blickling Hall, as did the Prince of Wales for Fort Belvedere.

Her own garden was lovely. It had a very formal layout with very informal planting. That's what I liked. And she used common plants, not rare or precious hybrids, allowing them to grow luxuriantly in the formal layout. Those were the kinds of borders she planted for me at Kelmarsh, overflowing with the old-fashioned plants and flowers I loved. But Norah was more than just a gardener; she was a much bigger person, very well-rounded. She had more facets than someone like Gertrude Jekyll. For instance, she was a great musician; she could draw and paint; she was the best letter writer. She could create atmosphere. And she could cook like no one else; I still use receipts she gave me back then.

Under Nancy's direction this ensemble converted Kelmarsh Hall into the most inviting hunting box in England. After seeing the results, the Duke of Buccleuch—who owned four of Britain's palatial treasure houses, including Boughton, ten miles from Kelmarsh—told Lady Astor that her niece was "going to cost us all a fortune" in redecorating. Gone were the drafts, the congestion, the lukewarm shaving water, the line for the bathroom every morning prior to hunting and every evening before dinner was announced. Old-fashioned discomfort, almost a national institution, was banished at Kelmarsh in a single season. When painting and upholstering had ceased and the furniture and objects expected in country houses were dovetailed with those conveniences that were not; when a large staff remarkably adept at the smooth running of the house was in place; when the day's fresh flowers were arranged; when all this was accomplished, Kelmarsh Hall dazzled and soothed each of the five senses simultaneously. Nancy made her house over to please—to please herself and anyone else who stepped over the threshold.

THE HUNT FINISHED for the day, exhausted riders would walk from the chilled Northamptonshire twilight into the serenity of the Kelmarsh great hall—out of the biting wind into glowing warmth. Twin fireplaces blazed with orange-hot coals and snapping chunks of firewood. Brightly upholstered, down-stuffed easy chairs and sofas framed each fire. Huge flower arrangements spilled full-blossomed geraniums onto the marble tops of two matching gilt eagle-base tables. Two more tables, these stretching the entire width of the room, were set with a hulking eighteenth-century samovar and dozens of china teacups and saucers; next to the tea sat all the silver dishes of scrambled eggs, bacon, sausages, scones and pastries that Alfred Munnings remembered at Cottesbrooke, everything kept at the right temperature by paraffin lamps. The riders had been five or six hours in the saddle and had eschewed a real lunch. Hungry, splashed with mud and their hunters' sweat, Pytchley followers found salve when they entered Kelmarsh.

The effect Nancy had on the whole house was most succinctly represented in this hall. Here was the mood of the place in one room: unhesitatingly welcoming, absolutely surprising, unashamedly elegant; a rich but fresh setting made from the melding of textures and colors; a mélange of pinks, yellows, greens, Savonnerie carpets, silk brocades, damasks, painted canvases and carved woods. The formality and dignity expected in a gentleman's countryseat remained intact; they were echoed in the order of Gibbs's design and reverberated in Nancy's pairing of tables and balancing of chairs. However, a wonderful ease and tranquillity undermined the usual stiffness of such a reception room. When Nancy was finished, it became a room where an army captain, a debutante or the Admiral of the Fleet might enjoy their tea and bandy about the day's chase as the Trees' two sons played underneath the tablecloths with their young friends.

I painted the hall at Kelmarsh pink. I never thought twice about using bright colors in old houses. The pink I used was an Italian pink, a light terra cotta. The idea came from Lady Islington's house Rushbrook Hall, a house built for Henrietta Maria, Charles I's wife. Anne Islington was the person in England who had the very best taste and the very best color sense. She and Lady Rosemary Dudley were people from whom I learned a great deal when I arrived here; they were always generous with their knowledge about decoration. Lady Islington allowed me to send Kick to Rushbrook to analyze the pink so that I might reproduce it. When he was finished, the effect of the room was breathtaking.

I then filled the hall with the three things that were essential to me in any room: real candlelight, wood fires and lovely flowers. Those were my tricks. There were always wood fires burning on cold days and in the evenings, and after dark the carved wooden chandelier that I bought for the hall was always lit. On the two Kent eagle side tables I bought from Lord Hampden's house, the Hoo, I always kept great raffia baskets of clashing pink geraniums, and in the corners of the room, in pots or big jars, I had forced standard lilac, liburnum and crab apple trees flowering in the dead of winter. You didn't see that anywhere else. I used to fix the baskets of geraniums myself, with flowers from the greenhouse. I did most of the flowers in the house in those days, and not just flowers like I've got here that I don't have to worry about . . . anybody can have a whack of flowers that stick straight up. At Kelmarsh I used to really arrange them and get the right flowers for the right room. I knew what I wanted in the rooms; I knew what flowers each room ought to have. I was very careful about that and very particular about the containers I used. If I couldn't do the flowers for the house at a particular time, the gardeners did them. I used to buy colored books of Dutch flower paintings to give to the gardeners to look at so they could learn how to arrange flowers like I wanted. I was quite good like that, making other people do it for me. If the gardeners were doing the flowers, they did it very early in the morning and put them out before we got up.

I supposedly had a very good eye for color. Along with the pink walls and the yellow laburnum, I had two chairs covered in the most wonderful tangerine velvet, another in an emerald green, one Queen Anne wing chair in bright yellow brocade, and a chair and a sofa in striped fabric I bought in Italy. The most comfortable chair in the

The Munnings portrait of Pytchley huntsman Frank Freeman hung over one of the great hall's fireplaces. "There was a fox that used to beat Freeman regular at Kelmarsh, and one day blowed if Mr. Tree didn't find him in the front hall, a-waiting for his tea, bold as brass" (Paget, *Rum 'uns to Follow*, p. 70).

house was a long-seated one I bought from General Trading in Mayfair that I still have. They called it their "hunting chair," and it was covered in yellow. The curtains were lovely white brocade—Elden made them—and in front of the door, to block the draft when it was opened, I had a black lacquer Venetian screen with a scene of white horses and little men in red coats painted on it. If the hunt ended near Kelmarsh, dozens of riders would come to the hall for tea. When you added the men in the scarlet coats and Ronnie and Jack Lowther in the burgundy Lowther-red the Masters wore, it was an extraordinary sight, a very attractive picture.

Munnings wanted to paint the hall with everyone in it. He thought it would make a marvelous painting, all the hunting people in red coats in the pink hall. But he had been at Kelmarsh for what seemed like weeks by then, painting Ronnie. Every night he was in the cups and got rather bleary-eyed. I thought, "I'll be damned if he stays here any longer." I wouldn't let him paint the hall, because I wanted him to go. What a pity it is; I wish I had let him do it. It would have made a wonderful record of the day.

The great hall's decoration must surely have startled even the most cosmopolitan of the Trees' guests, not to mention the hardened foxhunting gentry of Northamptonshire; its color seemed almost subversive. All of the principal ground-floor rooms were made over with the same inspiration. Opposite the front door through double doors was the drawing room.

The idea was that when you came in after dark, you would look from the front door through the pink hall, with its fires and flowers, into this wonderful drawing room, painted what Paul Phipps called "the soul of blue," lit only by candles. The blue and the candlelight created something atmospheric, I don't know how to describe it, but it filled up the room like a mist.

Just as the pink hall warmly embraced a cold, tired rider after a day in the field, the drawing room set a delirious, romantic mood for the late evening's entertainments at Kelmarsh.

Sometimes we would dance after dinner to music from the victrola, or sometimes we would have a band. I kept the drawing room frightfully bare of furniture, because we liked to roll up its lovely Aubusson rugs and dance on the oak floor. I also had musicals once or twice while we lived at Kelmarsh. I brought in a quartet or a man who was rather an admirer of Aunt Phyllis's to play the classical piano.

Other nights we played paper games like telegrams and word-taking and word-making. And you would have witty acting games like "In the Manner of . . ." or charades. My cousin Joyce Grenfell was very good at those. The funnier they were, the better. I remember Countess Helene Potocki invented a game called "*Coco est bien assise.*" Everyone sat in a ring, and a blindfolded person went from lap to lap guessing who they were sitting on; the only clue was the owner of the lap with a disguised voice saying "*Coco est bien assise.*" We had a game where the women would stand behind a cloth and put a knee up to a hole in the cloth and the men would have to guess whose knee it was. Husbands could never tell their wives by the knees. Another one was when two people left the room and then came back pretending to be famous characters—they might be God and Moses. They'd carry on a conversation in the way of the two people, and you'd have to guess who they were. It was amusing, and it kept your mind working. Of course, the cleverer the people, the more amusing it was. You see, there was no television then, radio was in its infancy, and when you stayed somewhere, you usually were deep in the countryside, far away from everything. And there was no question of going out and talking tête-à-tête; you entered into things.

We also had parties for the children in the drawing room at Kelmarsh. The Lowther children would come; young MacDonald-Buchanans, whose parents took a house at Guilsborough before they bought Cottesbrooke from Bobby Brassey; little Johnny Spencer—Princess Diana's father—who was Jeremy's age. I used to call Jeremy and Johnny the roly-poly puddings of Northamptonshire because they were such plump little boys. When the Duke and Duchess of York took Naseby so he could hunt with the Pytchley, Princess Elizabeth came to the children's parties. Our neighbor Marjorie Henderson—she was one of the beautiful Garrard sisters from Walton Place—was a genius at organizing them and arranging games like "pass the orange" and "sardines." We used playing cards to choose dancing partners. You would pick a card out of a hat, and the person with the matching card was your partner. A little boy came up to Aunt Phyllis at one party and asked if she had the two of diamonds. When she said she did, the little boy said, "Then will you take me to the lavatory?" Miss Waddington held dancing classes for the children in the drawing room; she was the sister of a famous tenor singer of the day. Each week she gathered the children at a different house nearby and taught them to dance.

There were also three smaller reception rooms on the ground floor of Kelmarsh. Each had a specific use in the day-to-day life there, and each, as Nancy decorated them, a distinct personality. In the southwest corner of the house, opening onto the great hall, the Chinese Room had the house's most striking character. In her tireless scouring of the country Nancy had found a room at Kimberley Hall in Norfolk hung in a particularly fine late-eighteenth-century chinoiserie wallpaper; the room dimensions had matched those of the Kelmarsh room perfectly, and the owner had agreed to part with the paper as well as the room's carved mantelpiece. Hand-painted and mounted on canvas stretched over wooden frames, the paper displayed a distinctly Occidental impression of the Orient. Miniature putty-faced figures with long braids and pinched eyes posed beneath foliage that climbed to the room's cornice. Leaves and fruit-tree blossoms washed the walls in subtle pastels; exotic birds hovered and perched within the branches. In the morning, sun poured through the tall sash windows; at night, like the rest of the downstairs, Nancy lit the Chinese Room with the candles in the crystal chandelier.

I kept rather strange flowers in the Chinese Room. I would have orchids from Ronnie's cymbidium house, sealing-wax red anthuriums and amaryllises. We would meet for cocktails there before dinner, or if someone wanted to play bridge after dinner, they played there.

The Trees commissioned the American architect William Delano to convert the billiard room, across from the Chinese Room, into their library. His plan would prove the most imaginative and extensive alteration to the house. Originally it was a square room with an incongruous rectangular alcove; Delano used paneling to make the alcove oval-shaped, then lined the other walls with Georgian-style bookshelves and paneling. With Delano's improvements and Nancy's decoration, the room became an eye-catcher instead of a relative eyesore.

I filled the library with odd-shaped but very comfortable chairs and covered them with different colors of leather, linen and chintz. I thought the different shapes looked better than plain chairs, and I liked an unevenness by the fireplace. There was a funny half-moon-shaped chair, a cockfighting chair, a tub chair and then a very plain but very comfortable deep-seated easy chair. I had a gout stool as well, the kind from the eighteenth century people used to put their feet up on. I used to collect them.

Shelves from floor to ceiling held our books, and on the far wall there was a map of Pytchley country we commissioned a painter

The Chinese Room at Kelmarsh—"Really the prettiest room in the house," wrote Nancy. The wallpaper and the Russian Aubusson carpet, both made in the eighteenth century, were well faded.

called Colin Gill to make for us. The Prince of Wales had a picture of Quorn country at St. James's Palace by the same man, and he told me who had done it for him. It was a huge cartoon, showing the details of the houses and spinneys and coverts, the pack of hounds and a group of followers on horseback.

A door in the corner of the library led through to the blue drawing room, at whose far end another door led to a small sitting room. In contrast with the dark, masculine colors in the library, this room, looking over the lake and the back pastures, was decidedly feminine.

Jubie's mother called it her "boudoir." I used it as my sitting room. On either side of the door to the dining room I had two old Adam bookcases, painted cream and black with a lavender-colored band. The rug had rows of flowers in it; it's still one of my favorite rugs—I have it in my bedroom here. Then I covered the sofa with a striped, sort of blue with yellow material from the eighteenth century. The walls were painted the palest green, the color of a new leaf. It was a very pleasant room to sit in.

One final room on the main floor of Kelmarsh Hall was of the utmost importance to a house and a hostess so often in the throes of company. The dining room as Gibbs planned it was to the right of the front door, balancing the Chinese Room and sharing its proportions. It was entirely too small for the Trees' hospitality, though, so during their tenancy it was used as the day nursery and schoolroom for the children. Instead, Nancy co-opted the ballroom for her dining room. When Richard Naylor lived at Kelmarsh in the mid-nineteenth century, he built the ballroom onto the north end of the garden facade, an addition many house owners in Victorian England undertook to accommodate the occasional dance. For the Trees and their generation, the dinner table was the more central stage of Friday-to-Monday house parties; the ballroom at Kelmarsh, second in size only to the great hall, made the ideal theater.

The dining-room chairs came from Lord Chesterfield. They were heavy Chippendale, carved with wonderful grotesques in all four knees and covered in a sort of dirty dandelion-colored leather. I painted the walls olive green; Mrs. Bethel made the curtains in a buff color, like old gold, with a red fringe. I red-marbleized the fireplace, and the lovely Regency coal scuttle was gilt on a red background. I hung a painting of the Duke of Marlborough at the end of the room in an arched recess, and the little girl over the fireplace was one of the Fanes. I bought her from Lord Westmorland.

Saturday night dinner parties were *the* event in the long winter months in the hunting shires.

During the week, as everybody had been on horseback all day, we were quite tired and didn't do very much. After tea you'd have a hot bath; I used to put crude Epsom salts in my bath, so I was never stiff. The dinner was at half past eight; then we'd be in bed quite early. It wasn't like London, where we'd be out all night; we were too exhausted. All our friends lived the same way. But at the weekend, when the house was full, we would invite neighbors and some of the officers from Weedon and have a dinner party.[15] Everybody dressed up in long dresses and dinner jackets and met downstairs around half past seven or at eight, when the others started arriving.

When the mahogany table in the dining room was fully extended, its four leaves in place, it easily seated twenty.

We served cocktails in the Chinese Room, which were quite new then. Everybody was crazy about old-fashioneds.

There were all ages at our dining room table on those weekends. Because it was a big house we weren't confined to our generation like one is now. The youngest were my cousin Wissy Astor and her friends like Esme Glyn, Lord Wolverton's daughter, and Davina Erne, Lord Erne's daughter. Lord and Lady Ilchester, Lord and Lady Islington, Maldwin Drummond, Kitty Rothschild, the Duke of St. Albans and Lord Berners were some of the older people who came to stay at Kelmarsh. Gerald Berners had a sparkling sense of humor and was thought rather eccentric. In the back of his Rolls-Royce he installed a piano so he could compose his operas on long journeys. Elinor Glyn was another guest of ours at Kelmarsh. She was the famous authoress of the novel *Three Weeks.* She had the most beautiful green eyes and was marvelous at games, jumping right in with all the young at charades.

Grand Duke Dmitri, Burgie Westmorland, Violet and Rudolf de Trafford—Rudolf had been Ronnie's best man—Nada and George Milford Haven, Rhoda and Oswald Birley and the Somersets were my earliest friends in England. They had all stayed with us in Virginia, in New York and in Long Island before we settled here.

In the Trees' dining room the very glamorous and sophisticated met the old-guard of Pytchley country. They had hunting in common, and the marvelous fare Nancy always served. Food at English country houses was notoriously mediocre at best, but Kelmarsh became known as an exception. One dinner menu might include fish soufflé to start, *langue de boeuf* in Cumberland sauce, *potirons au plat* Cliveden, potatoes *dauphinoise* and *glacé suprême* Alaska; another, consommé with poached egg, *suprême de lièvre* (hare), "Modern Ambrosia," baked-grits soufflé and chestnut-and-orange compote. When they were finished with dessert, at a signal from Nancy the ladies would move into another room for coffee, leaving the men alone with their cigars and brandy.

There was always delicious food. We brought Elise Dufour with us from America when we moved. She had grown up in Basque country and was a marvelous chef. She made it all easy for me. I only needed to approve of the day's menu when she brought it up to me every morning in my room. She took care of every meal with the three people she had in the kitchen underneath her.

Lunch was rarely served in the Kelmarsh dining room, with the Trees and their guests in the field hunting to hounds. They might have a sandwich at around two in the afternoon, when they changed their horses, or wait until tea. But the men had their breakfast in the dining room.

Breakfast was laid out at nine, before hunting. They came in when they were ready, helped themselves at the sideboard and sat down wherever they wanted. It was informal in that way. Silver dishes on hot plates had eggs with bacon, kidneys, sausages and toast, and there was cereal, juice, fruit and coffee and tea. We had done it that way at Mirador; I should think it was an English custom the aunts brought back with them when they visited. In Virginia people generally sat down and were waited on. Breakfast for the ladies at Kelmarsh was always served on trays in bed; a maid brought them whatever they liked.

IT WAS NO WONDER that the ladies ate their breakfast in their bedrooms; Nancy had decorated them with the same dash and comfort she had used on the rooms downstairs. Again, Kelmarsh was unique. Bedrooms in large country houses, like the drafty great halls and dining rooms below, were legendary for offering little or no respite from winter. It was especially true in the hunting houses of Northamptonshire and Leicestershire, where tempests blowing inland from the Wash easily breached window and door frames; their bedrooms, no matter how opulently appointed, were mainly sleeping quarters. Perhaps hunting folk were up and in their saddles each day because their rooms were so cold. At night, hot-water bottles, bed warmers, sleeping caps, curtains surrounding the beds and layers of blankets had to suffice in the finest manor houses; upon awakening, even the richest landlords dressed close by the fireplace. **People thought it was unhealthy to have heat upstairs. When I went to stay with friends when we were hunting, the houses were so cold I had to get under the bedclothes to put on my top hat and veil.**

Nancy spoiled the "hard-bitten" hunting elite. Everyone still awoke to a fire—the Kelmarsh housemaids slipped in and lit them at dawn—but radiators took the nip out of the air as well, and kept the rooms dry, while fitted carpets and rugs covered cold, bare floors. Nancy furnished each of these rooms as combination bedrooms and private sitting rooms. They were big enough for both. At the foot of the generous four-poster beds there would be a chaise longue or a deep-seated chair with an ottoman to stretch out on before dinner. **I'd have killed anyone who got onto one of my lovely bedspreads in muddy hunting clothes.** More chairs surrounded the fire. Each room had a desk and ample Kelmarsh Hall writing paper; each had books and a reading lamp at every possible resting spot. There was always a bottle of drinking water and a glass next to the bed, and every room always displayed an abundance of fresh flowers from the garden. Hanging on the wall next to the beds, silk bellpulls with gilded tassels could be used to summon a maid or a valet if anything was ever wanting.

Alongside the comfort came the style, which everyone who ever stayed at Kelmarsh agreed was dazzling. In decorating these rooms Nancy avoided the previous few generations' bric-a-brackishness, and splashed new life onto tired walls. To the left of James Gibbs's staircase, one room looked out over the lake and the garden. **I called it the Shrimp Pink Room because the walls were painted the pale, pale pink of the back of a shrimp. That was a lovely color. The bed had a pale tea-color fabric, like ivory, and the curtains were piped with a ribbon the same color as the walls. I had beautiful eighteenth-century Italian furniture in that room, three pieces that matched, painted pale green. They looked like Adam. The pictures by the fire were very pretty French pictures of flowers.**

Across the hall, with windows facing the elm-crested fields over the road, was the largest guest room, the Blue Room. **I painted it a marvelous aquamarine, and I covered the bed with a lovely chintz I found through Mrs. Bethel that was yellow with pink and red roses. The pelmet had a ruche of** blue around it. You used a room on the top floor for a dressing room if you stayed in the Blue Room. Everybody had to have a dressing room.

There were other "good" guest rooms on the top floor, alongside rooms for the Trees' and their guests' servants. When he and his wife, Mary, were guests of the Trees at Kelmarsh, Oliver Filley slept in a room on the south end of the top floor. Alfred Munnings, ensconced in Kelmarsh hospitality while painting Ronald Tree's portrait, jotted notes on Kelmarsh stationery of a scene he witnessed in Filley's bedroom:

> Breakfast . . . Ronnie Tree in bird's-eye blue. This afternoon . . . the butler with Mr. Filly's [sic] hat in his hand—the brim all smashed in . . . Ronnie Tree in his slow deliberate style of speaking: "Ye-es; b-a-a-d fall . . . Horse rolled on top of him for quite ten minutes— very serious." . . . Later on, up in Oliver Filly's [sic] bedroom . . . Bed encased in shiny chintz, lily of the valley pattern. Boots and trees on floor; spurs, gloves, etc., on chest of drawers . . . Doctor—"water on the knee, he can't possibly go away in the morning." . . . Lord Some- one and others there. Enter Mrs. Filly [sic] in black . . . Two men in scarlet one in black. Mrs. Tree in white silk flounces with black vel- vet coat—very charming. Miss Grenfell in velvet.[16]

Guests found themselves encased in chintz, silk damask and Irish linen when- ever they slept at Kelmarsh Hall.

> It started first thing in the morning. A housemaid would come in and light the fire before you got up. The ladies would be brought their breakfast when they were ready. There was always a small vase with a flower on the tray; a newspaper if you wanted. I was brought my mail. Then your lady's maid would lay out your hunting clothes and help you get dressed. The gentlemen were looked after by their own valets, whom they brought with them, or if they hadn't a valet, one of our footmen would valet them. When you came up from tea after hunting, the fire in your room had been lit again and the maid had turned on the water in your bath. Then she put out your under- clothes and your dress so you could get changed for the evening. The valets or the footmen did the same for the men. They shined their shoes, pressed their clothes, packed and unpacked for them. One of their biggest jobs was cleaning our boots and hunting clothes. Dur- ing dinner the maid would come and straighten up your room and turn down your bed. The butler and the housekeeper kept every- thing running smoothly. All you really had to do yourself at Kel- marsh was digest your food.

The Blue Room at Kelmarsh

. . .

NANCY'S OWN BEDROOM was above Mrs. Lancaster's old boudoir, at the end of the second-floor hallway. It was this single room, more than any other in the house, that displayed the mood and taste considered the height of chic in the era between the wars. In it, Nancy arranged a deft marriage of eighteenth-century refinement and Roaring Twenties glamour; she took the typically sumptuous materials and shapes of the Georgians and created with them a subtly *avant* impression. She wrote at the time that the room was composed from a combination "of all different whites. The walls look like ice; they are hung with silk; the curtains are the same. The valances and the fringes are old silver from altar cloths and quite lovely. The bed is cream brocade with old tarnished silver fringes and valances and four gilt ornaments on the corners. It is really lovely. [It] has two lovely gilt mirrors and is very mellow, pretty."[17] "Lovely" and "mellow," yes, but more so: stunning. And this

Fine Georgian furniture, a trompe l'oeil painted fireplace and a zebra-skin rug lived side by side in Nancy's bedroom.

was at least three years before the decorator Syrie Maugham finished her famous all-white sitting room in London.[18]

Because there was no paneling in the room, I covered the walls with this beautiful white silk that a woman in Versailles had woven by hand. Cole Porter's wife, Linda, told me about her; she had marvelous materials. The silk was pure white like ice; there was no cream in it at all. It shimmered. There was a slight glint of gold in the room, but it was reflected from the old gilt mirror and picture frames and the gilt finials on the corners of my bed.

The bed was grand yet understated in design, again, typical of the late eighteenth century. Nancy mustered its components especially for the room. I started from scratch with a frame I bought, added the damask curtains with an old silver fringe that came down the sides and along the bottom, and for the back and the cornice I used damask with a design of old silver embroidered in it. The important thing was it was all old silver; its age and tarnish were its charm.

The curtains were of the same white silk as the walls, the pelmets made of old silver lamé, and the fitted carpet was white. Black eighteenth-century nightstands, a pair of fire screens with black backgrounds and the wonderfully incongruous black-and-white zebra-skin rug in front of the fireplace all punctuated the cool, silvery scintillescence of the room with a strong exclamation point, yet never distracted from an overall harmony, an overall elegance. Of an evening, a blazing fire reverberated off the walls and the drawn curtains.

Paul Phipps concocted the small bathroom adjoining Nancy's bedroom. It was a series of large, mirrored cupboards, two on the left and two on the right, with doors that opened from the middle. Behind one door was the lavatory; it had an old mahogany seat and a stirrup-pump flush. Next to that you opened the door to find the washbasin; the doors across were for my bath. When you closed all the cupboard doors, all you saw was mirrors. It looked like a hall of mirrors with my dressing table and another mirror at the end.

An abundance of bathrooms at Kelmarsh was one more pleasant surprise for the Trees' house guests. Nancy added three baths on the main bedroom floor and another two on the top floor. Even the most sumptuously decorated, extravagantly run country houses of the day still came up short on bathrooms. Many houses were simply built before the invention of modern plumbing; succeeding generations made do with washstands and *pots de chambre* that were attended to by housemaids. Where there *was* plumbing, there never was enough. There would be two baths in little rooms next to each other, and two loos in another part of the house next to each other, and that would be it. Rooms didn't have their own bathrooms attached; they didn't have bathrooms like we're used to now. So people would rush to the lavatory or rush to the bathroom to get ahead of the line. Even at a big house like Cliveden there were only two baths to a floor. You'd see breadlines outside the doors, with people in their dressing gowns, carrying their sponge bags, waiting for a bath. The Victorian water closets were very comfortable, though. They had encased seats of dark mahogany that filled the width of the closet, so you had sides roomy enough to put your books or papers on.

Nancy contrived her bathrooms as carefully as she did other rooms. The tubs were always long, deep and encased in paneling like wainscoting that provided shelf space for bath salts and bottles of essence; sinks were installed in mahogany tables like the old washstands; there was always an extra table, an armchair, rugs on the floor, mirrors, pictures and prints on the walls, curtains made of crisp linen with machine-scalloped edges in colors to match the color of the adjoining bedroom. She installed heated towel racks. The water was hot, the floors were soft under bare feet, the towels warm and dry. There were even working fireplaces in some of the bathrooms. **People seemed to like staying at Kelmarsh.**

Nancy's eye for every detail equaled her perfectionist inclinations: She would have a room or a hallway painted and repainted, or a bed in the garden planted and replanted, until they matched her ideal. Though she finished decorating the entire house in a matter of just a few months, not even the tiniest feature was taken for granted. For instance, every door on the first two floors of the house was painted in two or three shades of white or beige to give them depth and a character of their own. The only electric light in the drawing room came from the bowl of a crystal chandelier Nancy thought to wire and from a pair of fine George III gilt torchères she had bulbs installed in. She never hesitated to alter valuable antique furniture to fit her needs. She also had tin containers for the begonias in the drawing room painted the same blue as the walls.

When she replaced the tall windows in the drawing room that opened onto a back terrace, Nancy had the new ones constructed with three sashes, so the windows might be raised high enough to use as doorways in the summer months. Fitted carpets around the house were dyed or faded to a "dead mouse" color. **It wasn't brown or black or the usual gray, but exactly the color of a dead mouse.** Others were "no color" or "elephant's breath." These shades acquiesced to the Aubusson, Bessarabian or antique hooked rugs in every principal room, bedroom or bathroom in the house instead of competing with them. Baseboards in large rooms were painted "bad mourning," the kind of off-black that sun-faded widows' weeds became. The books in the library were all wrapped in matching leather bindings. And even though the old servant-paging system was made redundant by a modern electric contraption, Nancy left the original bells and their bouncing coils in place, along with the wooden plaques below them that identified each room. Nancy sought out every corner, every niche, seen or unseen, in which to ply her imagination, to express a boundless repertoire of effect.

THE GARDEN AT Kelmarsh was one last "room" Nancy approached, a continual source of immense pleasure and tranquillity both for her and for anyone who strolled along its paths. An ocean of yellow and white daffodils blossomed every spring. **We used to ask our friends to "come see our daffs" along the oak walk. It's good soil for bulbs, because it's heavy clay.** Nancy ordered and planted 500 daffodil bulbs her first autumn at Kelmarsh, as well as 500 tulip bulbs, 650 hyacinths, 300 freesias, 100 scillas, 100 snowdrops, 400 crocuses and 300 lilies of the valley. **I planted snake's-head fritillaria along the drive. They eventually seeded themselves, because there's very bad drainage there and fritillaria love wet ground. The only place I've seen more is along** the Thames at Oxford. I planted an enormous hedge of pink and white rhododendrons along the Northampton Road.

Nancy also created a small fan-shaped rose garden with beds and box hedging that pushed outward from a patch of turf and a shaded niche cut in a box wall. Facing the Kelmarsh parish church from there, one met with a view that uncannily resembled a Constable pastoral. **I planned that as a spot where Nanny Weir could take the children for some sun on summer afternoons. I only used old roses, even though they were hard to find in England. I'd grown up with old roses in Virginia, and that's what I liked. They weren't at all special roses, just the old type that no one else had back then.**

We had a wonderful head gardener at Kelmarsh named Williams. He was there when we took the house; then when we moved to Ditchley, we took him with us. He was such a nice man, but he was often frustrated working for me. He used to give notice all the time because I told him to do so many things; it never made him very happy when I asked him to move trees that I thought were in the way. He only ever did half of what I told him, though; he was deaf as a post and didn't wear a hearing aid, so either he didn't hear most of the time or just didn't bother with most of the things I said. It worked out very well that way; we became intimate friends.

Williams worked from two greenhouses—a large one with a boiler to heat it in winter and a smaller one next to it, both surrounded by cloches and cold frames—in the middle of the kitchen garden. Enclosing this two-acre garden-within-a-garden were high walls: patched, repointed, buttressed and bleached by the sun over the decades like an ancient fortress, extra bricks and plain stone cornices used and reused until they crumbled. The kitchen garden produced something—generally a cornucopia—all year long, from brussels sprouts and artichokes to Nancy's favorite, sea kale. One corner was reserved especially for berry bushes: blackberries, raspberries and gooseberries. From May to October, a giant, dappled green wreath of foliage from the various trees that stood guarding its walls ringed the entire kitchen garden.

The overall garden at Kelmarsh was small, but there were a number of paths to take, making it seem more intricate. One route to walk was through the painted wooden door in the corner of the kitchen garden wall nearest the house; down among its steeply sloping beds; along box-hedged paths; past espaliered fruit trees rife with pears, apples and plums in the summertime; past the rows of vegetables, a small pet cemetery and a swatch of *fraises du bois*; through the jasmine-draped conservatories, with their supporting stanchions of sculpted Victorian cast iron, grape vines, clay pots brimming with every sort of flowering plant and standard tree; then back on a path with cutting flowers along both sides of it to Ronald Tree's cymbidium house.

Another way was to walk outside of the kitchen garden, to the south and east. Here were some of Norah Lindsay's borders, which Nancy had her gardeners pack with choice annuals and perennials. Clematis and climbing roses inundated the old brick wall on this side. This part of the garden was enclosed by an even taller "wall," this one of boxwood, holly and yew. The three evergreens grew together, intermeshing like a jigsaw puzzle, and when they were clipped twice a year, they became a solid mass of contrasting texture and hue. The odd strand of ivy grew along it here and there, or the invasive Virginia creeper, which produced such lovely flowers but strangled its host. From the borders the path carried on underneath a topiary loggia into a "hallway," this decorated with more of Nancy's old roses framed in slow-growing box hedges. This section ended in a latticework summerhouse, an ideal trellis for more climbers.

Following the perimeter wall of the kitchen garden, one was led down three brick steps into the fan-shaped rose garden, then turned sharply to the right to descend a wider footpath toward the tennis court. On the left was a pasture, interrupted here and there by a gnarled oak; the cows and bulls were kept from the garden by a ditch and fence typical of Pytchley country. The ribbon of lawn between the pathway and the fence was planted with scented bushes and some of the hundreds of bulbs. During high summer, the long, wide herbaceous border to the right of the path filled out. The beds sloped inward, and Nancy and Norah planned it so that as one grouping finished flowering for the season, another display nearby took its place; this went on over and over again like perfectly choreographed fireworks well into late autumn. Mrs. Lindsay espoused an overall formality, but "spontaneity in the planting, as though the flowers and trees had chosen their own positions as well,"[19] was an ideal that seemed to approximate the easy, timeless mood Nancy so loved in a garden. A hidden flagstone path passed between the border and the brick wall: a secret trail or an access for gardeners.

None of it was grand, none of it an exhibitionist display of hybrid, trend or drawing-board trickery; it was simply a lovely, comfortable, seductive place to be. "You feel you never want to leave this source of enchantment where peace and beauty beckon. . . . this is what you have missed and what, unconsciously, you have been seeking all your life."[20]

PART THREE

We were young, and the business of life was hunting. In such a climate not even the primmest and most precious of gardens were sacred. Hounds and then horses followed wherever Reynard led them; it was not uncommon to find him resting by a topiary swirl or holed up in a sunk garden among tree

Norah Lindsay suggested that a tall, old wall of yew should be sculpted into a topiary loggia.

peonies. In the eyes of the truly dedicated members of the Hunt, lolling about on a bench near a river or sacrificing a good morning to a book seemed a cruel and unnatural diversion from the forward-going momentum of their time on earth. These were an ever-active people. Taking joy in the work of decorating and restoring an old house was understandable, but resting on its threshold inexcusable.

Sunday afternoons after church and lunch we'd go for a walk to see the fences we'd jumped over when we were hunting the day before. You always thought you'd jumped the biggest fence in the world, then you'd get there and it seemed hardly bigger than a ditch. We'd also take our long dogs and course hares in the big fields around Kelmarsh. These same pastures had been marched over for centuries by sportsmen as they hunted rabbits with greyhound or lurcher couples. Michael Drayton spoke of it in the 1620 edition of *Polyolbion*, a book-length description of England in verse:

> *With Kelmarsh there is caught, for coursing of the Hare,*
> *Which scornes that any place should with her Plains compare.*

On a winter's day, when an extended frost made the ground too hard for the horses' hooves and hounds' pads to foxhunt, there was skating on the lake

Topiary swirls and standard rosebushes furnished one of the Kelmarsh garden rooms.

at the back of the house. Neighbors and their children, as always, joined the party. During the summer, between hunting seasons, Kelmarsh's inhabitants and guests rowed on the lake, swam in it or sat by it on benches under oak trees, reading and picnicking among swan, geese and duck families. Above them was an army of invisible songbirds, their constant calls and jeers drifting down from the treetops. At the bottom of the garden a lawn, kept perfectly rolled and tightly clipped, served as a tennis court. One team faced an herbaceous border; the other looked out onto a field of lazy park whites.

But the better part of the Trees' seven years at Kelmarsh Hall revolved around horses and riding. Polo playing, racing, showing, driving and hacking filled the spare hour not taken up by hunting to hounds. Ronald Tree was a patron of the Manton Stables; his racing colors for life were canary yellow with an azalea pink sash. Cecil Boyd-Rochfort trained Nancy's colt Stray Melody (by Meloa and Stratford). She bought the Meloa colt at the July sales at Newmarket in 1930; he eventually won a number of races, including the Hyde Park Stakes over a favorite called Dictator, and a Doncaster Foal Plate. At Brighton, Stray Melody "carried off the palm in the matter of looks"[21] and won the Steyning Plate "in brilliant style."[22]

Most years the Trees attended the races at Ascot, the Grand National at Aintree and the sales and races at Newmarket. They also traveled to Ireland for the Dublin Horse Show, where the world's finest hunters were bought and sold, and on occasion visited the International Horse Show at Olympia. One year Nancy's cousin Bill Astor asked Ronald Tree to serve as judge for Oxford's annual Trial of Hunters. Another year Tree was appointed Race Steward of the Weedon School Point-to-Point, an old-fashioned, single-race steeplechase; with no track for the race, the riders used the steeple of a distant parish church as their point of navigation, taking their own line to the finish.

Nancy was a spectator at these social and sporting events, though once in a while she competed as well. In the Langhorne tradition she was elegant and poised in the saddle, and fearless despite the accident that nearly crippled her. She entered hunter trials from time to time, including the 1932 Grafton Hunt Hunter Trials Open Championship, where she rode her horse Cherokee. The cross-country course was particularly rigorous, with high hurdles and water obstacles, a test of the strength and agility of the rider and mount rather than mere showmanship. Out of fifty-three competitors, both men and women, Nancy finished first. She also won the Lady's Class Hunter Trials on Hiawatha and was fourth out of twenty-four on Seminole at the Royal Horse Show at Derby. She always rode sidesaddle.

I always had frightfully good hunters. We bought them young, and I had a marvelous man named Pringle, who made them for me. Mostly I gave my horses American Indian names like Cherokee and Seminole and Hiawatha, which the English could never pronounce. I also had Schoolboy, whom I brought from Virginia, Sweet Pepper, Brandy Wine, Happy Days and Guardsman. You had to have a lot of horses if you were hunting four days a week and riding two different horses a day. Blue Ridge was the best horse I ever had; I had Munnings paint me on Blue Ridge. And I had a wonderful horse called Spectacles. He'd see a fence and just couldn't hold back; there was no jump that he couldn't jump better. He was the ugliest horse in the world, though, with the rings around his eyes. I showed him to a friend and said how he was the best hunter I'd ever had, and he said to me, "He's so common, he's got hair under his arms."

Because I always had wonderful horses I didn't have many bad falls, considering the country. The worst accident I had in England was when I jumped a fence and hit the branch of a tree with my face. It knocked me back in the saddle but not off my horse. I thought I was hit across the mouth. I continued on, though, going across the field, thinking, "My God, all my teeth will come out." I was terrified. But I went on hunting. That was Saturday.

The next day my whole head felt like it was full of tissue paper or bits of broken glass. Monday morning I rang up Gillies, who was

"There is nothing like hunting, and I had the best of it," said Nancy. "I lived in the best hunt country, owned the most wonderful horses and was always surrounded by the most pleasant and charming friends and staff." Standing next to a Kelmarsh groom is Lady Alexandra Metcalfe.

the surgeon who did all of the airmen. He was the first person who reconstructed faces. A man answered the phone and I said, "Look here, I've got no upper lip at all anyway, and if I've broken my nose, which I think I have, I won't be able to open my mouth. I'm coming up to London tomorrow and I want you to tell Dr. Gillies it's very important. There isn't any more room for my nose." I went up the next day, and the door was opened by a man whose whole face had been reconstructed; he had been an aviator. I felt so ashamed. I had spent an hour on the phone with this poor man discussing my beauty problems.

When the doctor got to me and took X-rays, he found that I hadn't broken my nose or my mouth at all: I had cracked my skull and all the bones along my cheeks and eyes. I was very lucky not to have been blinded. I had felt it in my mouth because the mouth is the nerve center. While he set the broken bones I was under anesthetic, and I remember him saying to me, "If you let me operate on your nose, I could fix you for the movies." I said, "What would you do? I have no upper lip." He said, "I'll take some of your behind and give you a longer upper lip." I couldn't possibly let him do that. I said, "I'm still young enough to be kissed, and if someone kisses me and I know it's my behind they're kissing, I'll die laughing."

My cousin Jakie Astor said to me after the accident that I left that morning an attractive woman and came back an old man.

The amusements of life in the English countryside came with responsibilities for a Joint Master and his wife. The Trees found the time to make trips to Paris for Nancy's wardrobe, to Deauville for Ronald's polo, to the English coast in the summertime and to St. Moritz in the winter. They also continued to stay at Nancy's beloved Mirador at least twice yearly. But the concerns of the Pytchley occupied a great deal of their time. The Pytchley Point-to-Point Races, for instance, required an energetic push to get started again as an annual event. These meets had waned during the years of the First World War and were only reestablished through the efforts of the Joint Masters and the Hunt Committee. The Master was responsible for the health and breeding of the hounds as well—bloodlines, "puppy walking" and training—and the large stable of hunters required for the huntsman and the other hunt servants.

Ronnie and I didn't only see the people we hunted with. As Joint Master you've got position in the country, so you don't just get to know the gentry; you must know all the people. You had to get to know all of the farmers, and have a good relationship with them, because it was through their kindness that you hunt over their land. And it wasn't just a "Hello, how do you do?" You had to be in constant contact with them. Ronnie would go to the market days in the villages to meet with the local farmers and speak with them, get to know them and discuss their problems. He would visit them at their farms.

I would go around with him sometimes. I would talk to the farmers as I would the people in Virginia . . . quite naturally. But I quickly found they didn't do that here. The men farmers were amazed by me. I don't think they were used to being addressed in such a friendly manner by a lady. They looked rather shy and startled as though I should only be speaking to the female of the species. Back then England was very old-fashioned. It hadn't changed its ways for centuries.

As the Master's wife and lady of the house at Kelmarsh I was meant to take on certain duties. People in the country in England lived there all the time, not like in America, where they have houses in the country that they only visit for holidays and on weekends. Kel-

Spectators at a Pytchley
Point-to-Point included
Ronald Tree's stepfather,
Admiral Beatty, second
from left in the back row.

marsh was our full-time home, and we were part of the goings-on. I
remember right after we moved to Kelmarsh a lady from Clipston
came to me and said, "Since you live in the big house, you have to be
the chairman of the nursing." Then she said, "Here is the agenda."
I'd never even heard the word *agenda* before, but I learned fast.

An endless array of country fairs and dinners faced the Joint Master and
his wife. In September 1927 Captain and Mrs. Middleton of Haselbech
hosted a garden party and clay-pigeon shoot for local farmers. The Trees
were in attendance, helping with the proceedings and representing the
Pytchley. Shooting competitions were thought by the Hunt Committee an
excellent way for the Master to exhibit neighborliness to the farmers. The
farmers brought their own guns, the host provided the shot and the Joint
Master contributed the clay pigeons. The Middletons' house in Haselbech,

built by the captain's father, Bay Middleton, offered a beautiful prospect for shooting clay pigeons. The targets, thrown out over the steep, downward-sloping fields behind the house, sailed on the air in the direction of Cottesbrooke until they were shot from the sky. Other years the Trees were the hosts at Kelmarsh.

The Joint Masters gave "earth-stoppers' dinners." Earth-stoppers were local laborers—like fence menders, gate closers and terrier men—employed by the Hunt. They plugged holes and burrows where a fox might go to ground during a chase. The pub dinner cost 30 pence, and the bottom of the engraved invitation read, "Earth Stopping money will be paid at the Dinner, when information as to any litter of Cubs in your district is requested please." The Hunt, while Tree was Joint Master, also reintroduced hedge-cutting competitions for the farmers and farmworkers. The event, which often attracted as many as 150 participants, offered a double dividend to the Pytchley, as the day resulted in better hedging in the country they rode over and closer ties to their neighbors.

The hedge cutting was held in the fields near Clipston, a village just north of Kelmarsh with a few lovely Georgian and redbrick Victorian houses and cottages surrounded by the most tranquil of landscapes. There the Pytchley also sponsored the Clipston Agricultural and Horticultural Show every year. It was one of Midland England's biggest farming exhibitions, with dozens of categories, for everything from yearling horses to potatoes represented. The president, Ronald Tree, and the judges awarded trophies for best beast or sheep, and best pair of bullocks or heifers. The Trees donated silver cups given as prizes. The gardeners at Kelmarsh won a number of ribbons and citations over the years for the vegetables they raised, and the Trees won for their Thoroughbred geldings and mares. **Jubie used to say the reason we always won prizes for our vegetables at shows was because our gardener Williams had so many friends in the garden world who would send him their prizewinners whenever there was an exhibition. He said none of the vegetables were ever born in the Kelmarsh garden; they were collected.**

The hunt community's biggest event of the season, other than the meets themselves, was the annual hunt ball. Four to five hundred members and their guests attended the Pytchley Ball each January at the Northampton Town Hall, arriving around ten o'clock to a crowd of townspeople standing in St. Gyles Square looking on as if at a Hollywood premier. Inside, the Great Hall of the dour nineteenth-century brick building was transformed, with billowing damask festoons in the Pytchley's crimson and white draping the walls and the iron balustrade of the gallery, as well as hundreds of red and white chrysanthemums, hyacinths and potted tulips.

The men dressed for the occasion in hunting-pink tailcoats, with collars the colors of their particular hunt.[23] The ladies' gowns for the Pytchley Ball in 1929 were "exquisite, of ankle length, of course, with dipping hemlines. Fairy-like materials—lace, georgette, chinon, net—had pride of place."[24] For their hair, "the mannish shingle" of the early 1920s "has nearly disappeared, and in its place has come a long shingle, which is very pretty. Many had coils not over the ears, but at the back of the head." The society reporter for the Northampton *Echo* also called attention to the "ropes and ropes of pearls and diamond tiaras."[25] A description of Nancy's attire headed an endless list of what every woman there wore that night.

> Mrs. Ronald Tree's picture-like beauty was suited to perfection by her pure white gown. At the left side were quite exquisite panels reaching to the ground. The collar was scarf-like. On one shoulder was a shaggy posy. She wore an exquisite necklace of rubies and pearls, and several bracelets of diamonds and pearls.

On the front steps of Kelmarsh Hall, Michael, Ronald, Nancy and Jeremy Tree, c. 1928

The ball itself was electric, a wondrous gathering of like minds and spirits swirling, dipping and quick-stepping amid wisps of burgundy and rich cream, the sparkle of precious gemstones. Caught in the fabulous spell of the era and the place, they stayed until sunrise, dancing to fox-trot after fox-trot called "Sweeping the Cobwebs off the Moon," "Sweet So-and-So" or "Varsity Drag." If a couple dancing were keeping a respectable distance from each other, you could be sure they were having a love affair. Remarkably, many of the guests made it to the meeting of the hounds the next day; the Pytchley set out after its fox only a half-hour late.

Kelmarsh was quite a life . . . it was very pleasant. Maybe it was because we were so young, but the whole world seemed young to me then.

What also made it wonderful at Kelmarsh is that Ronnie and the children and I were all living the same life together. The boys hadn't gone to Eton yet, and Ronnie's work was right there. We were all doing the same things, and the house was full of friends doing the same things . . . all the big houses in Pytchley country were full of people doing the same things as us. It was a marvelous period . . . a marvelous period in my life. Maybe the happiest.

I remember most the leaves falling from the trees in autumn. I remember the row of elms on the hill above Kelmarsh . . . they were what you saw first whenever you were coming home. And I remember coming in from hunting, tired and hungry, to find a hot bath and a delicious meal. I don't think anything felt as good. That was heaven for me.

DITCHLEY PARK

"There was something very attractive about working with Ronnie
and Nancy," said the garden architect Sir Geoffrey Jellicoe.
"They were a remarkable couple in that they were full of the joy
of life and the essence of living. I found them very knowledgeable
as well; I ended up learning a great deal working with them.
And if something wasn't right, if the material wasn't absolutely
top brass, they'd have it pulled down and start again."

PART ONE

RONALD TREE gave up both the Pytchley and Kelmarsh Hall in 1933, the year he found "a great house and a new vocation." It happened overnight. That March he led the field as Master of the Foxhounds for the last time, having announced his retirement the preceding autumn. In June, only two weeks after he and Nancy had stopped at Ditchley Park in Oxfordshire for a picnic, Tree bought the entire three-thousand-acre estate and its two-hundred-year-old mansion without even seeing the inside of most of the house. Three months later, in August, the member of Parliament for Market Harborough quit his seat because of his health, and in September Tree was chosen as the National Conservative candidate to replace him. Ronald Tree was a member of the British House of Commons in November, replacing the MFH after his name with an MP. There had barely been a moment to draw a breath.

His timing was perfect. The 1920s had been foxhunting's most splendid era. It had also been the last when its followers would ride freely across the countryside, galloping as they willed over anyone and everyone's land oblivious to care and consequence; the world around their Gardens of Eden had changed too dramatically for such independence to go on unchecked. The

"When Nancy and Ronnie arrived it came to life," wrote Deborah Devonshire about Ditchley Park, "and there they created perfection."

Depression played the biggest role, ruining the farmers whose land they hunted over, as well as their own fortunes. Some were forced to plow up their turf fields because beef prices were too low; others were forced to sell altogether. The hunt would never again have the influence it once had; its fate would now be in the hands of city folk.

The 1932 Pytchley Point-to-Point meeting was canceled, as was the hunt ball. Stable stalls at the big houses were empty for the first time since the Great War, and many of the hunting boxes were left unlet, their heavy damask curtains drawn and their furniture covered with dust sheets through the long Midlands winter. Prince Albert—the Duke of York and future King George VI— chose not to take a house in Pytchley country for the 1931–32 season and never returned. His family had "decided upon heavy sacrifices in the interest of the nation." The Duke wrote to Ronald Tree: "It had come as a great shock to me that with the economy cuts I have had to make my hunting should have been one of the things I must do without. . . . And I must sell my horses too. This is the worst part of it all and the parting with them will be terrible."[1] His younger brother the Duke of Gloucester closed his own hunting stables in Melton Mowbray as well, and Earl Beatty did the same at Dingley.

The reason for Tree's departure had little to do with the decline of the institution, however. He had always seen the job of Joint Master as a stepping-stone and training ground for entering politics. "A good MFH," he wrote, "had to show an interest in the lives and problems of the farmers; discuss prices, wages, all aspects of government policy," a relationship very close to that of local MP. The vegetable judging and hand-shaking with earth-stoppers schooled him in the art of diplomacy and vote gathering. As Master he had also met the powers behind the politicians. "The position of MFH put me in contact with a great many well established and influential Tories in the country, many of whom were either politicians themselves, in local or national government, or took part in the country's social life."[2]

Tree had been active in the community outside of his responsibilities as Joint Master. Among his many charitable contributions was a gift, in the early 1930s, of £1,000 to build a nursery school in Kettering, a large town in Pytchley country. He had tried to make the gift anonymously through Lady Astor's secretary, but when word reached the town fathers as to who had made the donation, they insisted on naming the school the Ronald Tree Nursery School. He also supported the traditional rural events, donating silver prize trophies to agricultural fairs and horse shows, even a Ronald Tree Trophy to the Wigston District knockout skittles competition. He fashioned himself an old-style country Tory with a strong sense of noblesse oblige. At about the same time, Nancy donated $1,000 to the high school in Greenwood, near Mirador; her loyalties would always remain in Virginia. The money was used for the installation of the building's first pipes and central heating. **Fortunately, they never named it the Nancy Tree Plumbing.**

Despite his experience, Tree discovered himself a wobbly novice when he was chosen as the National Conservative candidate for Harborough in 1933. The thirty-five-year-old's first speech was anything but a success. "Nerves . . . got the better of me. I got up, sputtered out a few inaudible platitudes and sat down, much to the surprise of the local press who had come out to assess the abilities of their new candidate and were not impressed."[3] The candidate's wife was also called upon to campaign and to speak to local organizations. **At the beginning of the campaign Ronnie unfortunately got the flu and I had to speak for him at his first meetings. Our constituency was made up of lots of small factory towns and agricultural villages. I thought all the voters would be exhausted after their day's work and want to go home, so I made my speeches short and easily digestible. My first speech, which I** thought excellent, a quick "in and out," was full of clichés like "A rolling stone gathers no moss," and "Don't change horses in mid-stream." I imagined that was just the thing required; I had no idea they expected much more. With practice Nancy became an important asset on the hustings for her husband. The Market Harborough *Advertiser* reported in March 1935: "Mrs. Tree is a welcome visitor wherever she may go in the Division. Her natural friendliness prevents any shyness, and her wit and charm enliven any gathering. During this election she proved herself a valuable ally to her husband."[4]

During the campaign Kelmarsh was full of people helping with canvassing for votes before the election, full of cabinet ministers and Members of Parliament who came to speak on Ronnie's behalf. There was a great deal of excitement, but it was all very serious. What was new to me and what I, being an American, thought very strange was that we also had members of the Opposition, like Nannie's friend Philip Lothian, who had come to speak against my husband, staying with us at Kelmarsh as our house guests. That to me was very English, that they could divorce the issues and not make a campaign personal.

Tree's victory by a healthy majority was a boon to his party and the answer to his own lifelong ambition. "I had done what my grandfather had hoped of me, and I had done it in my father's country."[5] It also had historical significance. Ronald's election to the House of Commons gave the extended Astor family six seats in Parliament, a number unprecedented in the twentieth century. Sitting on the backbenches in the Commons were Lady Astor, her brothers-in-law Major John Jacob Astor and Lieutenant-Colonel Spender-Clay, her son-in-law, Lord Willoughby d'Eresby, and her niece's husband, Ronald Tree; Viscount Astor sat in the House of Lords. After the 1935 general election Lady Astor's son William further swelled the ranks. More were on Tree's own side of the family. His stepfather, Earl Beatty, who had retired as First Sea Lord in 1927, sat in the Lords, and in 1935, his son and Tree's half-brother, Viscount Borodale, gained a seat in the Commons. All of Ronald's relations represented in varying degrees of enthusiasm the Conservative platform; indeed, they were a kind of last vestige of Britain's ruling class. Ironically, five out of nine of the members were full-blooded Americans, and a sixth was half.

Family ties, though, did not predicate political agreement among them in a Parliament bitterly torn over a number of debates, including the dissolution of Great Britain's empire; domestic programs, such as day care and compulsory schooling; how to solve high unemployment and the national debt; and, the most volatile topic of all, Adolf Hitler. Winston Churchill thought the Parliament of those years spineless, lacking in fight; despite his disdain, however, an extraordinary group of historic figures met at Westminster. Ronald Tree took a seat that November behind the likes of David Lloyd George and Austen Chamberlain; Stanley Baldwin, Ramsay MacDonald and Neville Chamberlain; Clement Atlee, Anthony Eden and Harold Macmillan; not to mention Lady Astor, and the greatest British statesman of the twentieth century, Churchill himself. Tree gave up the tranquillity of the countryside to get there—the soil and the hard saddle—but in doing so, he joined the British march into the uncertain future.

Nancy thought it a high price to pay, giving up the hunting, Northamptonshire, their friends there and a life that husband, wife and children shared equally . . . all for the endless appearances and countless constituency at homes of the political arena. She played the role of MP's wife, though, with the same élan and spirit she had displayed in the hunting field—in the newspaper photographs of the day, Nancy stood out like a beacon from the dowdy men and women, dressed in her Schiaparelli suits and smiling knowingly under the tilt of her hat—but she never enjoyed it. She also deeply loved Kelmarsh Hall itself and hated to have to move. The house had become their home, a bewitching place with a special atmosphere they had worked hard to create. But Kelmarsh belonged to Jubie Lancaster: Ronald believed it was time to farm his own land after seven years as someone's tenant.

> I looked at a lot of houses in those days, some that were for sale, others just because I love houses. We looked at Fawsley because we lived nearby. There, they had very nice Georgian stables and a lovely park with huge old cedars of Lebanon; we used to have picnics there in the springtime when all the wild cherry trees were in bloom. We never seriously considered buying Fawsley, though. It was mostly a Victorian house done up in the nineteenth century for a visit by the Queen.

> We had known about Ditchley and that it would be on the market for over a year. Our friend Reggie Cooper had sent us a picture postcard of it, saying that as we wanted a Georgian house, Ditchley was a particularly beautiful and untouched example. But Ditchley was in Oxfordshire; in those days I was rather a hunting snob and couldn't imagine living where the country was so close. I just stuck the picture on one of the mantels in the hall at Kelmarsh and forgot about it.

> When we eventually went to Ditchley, it wasn't because we wanted to buy it. Ditchley interested me because of its Virginian connections. The land first belonged to a Sir Henry Lee in the sixteenth century. The Lees in Virginia were from the same family; there was even a house called Dytchley that one of Robert E. Lee's

cousins built. In 1933 the Ditchley in England was still in the same family. The first time we saw it, the old butler brought me a postcard his master had sent him when he had traveled to Virginia in the 1870s to visit his relatives there. It said how miserable postwar Virginia was, and how desperately he wished that Dytchley was as comfortable as "our Ditchley."

The afternoon we saw it was a particularly hot early summer's day in June. It was so hot I remember taking my bathing suit with me. Ronnie and I and Crawley de Crespigny were driving from Kelmarsh up to London and decided that we would stop to see the house on the way. We packed a picnic lunch. That time of year England is at its most beautiful, and Ditchley's park, even though it had been neglected for years, was enchanting. We ate our picnic on the grass in the front lawn among white deer and gnarled oaks that reminded me of *Hern the Hunter*. When we finished, I decided to walk right up to the front door of the house and ring the bell . . . we all wanted to see inside, but women being bolder than men, I took the initiative. The butler answered—he was as old as God and wore an ill-fitting red wig on his head—and I launched into a bromide about being from Virginia and having Lee cousins and couldn't we please come in and see the house. He was unmoved and very protective. His master, Lord Dillon, had died recently, and the house was a shambles.

That day, though, Lord Dillon's heirs were at Ditchley, "counting their possessions if not their money," as the nursery rhyme goes. They were going to sell the house and the land, but they wanted to sort through all the furniture and the paintings. When we were introduced to them, it turned out that one of the Dillon relatives had served in the Grenadier Guards under Crawley in the First War; Crawley—General Sir Claude Champion de Crespigny—was a great soldier and had distinguished himself in France. Because of Crawley, the Dillon heirs opened wide the doors to the house and brought out champagne for us in a gilt trophy given to their ancestor by Charles II.

Ditchley was very beautiful, particularly as it hadn't been touched for a century, but it was not at all my type of house. It was much too grand and formal. Kelmarsh was my idea of a house in the country. Ronnie had a different idea, though. Two weeks after we had our picnic at Ditchley, he came into my bedroom in London, where I was in bed ill with the flu. He was white as a sheet. That's when he told me he'd just paid the £30,000 he had inherited when his mother died for the house and the estate. He hadn't even been back to look at it a second time.

Tree was smitten the moment they drove up to Ditchley that afternoon. Dangerously lost in the house's romance, he believed it a "Sleeping Beauty waiting to be called back to life."[6] It certainly was magnificent, standing at the edge of a slope in the landscape, a great central block with a wing attached at either side like a huge, perfectly balanced set of scales. Ditchley was a small palace, austere yet dignified, subtly decorated with quoins and keystones and the urns and statues that crowned its boxlike form, a house designed in the richest of architectural epochs by one of the period's masters.

Inside, though, the house presented a somewhat different prospect. This, too, was splendid, its grandeur intact after more than two hundred years; but the interior had been left to neglect and lay buried beneath a thick pall of tarnish and distress. Tree described what they saw that day as "an unforgettable picture of magnificence and accumulated junk." There was fantastic plasterwork and gilding in the ground-floor rooms the Dillons let them see, yet none of it had been painted or cleaned in generations. Ditchley's two small libraries were astonishing, "so cluttered with books, learned magazines and treatises left behind by the late Lord Dillon that it was almost impossible to find one's way through them."[7] That afternoon a large collection of paintings remained hanging as it had been for decades; Lord Dillon's heirs would sell many of the pictures before they gave up the house, but at this point the faces of their ancestors still glowered down from the walls, proclaiming the long history of the house and its people. Sir Henry Lee, the self-appointed champion of Queen Elizabeth I and founder of the family line at Ditchley; a bare-legged, barefooted Captain Thomas Lee of the Queen's Kerne; a pair of Elizabethan ladies dressed in tight bodices and stiff collars, called the Fitton Sisters; King Charles II in his ermine robes of state, his mistress Barbara Villiers and their illegitimate offspring the Duke of Grafton and Lady Charlotte Lee—all were represented among the pictures. A seated portrait of the 2nd Earl of Lichfield, Lady Charlotte's son, held pride of place in the enormous great hall. He had decided the grandson—legitimate or not—of an English king deserved a more fashionable home than the sixteenth-century timber house he had inherited from his father, and in 1722 he commissioned James Gibbs to design the one the Trees would buy.

Elizabeth, the Electress Palatine and Queen of Bohemia, Charles II's and James II's sister and great-aunt of the 2nd Earl of Lichfield, was also at Ditchley that afternoon. She was painted as the "Winter Queen"—old and frayed after her family's exile during the Cromwellian Protectorate—and seemed to frown disapprovingly at being left hanging alongside her brother's mistress and his bastard progeny.

The Dillons came into the estate when the 4th Earl of Lichfield died, in 1776, without a male heir to succeed him. The house, then about fifty years old, was inherited by his niece, another Lady Charlotte; she had married the 11th Viscount Dillon. Irish aristocrats and landowners and, like the Lees, Royalists and Jacobites, the Ditchley Dillons used the surname Dillon Lee for the next one hundred years; the 17th Viscount—the last Dillon at Ditchley—was called by his parents Harold Arthur Lee Dillon. Lord Dillon's sitting room, library and hallways were crammed with more family, friends and connections when the Trees and General de Crespigny were given their tour. Distant cousins and ancestors lived in the dark, wood-paneled stair hall: a Lady Lee, who would by successive marriages become the Countess of Sussex, of Warwick and of Manchester; an Admiral Byng, who was court-martialed and shot; King Charles I, beheaded by the Parliamentarians, here painted with his brother Henry as young children; Arthur Richard Dillon, the Archbishop of Narbonne and member of France's Assembly of Notables; Anne Vavasour, Anne St. John, Anne Danvers; Katherine of Braganza, Archbishop Warham, King Henry VIII—each room and every corridor of the two-hundred-year-old house sheltered pieces of a three-and-a-half-century family saga laced with chivalry, exile and lost causes. Ditchley brimmed with eidolon and wraith that afternoon, romantic spirits with names and faces.

The general condition of the house in 1933 exaggerated the effect of room upon room of costumed figures and stately profiles, heightening the impression of timeless isolation. As the old paintings were diminished by coats of grime and opaque varnish, the original colors and details of the house itself lay buried, their glimmer hidden from sight. Ditchley's heyday had died with the 4th Earl; after him the house fell into a century and a half of a slow, benign decay. The 11th Viscount Dillon and Lady Charlotte stayed there, but Charles, the 12th Viscount, indebted, preferred Ireland and Belgium. Following generations of the Dillon family returned, but very little was ever allotted for improvements. A conservatory was added in the nineteenth century, but there was no other alteration to Ditchley's exterior or interior.

The rooms with painted walls—as opposed to wood paneling or fabric— had been renewed from time to time, but the original, vivid eighteenth-century interior was dulled by a heavy film of Victorian dirty-white, gray and gray-green. By 1933 even that dreary scheme hadn't been repainted for some time, so the large rooms lacked any luster whatsoever. At the same time, the walls, the floors and the upholstery were in a severe state of disrepair. Cracks had appeared around many of the elaborate plaster overdoors; curtains were torn or unraveling; furniture was worn and stained. But instead of being overwhelmed by the dereliction that afternoon, Ronald Tree envisioned the wonderful house beneath the clutter, imagined its potential. To the true admirer of Georgian taste, Ditchley was a clean, untouched example of that age's superior architecture and decoration. There were few such remnants left in 1933.

Ditchley's decorations—still intact in 1933, though in dire need of careful attention—were contributed by a few of the Hanoverian reign's leading craftsmen. Lord Lichfield, Gibbs or Ditchley's contractor, Francis Smith of Warwick, hired William Kent and Henry Flitcroft. (Gibbs was a Tory and a Catholic like Lichfield, while "Il Signore" Kent and "Burlington Harry" Flitcroft were disciples of the very Whiggish Earl of Burlington. Thus the house was not completely the English Baroque of the past generation, nor the Palladian of the next—not of the old Tory sensibility nor of the emerging Whig taste—but a combination of both.) Kent, the artistic jack-of-all-trades of his day, offered the design for the great hall's ornamentation and painted allegorical scenes from the *Aeneid* for an oval in the ceiling and frames in the wall. Kent may also have designed the heavy gilt furniture for the hall, still there in 1933. Three Italian *stuccatores*—Giuseppe Artari, Francesco Vasseli and Francesco Serena—executed the room's plasterwork to the architect's strict specifications; then, freed from the constraints required in a respectable entrance hall, they covered the adjacent saloon from its marble floor to its rafters with exuberance.[8] The saloon was a small room, and the effect of their collective imaginations was almost claustrophobic, a nearly comic display of the plasterer's craft gone haywire.

Ditchley was not as grand as its immediate neighbors Blenheim Palace and Heythrop, but it was filled inside and out with all the details at which the Georgians so excelled in the decorative arts. Many of the mantelpieces in the house were designed by Flitcroft and carved by the sculptor Henry Cheere. The one in the Velvet Room dripped with fruits and flowers; that in the White Drawing Room, thought to have originally been the house's dining room, had a head of Bacchus carved at its center. Neither of these mantels could compete, however, with the Rococo panels above each of the doors in the drawing room, while the skill it took to carve and gild each of these was in turn surpassed by that obvious in the fantastic Chinese rocaille installed either side of the fireplace in the Tapestry Room. Here the craftsman subverted the natural properties of his medium, creating outlandish chinoiserie carvings so light to the eye that they seemed to defy gravity.

The house's exterior was brusque, though two hundred years had mellowed it. The gray patina of the lead statues of *Fame* and *Loyalty*, mounted on the front facade's parapet, rhymed now with the golden yellow stone; full trees gathered around it like a great, green greatcoat. After two centuries Ditchley was at peace with its surroundings; sublime. Ditchley's new landlord also bought for himself a few of the duties and perquisites associated with Britain's country houses: ancient traditions of power and patronage.

PART TWO

In November 1940 Harold Nicolson stayed at Ditchley. He was an MP and by that time had written a dozen or more books. He was also somewhat of an expert on old houses—he and his wife Vita Sackville-West had spent a good part of the preceding decade restoring the castle and creating the exquisite gardens at Sissinghurst—so when he looked at what Nancy and Ronald Tree had accomplished at Ditchley, he did so with a critical eye. Nicolson and Tree had driven to Ditchley from Leicestershire, where they both had their constituencies; it was the early months of the Second World War, the beginning of the bleakest winter in recent British history. In his diary that day he recorded his thoughts on the German bombing of Leicester and his impressions of the prime minister, Ditchley's guest of honor that weekend. He wrote of the approach up Ditchley's drive, with the house blacked out as a precaution in the event of an air raid: "The great mass of the house is dark and windowless, and then a chink in the door opens and we enter suddenly into the warmth of central heating, the blaze of lights and the amazing beauty of the hall." He continued the entry with a list of the other house guests, and mentioned that Michael Tree had just had an operation. Then he wrote: "The beauty of the house is beyond words."[9]

Lord Chandos, who also stayed at Ditchley during the war, wrote that Nancy's "taste had set it off to perfection. The furniture, the carpets and the pictures had been chosen with fastidious knowledge and discrimination, and all the embellishments were placed with an unfailing eye and contributed to a gracious, aristocratic but lived-in harmony. From the moment you went into the high stone-floored hall . . . you felt a certain pride and satisfaction at having been asked."[10] William Paley, who was invited to the house for a weekend after meeting the Trees in London in 1942, admitted that Ditchley would serve him as an ideal: "I think I learned more about living and about the way things should look if they are to be beautiful and well-run by my visits to Ditchley than almost any other way I can remember."[11] Even James Lees-Milne, who visited hundreds of Britain's stately homes while helping to found the National Trust, thought the interior of Ditchley as the Trees decorated it "perfection. Exquisite furniture and fabrics, many original to the house. I have never seen better taste. Nothing jars. Nothing is too sumptuous, or new."[12]

It proved an immense task, raising up the near ruin to this blissful height. In 1933 there was a great deal to do, and a great deal of house to do it to. The simplest decision Nancy and Ronald had to make was their first: painting the brown window frames on the outside of Ditchley white, transforming the house from somber to "light and inviting."[13] Labor was abundant and cheap in 1933;

nevertheless, the house presented eighty-six window frames to be painted in the entrance facade alone. Sheer size was part of the point at Ditchley; though it might very well have fit into the courtyard of some of England's massive residences, the width of its main block alone nearly equaled the entire length of Kelmarsh Hall. The interior walls on the ground floor of Ditchley were so thick that passing between rooms required opening two heavy mahogany doors separated by a space large enough for a person to stand in it. The master-bedroom floor comprised eight huge bedrooms and dressing rooms, twice as many as at Kelmarsh, with twenty smaller bedrooms on the top floor. Fifty fireplaces could be lit at once in the main block; once Nancy was finished, there would be almost as many sinks.

Every corner and every cupboard had to be mulled over, seen to and furnished to one degree or another, from the timbers in the rafters down to the pilings in the basement. Every reception room, every bedchamber, every hallway, cubbyhole and cabinet required time and attention, not to mention heat, electricity and plumbing. **I had a marvelous linen closet on the top floor of Ditchley. It was big enough to walk into and close the door. The children used to use it for "sardines." I bought paintings on paper of blue horses rearing and prancing that Vera Lombardi had painted, and I pasted them on the cupboard doors in the linen closet and on the shelves.** Nothing, no matter how minor or utilitarian, was ignored. This included the service rooms traditional to an English country house, from the gun room to the butler's pantry, as well as the string of estate outbuildings and dependencies: the bothy, barns and stables.

When Ditchley changed hands, all of the rooms were filled with the belongings of a family who had lived on the estate for 350 years and in this house for more than 200. It seemed they had thrown little away over the years.

The house was crammed with furniture. Our plan was to buy Ditchley with furniture but let the new Lady Dillon go through it first and pick out a few of the important family pieces; I didn't want to go to town with the Dillon heirlooms. Ronnie said to me, "Look here, Lady Dillon has been all over the things at Ditchley and put her initials on all the family things she'd like to keep." He said, "I don't think she knows anything about good furniture, but just go down and have a look." So I went down to see what she'd picked out, and after looking at it said to myself, "If this is Ronnie's idea of someone who doesn't know anything about furniture, take me home." I've never seen a woman with a better eye for what's what! Anything that was of any value at all had "K.D." for Kate Dillon on it. So we decided then that we would buy the house either with

everything or completely empty: one or the other, it was their choice. In the end they decided to sell it lock, stock and barrel.

The original furniture, like the intrinsic decoration of some of the rooms and the architectural integrity of the structure itself, created questions about what was historically important and irreplaceable versus what was aesthetically pleasing: what to leave as is or restore, what to scrap or replace. Decorating Ditchley required Nancy to wear the various hats of architect and archaeologist, as well as interior designer. It also included addressing the house's value as a historic monument when some in England were just waking up to the importance of such treasures. The year after the Trees bought Ditchley, *Country Life* magazine published an article about the house with photographs of it as it was when old Lord Dillon lived there. The historian commented that "the completeness with which Ditchley had been preserved as a typical Early Georgian seat must arouse some inevitable regrets over the dispersal of its splendid contents last summer and the break in a continuous descent going back to 1580." The article might have continued as a eulogy from there; however, he added, "this regret is greatly tempered by the knowledge that the house has found a new owner in so short a time and one so . . . discerning."[14]

Others had restored or were restoring some of Britain's antique houses, repairing their walls and roofs with care and furnishing their rooms with period decoration. The gardener Norah Lindsay and her husband, Harry, had at Sutton Courtney, as had Lawrence Johnston at Hidcot and Harold Nicolson and Vita Sackville-West at the Long Barn at Knole, then again at Sissinghurst. Percy Fielding had bought an isolated, moated Tudor mansion in Oxfordshire and started resuscitating it in 1920. Called Beckley Park, this fairy-tale manor house, with its massive peaked roof and thick walls, became one of Nancy's favorite houses in England—one she loved to take friends to see—so much so that when Lady Astor asked Mrs. Fielding if she ever opened Beckley to the public, she replied, "I don't, but Nancy Tree does."[15] Colonel Reginald Cooper, the man who originally sent Ronald and Nancy the postcard of Ditchley, had restored three country houses by the beginning of the Second World War and would take on a fourth afterward. About a dozen people, most of whom Nancy knew, were addicted in this way to history's charm—a clique of romantics drawn to often hopelessly crumbling edifices. They preferred looking backward for aesthetic pleasure instead of toward Modernism, and in doing so were ahead of their time.

Nancy knew well and admired two other houses saved from twentieth-century ignorance that were closer in scale to Ditchley. In both cases the houses had been inherited. In 1913 the Marquess of Cholmondeley gave his heir, Lord Rocksavage, the family's colossal ancestral seat as a present when he married Sybil Sassoon. (She was the sister of Sir Philip Sassoon, another restorer of country houses.) Houghton Hall was built by Robert Walpole, and though much larger than Ditchley, it was designed in the same grandiloquent, early Anglo-Palladian period. Kent supplied paintings and decorations there around the same time he did at Ditchley. Lord and Lady Rocksavage (later, the Marquess and Marchioness of Cholmondeley, after he inherited his father's title) tended to the huge palace for the next fifty years, strengthening its foundations and adding to the collections that had ebbed and flowed over the years, as no one had since the first Lord Cholmondeley in the 1790s.

The second house was Uppark, a William and Mary building that had survived unaltered from the time of a decorative splurge in the eighteenth century with barely a stick of furniture rearranged, let alone replaced. Uppark was "made up of the elements of a mirage," wrote Christopher Hussey; "it shimmers in the hot aromatic air, suspended in time: so little has changed within, you could swear that you are imagining it, that it is a reflection, a ghost, of a house that stood somewhere two centuries ago but not here and now."[16] A teenage Emma Hart—the showgirl who became Emma, Lady Hamilton—danced on a table at Uppark in front of its young owner; her table remained in place in 1933, and his chair was still offered to house guests.

Uppark lasted so long untouched through the eccentricities of fate and the stout health of its owners. The Sir Harry Fetherstonhaugh who brought young Emma to Uppark as his mistress eventually married the daughter of his estate's dairy maid when he was seventy-four and she still a girl. The house passed to his wife when he died, then to her younger sister, a span of time that carried the countryseat, just as "Sir 'Arry 'ad it," almost to the end of the nineteenth century. Uppark's twentieth-century owners, Admiral Sir Herbert and Lady Meade-Fetherstonhaugh, considered the interior of the house sacrosanct. Beginning in 1931, they reinvigorated it, silken thread by silken thread, a painstaking pursuit that left Uppark "the kind of house you feel you might look through the window into the life of another age."[17]

Though its decoration was influenced by its pedigree, Ditchley became more of a personal statement of Nancy's taste. Historic authenticity was but one minor element in decisions regarding the house—and even then, only because an authentic piece of furniture or a period color scheme was the most attractive for the spirit of the house. She did draw her inspiration from the past, but Nancy was never a slave to academic predictability.

I didn't want Ditchley like a museum. I've never been a person who liked period rooms. I can't think of anything I had at Ditchley that wasn't eighteenth century, but the eighteenth century was one

hundred years long, and the taste of the early part was very different from the later Regency taste.

The first person in New York who had period rooms was a
friend of Henry Field's mother named Mrs. McKee. She was one of
those women of forty who were crazy about men . . . young men,
old men, any kind of men. I remember when Henry was ill, she used
to send him bunches of pansies in the hospital, while she also made
a great impression on Henry's stepfather, Maldwin Drummond. She
owned a Queen Anne house in Mount Kisco and had it completely
done up in the Queen Anne style. She collected Queen Anne furniture, the curtains were Queen Anne, the needlework was Queen
Anne, everything . . . it wasn't a very large house, but it was Queen
Anne until Queen Anne herself would have been seasick. I never like
that. I like continuity, the feeling that people have added different
things to the house, that things flowed in over time.

The saloon, the room at the center of the ground floor that opened onto
the back lawn and the lake, became a medley of what was already at Ditchley
and what she brought to the house with her: one part restoration and two
parts Nancy's own style. The Italian plasterers' effusiveness dominated this
ecstatic reception room, its stucco so rich and ornate it bemused even the
most disciplined eye. In the ceiling alone there were a dozen putti, with at
least that many around the life-sized figures along the walls, on the mantel
and near the recessed buffet. Pilasters with Corinthian capitals striped the
walls, and each of the three doors into the room were piled high with either
the arms and coronet of Lichfield, or lions, harpies and more swags. The
saloon was bursting its seams as well with Lord Dillon's billiards accou-
trements and pieces from his antique armor collection.

Nancy swept the saloon clean of furniture and collected clutter; she then
performed a bit of archaeological detective work when she took a twopenny
coin and began scraping at the two centuries of paint covering the walls, hoping to find somewhere underneath it the bold palette typical of the early
Georgians who built Ditchley. These rooms were created with exuberance in
mind: The subjects of George I and George II were shy neither in their living nor in their decoration. Nancy struck what she was looking for eight coats
below the contemporary surface: a vivid orange streaked with ocher that suggested the arid chambers of Palladio's Brenta villas. The Trees restored this
vibrant ruddiness to the room; the gaudy plaster, painted with a fresh coat of
white, now made perfect sense.

We used the saloon for tea when we had large parties, or for dinner in the summertime. It was especially lovely when it was warm

enough to throw open the doors to the back terrace. Stéphane Boudin had given me an eighteenth-century book where we found the design for a table that one enlarged by adding different shapes to it. I had it copied and a cloth made to fit the several sizes we would need. It was particularly attractive and unusual and was always decorated with layered pyramids of fruit. I also had the set of wonderful Louis XIV armchairs of yellow and gold painted wood that I found in Italy and first used in the saloon at Kelmarsh. On either side of the garden door I put a Moorish bust on a marbleized column. They had marvelous black marble faces, mother-of-pearl eyes and wore yellow marble coats. I bought one of them and gave it to Ronnie; the other had been Lord Dillon's. Boudin found the perfect rug for me in Paris. It was an early Aubusson with faded gray, green and blue vines and flowers in geometric patterns.

Among the Whiggish brilliance and twentieth-century chic, Nancy left a few poignant remnants of Ditchley's earliest history in the saloon exactly as she had found them. Six pairs of antlers, blackened with age, from stags that King James I had chased as a guest of Sir Henry Lee three hundred years before were mounted at eye level on the orange walls, between the white plaster pilasters. Under each of the trophies a plaque engraved in an uneven hand with doggerel verse told the story of the chase.

> *1608 August 26 Munday*
> *King James made me run*
> *For life from Deadmans Riding*
> *I ran to the Goreil Gate,*
> *Where Death for me was biding.*

The room succeeded because no individual element—no matter how extraordinary—stood out over the rest, but all blended together in a harmonious composition of architecture and decorative art. For all its eighteenth-century "authenticity," with a fire lit or the door opened to the scented summer air, there was nothing still or museumlike about the saloon.

In rooms where historic stateliness was most evident, the original grandeur might easily have defied any efforts to humanize them. The first glimpse a guest had of the Ditchley interior was of the great hall as he entered the front door. The hall was imposing by design: a tall, tall ceiling with Kent's oval picture of Olympian gods and goddesses at its center; a suite of grandiose plasterwork figures and classical architectural accents; and yards of gold leaf covering every detail from the flutes and capitals of the columns to the swags draping the walls. It made a very powerful impression. Walking into this life-sized allegory of universal order created the very opposite impression from that Nancy preferred: It was cold and forbidding.

As an antidote to pomp, Nancy turned to bright color. She used as her cue the portrait of the 2nd Earl of Lichfield hanging above the fireplace, in which he wore a crimson frock coat; Nancy borrowed this red and spread both subtle dashes and great swaths of it around the room. Magnificent blood-red velvet curtains draped the windows either side of the front door, while the heretofore aloof Kent benches had their cushions reupholstered in scarlet damask. At the center of the floor they placed an early Wilton carpet with a faded *rouge* ground that softened much of the hard marble. In the middle of the carpet sat an exquisite eighteenth-century French ormolu-mounted writing table, its chair and stool also covered in red damask. Red tied the room together like a drawstring, complementing the inordinate amount of gilding while fervidly attacking any chill. A Venetian screen fourteen feet tall by twenty feet across, painted with perspectives of Palladian interiors, was placed directly in front of the oak entrance door, "to keep out the biting east winds."[18] Great sprays of fresh flowers in a huge urn became a pleasant introduction to Ditchley for the family's guests.

Nancy had to work with and around the original decoration in the White Drawing Room, the most regal of the reception rooms. The woodwork and plaster were the finest in the house; practically life-sized oil portraits of Charles II and his unofficial family painted by Kneller and Lely had a dominating presence, as did the carved marble fireplace. It was as much what she left alone as what she changed that succeeded so well in the White Drawing Room. **I refused to paint any of the woodwork. The woodwork was what John Fowler and I would later call "Ditchley white." It was a sort of dirty, not-quite-gray white, like white beneath a shadow. Around all the doors and frames and on the carvings above the doorways was lots of original gold leaf. I wouldn't touch any of it: New gilding looks like a gold filling in a tooth. Instead, I had it all scrubbed.**

She did rid the room of most of the furniture that had been left behind. **The tables, chairs, mirrors and candle sconces were mostly nineteenth-century French Charles X, a style later than I liked. We bought two fine Kent glasses that fit the room better, and underneath them I put the pair of Kent tables I bought from Lord Hampden's house for Kelmarsh; they had yellow marble tops banded in brass, which was very unusual, supported by white-and-gold eagles. These suited the room much better than Charles X. I also replaced the two long, armless banquettes under the portraits of Charles II and Barbara Villiers. Under the king I put a piano, and under his mistress a Kent table. I used the two antique banquettes in the male servants' bothy: I had the chicest bothy in England.**

The addition of rich color would again prove the best cure for any off-putting formality, even though bright color in rooms such as these was practically unheard of in the 1920s and '30s. Nancy used red velvet curtains bought secondhand for the White Drawing Room's three tall windows that faced out onto the garden. With a bold stroke she reupholstered two easy chairs by covering their frames in red silk and their cushions in white with red piping. The two sofas either side of the fireplace were of the same combination: half red damask and half white. She designed them herself in a Georgian style with double-hump backs, scrolled arms and wavy skirts; the Parisian decorator Stéphane Boudin had them constructed for her. These plush, irresistible fixtures sat alongside the Kent tables, mirrors and six Kent chairs with faces carved in their gesso knees. A crystal chandelier the Trees found for the Kelmarsh saloon, with translucent stems and teardrops of shimmering cut glass, finished the room.

During Ditchley's first century the Velvet Room served as the State Bedroom. It was a small chamber next to the White Drawing Room, originally decorated and furnished for a possible visit by a monarch. But by the early nineteenth century the state tester bed had been disassembled and removed, and the room became another reception chamber along the house's western enfilade. For the Trees it became the corner of the ground floor they used the most. **We sat in it every night. England is so cold in the winter, but that room was the warmest in the world. It was cozy, but I have to say I never liked the velvet.**[19] Like the wallpaper in the Chinese Room at Kelmarsh, the velvet wall hangings illustrated a Western version of an Eastern theme. Repeated over and over in very loud cut and uncut velvet was the Hindu god Shiva, angrily flailing his many arms, hands holding bows, arrows and swords. While this choice of decoration suggested the mid-Georgians' love of the exotic and outrageous, it also reflected the taste of a man who had spent most of his life below the decks of British men-of-war. The 2nd Earl of Lichfield's brother, Admiral Fitzroy Lee, was commander of the Mediterranean Fleet in 1738 when he bought the fabric in Genoa for the exorbitant price of £292; he probably thought it would give his brother's Oxfordshire house the feeling of the Italian villas their generation so admired. The loom on which the pattern was woven was destroyed when enough fabric was made to furnish the State Bedroom, guaranteeing that Ditchley would be the only house with such decoration.

In the Velvet Room Ronnie wanted to get a red lacquer desk. I thought that was too eye-catching. An old, faded walnut desk of the early eighteenth century was better with all that *mouvement* than something that when you came in it took your eye from the general flow of things. I like rooms that flow. I never liked things in a room that when you came in they struck your eye.

She covered nondescript easy chairs with monochrome damask and arranged them near the fireplace. Tables were piled with books. She also hung a portrait of Sir Henry Lee and his mastiff Bevis, along with the charter for the Ditchley land given to Sir Henry by Elizabeth I. On the floor by the fire was a painted nineteenth-century helmet-shaped coal bucket, and on every table, as in every room, were fresh flower arrangements.

Next to the Velvet Room on the south front of the house was a room variously called the Tapestry Room and the Chinese Room. In Nancy's day it was known as Mrs. Tree's Sitting Room and was used as her office. She sat at a splendid kingwood-and-ormolu *bureau plat* in an eighteenth-century Austrian fauteuil and wrote letters, paid bills or spoke with the servants regarding the housekeeping. Busy seventeenth-century Brussels tapestries by Dogus de Vos had been made for the decoration of this smaller reception room, but Lord Dillon's heirs had sold them; when the Trees took up residence, they found large stretches of unpainted, unplastered wood planks where the hangings had been.[20] A portrait of James II as the Duke of York that had sat above the fireplace for two hundred years had been sold to Queen Mary. The room was void of its most domineering decorations. What the Dillons had left behind, though, was all the astonishing Rococo carving that had flanked the tapestries and the York portrait: the exotic chinoiserie rocaille that seemed to descend the walls in diaphanous ribbons feathering in an imaginary breeze.

The Rococo taste in England in the eighteenth century was decidedly of French influence. Appropriately, Nancy brought a Parisian decorator, Stéphane Boudin of the firm Jansen, to work with her in this room. Boudin was "arguably the most brilliant decorator of his generation in the French Classical style in Europe."[21] He would from the 1930s through the 1950s work for "all the French heavy guns," as Russell Page—who also worked for the Trees at Ditchley—put it. Boudin's other clients of international taste and fortune included the Duke and Duchess of Windsor, for whom he found the Mill at Giff-sur-Yvette; Olive, Lady Baillie, at Leeds Castle and in London; Henry "Chips" Channon, for whom he created an elaborate Rococo dining room in London; even Elsie de Wolfe at the Petit Trianon in Versailles, where he designed a party. At the House of Jansen's atelier in the rue Royal, the firm offered every deluxe accoutrement of the Classical style imaginable, as well as a library of research resources. Turning to Paris for a contribution in the decoration of Ditchley was entirely in keeping with the Trees' passionate leaning toward eighteenth-century English taste, for the Whigs looked across La Manche as well for inspiration and were equally Continental in their sources.

I loved Boudin; he was charming and most enchanting. He begun by selling fringes for Jansen, then educated himself up the ranks until he was president. He had the most extraordinary good

taste and understood about color. Color was what interested me, so
we got along very well. The first time I heard of him and saw his
work was through a friend of my aunts' from New York who'd
moved to Paris, called Kitty Havermeyer. She had discovered
Boudin. He did her house in Paris, and everybody thought it was the
last word . . . simply wonderful. I used to go to Paris quite often in
those days, and when I was there I would visit Jansen. I bought a
great many remnants of very early Aubussons there; early Aubussons, not the late ones with floral patterns but early ones that looked
very crude. That's how I met Boudin; he became a great friend.

As she had with Mrs. Bethel at Kelmarsh, Nancy used Boudin sparingly;
he was not so much a decorator at Ditchley as a contractor. **I knew what I
wanted; I didn't want any decorator's idea of how it ought to be.** Nancy
needed a shop to complete her ideas for certain rooms at Ditchley, and there
was no better than the House of Jansen. **Boudin made the pelmets and curtains for my sitting room from old satin I had. I took the idea for the pelmets from an old book of Chippendale designs that I found. He hated the
designs for pelmets in that book; he would never have used them himself. He
only liked simple French headings. He also couldn't bear Kent furniture. He
hated anything to do with Kent; he thought it appalling. He used to say to
me, "I can't get over how you like Kent furniture." But they were the thing
for that house. They're very English, and certain houses needed them
because the rooms were enormous, like the hall at Ditchley. Boudin was very
nice and he adapted.**

    **One thing Boudin did teach me was that Victorian damask was
of frightfully good quality. It's much better than present-day
damask . . . it lasts longer. We bought spools of red Victorian
damask—you could get it very easily in those days—had the color
bleached out of it, then put it on my sitting room walls. That was a
huge success. Bleaching it gave it a wonderful ivory color, a sort of
hardly pink.**

Nancy's sitting room was the most feminine room in the house. The
thicker, harder limbs and edges of the English furniture throughout some
of the other rooms melted into the graceful curves of the Austrian fauteuils
and the doe-thin cabriole legs and ormolu trim of Nancy's writing table. The
muted colors she chose further softened the room's character: pale yellows,
golds, whites and pinks. An eighteenth-century Axminster needlework carpet
made of the same colors and woven with birds, bouquets of flowers and wheat
shafts held the room together like a great frame around a family portrait.

It was lovely. The most stunning decoration in the room, however, remained the Chippendale rocaille carvings that had been there for nearly two centuries. They had once hung in narrow strips of wall space crowded into corners by the huge tapestries; now they became features in themselves, stepping out from their almost-pink damask backgrounds.

Because of the quality of every element in this room, nothing stood out on its own; nothing, not even the rocaille, seemed exaggerated. If anything pulled at the eye, it was the few dark pieces of furniture—kingwood and black lacquer—Nancy placed in the room like commas to keep it from being too soft or confectionery. Even these, however, melded smoothly into their surroundings, with their ormolu mountings mimicking the room's carvings. The only incongruous detail was an odd Victorian tablecloth covering a round lamp table against the wall. Around the cloth's skirt was a parade of dogs standing on their hind legs, all dressed in the finery of ladies and gentlemen of the nineteenth century; its inclusion was a gesture typical of Nancy's sense of the ridiculous.

The Breakfast Room was directly across the great hall from Nancy's sitting room; because of their corresponding positions in Ditchley's Palladian master plan, the two were of the same dimensions. For the Trees the Breakfast Room served as a family dining room. **If we were eight or more, we used the big dining room, but when Ronnie and I were alone during the week, we ate in the Breakfast Room.** This was the east side of the house, where the rooms mostly lacked the fine plasterwork or fabrics decorating the rooms to the west. The lords Lichfield seemed to have concentrated on the western enfilade first, running low of funds when it came to the eastern rooms.[22] The 17th Viscount Dillon made up for what was lacking by decorating his Breakfast Room with the dour faces of his ancestors as painted by Kneller, Lely, Wooton, Holbein and Stoop.

I painted the Breakfast Room tan and gold, covered the walls with old Hogarth prints that I found in the attic and furnished it entirely with old walnut chests, chairs and tables. It was a charming room. Louise Boulanger, the famous Paris dressmaker, had an early walnut billiards table where she displayed furs. I thought it would make a marvelous dining table and asked her to sell it to me.

The "beautiful" furniture at Ditchley, the "important" furniture, if it was bought, was mostly bought by Ronnie, except for that billiards table and for the set of chairs that we had in the saloon. Ronnie was much more interested in "good" things than I was. He had a marvelous eye for *bibelots*. He knew just by looking at it how good a painting or a piece of furniture was. But I imagine that if Ronnie were getting furniture without me, it would be too good. The rooms would be too much of one . . . price. He wouldn't know

how to put an ugly thing in a room to enhance the beauty of the good things. I think that's the one quality I have . . . I can mix things. If Ronnie and I had gone into business together, I'm sure that we would have made a big success.

They used the long dining room whenever there was a house party. Here the Trees memorably entertained their guests on weekends, when Ditchley brimmed with friends and relatives and Ronald's political colleagues. Answering the butler Collins's call that "dinner is served," ladies, beguiling in evening dresses, streamed through the doors, escorted by men tucked into starched black and white. Saturday night dinner was the climax of any weekend.

Ronald sat at one head of a table that might be stretched to seat as many as thirty. Nancy presided over the other end. And though dinner at Ditchley was as choreographed by tradition as at every other grand country house in England, Nancy brought to it a certain light touch. "There was always an element of fun at the table there you didn't find elsewhere," Nancy's first cousin David Astor remembered. "Both Nancy and my mother at Cliveden would talk right up the table instead of only to the man on their right or left, making the whole occasion more amusing because everybody joined in. The two of them liked a sort of free-for-all." Elizabeth Winn, a young niece, thought Ditchley was "a bit more fun" than Cliveden or other country houses because "anything went. It really didn't matter what you said there. As Bobbie Shaw used to say, 'There's no too far.' "

The dining room sparkled on a Saturday night; candlelight reflected gilt wood, silver, crystal and china and bathed the green livery of the Trees' three footmen waiting table. The room shone with magnificence and warmth. This effect was somewhat of an illusion, however, the creation of a magician's mirrors, for in the daylight the dining room was the least inherently beautiful room downstairs. There was no dramatic ceiling plaster in the dining room, no *boiserie* or rocaille; even the fireplace was flat. It was the hostess's decoration of the old room that provided it with personality. She started with the same upholstered chairs she used at Kelmarsh, their thick, carved legs splayed outward, their wide seats and high backs covered in "dirty dandelion-yellow" leather. Her curtains, too, were yellow—yellow silk damask that leapt from the green-gray walls and the Ditchley-white wainscoting. At the library end of the room was a typical Kent console, set with a few large pieces from Nancy's collection of red-and-blue Queen Charlotte Worcester china. Above it was a picture by Tiepolo of a halberdier that Ronald bought for his collection, a section cut from the painting *The Finding of Moses*. On either side of the Tiepolo hung two Russian ormolu-and-crystal candle sconces they had bought for the saloon at Kelmarsh.

On the side wall hung two Lee family portraits. These were not pictures the Trees found when they arrived; Nancy bought them at a house sale at Hartwell House, a stately neighbor of Ditchley's in Oxfordshire whose heiress Sir Thomas Lee had married. The portraits of the eighteenth-century noblemen were in themselves appealing, but it was their Kent frames—carved with eagles clutching weightless swags in their beaks, borders of fruit and acanthus leaves—that attracted Nancy's attention. The paintings' soft style and the sculptural presence of their frames added to the levity of the room's atmosphere, already magnified by the twenty candles burning in the chandelier above the heads of the dinner guests. In this surrounding they drank champagne and ate the pheasant taken in the fields outside the house, the fresh vegetables, fruit and dairy cream.

The dining room, as with every room in the house, became a repository for the *objets* Ronald and Nancy each delighted in. The Trees were collectors as avid as their eighteenth-century counterparts. The Tiepolo, the china, Kent's pieces and especially the Russian candle sconces exemplified their taste in decoration as well as their appreciation of owning beautiful things. Tree admired "good" furniture, but even more so fine pictures. Ditchley was a marvelous house in which to spend a rainy afternoon discovering examples of eighteenth-, nineteenth- and twentieth-century fine art along the hallways and staircases and in the long line of rooms on all three floors. There were two Wright of Derby portraits in a smaller, silk-hung reception room called the Blue Parlour, and an Amigoni and a pair of Giovanni Domenico Tiepolos in the Chinese Room. Ronald bought his own Kneller, a de Troy and two Migliari views of Venice. Around any corner one might spy a drawing of Salisbury Cathedral by Constable, the Géricault called *The Deluge*, a Tiepolo study for *The Entombment* or a Morisot sketch in colored pencil of a *jeune fille*. He owned a Jack B. Yeats, an Augustus John, an Alfred Stevens, a Victor Pasmore and a Graham Sutherland, as well as dozens of unattributed but agreeable portraits, pastorals and other pictures and conversation pieces. To these he added his Munnings pictures and a very small, very sensitive bronze head by Rodin from 1886 of Pierre de Wiessant.

Nancy's overwhelming zeal for collecting excluded the fine arts. **I don't particularly like pictures. They're static. But I like them as decoration, for their colors. The most humiliating thing that's ever happened to me was when I was doing up Kelmarsh, I went into Christie's, where, hanging in the sales room, was a picture that I recognized. I burst out, "I *do* want that picture; it's exactly the color I want. It matches my curtains." My dear, it was a Van Dyck and it sold to some important museum for a tremendous amount of money. Ronnie was so ashamed of my saying that. He loved pictures. He bought an Etty for Ditchley of the back of some naked woman that I really** couldn't bear. I said I thought she looked like a line of toothpaste on a toothbrush. But he did give me a watercolor that I liked very much. He thought it looked like me lying in bed drinking coffee. It was a little Whistler.

Preferring the decorative arts, Nancy collected antique fabrics—old chintzes, damasks, laces—squirreling them away by the trunkful. She bought them at every opportunity and would later use what she needed in the decoration of houses. French bedspreads, eighteenth-century fire screens and old painted coal buckets, if they had charm, were all objects she looked for at sales and in shops. The carpets and rugs she bought were without exception exquisite: from the early Aubusson remnants from Jansen, to Bessarabian and Savonnerie rugs, carpets and runners. One George II needlepoint carpet had rows of Chinese vases on a blue-and-gold ground inside a black trellis. Nancy also owned a collection of silver, gilt-metal, gold, enamel and tortoiseshell spice boxes, snuffboxes and cigarette boxes, along with other smaller objects of virtu that she would place on shelves and dressing tables throughout the house. Nancy had a collection of geranium varieties as well, and she kept a tall pile of gardening hats near the garden doors.

Her dining services at Ditchley were more a collection of fine antique china than anything utilitarian. It was all early Queen Charlotte–pattern Worcester china from the first period to the turn of the nineteenth century. Referred to as the "rich Queen's pattern," the "Wheel" or the "Whorl," its design was composed of swirling spokes of red, pink and gilding with an underglazing blue that radiated from a circle or oval. She bought dozens of different sets: dinner plates, tea services, waste bowls, dessert services; coffee cups and coffee cans, all with their saucers; butter tubs, hot-water jugs, sugar bowls, sauce terrines and baskets; oval, square, rectangular, diamond and shell-shaped plates and platters; soup dishes, eggcups, milk jugs, bouillon bowls, jardinieres, sweetmeat dishes, junket dishes, potpourri vases and candelabra. The Georgians who made the Whorl had a piece for every conceivable possibility. Nancy also collected something from almost every other European and English china factory of the eighteenth and early nineteenth century, along with a number of pieces of Chinese export. Vessels from Spode, Sèvres, Saint-Cloud, Caughley, Davenport, Dutch Delft, Derby, Bow, Leeds, Minton, Miles Mason, Meissen, Wedgwood and Coalport were spread around the house. Nancy had cabbages, ducks and cockerels from Chelsea on the shelves in Ditchley bathrooms.

Her real passion, though, was furniture. At first she sought for it simply to bring her new houses to life. Not only did the Trees have Ditchley, but they kept Kelmarsh ready in the years immediately after they'd left it, replacing pieces taken to Ditchley so it might be sublet while there were a few years left on their lease. Nancy also decorated their London town house in Queen

Anne's Gate around the same time: another dozen and a half empty rooms to fill. But she didn't stop when these jobs were finished. Edith Bridges, who was a housemaid at Ditchley for Lord Dillon, then for the Trees, recalled: "Oh, on a Friday, dear oh dear, Mrs. Tree used to come down and say, 'There's a lorry-load of furniture coming.' My god, we used to dread that. We would have the rooms all ready for the house full of people that were coming that evening, and she'd get this lorry-load from Partridges or somewhere in London. She'd get the men—Collins, the butler; the footmen and hall boy—to lump the stuff up the stairs. She'd say, 'No, it doesn't do there. Take it to such-and-such room.' First it was downstairs that filled up, then upstairs. I think they all got a bit fed up with it. Oh, boy. She's a real one for furniture."

Ronald thought Nancy ought to go into business for herself. She bought furniture for Lady Colefax and for the American decorator Marian Tiffany and helped various cousins and friends decorate rooms in their houses, so some of the furniture she found did go elsewhere. The market offered infinite possibilities to a buyer with even modest wherewithal—the Depression, escalating land and inheritance taxes, the immense shift in the political and economic order in the British Empire, all took heavy tolls from the once-sheltered paradises of English country houses. Estates in the same family for two, three and four hundred years had their gates forced open, their contents and collections dispersed. Because there was little money to spare in Europe among those who would traditionally have taken notice, and only limited general interest in antiques, a few like Nancy and a prophetic museum or two had the entire field to themselves. Between them, the Trees compiled what most families took generations to accumulate. In its size and breadth it appeared as though the contents of Ditchley had been in place for exactly that long, with things added piece by piece, year after year.

The last of the grand ground-floor rooms, the library was nearly fifty feet long and lined from wainscoting to ceiling with inset rows of bookshelves. Its length was the result of the Trees' combining Lord Dillon's two smaller libraries by tearing down the wall between them.

The library was a mistake. It wasn't my doing; Ronnie wanted it that way, and after all it was his house. You see, Ditchley was perfectly symmetrical. My sitting room and the Velvet Room on one side were diagonally balanced with the two small libraries, just as the Breakfast Room and the long dining room were across from the Blue Parlour and the White Drawing Room. I thought that symmetry should never have been destroyed. There was also the most beautiful plaster ceiling of Leda and the Swan that I've ever seen in the first library. They swore to me that they could take it down and not break it. It broke into a thousand pieces. It turned out to be a

lovely room, but I always thought destroying the smaller rooms was a great error. When you get such a wonderful old house as Ditchley, you shouldn't make big changes just to get something you want. We should have kept the symmetry . . . I felt very strongly about that.

Ronnie also wanted to get rid of all of Lord Dillon's marvelous old books. A lot of them were in German and Italian, but they were bound in old vellum and old leather. I love old, starved leather. I like decay. . . . Lord Dillon also had all the eighteenth-century *Gentleman's Magazines* in his libraries. I thought they were fascinating. They had the most interesting tidbits of gossip and had articles in them like someone writing on how he dyed his wife's hair or got hairs off his wife's face. Instead of throwing it all away, I made a library for myself in the old kitchen wing, where I would go and sit and read them.

They bound Ronald's own books, thousands of volumes of literature and history, in French morocco leather and English calf. They were immaculate, row upon row, like the rest of this very masculine room. For furniture she took a set of six Georgian chairs they found scattered in different rooms throughout the house and a large sofa, and had them covered in scarlet leather tacked down with brass nails. **I had trouble getting that leather; I wanted it very thin. Then I found a man to antique it for me.** These she grouped around one of the fireplaces and a Hepplewhite desk they bought. The desk was oval and had kneeholes for four people to sit at it at once. Walnut tables of various sizes and uses filled up the rest of the immense room, as well as side chairs, armchairs and slipcovered easy chairs and sofas. There were miscellaneous books piled about, current novels and biographies, the requisite globe, a Dutch study in oil on canvas of horses in different frolicking postures. Above each fireplace was one of Tree's Munnings portraits that he commissioned for Kelmarsh: the one of Frank Freeman, the other of his wife and eldest son. **I thought the room charming the way we did it . . . but it looked like anyone else's.**

The cascade of beautiful reception rooms ended where it began, with doubled doors leading from the library into the pumpkin-colored saloon. Each room along the way was a surprise; each, in its own way, was richer than the last or the next, an expression of historic grandeur and "Indian Summer" glamour. All of them were comfortable and inviting. The burden of Ditchley's dereliction became its blessing, for unlike so many of the grand houses buried in England's countryside that many of the Trees' young friends were inheriting, Ditchley, as they re-created it, reflected the verve of the moment in its rooms and the slow relaxing of repressive formality. Other houses were weighted down by their past and their vast treasure troves of art and decoration to such a degree that in the 1930s they were little more than private museums, their most frequented areas being small private apartments or the nanny's sitting room. Ditchley possessed order and tradition in its foundations, but everything inside it was arranged anew and afresh in a style as alive and fantastic as the era.

TWO MAIN STAIRS led to the bedroom floors; neither, though, could be construed as "grand staircases," because Ditchley's architect, James Gibbs, had believed that steps should be unobtrusive, off to the side, functional. There were four flights of back stairs as well, inside the four exterior "towers" of the main block. These hidden stairways, which climbed from the ground floor to the top of the house, were made from unpainted pale oak and had to be laboriously scrubbed like a butcher's block. Mostly the servants used them, to pass from floor to floor undetected by the family or their guests. At each storey the tower steps shared the space inside the tower with tower rooms; the tower rooms were used at various times in Ditchley's long history as private cabinets, closets or dressing rooms. On the ground floor Nancy turned one of the tower rooms into the apple-green-and-white Writing Room and another into the Bridge Room, with gros point needlework upholstery and a display of Dutch Delft and Chinese export on its walls. (In these two out-of-the-way rooms she was decorating as much for the pleasure of it as for the results; each might very easily have been overlooked, their doors shut and their space used for storage, but to Nancy they offered more canvas on which to paint.) The steps next to the Writing Room went up to Nancy's bedroom and continued to her lady's maid's bedroom on the top floor; next to the Bridge Room, they passed Ronald's bedroom on the way to his valet's quarters.

The tower rooms on the bedroom (second) floor provided the perfect answer to the shortage of bathrooms in the mansion. These four paneled cabinets—along with two interior dressing rooms—allowed them to plumb the house without carving up the antique interior.[23] **At Ditchley before we did it up, every room had a very attractive early Georgian armchair, which had a seat that lifted up and you found a *pot de chambre* underneath. That's all there was. You used them right there in the room you slept in. Also at Ditchley there were very high beds, which had mahogany steps to get into them. Underneath the second step when you lifted it was a slop drawer, which you used in the night if you had to. The housemaid had to empty it in the morning, which must have been a horrible job.**

The tower rooms upstairs were all charming little closet-rooms with paneling on the walls and their own fireplaces like those downstairs. I put in tubs, the freestanding tubs with tin feet I grew up

with in Virginia. As there was space between the bath and the floor and because it's rather a bore to get down and clean underneath them, I had them enclosed in wood paneling that matched the walls in the room. The idea was to save labor and to make them very much nicer to look at.

I used the *chaises percés* for the lavatories, substituting for the chamber pot a modern fixture with a tank at the back . . . so the loos we installed at Ditchley were actually lovely chairs, as they always had been. I made the washbasins from tables we cut the center out of. For the walls and the floors I decorated the bathrooms much as I would any other room, hanging pretty paintings and prints, putting down good rugs, maybe a walnut chair and a table. I had very pretty curtains in all the bathrooms, made of white linen sheets that had machine-scalloped edges of different colors, some brown, some azalea colored, some blue.

Deborah Mitford, later the Duchess of Devonshire, was astonished at the difference between Ditchley's bathrooms and those of her family's manor house nearby. She was a friend of the Tree boys and would stay at Ditchley on weekends. "The bathrooms were little works of art, much more like sitting rooms than bathrooms. . . . A far cry from the cracked lino and icy draughts to which I was accustomed."[24] She had grown up at Swinbrook, her father's seat ten or so miles from Ditchley; its "icy draughts" were far more consistent with English country house living than Ditchley's fireplaces, radiators and fitted carpets.

In the bathrooms the hostess saw to every detail for her guests. Elizabeth Winn remembered this "marvelous lavatory paper that came in little sheets that the housemaids would arrange in a swirl on a lovely china saucer. They always left a lavender bag on top. And there used to be cigarettes in china boxes beside the old mahogany loos. I used to sit there and smoke like mad for hours. Aunt Nancy said that she couldn't understand why I was in the loo so long; she thought there was something wrong with me until she saw the smoke coming through the keyhole one day." When guests returned to their rooms at the end of the night, their toothbrushes were carefully laid next to the basin, toothpaste already squeezed on them by a housemaid or footman.

Nancy's own bathroom and bedroom were at the northwest corner of Ditchley's second floor. The bedroom's large windows overlooked the garden's formal parterre and crescent pool; idyllic pastures stretched into the distance. The north-facing window in her bathroom looked to the tranquil serpentine lake Capability Brown had created two hundred years before. **In my own bathroom I put the washbasin in the top of a circular Japaned cabinet; the loo was** made from one of the Charles X armchairs the Dillons used in the White Drawing Room. My bath was a copper tub set inside an eighteenth-century French chaise longue with a cane top that I had found in Lyon. You lifted the cane back to get into the tub, then put it down to cover yourself up. I could receive people while I was in the tub if I wanted, it was quite respectable; when the top was down, you couldn't see anything at all. You could also fold down the piece of the top that covered my chest, making a perfect book rest. That was very pleasant, to sit in the hot bathwater and read. I think it was one of the prettiest rooms in the house. I had lovely mirrors that I had made out of Chippendale picture frames over the corner fireplace and the washbasin, and a very beautiful Bessarabian carpet on the floor.

Nancy's bedroom was paneled with wooden sections left from Sir Henry Lee's Tudor mansion after the 2nd Earl of Lichfield tore it down. I could never decide if it should be painted cream or coffee colored. I was always experimenting. In the end each panel seemed to be a different color, but it worked out very well. My bed and curtains came with me from Kelmarsh; the carpet was an ornate Savonnerie with blue ribbons crisscrossing to make squares, then roses inside the squares. Because the rug had a design and the walls had paneling, I decided the curtains on the windows and on my bed were too plain. I had Boudin machine-stitch designs all over the silk for me. White stitching. I wanted to create movement. I had learnt from going to Houghton that to make a room quiet, to make it harmonious, you never wanted to have only one *mouvement* thing like the Savonnerie rug that would stand out. You must have *mouvement* everywhere.

Nancy also had in her bedroom a pair from a set of six black lacquer chairs that she bought from Edward Hudson of *Country Life*. They were perfect examples of the furniture she was drawn to: George II arm- and side chairs with backs, arms and skirts of interlacing loops and swirls and gamine cabrioles. Leaves and flowers decorated the black ground, and Nancy covered their dished seats with a rose-and-white-striped fabric. These chairs were indescribably lovely and completely unique.

Her bedroom and Ronald's, next to it, were large enough to take up the entire width of the house above the White Drawing Room and the Velvet Room. His bedroom and dressing room faced the parterre to the west, as did Nancy's. His bathroom overlooked the approach to Ditchley; the cricket pitch in front of the house, which his gardeners kept as pristine as a putting green; and the avenues of plane trees planted two and a half centuries before, which had, by 1933, reached magnificent stature. The sashed windows in these and all of Ditchley's second-floor bedrooms were the same size as those in the grand reception rooms below. All around the house they afforded splendid views of Ditchley's three thousand acres while allowing floods of light into the rooms. Their eighteenth-century panes of glass had dappled surfaces, uneven, and were permeated by the tiny air bubbles frozen there when they were handmade.

Ronnie's bedroom was very nice. Its paneling was painted a sort of green, and he had a funny, perfectly charming eighteenth-century bed shaped like a sleigh and painted to look like bird's-eye maple. It was beautifully done. The cupboard for his clothes was also very pretty: It was made of pale wood, not pickled wood or mahogany, but a light old pine or walnut. The curtains in Ronnie's bedroom were an old chintz of a green background with a brown speckle and white four-leaf clovers.

The six other bedrooms on the second floor, and the many smaller rooms on the third, were decorated with equal flair and with the express purpose of providing comfort and pleasure for every guest who slept and changed in them. Many of those who stayed at Ditchley either owned country houses of their own or were regular house guests among the interconnecting circles of English society, but no matter how used one was to great mansions and the life within and without, Ditchley never failed to impress. The style and warmth, especially of its bedrooms, stood out dramatically from what guests usually found when a footman led them to their rooms in someone else's house.

"I'd never seen such huge square down pillows as Nancy went in for," wrote the Duchess of Devonshire, "nor the Portault sheets, decorated with carnations or trailing blue flowers of M. Porthault's imagination and scalloped edges of the same color. Nor the puffed-up eiderdowns covered in pale silk with tiny bows where a stitch held the down in place."[25]

In the Blue and White Bedroom Nancy took her lead from furniture left behind by the Dillons. The Trees found among their new treasures three large four-poster *lits à la polonaise*, which Ronald thought were of "a most unusual design, possibly made by Hepplewhite, having a round cupola-shaped top held in position by semi-circular iron rods."[26] One of them was still draped with 1830s blue-and-white Whillemot Gothic chintz in perfect condition. Nancy retained the century-old chintz hangings and curtains, then lightly spread similar color throughout the large bedroom: in the pale blue piping on the white windowseats, in the pattern stitched in the dressing table skirt, in the bellpull next to the bed, even in the pair of porcelain wastebaskets and Bristol glass table lamps. The Blue and White Bedroom was a perfect example of Nancy's style of "restoration": never confining a room to a specific period but, rather, drawing from a more pleasing and perhaps more accurate sensibility of layered eras and styles. Here the change in mood and purpose between Kelmarsh and Ditchley became clear as well. The chaise longue always at the end of a Kelmarsh bed, where an exhausted hunt follower might stretch out with his boots on after tea, gave way at Ditchley to a writing table.

When Winston Churchill stayed weekends at Ditchley in the first year and a half of the Second World War, he was given the Yellow Bedroom on the lake side of the house. Here the prime minister "would wake between eight and nine, and have his breakfast—a big one, bacon and eggs and marmalade . . . , and if there had been partridge at dinner, he would carefully have half the bird kept for his next day's breakfast. He would spend most of the morning in bed . . . then he would work on his boxes with a secretary. . . . He would never appear before lunch."[27] His bedroom at Ditchley, as at Chartwell and Chequers, was his most important inner sanctum. The bed in the Yellow Room was a tremendous four-poster the Trees had brought from Kelmarsh. Hung in yellow moiré, it was surmounted by a near-royal cornice and hangings made of the same moiré, with fringing, carved curlicues and finials suggesting the fleur-de-lis. Beside the bed—the four-poster being so high off the ground—Nancy placed a small bed-step. **I have it here next to my bed now; my poodle used to use it to get onto my bed. It has embroidered cushions on the steps. I imagine Winston must have used them to kneel on and say his prayers.**

Any of the second-floor Ditchley bedrooms might have been suitable for a prime minister in their architecture and decoration. Each was steeped in the parade of exquisite furniture and sumptuous luxuries, and every guest was looked after like a premier by Ditchley's indoor servants. Not quite the same grandeur, but certainly all of the comfort and personality, was carried up into the smaller bedrooms on the top floor, where mostly younger guests would stay: schoolchildren, single men, young nieces, nephews and cousins. The nursery was on the side of the house above the Trees' bedrooms; it comprised a large bedroom for the boys, a sitting room and a room for Nanny Weir.

On the other side of the house were the various quarters for Ditchley's indoor staff. Edith Bridges remembered the layout of the top floor, where "the whole staff was and some of the gentry, too. There was one bedroom which three of us girls shared and another which three of the boys shared. The housekeeper had her own rooms. The head housemaid had a room to herself at one end of the back landing; then there was the two footmen in the next rooms, a cook next to them, then the hall boy and the odd man. Farther along the top landing there was a bedroom where they used to put a couple of the maids when guests brought their own with them." Servants had little time to spend in their rooms, but unlike those in most large country houses, these bedrooms, too, were thoughtfully decorated. George Washington was one of Ditchley's footmen and later Ronald Tree's valet. Upon his hiring, he was immediately taken to his quarters: "I thought I had been put temporarily into one of the guest rooms. It had a fitted Wilton carpet, a comfortable bed with matching chintz valence, bedspread and curtains, an antique chest, fitted wardrobe and wash basin, and of course central heating, an untold luxury for any servant's room at that time."[28]

Washington unabashedly admired the mistress of Ditchley Park. "Everyone adored her, perhaps the men more than the women. The picture of her sitting side-saddle on her horse before a hunt, immaculate in her top hat and veil and wearing a blue coat and long skirt, is one I shall take to the grave with me." He also appreciated the way the large house was run. "[Mrs. Tree] commanded us all, but in such a charming way that made it impossible to refuse her anything she asked. It was, 'Could you spare a moment,' or 'Would you be so kind as.' She hardly ever rang a bell, she would telephone or try to find you. She really didn't give orders, she only asked favours. But she was sharp. We used to say she was blessed with two brains not one, and that you needed a pair of roller skates to keep up with her."

THE STAFF AT DITCHLEY was an inextricable element in the house's aura and allure. The newly refurbished mansion was run like a ship of the line, with the butler Collins and the housekeeper Mrs. Hayes on the bridge. To make it work smoothly, they utilized domestic skills and a professional hierarchy older than the house itself. The men answered to Collins, "a remarkable man," as Tree described him. "A man of great judgment, with a tremendous capacity for detail."[29] Under him were the three footmen, who looked after the reception rooms during the day and valeted male guests who brought no valet of their own. They laid the table for breakfast, lunch and dinner, then carried the food through from the kitchen and served it. The footmen cleaned plate, silver and candelabra with the help of the pantry man. The footman with the least seniority helped bring coal and firewood to the dozens of fireplaces throughout the house, while the most senior drew and closed the fancy damask curtains. Ronald's personal servant, who generally answered only to his master, acted as an extra footman if the need arose. Underneath the footmen were a hall boy and an odd man.

Mrs. Hayes was in charge of the linen and of ordering whatever supplies housekeeping might need. She had a corps of housemaids in her charge, starting with a head housemaid and descending through the first, second and third housemaids. The lowest maids on the ladder undertook the grueling task of cleaning and blacking the grates in all the fireplaces, a job they had to complete before eight in the morning and that often took two or three hours. The others dusted, cleaned, polished and vacuumed every corner of the reception rooms before guests came downstairs for breakfast. Housemaids slipped into

Collins, Ditchley's vaunted butler, with a tray of milk punch, May 1938

bedrooms at dawn to lay and light fires, then returned after guests left for the day, to air and make the gigantic beds, clean these grates and lay the evening fire. Beyond her regular duties, a housemaid served as lady's maid for a guest who came without her own. The most senior housemaids looked after the most important guest rooms and the ladies staying in them; the lowest-ranking housemaid waited on the housekeeper and the other senior servants.

Independent of the hierarchy were Nanny Weir—**she was a marvelous old woman with white hair who looked just like Queen Mary**—and the head chef, Monsieur Sier, who had a kitchen staff of his own. Sier would travel back and forth from London to Ditchley whenever the Trees did. He replaced Elise du Fore, who retired when the Trees moved from Kelmarsh, suggesting she was too old for such a large house. Most head chefs prepared a menu and presented it to the house's chatelaine every morning in her boudoir. **I hated that, so I sat down for two weeks and made a menu book. I listed first courses, main courses and all the sweets. I did it for lunch, dinner, teas, high teas, suppers before the theater, Christmas dinner. I would tell my cook, "Any of these things suit me if you serve them just as I've written it down." I didn't really want anything to do with the kitchen.**

Luncheon menu number fourteen began with "Mrs. Gibson's Egg Dish," and included brochette of liver with mushrooms and onion rings, "Mrs. Gibson's Carrots" or "Savoy Cabbage," yams baked in oranges and sweet griddle cakes with maple sugar or maple-sugar toast. For a buffet luncheon Sier could serve pâté de fois gras, cold smoked turkey and smoked ham, a mushroom ring with peas, a lettuce and watercress salad and pumpkin pie. There was a distinctly Anglo-Virginian flavor to the meals. For dinner, menu number one started with lobster milk toast and continued with roast chicken with prunes and cauliflower crumbs; dessert was a guava mousse or apple strudel. Another dinner party menu included borscht soup, pheasant, wild rice, creamed celery, "Orange l'Arab" and champagne. The kitchen at Ditchley, below the dining room in the refurbished cellar rooms, would prepare the meals for as many as thirty or just one. Most of the produce was grown at Ditchley on the farm, in the kitchen garden or in the greenhouses. The game was shot on the estate, the lamb raised there. **We did have to buy the meat. I thought English meat didn't hang enough. It seems to me we used to get meat from the Argentine.**

There was a separate cook for the staff's meals. They liked quite different foods than what I liked; they didn't like to have our leftovers. They liked a good hot meal, stews, that sort of thing. So I had another kitchen and a kitchen maid who cooked for them, and I worked out another menu. One had all sorts of dining rooms in those days. The children had their own dining room, the housekeeper had hers, the staff had their hall and we had two of our own.

Living in cottages or in the bothy down below the farmhouse in the stable yard were the outdoor servants. Jack Boneham was the head groom. He and four undergrooms took care of the stables, saddlery, livery and coaches, the fourteen or so hunters Ronald and Nancy and the boys kept and Nancy's two high-stepping ponies. There was one chauffeur at Ditchley for each of the Trees' two dark green Rolls-Royces; a small tree was painted where a coronet might have been on the car doors. Another driver was employed at Ditchley for the house van. The unmarried undergardeners lived in the bothy, while Williams, the head gardener, had his own cottage. Mr. Starling, the head gamekeeper, lived in a house on the estate with his sons, the underkeepers. Farmworkers lived in the two villages, Enstone and Spelsbury, that belonged to Ronald Tree and his Ditchley estate.

When we came to London, we had a whole family of secretaries. Mr. Bolongaro had been with Ronnie's father for fifty years. Ronnie gave me his brother as secretary, who was absolutely half-witted. I had some really rum secretaries, but Ronnie's Mr. Bolongaro was wonderful. The half-witted brother then married the children's French governess, who had had a love affair with the man who was teaching the boys how to play tennis; we had a tennis professional

down to teach the boys to play the right way. That governess was the sister of Ronnie's mother's two boys' governess . . . the Beatty boys' governess; my children never learned any French, but Mademoiselle became very proficient in English and married Bolongaro's brother.

Edith Bridges was hired as a housemaid by Lord Dillon's housekeeper in 1931, when she was sixteen years old. She began as the fourth housemaid:

The house was a different place then. We had to go to bed with lanterns or candles because there was no electric light. Of course, when you opened the doors, out went the candle because of the draft, so we had these lanterns. Downstairs they had what you called a tilling lamp, something like an Aladdin lamp it is; you have to keep on pumping it up, but they gave a very good light.

When the Trees came I stayed on. I was with them for thirteen years. I left in 1945 when my husband came back from the war. I remember the very first day they came to look at the place. They had lunch out in the park, out under the trees to the righthand side of the mansion. They had two dogs with them, that's why the old butler, Mr. Russell, wouldn't let them into the house.

I had a nice time at Ditchley. I enjoyed it. You worked hard. We used to work hard all the week and get ready for the people coming in at the weekend so that we didn't have to do it all on Friday morning. Sweeping and dusting, making the beds, changing them—'course, they were some beds to make—doing the bathrooms, putting all the clean towels out, all that sort of thing. We used to try and work it so that two housemaids were on and two were off; that way, we got every other day off. We could have a little bit of free time because at weekends you couldn't.

I was the fourth housemaid when the Trees took over. Then the head housemaid left and the second one took over from her and the third took over her job and I took over the third. Before I left them, I got to the head. I was very pleased about that. The job got a little easier as you moved up. You didn't have so many grates to clean. They had a lot of fires, the Trees did. All day long. They had the bedroom fires going and the bathroom fires. When you're the fourth and the third, you share them between you. And we had to scrub the back steps once in a while. My goodness, they took some doing from top to bottom. The front stairs, the brown stairs, they were nice. It was a lot of polishing, but we did it. We worked hard there, but I mean, we had the pleasure of it.

I looked after Mrs. Tree many a time when her maid was out. She was always so charming. It used to worry me, though, when I had to look after her; one used to think, "Should I put the jewelry in the safe or take it and sleep on it? If anyone gets in and gets at the safe, they'll have me." It used to worry me, because she had some lovely things.

Her clothes were all in the cupboards on the landing, and she had one cupboard in her bedroom. She's got a lot of lovely clothes, oh, lovely. I know this one dress, cream with a pink stripe down, and around the bottom was green. She used to wear that a lot. She was good. I mean, you put out anything for the evening and she'd wear it . . . she'd put it on, she wouldn't change it. Some of the ladies that we had, you put one out for them and they wouldn't touch it; they've got to get another one out. Not Mrs. Tree. You just used to think, "I wonder what she'll wear tonight?" and put it out, and she used to wear it. She wasn't hard to please; no, she was very easy.

I imagine running a big house is like running a business. You get very good people at the head of each department and let them run it. When I came over to live in England between the wars, there were generations of trained people who knew what was expected of a butler, what was expected of a footman, what was expected of a housemaid. That was the important thing. The machinery was there. A house was like a symphony orchestra; everybody knew their parts. I just had to fit into it.

So much relied on the butler. I said to somebody the other day, "I'm not so good at husbands, but I was very good finding butlers." At Mirador I had Stewart Wood. At Kelmarsh we first had a very tall old butler who had been with Lord Wilbur. He left Lord Wilbur's because he was found drinking the children's milk in the kitchen. Collins came to us at Kelmarsh as Ronnie's servant. He was a very distinguished gentleman, one of the best-bred and handsomest people you ever saw . . . and one of the best friends I've ever had. He came from Lord Lonsdale's, where his family had been for years; he no doubt had Lonsdale blood in his veins. His brother was the butler there, and his father the headkeeper for Lord Lonsdale's shoot. He came to us from being a Life Guardsman, the batman for our friend Bobby Jenkins, who lived at Lamport. He asked to come to work for Ronnie because he rather took a shine to my maid Nellie Meats. Collins became butler at Kelmarsh the second year we were there, then ran Ditchley beautifully. He was very efficient and extremely well trained. And he was loyal. He grew up with us, you see; he was our age. He adored Ronnie. They're buried practically on top of each other in Spelsbury.

You didn't pay people much, but it was a great thing to get into a big house. You were well looked after. You had class distinction as you went up the ladder. You demanded your rights within your position, whatever your position was on the scale. You had a profession you were proud of. It was like an office. And they had quite a gay time amongst themselves. We had a very big stable and a lot of gardeners. I remember when the grooms were exercising the horses, the young maids waving at them out the windows. It was a very good marriage market for the maids, because you hired very good-looking footmen. Always my kitchen maids were married to the footmen, again and again.

Life was so different; the younger generation in England would not know what I'm talking about. Nobody lives like you used to live, where you have underpinnings beneath you, where you expected your bed to be turned down and curtains drawn at a certain hour. It was a regular routine. Now people draw them themselves. I was amazed when I went to Newport not long ago . . . when I went out to various people's houses, they all had the same butler working for them. He went from house to house.

No friends I've had have taken the place in my affections of the people who worked for me. They are something that is beyond price.

THE FINAL MEASURES in Ditchley's recipe, a large part of what made the place so rapturous, so paradisiacal, were the gardens and the park. Called "pleasure grounds," they were aptly named for the ecstasy they offered the senses. Here, during all four seasons of the year, parterre and footpath alike never ceased to provide enchantment, contentment, a "perpetual refreshment to the spirit." They were perfect companions to the interior of the house as the Trees remade it, a continuation of its comforts and its grandeur. Of course, the gardens were very much born of the same sensibility as the decoration. To create them, the Trees turned directly to the eighteenth century while subtly implying within their borders the passing of a hypothetical two hundred years. They rewrote the history of the old estate, gave it new origins; they made the park true to its past, yet true to its great age as well.

The Trees found very little in the grounds when they bought the house, "only a few flower beds set higgledy-piggledy on a grass lawn looking unkempt and uncared-for"; "a dilapidated conservatory look[ing] as if it would soon fall down"; "vistas . . . totally obscured by self-seeded trees and bushes."[30] Beneath the neglect, a skeleton of a planned landscape did exist. Long avenues of beech trees had been drawn onto the parkland before the Gibbs house was built. **The most lovely effect—my favorite view—was from the front door looking over the wide grass lawn, over the cricket pitch, down a broad avenue, to the night sky in the evening.** Two and a half centuries later, these trees scraped the sky, so tall only the huge chimneys in the top of the house could be seen above them. Old oaks mottled the pastures around the house, their bottom leaves and shoots eaten by deer. On the other side of the house, the remnants of the Heythrop light remained just discernible, a straight ride scratched through the thick forest north of the house in the direction of Ditchley's second grand neighbor. This vista, also imposed in the eighteenth century, was now mostly grown over. So was the vista that balanced it to the northwest, leading from the house to a round Palladian temple on a rise behind the man-made lake. The folly had been so ignored over the preceding decades, it had almost completely disappeared into the landscape around it.

Though she preferred formality, Nancy saw charm and a certain honesty in the dereliction, in the toll that time had taken there. Such blatant anarchy was antithetical to Ronald's ideal, however. He was the "pure Palladian" and would insist on imposing order on his park, an order befitting his house. They asked their neighbor in London, *Country Life* editor and publisher Edward Hudson, whom he might recommend to help compose appropriate gardens and landscape. Hudson suggested a young architect named Geoffrey Jellicoe, who had recently finished a book on Classical Italian gardens, someone who could work in the right idiom and style. Jellicoe remembered their first meeting:

> When Ronnie called and asked to see me, I wasn't completely raw— I'd been in practice for two or three years by then—but I was rather frightened. You see, they were staying in their house in Queen Anne's Gate when I went to see them, and it was evident they were very wealthy indeed. When I arrived, however, and was shown in by the butler and Ronnie and Nancy introduced themselves, I was delighted to find they had each bought their own copy of my very expensive book. I thought, "This is terrific."
>
> I think Ronnie and Nancy belonged completely to the world of the 1920s. It was when most people were still thinking along neoclassical lines, looking back instead of forward. In many ways they lifted themselves above that, but the new world of thought and of psychology and so forth just hadn't broken on them, and I don't think it has with her even now.

Despite his having published a book on Classical gardens, Jellicoe's artistic sensibilities couldn't have been further from the Trees' own. He would spend his career, one for which he was knighted in 1979, transposing the tenets of Modernism onto the landscapes he worked with—the polar opposite of his future employers' vision.

> The two of them were a pair, a marvelous pair; they were different, but they absolutely complemented each other. You see, he thought along heroic terms, and she more domestic. That's why Ditchley suited him so and not her. It was tangible. She would come in and touch things, touch the flowers and things like that, while what I remember about Ronnie back then is his once telling me that Ditchley was all right, but the larger the place, the happier he would be. He would really have liked a house like the one next door.* He was firmness; she was delight. I think that's quite a good way of putting it.

Jellicoe found a sketch among James Gibbs's papers at the Soane Museum of a terrace for the garden front of Ditchley—a plan never carried out. His reinterpretation of Gibbs's terrace, which Tree called "Jellicoe's great achievement" at Ditchley, relieved an awkward "twist in the land" that betrayed the relationship between the house and its landscape. They moved tons of soil, leveling off ground that had previously sloped gently downward, creating a massive, three-hundred-yard-long grass embankment. The west end terminated with a second neoclassical folly the Trees found buried in bushes in their park. A stone terrace was laid directly behind the house, outside the windows of the saloon, using flagging from the basement.[31] A pair of magnificent reclining lions that they bought in Venice—one smiling, the other in a grimaced howl—flanked the steps.

Parallel to the terrace, shooting out from the western facade, the Trees installed a long sunk parterre. It was a study in formal French garden composition; early Georgians would have appreciated its rapport with Ditchley's Palladian architecture—that is, before the Landscape Movement took hold of their imaginations and judgment. From Wrest Park, a mid-nineteenth-century house in Bedfordshire, Ronald and Nancy bought stone outlines for the parterre that consisted of four square sections, each divided into diamond and triangular pieces by carved stone borders; a mile of this stone edging separated gravel paths and lawns from flower beds, instead of the usual box hedging. The Trees planted the beds with flowering annuals. Cone-shaped yew topiaries, a double line of low box, pleached lime trees and a yew hedge

*Blenheim Palace.

framed the parterre in quadruplicate. At the end farthest from the house, the parterre ended in a half-moon swimming pool. Arcs of water gushed from urns on the pool's rounded side; concealed in the stones on the flat part, facing the house, were *jets d'eau* that threw up a curtain of misty water, hiding the pool from the house or drenching, upon command, an unsuspecting visitor. At night spotlights set the mist afire.

Of the three thousand acres that made up the estate, at least one hundred were set aside for the pleasure grounds, so there was a great deal to do to bring the gardens and park to the state the Trees envisioned. Work went on steadily for more than three years. Lord Dillon's conservatories, built outside the west wing and the quadrant leading to it from the house, were ripped down. Part of the wing became an orangery. During the summer eight orange trees potted in lead jardinieres were arranged along the stone terrace at the back and a second stone terrace on the side of the house; when weather began getting cold, the trees were lifted by winch onto a wagon pulled by Persian draft horses, then hauled into the orangery. Paul Phipps turned what had been the quadrant conservatory into an inviting summerhouse. Floor-to-ceiling French doors that could be thrown open on hot afternoons now spanned the pathway. Twin columns created a gracefully curving loggia; windowpanes and stone steps bowed along with the quadrant's sweep.

Nancy, Geoffrey Jellicoe and Jellicoe's partner, Russell Page, created a beautiful garden room at the end of the orangery, parallel to the sunk parterre. Jellicoe considered it his favorite pause in the vast Ditchley layout; Nancy simply referred to it as "my garden." **I asked Jellicoe to copy the design from a Kip's View I had of Grimsthorpe. It was very simple and very formal, straight paths cutting through triangle-shaped beds. Jellicoe wasn't interested in flowers, so he had with him a very creative man who did his planting called Russell Page. Page later wrote the best book on gardening that's ever been written . . . *The Education of a Gardener*.**[32]

> **I told Page I wanted it like an old-fashioned curé's garden, and, as he did it, that garden was the loveliest part of Ditchley. Along with his planting, he did something I thought very clever. He made the edges between the paths and the beds from green boarding. It was an eighteenth-century trick that allowed the plants to spill out onto the paths the way I like. A low curb of green boarding with low box hedges . . . I thought that very attractive.**

To fill the 14 beds of the Orangery Garden, Page proposed, and Ditchley's gardeners planted, more than 1,500 plants and flowers of 72 different varieties. They used vast numbers of salvias, lychnises, veronicas, campanulas, tradescantias, aquilegias, anemones, delphiniums, acanthuses, clematises,

Groundwork for the sunk parterre, under way around 1934. Lord Dillon's glass conservatory quadrant, between the house's main block and its wing, has yet to be demolished and replaced.

The garden facade of Ditchley. The terrace and the second flight of steps linking the architecture of the house to the parkland around it, as well as the potted trees and the pair of Venetian lions, were all added by the Trees.

The sunk parterre and crescent pool as seen from Nancy's bedroom window. The planting had only just been completed and the rows of lime trees and the hedges had yet to reach maturity.

The lead statue of *Fame* on the roof of Ditchley and one of the park's ancient lights. "I used to stand in the doorway and look down the avenues," said Nancy, "and think it's the most beautiful place in the world."

euphorbias, sedums and dictamnums. They planted 800 tulip bulbs; 1,500 mixed bulbs, including muscari and fritillarias; 1,000 narcissus, crocus, iris and lily bulbs; as well as scores of bushes and shrubs. In exactly the manner Nancy loved, plants tumbled into each other and out onto the paths, mixing, jostling for sunlight, closing up even the smallest hint of the earth below. Each bed produced a continuous show of color and fragrance through the spring, summer and autumn.

Nancy, Jellicoe and Page collaborated on one other entrancing corner of the Ditchley estate. Within the square formed by the old walls off Lyon's Court—an area that probably was once the laundry yard—Nancy conceived, Jellicoe designed and Page executed a most extravagant herb garden. The plan called for breaking up the yard into no less than forty compact square and rectangular beds, surrounded by low, slow-growing box hedges. The beds moved outward from a round pool at the center. In April 1938 Page wrote to Nancy: "I enclose the plan of the Herb Garden done on the very small clump principle as you wanted, and all very much mixed up. I expect the best thing to do would be to accumulate the plants gradually and plant them out in rows as it may be that eventually you will like to have, for instance, all the mints collected together, all the thymes and so on. In any case it is a very formidable document!" The list included 250 varieties, from *Angelica archangelica*, *Verbascum thapsus* and *Artemisia abrotanum* to horseradish.[33] A small summer-house was constructed inside the herb garden; there Nancy could retire in complete privacy. **It was the prettiest herb garden I have ever seen.**

Elsewhere on the estate, the Trees kept a large kitchen garden, a cutting garden for flower arrangements and a network of greenhouses. They placed the cricket pitch in front of the house to mimic the circle formed by the quadrants and bullring. They tidied the two-centuries-old grass rides and towering avenues, trimmed for the first time in decades. They cleared away the overgrowth along the original vistas, freeing the temple and the view of it from the upper storeys of the house. (During the Second World War Italian prisoners were pressed into helping with the clearing.) At one point, the Trees, along with Jellicoe, attempted to lengthen the lake; Nancy suggested the change. The man-made body—supposedly designed by the Georgian landscape architect Capability Brown—inexplicably stopped where typically it should have snaked on so that it might appear as a slowly ambling river, "a silver slither across the landscape." **I thought we could enlarge the lake if we cut a hole in the embankment on the side nearest the house. It would then flood the little valley, leaving the old beech trees to be surrounded by the water. We did it during a very hot, dry summer; it looked marvelous when we did it, exactly what we wanted. The next morning Ronnie rushed to me rather agitated, saying, "Look out the window; the lake has disappeared." I** tried to reassure him by saying we couldn't possibly see the water from downstairs anyway, but when we went upstairs, it was true, the lake was gone. That day our neighbor Mr. Gaskell, who had a farm three miles from us, phoned up to say his cows were knee-deep in water. "The only satisfaction I have since had," wrote Geoffrey Jellicoe about their attempt to enlarge the lake, "is that Capability Brown . . . must have had a similar experience."[34]

Taken as a whole, the Ditchley gardens and park—now perfect complements to a country palace—were rendered by the Trees on a scale few would even bother to envision in the 1930s. They had moved the earth in the wholesale fashion great British landowners of the preceding centuries had, with equal confidence, equal knowledge and equally delightful results. But more so, Nancy's imagination was drawn to the details, the little medleys she or a guest might come across as they wandered the park. As inside the house, every conceivable empty space was an opportunity. More than in the grand parterre or the terrace, her taste for how a garden ought to be was found in small compositions of delicious-smelling nicotiana, heliotrope, lavender, lemon verbena and sweet sultan underneath the windows of the house. They gave Ditchley the personality she sought. Spreading and drooping wisteria and jasmine on a wall or around a tree, or a Gloire de Dijon rose climbing over a Portland stone pediment, were enlisted in taking a site that was somehow neither of today nor of yesterday and blessing it with an indescribable essence of passing time, time past and timelessness.

THE TREES CELEBRATED their newly completed house with a spectacular summer ball. Given in June of 1937 at the end of Ascot Week, it was conceived on the same scale and with all the splendor of the great parties of their parents' generation. One thousand guests attended. Many drove down from London, automobiles making a quick trip possible for the first time. Others came from neighboring country houses like Blenheim Palace, which were filled for the weekend. Every inn for miles around, including those in Oxford, was completely booked.

Arriving after dinner, guests drove up the long, tree-lined estate roads to find every room at Ditchley lit brilliantly from within, their curtains pulled back. Cecil Beaton thought the effect that of "an enormous eighteenth-century doll's house of honey-colored stone. . . . Through the tall windows the gold ceiling and chandeliers sparkled. Canopied beds could be glimpsed upstairs; the great front doors stood open to the steady stream of guests and the balmy velvet evening. Yellow roses tumbled over the balustrade at the entrance steps."[35] Downstairs rooms were illuminated by candles, and each was graced with flower arrangements by Constance Spry. Ronald remembered that "the smell of lilies in the drawing room was almost overpowering."[36]

Nancy Tree in the gown she wore for the 1937 Ditchley ball, photographed by Cecil Beaton

Ladies were asked to wear red and white, and almost every one did. "Most of the great beauties of the epoch were there," wrote Tree, "among them: Diana Cooper, Elizabeth von Hofmannsthal, and her sister Caroline Paget, Sheila Milbanke, Lady Plunkett, Mrs. Churchill and Merle Oberon."[37] Lady Diana Cooper and Lady Ravensdale dressed in red, while the Duchess of Sutherland, the Duchess of Westminster, Clementine Churchill and Lady Colefax wore white. *Vogue* thought Lady Caroline Paget, "in a candy-stick pink and white striped dress with a garland of flowers falling off her shoulders (a dress designed by Rex Whistler), was the woman most remarked."[38] Men came in traditional white tie or military dress uniforms, though Oliver Messel, the party's designer, flouted convention by wearing a suit of white serge and a red tie, to match the party's theme. One peer of the realm, on catching sight of Messel, pronounced, "Fellow ought to be thrown in the lake."[39]

Nancy, in a red-and-white gown, received her guests in the Blue Parlour. They then proceeded through the White Drawing Room and out the garden doors into a white muslin ballroom erected on top of the flagstone terrace. The marquee was the creation of Messel, considered the most talented stage and costume designer in Britain. The *Vogue* journalist described how it was "garnished with garlands of flowers and gold fringes. Along the walls were papier-mâché busts of negroes dressed up with fantastic hats, mantillas, tiaras, necklaces, and ear-rings, perched up on marble painted columns."[40] The orchestra was positioned in what looked like a rose-encased birdcage, and the stone of the terrace was covered in a parquet dance floor.

During one orchestra break, long after midnight, the sky over the lake and the forest exploded into a breathtaking exhibition of pyrotechnics choreographed by the Trees' friend Anthony Head. Breakfast followed in the library; the dancing continued until dawn.

Nancy left her ball as the sun came up. She was to meet Lady Astor on board a liner bound for America, where they would visit Buck Langhorne, who lay ill in Virginia. She drove away from a party still in full swing, a ball in her magnificent new house lauded as "the best party anyone had seen in many years."[41] Geoffrey Jellicoe and his wife departed for London soon after, "wondering if we should ever see the like again."

"WHEN THE MOON IS HIGH"

I suppose one ought to have kept a diary. Things came so quickly; something was happening every day. But somehow, when it was going on, you didn't realize you were living in historic times.

DITCHLEY COULD ONLY have been in England: where the decorative arts of many different cultures could meld together so perfectly underneath one roof. The eighteenth-century England that Ditchley was born into had an arrogant, chauvinistic heart and soul, but a curious mind and body. An island protected—but isolated as well—from the rest of civilization by a great moat, it found itself starved at times. For nourishment its people went off on grand tours and expeditions, built colonies and an empire. When they returned to their mother country, they brought with them objects and ideas they found "out there," thereby renewing and replenishing their own culture. Even when England was at war it saw no contradictions in filling its drawing rooms with the delights of its enemy's genius. Most *things* English were *things* international.

Ditchley was a tall, proud, English stately home; but its design was Italian, its gardens and decoration Italian and French, while the things that filled it were from just about everywhere in Europe. The Trees themselves added another element, one of the ingredients that made Ditchley stand out so in their day: They contributed their own particular Americanness. They carried with them the Gay Nineties and Roaring Twenties of New York and the concise puritanism of New England. Most importantly, Nancy brought with her Virginia. The soft edges inside and out that tempered Ditchley's pompousness were Virginian; the extravagant hospitality that so brightly colored it was Virginian; the iconoclastic wit in the decoration and at the dinner table was Virginian. Everything Virginian, ironically, had once been English; the England that sent its people to Virginia was the same England that built Ditchley. Englishness and Ditchley had come full circle.

The wonderful and eccentric life led at Ditchley and in other houses like it did, however, find its origins in the British Isles. English rituals and sport grew organically from English soil; if they imported the decorative arts, they exported the country lifestyle. History played a part in it: English country house life had survived the civil wars, revolutions and invasions that had destroyed such privileges elsewhere. The French thought it banishment to leave the court at Versailles for their estates; the English reveled in the freedom of their own fields. Inside English estate walls, these islands within an island amid the most beautiful man-made settings on earth, they created marvelous distractions and pleasures for their own amusement. For instance, never was there a pastime so ideal for whiling away hours in the country as cricket. Cricket was a pure existential exercise. Country life was a distinct

A Ditchley house party in 1938, including the host and hostess, standing at left; Lord and Lady Erne, seated next to them; Anthony Eden, seated upper right; and Clementine and Winston Churchill in front.

style and sensibility, not the city transposed periodically onto a new stage. It had its own set of rules, customs and costumes. It had survived the centuries to reach its *fin de siècle* between the wars.

At Ditchley, "it was like a dream-world, something out of a film." Nancy danced with Collins the butler once a year, at the servants' Christmas party. A newspaper came on a lady's breakfast tray if she wanted one, next to the Porthault napkin that matched her bed linens and the "tiny flower in the tiny vase." Men's newspapers, set out in the breakfast room, were toasted and ironed. Cricket took all day: "Every Saturday in the summer months there would be a match against a local village team. The sound of ball against bat could be heard quite plainly from the house." Jeremy Tree tried to drive a miniature electric motorcar he was given all the way to London. Riders rode and walkers walked to Lee's Rest, Clark's Bottom, Bevis Farm, Norman's Grove, the Blenheim Gate, Henley Knapp or Deadman's Riding Wood, never leaving the Ditchley estate. "We used to love visiting Starling the game-keeper on a Sunday afternoon." A man might easily change his clothes four times in one day: for breakfast, sport, tea and dinner. "Michael was frightfully good at sardines. He always found a good spot and usually managed to get a pretty girl in there with him. It was all very innocent, though."[1]

The Midlands Counties Retriever Trials were held at Ditchley in the autumn of 1938; "Bitingham Scoonie" and "Birlingham Jerry," belonging to Bernard Brassey, were particular favorites. "Mercifully, our days at Ditchley predated the age of television and pop music." Ronald played New Orleans jazz and Big Band music on his gramophone for everyone to dance to after dinner. **I remember a party when we were all playing *The Game*. We were all cheating madly, and Rosie Cecil, who was up for the first time, was on the floor acting like a woman having a baby. An American girl who was a guest of ours said to me, completely in earnest, "We don't play it this way in Philadelphia."** Bridge, whist and "old bitch" were the card games of choice. "You think, 'Can I have lived through it, can I have taken part in that?' It does make one feel glad to have been there."[2]

Ronald gave Nancy a pair of high-stepping Hackney ponies one year for Christmas. **Their names were Lord Airlie and Romney Swell. Bertram Mills found them for Ronnie; they had been performing in a show. I remember looking out the window Christmas morning and there they were, drawn up in front of the house with a little boy in a top hat—what they called "a mon-key"—sitting behind in a cart. They really pranced; they were terrific.**

I don't know a thing about driving, I certainly wasn't a seasoned whip, but I used to drive down the road to Blenheim or drive across the park. There were huge rabbit holes in the park, and why we didn't turn over I'll never know. The boy in the top hat whose job it

was to get out and hold the ponies was scared to death; he was ready to fly off the back.

I took Mrs. Keppel for a ride when she came to stay with us; she was the famous mistress of Edward VII. I was very fond of her; we had stayed with her in Florence, and she had rooms next to ours at the Ritz during the war. She was also fearless about my driving; she barely turned a hair.

That day she wore a great big hat, which was fashionable then, to go along with her great big bosom that was pushed up by stays. As we bumped across the fields the brim of her hat would come down and touch her bosom. It was the time of Edward VIII's abdication, and as we went she was telling me things like "Ah, this Mrs. Simpson, I could tell her a thing or two if she'd only talk to me. Now, Charles II had the right idea; he made them all duchesses." Then she said, "You know, Nancy, I like old George," George was her husband, "but I like a man with a dog whip. Edward was the man for me." All the while the cart was bumping up and down and the bosom and her hat were meeting together. . . . I couldn't drive to save my life.

Nancy shone as a hostess; her personality was at the center of the house's. "Nancy had quite a magical way of putting people at their ease and entertaining them without dominating them at all," remembered her cousin David Astor. "As a hostess she didn't play actively; she played the role very lightly. There was no direction thrust upon you when you stayed at Ditchley; you felt very much it was your house while you were staying there." Deborah Devonshire thought the same: "Nancy made everything seem so easy, as though it had fallen into place by itself. She was such a brilliant hostess, the way she used to make you feel that she was pleased to see you. And you weren't bossed about on weekends at Ditchley; you decided yourself on a variety of things to do."

Mary, Winston Churchill's youngest daughter, thought Ronald the consummate host, the two Trees a remarkable combination. "They were a splendid show, splendid at what they did together. They both knew how to entertain, what comfort was in a house and what makes an agreeable party; they did so to perfection. In a way they complemented each other. They were a formidable team." Mary Churchill was seventeen when she first stayed at Ditchley. At her initial encounter with Nancy she thought her "a bird of paradise. She was a sort of person I'd never seen before. I found her fascinating. I can't say I found her cozy, but she was always frightfully kind to me." Like Kelmarsh and Cliveden, Ditchley could be a difficult arena for the young. Much was expected of the teenage peers of the Trees' children; they were

Anthony Eden, MP, future prime minister, and Moggy Gage in the saloon at Ditchley in 1938. Eden had by then resigned his position as foreign secretary in protest over Neville Chamberlain's appeasement policy.

Another future prime minister of Great Britain at Ditchley: Alex Douglas-Home, second from left. Before the war he was Chamberlain's parliamentary private secretary and a supporter of appeasement. Ronald Tree is in the middle; the writer André Maurois is seated at right.

The perfectly manicured turf behind the house was ideal for croquet and lawn tennis.

Reading the Sunday papers on the back steps outside the saloon

treated and served like everyone else staying in the house. "Nancy was very clever about mixing people up at dinner," remembered Sarah Baring, one of Jeremy's and Michael's friends. "One was often put next to important people and forced to learn how to talk." Nancy could be intimidating to someone young or shy, just as she could be welcoming, talking down the long dining room table, picking out whomever she chose. She had a way of sensing vulnerability, like her Aunt Nancy. Sarah Baring thought, "Some people found Nancy draconian; not everyone understood her. She could find a sharp little pin and dig it in."

Joyce Grenfell used to stay at Ditchley for weekends or a holiday like Christmas. She was Nancy's first cousin, the daughter of Nora Langhorne and Paul Phipps, and was becoming by the end of the 1930s a celebrated actress and monologist in the vein of her mother's childhood friend Ruth Draper. Joyce became one of the most popular comediennes in England after the war, but to most of her family she was just doing what they'd always done for entertainment at Mirador or Cliveden or Ditchley: the mimicking and the skits. She stayed at Ditchley one week when she was performing in a variety show in Oxford along with the actresses Dorothy Dixon and Edith Evans.

> They stayed with me for a week . . . these three great actresses. The year I came out in New York with Babs Gibson, Dorothy Dixon was in a play that Babs and I went to see. We thought her more like Aunt Nora than two pins. She was dressed as a bellboy . . . ladies didn't wear trousers and tight little coats and bellboy hats back then. We thought she was the chicest number that ever was. I had a sort of hero worship of this lady.
>
> The only night that they let loose was the last night that we had dinner together. Ronnie was away. They let their hair down. I remember Dorothy Dixon got a little tiddly and put her foot up on the table and told us about the loves of her life. That was quite amusing.

Joyce and her husband, Reggie, spent a family Christmas at Ditchley in 1938. English Christmases for the extended Langhorne clan were traditionally at Cliveden, with Nancy Astor the center of the festivities, though the Trees usually celebrated their own Christmas at Kelmarsh or Ditchley. Inevitably cousins who had spent time at both compared Ditchley with Cliveden. David Astor thought Christmas at Ditchley "was as if we'd gone there every Christmas. It didn't seem different from our home, you see, because their family behaved just the same way."

Phyllis and Bob Brand, their children Dinah and Virginia and her son Peter Brooks came from their house, Eydon Hall, and joined the Trees, the

For the passage between the main block and the orangery, Paul Phipps designed a stone-and-glass summerhouse to replace Lord Dillon's derelict conservatory. On warm days its French doors were thrown open and its chairs placed on the flagstone terrace.

Grenfells and various Astor cousins for Christmas that year at Ditchley. Ruth Draper was there as well, and Bobbie Shaw, Nancy Astor's son by her first marriage. The Christmas day dinner was "dress up." Joyce wrote to her mother, Nora, that "Nancy was the best as Mrs. Rittenhouse. She wore a black velvet dress and padded her bosom and behind. Of course she looked very lovely with her hair pulled up off her face. She was very funny and a little outrageous. Billy [Astor], Reggie Winn and Jakie [Astor] were the Marx Bros. I was rather dreary as a 1900 lady with holly in my hair and the green velvet dress you sent me. Alice [Winn] made an incredibly mad Sur-realist picture."[3]

For a field sport, shooting supplanted foxhunting at Ditchley; plus-fours replaced breeches. As early as the winter of 1933, Ronald and Nancy were taking partridge and pheasant at their new estate, even though their house would remain uninhabitable for two years more. North Oxfordshire was not foxhunting country as the Trees were used to it; neither the "close" terrain nor the field of followers could compare with the sport or the society of the Hunting Shires in the 1920s. Nancy continued to hunt right up until the Second World War, when the horses were requisitioned by the government, but hunting was no longer a family vocation practiced in and around their own

Nancy Tree at Ditchley
in 1938

The actresses Dorothy
Dickson, Edith Evans
and Joyce Grenfell,
Nancy's first cousin,
at Ditchley

neighborhood. On her own, she sent her horses to the Warwickshire Hunt for the day by horse box, rode from Kelmarsh or hired stables in Guilsborough, at the center of Pytchley country.

Shooting parties were held all over Britain during the autumn-to-winter season; it was the British upper class's second blood sport. Saturdays and often Mondays the *pop-pop-pop* of shotguns and the *cockle-cockle* of game birds could be heard across the countryside. Extraordinary to Ditchley, however, almost unheard of between the wars, was that both Ronald *and* Nancy took up positions along the line. Shooting unquestionably remained a gentleman's domain, an out-of-doors men's club closed to female intrusion. It was an Englishman's institution, like the House of Commons before Nancy Astor; shooting though, unlike Parliament, was not accountable to the vicissitudes of democracy. Some women might shoot informally along the paths and in the spinneys of a park, and some shot clay pigeons, but their inclusion in organized, daylong shooting parties was limited to their joining the men for lunch at around one, then standing quietly behind their husbands and beaux in the line as they shot the afternoon stands. At home in Virginia Nancy Langhorne shot frogs and bats behind the house at Mirador with her father and brothers, but as Viscountess Astor, she never stood in at a partridge or pheasant drive, nor, when her husband took houses in Scotland, did she shoot grouse. But her niece Nancy Tree did break the barrier and by the early 1930s was considered one of the few "well-known women who can use a gun skilfully, safely and well, and hold [her] own in a man's shoot."[4]

Men hated women to shoot; they really didn't like women to do anything in this country. Here, if anyone is going into a good school or a good regiment, it's the boy of the family; the girl can slog it at home. But there were a few of us shooting between the wars. We were mostly women whose husbands had shoots of their own. Mary Marlborough was a very good shot; I shot with Mary at Blenheim. I was told that Lady Townsend was a wonderful shot. Debo [Devonshire, née Mitford] was just starting to shoot; she was having lessons at the shooting school. I also remember Antonia Frasier at the shooting school. Nannie never shot, but Aunt Phyllis did. She loved shooting and was a great shot.

I started when we lived at Kelmarsh and would take a place in Scotland for six weeks with Lord Beatty after the twelfth of August. We took Grantully Castle and a moor to shoot grouse three years running before the hunting season began. I shot with them every day. I said, "If you think I'm going to sit in this bog and knit, you're wrong. I'm going to shoot." But they always stuck me on the end like an extra gun. I was a good shot, though. Crawley de Crespigny taught me to shoot and gave me a marvelous pair of guns. I took to shooting in a big way.[5]

In September we shot partridge at Ditchley when there were fields of mustard everywhere and it was still warm enough to shoot in your shirtsleeves. That was wonderful. During partridge season we'd have our lunch in the field. The car would come down with the butler and a footman, and they would put out trestle tables and serve us lunch. Something else we could do in September which was very nice was to walk up fields and shoot. You'd go out with the head keeper, and he would beat up the hedgerows, and things would get up and you'd shoot. That was wonderful for the two boys; it's why Michael is such a good shot. Jeremy didn't pay a bit of attention, because he was already thinking about his racing.

In November you'd start to shoot the pheasant. I do remember one particularly good stand for pheasants at Ditchley. You stood on the other side of the lake, and the beaters drove the birds up over the house and the lake towards you. You got them quite high there.

It's rather fun when you have people to stay in the country if there's something you can all do together; something that will also tire your guests. We'd start quite early in the morning and have three or four stands for seven guns before lunch. When the party shot pheasant at Ditchley, it was late autumn and winter, so we'd have lunch inside. Sometimes we ate in the house if we were nearby, or in the cottage where we lived before the house was ready. Or there was a perfectly charming farmhouse that was supposed to be where one of the Lees had kept a mistress. The idea was, you wanted a warm room, hot food and a loo after being outside all morning. The butler and a footman brought down great thermoses of stew or something else hot, and baked potatoes. You had wine or sloe gin, and after lunch, cheese and coffee or a sweet like a pie. You kept a game book, where you'd record the day's bag. Once we got five hundred brace in a day . . . a thousand birds.

THERE WAS ANOTHER noticeable distinction between Kelmarsh and Ditchley, aside from the sport: a change in atmosphere. Part of it had to do with the houses themselves: Ditchley was a far grander, more imposing building. Part was the general disposition of the times: The Great Depression of the 1930s affected all levels of society. But more so, the difference was a result of Ronald Tree's career. While Kelmarsh was a romantic hunting box where everything centered on sport and sportsmen, Ditchley evinced a more serious nature, being the country seat of a hardworking and ambitious member of

Lunch in the field during a prewar partridge shoot: from left, Dorothy Beatty, Duff
Cooper, Elizabeth Koch de Gooreynd and Diana Cooper. "We had four game keep-
ers at Ditchley who organized our shoots," said Nancy. "Mr. Starling, the head
keeper, engaged the beaters who were usually schoolchildren and workers from
around the farm."

Parliament. As Tree's occupation turned from mastering hounds to mastering
legislation, his home evolved with him. Weekend house parties were as hospitable and Circean as ever—the place could never be bleak—but fewer of the
freewheeling hunting wags were included on the guest list, and conversation
abandoned the realm of the seven-mile gallop for the domain of low-income
housing and the League of Nations.

During one week in July of 1938, the Trees hosted at Ditchley a fete for
the Harborough Conservative Constituency Council and a large garden party
for visiting American members of the English Speaking Union. Ronald's
maiden speech in Parliament dealt with beef subsidies and farm prices. He also
entered into debates on the floor concerning rural conservation, education,
the Unemployment Insurance Act and Anglo-American relations. Tree's star
was on the rise. In 1936 he was asked to become the government Minister of
Pensions Robert Hudson's parliamentary private secretary: the minister's eyes
and ears in the Commons. It was the first step a "backbencher" made toward
joining a government. He retained the position as Hudson moved up the ladder as the Secretary for Health and then the Overseas Trade Secretary.

But Tree was decidedly outspoken on what was perhaps the decade's most divisive issue in Parliament and in public, an argument that came up time and time again in the Commons and managed to unsettle even the most tranquil of private homes: what to do about Hitler and Mussolini. It was a complex question touching upon all the strongest emotions bubbling beneath the surface of every Crown subject. If honor was at stake, so was domestic stability. Prime Minister Neville Chamberlain and his party believed that "peace at any price" was preferable to a repeat of the appalling carnage of the 1914–18 war with Germany. The Tory premier was joined by the far left, who feared that a strong British military could threaten their growing labor movement and lead to British fascism. Other "Appeasers" were pro-German, some anti-Russian. Opposed to the government, besides the minority party in the Commons, a small group of "Tory rebels" loudly advocated standing up to the dictators at whatever the cost, as well as the immediate rearming of British forces. History proved them right, but these "warmongers," as they were then labeled, were vilified as traitors to their party, their government, their class and their country for their opposition to Chamberlain.

Winston Churchill began the dissension with speeches that exposed the extent of British military weakness abroad. Independent of Churchill, a group of younger Conservative MPs began gathering in 1938 to discuss the grave danger as they saw it; Churchill was pointedly left out, considered past his prime. This group, referred to by its adversaries as the "Glamour Boys," was made up of young, educated, aristocratic members of Parliament, typical of those who had been Britain's ruling class a generation before. Lord Cranborne was one, along with Anthony Eden, Harold Macmillan, Leo Amery, Duff Cooper, Lord Wolmer, Ronald Cartland, Jim Thomas and others. Ronald Tree was included, and the Trees' London town house in Queen Anne's Gate became the meeting place. The Glamour Boys were sufficiently distrusted by their own government that Downing Street tapped the telephone at the Trees' house and had the entrance watched for its comings and goings.

Lady Astor was one of the most avid Appeasers, among other things because she was a devout pacifist. And Cliveden was indeed a house where Appeasers like Geoffrey Dawson of the *Times* or pro-Germans like Sir Neville Henderson and Charles Lindbergh were welcome. Prime Minister Chamberlain was a regular guest there as well. At the same weekend house parties, however, Anthony Eden and his wife were Lord and Lady Astor's guests, as at other times were Charlie Chaplin and George Bernard Shaw, all of whom were anti-fascist.[6] Nonetheless, the volume of her support for the government put her at odds with the Trees and left a cool relationship between Cliveden and Ditchley. The family took sides, like so many others, the difference being that this family had a number of members sitting in Parliament.

Feelings ran very high after the Munich Agreement, when the British government let Czechoslovakia go to the Germans and Chamberlain announced "Peace in our time." There was a good case for both sides, but unfortunately most people thought the same way Nannie did about Appeasement—that it was a bad wicket to go to war over Czechoslovakia. Others like us believed that by not going to defend the Czechs, we were losing all their arms factories to the Germans. We had had Jan Masaryk to stay with us at Ditchley quite a lot . . . we thought the government should live up to the promises it made to him and his country.

I felt strongly anti-Chamberlain. I was violent about it. Chamberlain was a hidebound, second-rate man. I thought the real person to blame, though, was Stanley Baldwin. He was the one who let the army slip, and he should have taken a stronger stand when the Germans went into the Rhineland. But our views were in the minority; most people were deeply relieved that Chamberlain had avoided war at Munich and thought anybody who opposed him disloyal. We were always great friends, but Nannie and I differed so on this that at the time I wouldn't have her in my house. Our friends the Wallaces had made Ronnie the guardian of their children if something happened to them—he was that close to them—but they wouldn't speak to him over Munich.

The one person who knew we had to stop Hitler from taking Czechoslovakia, who knew we ought to be arming, was Winston Churchill. He saw that before anyone else. But I can assure you—I used to be quite close to things in those days—nobody trusted him or liked him. He sat alone. In the year before the war, just after Munich, Ronnie saw him sitting so much by himself in the House of Commons that he felt sorry for him and asked if he and Clemmie would like to spend the weekend at Ditchley. It was a weekend that Anthony Eden was there and Bobberty Salisbury and others in the group. Anthony said to me the most extraordinary thing when we went for a walk in the woods. He said, "I'm rather annoyed with Ronnie for having asked Winston. I think Winston wants to get in on my bandwagon."

War was declared a year later, in the autumn of 1939. That morning I listened to Chamberlain's address to the nation on the wireless at our house in Queen Anne's Gate, then started to walk across Green Park to Parliament, where Ronnie had got me a seat to listen to the prime minister's speech to the Commons. I vividly remember noticing a little man in a raincoat walking just ahead of

Jan Masaryk, the foreign minister of the Czech government-in-exile, with the American columnist Dorothy Thompson at Ditchley in 1941

me as I crossed the park. Suddenly the air-raid siren went off, the first of the war. My dear, that little man disappeared in a second as if he went underground! I looked up and he was gone, along with everyone else. I seemed to be the only person left out in the park. It was terrifying.

The following weekend Ronnie and I had been invited to shoot at Hackwood with Lord and Lady Camrose. They had made the invitation months before. It never occurred to me with the war on that people would have shooting parties, so I didn't even bother to say that we weren't coming. It seemed the end of the world. To my horror, I got a telephone message from Lady Camrose, who was a very distinguished old lady, saying, "What time were we arriving?" They were waiting and they hadn't heard from us; they were still having their shoot. I had to write and apologize and say, "I thought war stopped everything." It's very British that they went on with their plans.

Ronald Tree's staunch convictions prior to the Second World War had a direct effect on his home and estate during the war. Because of political alliances he had formed, another chapter in Ditchley's 350-year history as a seat of power was written, while the fabric of the mansion's priceless decoration was saved from the dereliction that befell many other English country houses. When a German invasion of Britain seemed imminent, the government exercised emergency rights of eminent domain over the property of landowners—most noticeably, commandeering the country's manor houses. Such enormous buildings were as institutional in their planning as they were domestic, and their locations far from the city centers provided ideal headquarters for wartime operations. Some were taken by branches of the military, others by government ministries to use as hospitals, schools and shelters. Cliveden became a hospital, as it had in the 1914 war; Chatsworth, in Derbyshire, the temporary home for a girls' boarding school. The Duke of Buccleuch loaned Boughton to the British Museum as a place to warehouse their collection during the Blitz. Not as fortunate, Haseley Court in Oxfordshire had its lovely rooms divided into cubicles by the military and the lead removed from its roof. As at Evelyn Waugh's fictitious Brideshead, some owners were swept aside in the rush, and irreplaceable works of art and architecture were completely disregarded.

Ditchley's initial role was as a shelter for a nursery school. Rather than shooting with Lord and Lady Camrose, Nancy and some of the Ditchley servants zealously whitewashed unused rooms in the east wing in preparation for children being evacuated from London. **When they arrived, they seemed very young and pathetic. They were lost without their parents, such a long way from familiar city walls in a strange, houseless countryside. We also gave our empty cottages to evacuated families from the London slums.** After a few months of "Phony War"—fighting didn't begin in earnest until the following spring—evacuees were returned to their own homes, many of them more afraid of the quiet in the country than of the threat of bombs.

> **Something else I did at the beginning of the war, like so many others, was take Volunteer Aid Nurses classes. I did it in Oxford with Baba Metcalfe and Edwina D'Erlanger. We went to classes during the day and practiced bandaging each other in the evenings. I got a ninety-seven on my final exam, with the three points deducted because when asked to pour a level teaspoon by the examiner I got down on my hands and knees to get my eye level with the table. He penalized me for having no common sense at all.**

The Trees offered Ditchley to the Canadian Army to use as a hospital, but the house was thought too small. Instead, its primary war duty would be decided in the autumn of 1940 by Britain's new prime minister, Winston Churchill. Ronald Tree related Churchill's proposal in his memoir *When the Moon Was High*:

One dark November afternoon in 1940, I went down to the House of Commons on some Ministry of Information work and dropped into the chamber to listen for a few minutes to the debate. I had not been there long before one of the attendants sought me out and told me that the Prime Minister wanted to see me urgently in his room. This came to me as something of a surprise. Though the Prime Minister had visited our house on one occasion, and though we were on friendly terms, I was not close to him personally, and was far too junior in the Party to regard myself as one of his political colleagues. I was still further surprised by his first words to me: "Would it be possible for you to offer me accommodations at Ditchley for certain week-ends?"—and I can still recall the mystery and poetry with which he invested the phrase—"when the moon is high." He explained that German reconnaissance planes had flown over Chequers after the war started, taking photographs of the house and its surroundings. Shortly after the Battle of Britain began, he went on, bombs were dropped near the house, indicating that the Germans knew its precise location and were probably aware that the Prime Minister was in the habit of spending his week-ends there. The Chiefs of Staff became alarmed that there might be a heavy attack and had advised him, he said, to move to some other country house "when the moon is high" and visibility was likely to be clear. . . . I told Churchill, of course, that we would be delighted to have him, and asked him when he would be coming. Somewhat to my dismay, he asked if Friday would be all right, this being Tuesday.[7]

Ronnie rang me on the telephone and said, "Get everything ready. I can't tell you who's coming or what's happened, but every room must be ready Friday; we're going to be full." He couldn't tell me over the telephone for security reasons. I thought the house was going to be used by Lord Swindon, who was head of British Intelligence. The headquarters of MI5 was at Blenheim, and we assumed he would take Ditchley for himself, because during the week technicians began arriving to install telephone lines and scrambling devices. We did know whatever it was, we were going to be something very secret. I got the house ready in the next few days, and on Friday as I was looking out a front window I was simply amazed to find coming down through the avenue of trees an armored car with Winston Churchill sitting outside in a zoot suit with a huge cigar in his mouth. That was the first I knew of it.

Ditchley never skipped a beat with Winston there. He was a very easy guest. We still had our servants in the first year of the war, and the house was run as I always ran it. The schedule never changed. He would arrive at teatime or drink time on Friday evening and ask for whatever he wanted and get it, but anyone could. If he came at tea, he would sit and chat in the library, then go upstairs to lie down before dinner. Often Friday evenings were the most interesting, because there weren't so many important people; he'd just have someone he really wanted to talk to. There would be Duff Cooper alone with Winston—not talking about the war, though; rather, having disagreements about literature and history. It was very much more interesting hearing Duff talk to Winston than hearing Anthony Eden talk to Winston. Duff had fire in his belly and had just as strong ideas as Winston. It was like watching a tennis match.

According to Tree, Churchill took his breakfast in his room—the Yellow Bedroom that overlooked the lake—between eight and nine o'clock. There he would remain in his nightshirt until lunch, reading the newspapers and working with his assistants on his dispatch boxes. Lunch was served in the dining room, and if "he was in a good mood"—that is, provided he found something optimistic in the war news he had received that morning—he stayed at the table "talking into the afternoon over brandy, before disappearing into the Chinese Room with his private secretary."[8] The Trees gave the prime minister the Chinese Room, Nancy's sitting room, as a study whenever he stayed at Ditchley. At five, Churchill returned to his room for a nap, from which he emerged dressed in his dinner jacket, to be seated at the dining room table at eight-thirty. If for some reason he was delayed upstairs, he sent a message down telling everyone to go ahead with dinner without him.

What did change were the faces. The one thing that I insisted on when Ronnie told me Winston would be coming regularly was that it should not be considered our house party; Winston should take it over and fill it with his guests. I refused to put myself in the position of annoying all my friends because they weren't invited; I didn't want to seem as though I was using him for social reasons. The only people that I ever asked, and only if there was an empty bed, were attractive women. He liked two of them that I had again and again: Daphne Straight, who he said was so pretty she must have grown up under a mushroom, and Freda Dudley Ward, whom he loved and was a great friend. Those were the only two people I invited. The Cranbornes, my most intimate friends, and the Coopers came to

In front of the orangery wing, Prime Minister Winston Churchill inspects soldiers of the Oxfordshire and Buckinghamshire Regiments, who were assigned to guard him when he stayed at Ditchley.

The prime minister's armored car

Taking a rare break from his war work, Churchill with Diana Cooper in front of
Ditchley

The third Churchill weekend during the war, December 14–16, 1940: from left,
Brendan Bracken, the parliamentary private secretary to the prime minister; Viscount
Cranborne, the government's Dominions Secretary; Richard Law, the financial
secretary to the War Office; Winston and Clementine Churchill; Viscountess
Cranborne; Ronald and Nancy Tree

In the spring of 1941, the prime minister, an anti-aircraft gun and a snake, on the terrace overlooking the pond at Ditchley

stay; but Bobberty and Duff both had very big jobs, so they were invited by Downing Street.

Churchill stayed at Ditchley for thirteen Friday-to-Monday weekends between November 1940 and September 1942. After the initial house party—which Tree thought "went well . . . the Prime Minister intimated that we had given satisfaction by saying he would be back five days later, 'high moon, or no high moon' "[9]—the Ditchley visitors' book began to fill up with the signatures of the most vital members of Great Britain's war effort, as well as Churchill's personal entourage, like Brendan Bracken.

Britain's most important military leaders called on Churchill at Ditchley. Major-General Sir Hastings "Pug" Ismay, the chief-of-staff to the Minister of Defense, was often there. He married a cousin of Ronald's and had become the Trees' close friend over the years. Admiral Thomas Phillips, the commander-in-chief of the Eastern Fleet, was there for the prime minister's second weekend at Ditchley, along with Field Marshal Sir Alan Brooke. During the course of the war, Brooke would serve as commander-in-chief of the Home Forces and later commander-in-chief of the Imperial General Staff. **I remember telling Pug Ismay that I didn't think Alan Brooke was going to be a big success with Winston. They were sitting either side of me at dinner with Win-**

ston questioning him about the strength of the British Army somewhere in Africa. Winston was saying to him, "We're twice as strong as the Germans there, aren't we?" Brooke replied, "No, sir." Winston said, "But we are just as strong." Brooke said, "No, sir, we're half as strong." Brooke kept on contradicting Winston. But as it was, Winston liked his candor. Another weekend General Sir John Dill stayed at Ditchley, the CIGS (Chief of the Imperial General Staff) before Brooke. Dill was the most charming man, a great gentleman and much more tactful than Brooke. But he was very tired. Winston exhausted him. He would expect Dill, who was quite old, to stay up until three in the morning talking, and Dill wasn't taking naps all day like Winston.

At that point in the war they used to put a Churchill decoy around to try to fool the Germans. Because so few people knew where the real Winston was when he stayed at Ditchley, some branch of intelligence mistakenly put a decoy at the back drive of Ditchley. If the Germans had come after the decoy, they would have got Sir Eric Pound, the admiral; they would have got the head of the army, Sir John Dill; they would have got the whole bag of works. Everybody was there that weekend, and the decoy was two miles from the house. Peter Portal was also there, the head of the air force. He was a most charming man. I was rather in love with him.

British political and civil leaders surrounded Churchill at Ditchley. His first weekend there included Lord Lothian, the ambassador to the United States; Anthony Eden, then the Secretary of State for War; Brenden Bracken; and Jim Thomas, the Junior Lord of the Treasury. During that weekend Churchill began dictating a lengthy personal letter to President Roosevelt outlining his assessment of the war and his country's specific needs; it was this appeal that led to Roosevelt's drafting of the Lend-Lease Act. Lothian delivered the letter to the White House upon his return to Washington.[10]

Duff Cooper spent a number of Churchill weekends at Ditchley. Old friends of the Trees, he and his beautiful wife, Lady Diana, had also been guests at Ditchley before the war. The Coopers were close to Winston and Clementine Churchill as well, remaining loyal friends during the years of Winston's political isolation in the 1930s. On one of these weekends, the prime minister's arrival at the front steps prompted Lady Diana to "[throw] her arms around his neck and [shriek] DARLING, how glad we are to see you!"[11] She wrote of a stay in a letter to her son:

> Great Excitement last week-end! We went to Ditchley where Winston was staying. Golly, what a to-do! To start with, the Prime Minister has a guard of fully-equipped soldiers. Two sentries are at every

door of the house to challenge you. I look very funny in the country these days, in brightly-colored trousers, trapper's fur jacket, Mexican boots and a refugee head cloth, so that on leaving the house I grinned at the sentries and said: "You will know me all right when I come back." However, when I did return the guard, I suppose, had been changed. I grinned at what I took to be the same two soldiers and prepared to brazenly pass, when I was confronted with two bayonets within an inch of my stomach. They no doubt thought that I was a mad German assassin out of the circus.

Winston does nearly all his work from his bed. It keeps him rested and young. . . . There is also a new reverence for so great a leader, and that creates an atmosphere of slight embarrassment until late in the evening. Also instead of old friends the guests included people called DMO and DMI . . . and an enchanting king of the Air Force, Sir Charles Portal, with a wife I used to play with as a child. . . . Brendan of course was there, and Venetia, also Winston's wife and beautiful, animated daughter Mary.[12]

In the effort to win American support for Britain, Churchill continually met with delegates from the United States. Downing Street invited Averell Harriman, Special Representative of President Roosevelt, to Ditchley in April of 1941, the same weekend as Jim Forrestal, the under-secretary of the U.S. Navy, and General H. H. Arnold, the U.S. Army Air Force deputy chief-of-staff. Arnold and Churchill worked out an agreement whereby British pilots would be sent to America for training. Certainly the most significant of Churchill's American guests was Roosevelt's personal friend and envoy Harry Hopkins. He met the prime minister over lunch at Downing Street on Friday, January 10, 1941; then the two traveled to Ditchley for the weekend. Hopkins was in England to assess British morale and its material wants; in those three or four days spent with Churchill, Hopkins became convinced, and through him the president, that Great Britain could not only hold out against the Germans but, if allied with the United States, eventually win the war. During his stay the finishing touches were put to the Lend-Lease Act and the Anglo-American alliance was further cemented.[13]

Jock Colville attended Churchill that weekend as the prime minister's personal assistant. In his diary entries he noted the importance they all attached to the visit, as well as some of their schedule while at Ditchley. On Friday night,

before dinner we drank and thawed while Winston pointed out, in reply to Mrs. Tree, that Wavell had done very well but that the Ital-

The Chief of Air Staff, Marshal Sir Charles Frederick Algernon Portal, known as Peter, weeding in the sunk parterre at Ditchley in the summer of 1941

ians were the sort of enemy against whom any General should be only too happy to be matched.

Dinner was an exquisite meal at which I sat next to Mrs. Tree. Afterwards Winston smoked the biggest cigar in history and became very mellow. There was an interlude in which I talked to the exceptionally pleasant Dinah [Brand], after which Winston retired to bed with a very full [dispatch] box and in an excellent temper while I whiled away time arranging the box in the beautiful working room below.[14]

In the dining room Ronnie sat at one head of the table while I sat at the other, with Winston on my right. The first thing with him was that he would never speak until he had a glass of champagne. Always Pol Roger. He had his first glass with the soup, then he would speak. The other thing was, he never spoke to his left or his right; he only spoke to the person sitting opposite him. He only liked to talk across the table, so that the person he wanted to talk to was seated on my left. And he didn't talk unless he wanted to talk; there was no polite conversation. I would put a pretty woman on Winston's right, and they would always come to me after dinner and

James Forrestal, under-secretary, U.S. Navy, in front of the Venetian screen in the great hall at Ditchley in 1941

say, "I was so nervous sitting next to Winston; he didn't say a thing." I'd always reply, "You'd be extremely nervous if he did speak." Sitting where I did, I was literally in the middle of his conversations with people like Dill or Brooke. I had rather fun listening. It certainly wasn't just social conversation.

Following dinner during Churchill's weekends, the Trees showed a film in the great hall. It was Ronald's idea that this would be a splendid way of entertaining the prime minister, and as Tree was in the Ministry of Information, he was able to solicit the newest releases from Britain's film industry. The first film they screened was *Lady Hamilton*,[15] the story of Emma Hamilton and Admiral Nelson; the movie quickly became Churchill's favorite, much to the annoyance of his closest associates, who would later have to watch it over and over again at his request. They also screened *Gone With the Wind*, *The Great Dictator*, *Brigham Young* and *Night Train to Munich*. Churchill often invited his cousins the Duke and Duchess of Marlborough to Ditchley from Blenheim Palace for dinner and a movie. The films were Churchill's only recreation at Ditchley, other than the conversation he might find at tea or after dinner, his cigar and his whiskey-and-soda. During all the weekends he was there he left the house only once, for a walk in the pleasure grounds.

Isaiah Berlin came for lunch to meet Winston. He had written brilliant papers for the prime minister, but they had never met before. In those days Berlin was working in the British embassy in Washington, so when he returned to England he was invited down for lunch to meet Winston. Unfortunately, Winston got rather mixed up as to who he was. He asked him, "Which one of your musical comedies is your favorite?"

Another weekend included a visit from the Duke of Hamilton, the reclusive Scottish peer who, for reasons never explained, was chosen by Hitler's deputy Rudolf Hess as the middleman for a peace proposal to the British government. Hess had landed in a light plane on Hamilton's estate the night before, Churchill was informed while watching *Lady Hamilton*; the duke was then asked to travel to Ditchley to be interviewed by the prime minister. I remember Hamilton's arrival at Ditchley but did not then know the reason. He was immediately closeted with Winston in the Velvet Room. In another room Mary Churchill was refusing a marriage proposal, while in another room Clemmie was saying to me, "The man is charming, but his interests are more suitable to me than to Mary."

Rounding out the prime minister's visits to Ditchley was his family. His wife, Clementine, accompanied him on each of the weekends and went to stay once on her own when she needed a solo holiday. The Churchills' eldest daughter, Diana, spent a weekend there with her husband, Duncan Sandys, an MP and the financial secretary in the War Office. And Mary, the Churchills' youngest child, traveled to Ditchley for at least half the weekends her parents were in residence:

I remember Ditchley as a silver lining. During wartime all pleasures and glittering occasions were tremendously valued. Life had become infinitely drab. London was so dreary; everything was sandbagged, and there was the blackout. My parents were living in an apartment over the Central War Rooms that was made up in great haste because Downing Street was a totally unsafe structure. Number 10 used to practically collapse every time a number 11 bus would rumble down Whitehall, let alone when bombs went off nearby. But there was Ditchley, like a stage set. There was the glowing interior: I suppose it was the first dining room I'd seen in my life lit entirely by candlelight. Nancy had a marvelous cook and that wonderful butler Collins. I'm sure they conformed to all the rules about rations and everything, but all the sorts of things, the creature comforts, that had absolutely gone down the drain for everybody else remained encapsulated at

Ditchley. Nancy knew about civilized living even under those desperate circumstances. My father liked it very much, and Mummy, who could be very critical of that sort of thing, loved staying at Ditchley.

It was a great thing they did for us, having us to stay, because it meant Ditchley was invaded by a very rum collection—everyone from the scrubby eighteen-year-old daughter to the private secretaries and visiting field marshals. I mean, anybody you'd like to mention. Nancy was a wonderful hostess . . . but there was more to it than that. Somebody else could have done the hostessing in the sense of ordering good food and getting enough places put around for lunch; but what was special was that Nancy never seemed nonplussed by all the people, who they were or what they were doing. She wasn't fazed by any of that side of it. Consequently it was very amusing, because the people who came to stay—the admirals and the chiefs of staff—probably only saw my father for a bit of the time during the day, and the rest of the time they had a ball, because Nancy herself was very electric, amusing company.

The other thing was that everybody dressed up very much at Ditchley, and I don't mean in a common way. Nobody wore evening dresses during the war, but when you went to Ditchley, there was no earthly reason not to; it was a nicely heated house. Nancy always dressed beautifully; she had the most lovely clothes. I specifically remember one night Papa was sitting up very late, as he liked to do, with the other guests. There were ten or twelve people in the room. Nancy was fed up and wanted to go to bed. She was talking, and as she was talking she started undoing her cuffs, then, still talking, undoing other buttons. My eyes started popping out of my head: She was getting dangerously low. She then rose up and leant against the mantelpiece and very, very slowly started undoing her zip. I remember her yawning and saying, "I'm very tired; I think I'm going to bed," and she walked through the room, following the zip down with, I assure you, her clothes hanging by a thread. The dress must have fallen to the floor as she went around the corner. It was the most astonishing exit I've ever seen in my life.

Neither by design nor by choice, but as a result of war, Nancy Tree became "the most important political hostess in the country."[16] At the same time Ditchley joined the centuries-long line of great country houses where British leaders surrounded themselves with their allies and enemies alike, well away from the fray of the capital city. Ironically, the house whose function

Ditchley had usurped was that of Nancy's aunt and uncle: Cliveden had been at the center of Britain's political universe for the past two decades.

Nannie did know, because I told her, but there was no rivalry. She was never at all resentful of Ditchley, but she did resent that I wouldn't have her there when Winston was staying. She'd call and ask, "How many whiskeys are you letting him have?" and "Why don't you have me?" I said, "I won't because you've been insulting about Winston and insulting about Anthony Eden and I'm not going to play with you."

The bad blood between Nannie and Winston went back to when she first entered Parliament. Winston had been a friend of hers and had stayed at Cliveden many times, but when she took her seat in the Commons, Winston above all the other men hated a woman being there and showed it. She could take it: I don't think anyone else could have been the first woman member. She was very strong, and she gave as good as she got. But I know his being so rude disturbed her, and from then on they continually insulted each other. Whenever Winston spoke in Parliament, Nannie interrupted his speeches and tried to rattle him. The truth is, they were alike; they were both *enfants terribles.*

There was a temporary peace when Winston went down and stayed at Plymouth, Nannie's constituency. Plymouth had stood the most horrible bombing. It was simply flattened. The very next day Nannie took all of the people of Plymouth—most had just lost their homes and their businesses and people they loved—got them out onto the Hooe, which is a palisade above the sea where she had her house, and started them dancing. She said, "We are not downhearted, are we?" and led them in dancing. Winston was terribly impressed by that.

Though Churchill was the most notable "evacuee" of German bombing to stay at Ditchley, many of the Trees' friends, acquaintances and colleagues took refuge at the estate on the weekends when the prime minister was elsewhere, while others stayed week in and week out for the duration of the war. Ditchley offered a fleeting oasis—something rather illusory—within the pervasive gray-and-green drab. General Ismay returned often, as did Antony and Dorothea Head. **Pug chose Antony for the war cabinet after meeting him at Ditchley. Following the war, Antony entered politics, became Secretary of State for War, then Minister of Defense. When he retired they made him a viscount.** Nancy's friend Baroness D'Erlanger arrived in a car piled high with her belongings. She and her daughter lived in one of Ditchley's cottages dur-

Mary Churchill with her father's dog, c. 1940

ing the war. **I'll never forget Edwina arriving with her child, her maid and the bed-head from her London house that had *Enfin Seule* embroidered on it.** Noël Coward went for a weekend early in the war; Ève Curie, a daughter of Madame Curie, stayed with the Trees often, having been forced to flee France. David Niven spent his honeymoon with his first wife, Primula, at Ditchley. Niven was a friend of Nancy's Aunt Nora and enlisted in the same regiment as Michael and Jakie Astor. **I think it was Michael who first brought him to Ditchley. He thought he had charm, and he certainly did work it, didn't leave a stone unturned. He used to say, "I'm fighting the war for Ditchley." Full of baloney. I remember before he got married he fell madly in love with a girl who used to stay with us. Every time she went to put on her coat to go outside, she would find a note from him in her sleeve. It was all too obvious; you could see the workings of the machinery. He did, however, give up his career—he was the first of all those actors—to come back and fight.**

Ronald Tree's work during the war as the parliamentary private secretary to consecutive Ministers of Information—John Reith, Duff Cooper and Brendan Bracken—and as an advisor to the Ministry on American Affairs brought him into contact with many journalists covering the war for the American media. They invariably found their way to Ditchley. The "doyen" of the press corps, Edward R. Murrow, and Mary Welsh, the future wife of Ernest Hemingway, were both guests. Helen Kirkpatrick was a correspondent for the Chicago *Evening News.* Her office was across from the Trees' house in Queen Anne's Gate, and it was she who informed Tree that the government had tapped his phones. She was invited down often and, in a letter to Nancy in later years, especially recalled "sitting to the left of the house one warm Sunday morning: Ronnie, Jim Thomas, Dick Law and one or two other MPs, perhaps Bobberty, all discussing the necessity for getting Chamberlain out. [Nancy] had been cutting flowers and came wandering by, paused, heard the trend of the talk and announced: 'Why all this talk; you all know what you should do, now go ahead and do it.' It electrified them." She also remembered the image of Brendan Bracken sitting "perched like a great Buddha in one of [Nancy's] lovely four posters—reading from a red Gov't dispatch box."

Another journalist to visit Ditchley was North Carolinian Ben Robertson, covering news for *P.M.* In 1941 he published a first-person account of contemporary British politics and politicians called *I Saw England.* In it, with the ear of a fellow Southerner, he recorded the typical Langhorne repartee that he witnessed:

> One day [Lady Astor] told me that Lady Oxford had said that Nancy Astor was too stupid to think and too reckless to pray. I burst into laughter. "Brother, what are you laughing at?" inquired Lady Astor. (She calls everyone "Brother.") "I think it's funny," I said. "It is funny," she said, "but you laughed too quick."
>
> I like the quality she has of take as well as give. One time she said to her brilliant niece, Nancy Tree: "Nancy, you ought to get interested in politics." Nancy Tree replied: "I am interested in politics— I've been interested in politics for eighteen months, and during that time I have never seen a windjammer veer in the wind as you have." Lady Astor laughed.[17]

Robertson also wrote of Nancy Tree's main wartime occupation, one beyond looking after Ditchley and her guests: She commanded a corps of mobile canteens that traveled to bombed areas carrying food to the victims. Robertson was in Coventry the day after a German raid had all but razed the entire city:

> Near by there was a mobile canteen, and about it were tired, battle-worn men and women, eating bread and stew. Nancy Tree was there with her mobile canteens. She had been working all the night before and all that day, and with her were several farmers' wives from Oxfordshire, several footmen's wives, a groom's wife, and Leonora Corbet, the London actress, and the Duchess of Marlborough.

Nancy Tree playing darts with David Niven and soldiers billeted near Ditchley. In his memoir, Niven wrote of Nancy's "sublime taste," how "it was fascinating to rub shoulders with the greats" at Ditchley, and that Churchill said to him when they met, "You did a fine thing to give up a most promising career to fight for your country" (Niven, pp. 209, 211, 222).

Refugees from the Blitz: Baroness Edwina D'Erlanger and her daughter

Helen Kirkpatrick, correspondent for the Chicago *Daily News*, and David Bruce, right, who was then officially attached to the American Red Cross

The American journalist Ben Robertson, left, was a guest at Ditchley. He was killed when the Pan Am Clipper he was a passenger on crashed in Lisbon in 1941.

Nancy had her sleeves rolled up and was dipping out stew with both hands. She said never in her life had she seen such grateful people as these bombed citizens of Coventry. One man, she said, had told her he had lost his wife, his children, and his home, and when she had given him a bowl of stew he had asked her how much he owed.[18]

The Coventry raid occurred during Churchill's second stay at Ditchley; they had all heard the bombers flying overhead after dark.

I was called by someone at the YMCA, around four o'clock in the morning. I'd been up very late with a big party for Winston. Winston thought it wonderful and gallant that I got up and drove my canteens to Coventry; he didn't know I was kicked out of bed by Ronnie. I kept saying, "I don't want to go." Winston was leaning out of the window and waved as we went. He already knew about the bombing.

I was the first canteen into Coventry. It was like a theater without a backdrop. I'd never seen anything like it. It was just nothing. When I returned home, Winston called me in and questioned me about details of the condition of the city. That afternoon he motored there, hoping his presence would lift the morale of its citizens.

At its peak Nancy's corps included more than one hundred canteens—all of them financed by appeals she made to friends and acquaintances in America, some of them manned by farmers' wives and her women friends living at Ditchley.

We made our first canteen just after war was declared. Ronnie was convinced that the Germans would start to bomb London and other cities right away, and that there would be a need for mobile soup kitchens that could go right to the people affected. We were going to convert my old horse box that we had used for hunting—the military had come and taken all my hunters and shipped them out to somewhere like Egypt—but Ronnie's secretary, Mr. Bolongaro, found us an old fish and chips shop on wheels that was for sale.

One late May afternoon in 1940 I was suddenly called to the telephone from the tennis court, where we were playing with Anthony Eden, who was down at Ditchley for the weekend. Winston had just been made prime minister and Anthony was the Minister of War. On the phone was the area colonel for YMCA canteens. He said, "Mrs. Tree, will you bring your canteen at once to Churchill station." Churchill was a small village not far from Ditchley. When we arrived, train after train was shunting through Churchill, with soldiers and sailors in every type of uniform from every sort of regiment hanging out of the windows. Many of them were French. We couldn't make tea quick enough. I was there for a good twenty-four hours, night and day, but I had no real idea what was going on. It was the evacuation from Dunkirk. By the time I got back to Ditchley, the War Office had sent for Anthony, but at the time he had no idea either.

After Dunkirk the War Office saw the need for more canteens like ours and asked me to help organize a corps in connection with the YMCA. I raised funds by asking people to donate money in the name of someone like their mother or father or girlfriend, someone who was dead or someone they wanted to die, and I would put a plaque on the canteen that said, "This was given by Mrs. Jones in memory of Mr. Smith," something like that. I gave the person who ran each canteen the address of whoever donated it so they could write and keep them informed as to their wanderings. We had one given by the city of Richmond; a lot from New York; one canteen was given entirely by Germans in New York. Over forty canteens came from various chapters of Bundles for Britain. Others came from the Garden Club of Virginia, the Foxcroft Alumnae, Billy Delano, the Jockey Club of New York, Mary Filley, Charlotte Noland and so on. David Bruce gave us three canteens. When I sent letters to all these people asking for the canteens, they said I wrote so badly I must be honest.

Nancy's canteens followed closely on the heels of air raids at Portsmouth, Plymouth and Southampton. "I remember one morning very, very clearly," Churchill's daughter, Mary, said, "when I was having a lovely lie-in in bed and a late breakfast. I went to look downstairs for Nancy; I think I had broken something in my room. I asked Collins if he had seen Mrs. Tree and he replied, 'Mrs. Tree, Madame, left this morning before dawn. She's out with her canteen.' I remember it very clearly. The night before she was this extraordinary hostess in this *avant déluge* setting . . . then she was gone by two or three o'clock in the morning. She was the sort of person who did that sort of thing in a very wry, offhanded manner." Nancy was made a colonel in the Southern Command and was meant to wear the colonel's uniform. Since my hair and skin were very near the khaki color of the army uniform, I decided to opt for the whipcord suit and blue collar of the YMCA uniform instead. Aunt Nancy said to me, "As you are neither young, a man, nor much of a Christian, I don't know why you're dressed as one."

Nancy Tree in uniform

Nancy presenting her canteen volunteers to Queen Elizabeth

•   •   •

I remember thinking I was living very much the same life that my
father's mother led, who in the Civil War was on the plantation very
near Appomattox. She used to describe to me when I was a little girl
what life was like during the war: the children sent to a farm back in
the woods, a sort of shooting place, because they were afraid of the
danger, and how they took the silver and buried it in the garden and
planted peas on it. It seemed in my imagination that was very much
what was happening to us in England.

OTHER HOUSES

When I was at school at Foxcroft in 1914, a few of my friends and I went into Washington by train for an afternoon where we consulted Mr. Dodds the fortune teller. When it was my turn, he said to me, "You are going into decorating." I didn't know what he was talking about; it meant nothing to me at the time. Decorating as we know it now didn't exist. To me it meant plaster on the ceiling like icing on a cake. I thought he was mad. Then I bought a box of wonderful chocolates, got on a train and went home.

PART ONE

NANCY WAS ALWAYS "doing up" something from the moment she and Ronald settled in England. Kelmarsh and Ditchley were the most notable houses she decorated between the wars, but there were a number of smaller projects on which she bestowed her intuitive gifts. Possessed of a strong sense of what was beautiful in houses and how this beauty could be accomplished, as well as a compulsive urge to raid antiques shops and auction sales, Nancy created a number of "little gems," including cottages and London town houses for herself and Ronald, suites and individual rooms for her aunts Nancy Astor and Phyllis Brand, and at least one entire house for a friend. Her instinct for "knowing what a house needs" was just as clear and exceptional in a modest house as it was on a large scale.

Nancy turned the Victorian dower house at Kelmarsh, called the Wilderness, into a smart hunting box where her family could live while restoration and decoration proceeded at the Hall. She remorselessly smashed down walls to make larger, lighter rooms filled with pale colors, faded chintz and simple, painted fruitwood furniture, then added a formal box garden using a design from the Alhambra. (The box bushes were shaped into topiary teddy bears.) Once they had bought Ditchley and work had begun in earnest on the interior of that mansion, the Trees needed an on-site home where they could watch over the progress of their army of architects, contractors and builders: something similar to the cottage at Mirador or the Wilderness. For this purpose Nancy decorated the Home Farm farmhouse, in a hollow just below the main house's stable wing. Compared with restoring houses the size of Kelmarsh Hall or Ditchley, decorating the farmhouse must have seemed like child's play. It was pretty but plain, a frill-less two stories built in the shape of an L, with four strong chimneys and a solid, hipped roof. The house was faced in the same white-turning-golden stone as the manor house; beyond that, all similarities ceased. Inside, it had no intrinsic dressing for a decorator to sidle up to, no plaster or stucco work by a heralded eighteenth-century craftsman to tiptoe around. The farmhouse presented Nancy with a blank page to draw on: bare walls and ceilings, sloping oak floorboards and an orderless array of rooms, including one near the kitchen for the family cow. In contrast to bigger houses, where part of the work was to reinvigorate embellishments already in place, the farmhouse possessed no details. Likewise, it offered no clues to guide the decorator's hand.

To create one large central room, Nancy pulled down walls again; she then transformed the new living room into a tableau of *haute* taste.

> I had Kick paint the walls a dark, shiny green like the porcelain lamps you see in China. It was a marvelous color that gave the room a personality. Then I furnished it with antique bamboo armchairs I had collected and painted white, with the rings in the bamboo picked out in brown. The curtains and seat cushions were white linen, very cheap stuff like canvas. The curtains hung down very simply and had no pelmets. I always had very cheap things done for cottages; no silks or anything like that. The rugs were modern, white cotton fringed with claret red.
>
> Because I made the room from two smaller ones, it now had two fireplaces. They were completely asymmetrical to each other—one in one wall on the inside width of the room, the other at the far end of the length—making the room cockeyed. In front of the fireplaces I put the skins of zebras that I had shot during a walking safari in Africa.
>
> We would use this room for shooting lunches, so I had two corner sofas made to fit the angle of the room and two pedestal tables that had leaves you pulled out. End to end the tables seated about sixteen people; I used the sofas as banquettes. I covered them in the white linen, and the tabletops I painted a trompe l'oeil marble on a

dark green ground. I wouldn't hesitate to have furniture made for a specific room or a copy made of something I liked, especially in a cottage, where the good furniture I bought wouldn't fit in. You can't really have things copied now, it's too expensive, but then I would have what I wanted made to order and fabrics and rugs dyed or faded.

By the time I decorated the farmhouse at Ditchley, Mrs. Bethel had died; and as I didn't have a shop of my own, I used Syrie Maugham. Her people made the curtains for me, and the sofas; I found one of the pedestal tables in her shop. Mrs. Bethel had a great sense of history and a true feeling for houses, but Mrs. Maugham was much more original. She was the starter of crazes in decorating. When she had a blue period, everyone went blue. I think it was she who began pickling furniture. The pickling fashion was a shame; so much beautiful furniture was ruined that way. I preferred the old paint.

Before the war Mrs. Maugham asked me to go into business with her. She described it to me . . . she said, "If we go into business together, we'll have a big room and drape the whole thing with fabric like a circus tent. You'll sit in a booth at one end and I'll sit in a booth at the other, and we'll see our clients there." I can't imagine anything I'd have liked less. But I liked her.

What had been the dairy room in the farmhouse I made into our dining room. I had great fun with that. I got canvas and stretched it over the rough walls and got Kick to paint it in green stripes: wide, apple green stripes about an inch and a half or two inches thick. I copied the idea from some old Swedish wall hangings that Mrs. Maugham had in her hall in London. And again I used bamboo chairs and a table painted white with knots picked out in green. You could have ten people around the table at once. The floor I covered in Norfolk rush matting, and I had sideboards made for the room that you put the dishes on.

Once the Trees moved into the big house at Ditchley, the cottage was often loaned to friends. When they used it as a rest stop during shooting parties, its interior existed as a slightly exotic folly hidden beneath the common, flat, stone facade; the shiny green walls and zebra skins created an oasis of brilliant color in the monochromatic surroundings of an English park in winter. The guests spied the ordinary building standing in front of them that not many years before had housed farmworkers and livestock. Inside, they discovered a pasha's tent of luxury: two roaring fires, comfortable sofas and chairs, a table laid out with silver and crystal, and plates of venison stew.

· · ·

NANCY'S AUNTS AND COUSINS in England took advantage of her taste, borrowing from her know-how and her trove of ideas. At Cliveden before the war she decorated a suite of rooms for her cousin Wissy, and Lady Astor asked her to enliven a number of bedrooms at the Astors' palatial town house on St. James's Square in London. After Wissy married James Willoughby d'Eresby, the son and heir of the Earl of Ancaster, Nancy helped her with the dower house at his family's seat, Grimsthorpe Castle, where they lived.

Nancy not only helped Phyllis and Bob Brand with painting and furniture for Eydon Hall after they bought it; she discovered the house for them in the first place. **I saw Eydon one morning in 1927 when I was out hunting. We were in the far corner of Pytchley country, south of Northampton. It was extraordinary because the Pytchley ran into the Grafton as they hunted the neighboring country, and the two packs ended up chasing the same fox together. Without hesitating for a minute, our huntsman Frank Freeman took both packs and hunted them over a third country that bordered ours and the Grafton's, called the Bicester. There was an enormous field following them . . . it was a historic day.**

As we rode over the Bicester I saw this marvelous house on a hill that reminded me of Bremo, one of the most beautiful houses in Virginia. My mind is always on Virginia, there's no doubt about it; I'm always thinking of Virginia. At that moment I was torn, being the wife of the Joint Master of the Pytchley, whether I should continue on this historic chase or look at the house. I went to look at the house. I rode right up to the front door and said, "Can I telephone for my car?" That's how I got in to see Eydon. I wrote to Phyllis— she was mad about hunting but lived in Herefordshire, where nothing ever happens—and said to her that I'd found a house that looked like Bremo and that she must buy it. She wrote me back to tell me I was crazy, but when I returned from a trip to Mirador a few months later, Bob had bought her the house.

Eydon would come close to replacing Mirador in Phyllis's imagination. She pined for Mirador as all the Langhornes in England did, but as it had once belonged to her, there was an added element to her longing. On the outside Eydon possessed the same out-of-the-blue posture that many of the plantation houses in Virginia had; though it was surrounded by manicured parklands rather than wooded colonial wilderness, it too shot straight up from nowhere, a tall, square Palladian villa superimposed on the decidedly un-Italianate Northamptonshire countryside. Its two-storey entrance porch was a feature Virginian tobacco growers commissioned for their houses; its thin Doric columns were the first features someone approaching the house noticed. And age had tempered Eydon. It had been completed in 1791, and trees and the gardens had grown around it to give the estate the aura of continuity that graced many of the houses in the Old Dominion. Eydon became for Phyllis very much what Kelmarsh had become for Nancy.

At Eydon I painted the hall the same pink color I painted the hall at Kelmarsh. I painted Aunt Phyllis's sitting room, a rounded room in the bowed side of the house, a sulfur yellow. I also bought some of the furniture for Eydon. They brought most of it from Ferneaux Pelham, their old house—Phyllis had a very good eye for furniture—but I bought her a lovely four-poster bed and a very pretty eighteenth-century desk. I found two wonderful black leather chairs—I wish I had them now—their backs looked like giant mushrooms. She had them by the fire in the hall.

Eydon, Cliveden, Ditchley: There were as many extraordinary houses in the extended family as there were members of Parliament. (The Anglo-Palladian masterpiece called Nostel Priory was added to the list of family destinations when Nancy's sister, Alice, married Reginald Winn, whose family's ancestral home it was.) So for a brief moment in the first half of the twentieth century, the family in England lived somewhat as their forebears had in Virginia in the first half of the nineteenth, when brothers, sisters, aunts, uncles and grandparents all had plantations and plantation houses and each family regularly descended on the others like a plague of locusts. The contemporary evolution of their progress was an English version, though, rather more grand and refined; no one played the fiddle on the back porch of Earl Beatty's Dingley Hall.

One of the houses I was proudest of doing was also one of the ugliest. Champion Lodge had a ridiculous charm all its own. It was the best thing I ever did, but the house was perfectly hideous. A Victorian "monster"—dark, gloomy and haunted—the lodge sat upon a hillock surrounded by the fields and pastures of Essex. It was a typical smaller nobleman's house of the period: a linsey-woolsey of gables, bays, stained glass and conicals confusing the already distracted redbrick exterior—the antithesis of the Georgian order and grace found at Kelmarsh and Ditchley. What attracted Nancy to the place was what was inside, its personality. Something she loved emanated from the family that lived there. Champion Lodge was the seat of the de Crespignys, Jubie Lancaster's mother's family, the home of a unique race of soldiers and sportsmen.

When Lancaster first took Nancy to see the Lodge, in the 1920s, his grandfather Sir Claude Champion de Crespigny still lived there. Old Sir Claude had been the beau ideal of High Victorian adventurer, a true man of empire. Sailor, soldier, white hunter, foxhunter, bare-knuckled boxer, swimmer and steeplechase jockey: at home he was known as the "Sporting Baronet of Essex," while in the army he was called "Mad Rider."[1]

> Crawley used to tell me wonderful stories about his father, how when he was seventy he and another man went to the cliffs on the Isle of Wight, clasped hands and jumped into the sea together. That was the kind of thing he did, even in his old age. When Crawley was young, every morning Sir Claude would take his five sons on a steeplechase; that's where they all learned to be such fearless riders. They would all come back with broken noses and separated shoulders. Then in the afternoon Sir Claude would walk over to see Lady Warwick; he was rather keen on old Lady Warwick at one time. Every afternoon Sir Claude would walk the twenty miles to Warwick Castle to see her. And every afternoon his five sons would follow him. He was like an old duck with five little ducklings following behind him; they all walked twenty miles to see Daddy's girlfriend!
>
> I remember that Lady de Crespigny was very, very pretty. She was something to do with the Vivien family, who were all mad as hatters. She said to me once, "My dear, my hair is getting a little thin here in the front. Do you think if I *shaaaved* it back, it would grow thicker?" She was charming, and very old-fashioned. She made both the doctor and the parson go to the side door of the house . . . they weren't allowed in the front door. And she expected the people in the village to curtsy when she passed.
>
> I met most of the five sons. They were the best-looking, most fascinating men you can imagine. They were all named Claude So-and-So Champion de Crespigny, but they were called Creepy, Crawley, Phil, Vere and Norman. Every one of them was a marvelous jockey and polo player; they all went out to Africa to shoot big game; they all had tremendous military records. And every one of them was wonderful looking, the kind of men Uncle Dana drew. That ilk is gone forever.

Nancy decorated Champion Lodge for Sir Claude's heir, Crawley, after Sir Claude died in 1936. Brigadier-General Sir Claude Raul Champion de Crespigny, Baronet, CB, CMG, DSO, was an officer in the Grenadier Guards and a true hero of the First World War.

For his career as a professional soldier, before and during the First World War, General de Crespigny was made Companion of the Order of the Bath, the Order of St. Michael and St. George, and the Distinguished Service Order, in addition to receiving countless decorations, including the Queen's Medal with four clasps in the South African War.

I wish I had been born into that era. That's the sort of people I like. He was absolutely straightforward; there was no subtlety to him. It was quite easy for Crawley to say "Go to hell"; he meant it and wasn't afraid to live with the consequences. To him everything was bang, bang, bang; black is black and white is white, and he could care less what people thought. I was always very proud that Crawley de Crespigny was fond of me.

He really was my type. For instance, he went through the whole 1914–18 War with ulcers and never missed a day of duty. I admired his courage. But he was more than twenty years older than me, so it never would have worked. Besides being a soldier, he was his own white hunter; when he went into the African bush every year after big game, he was his own guide. He knew how to track every sort of animal there: lions, rhinoceroses, even bongos. In the early thirties, before we moved to Ditchley, Esme Glyn and I went on a walking safari with Crawley. We had around sixty native porters to carry our gear, but it wasn't the kind of safari where you rolled along in Land

"I've only got one talent," said Nancy. "I can feel a house . . . I can feel the personality of a house. . . . Champion Lodge had a ridiculous charm all its own."

Nancy Tree with
Crawley de Crespigny
at Champion Lodge
in the mid-1930s

Rovers and slept in treetop shelters. We walked the whole way. We walked ten miles in the morning and ten miles in the afternoon. We walked up lions the way we would walk up partridges in England. Once, we got into the middle of a herd of wild buffaloes. I was shooting left, right and center. I nearly died, I was so frightened, because they are one animal who will turn and stalk you right back. I also shot two lions.

Crawley found the game by following animal spoor. If the spoor was fresh, we knew what animal it was. I remember saying that if anyone had told me that my life would depend on the droppings of animals, I would have thought they were crazy.

Champion Lodge served as an enormous trophy case for prizes from various de Crespigny trips to Africa and for the commendations and mementos received from their careers in the military. **On every inch of every wall, right up to the ceiling, along the stairs and the gallery, were eighteenth- and nineteenth-century pictures and family portraits cheek-and-jowl with big-game trophies. There would be a portrait of some distinguished de Crespigny great-aunt with a huge bosom, then right next to her, practically coming out of the bosom, would be a rhinoceros's horn. I thought it was frightfully funny. There were animal skins all over the floor, mirrors mounted between pairs of tusks, and elephants' feet used for flowerpots. On all the sofas were cushions that Lady de Crespigny had made from the hatbands of her son Phil's sailor hats; he had been to sea since he was fourteen. Another feature Lady de Crespigny used was very chic: She covered the dining room chairs with the skins of zebras her boys had shot. They were frightfully modern, but they had been there for fifty years.**

Champion Lodge looked like a boardinghouse by the sea in America, but it had immense charm because of the de Crespignys and their history. It had its own aroma, and it seemed to me the key was to retain that aroma, not to try to turn the house into something it wasn't. Trying to make the interior Georgian would have been entirely inappropriate. So I left the awful carved staircase and gallery stained a sort of Pullman-car oak, because the color fit the house; and I left all the portraits and antlers. What I tried to do was to lighten everything up. I took old curtains that I found when we bought Ditchley, tore out the lining, and used the lining to make curtains for Champion Lodge. It was Victorian fabric, so it didn't spoil the atmosphere. I put a lot of old faded chintz in the sitting room; instead of new chintz I used it secondhand from Ditchley. The two sitting rooms on the ground floor were joined together by

Hunting trophies and souvenirs of empire cluttered the interior of Champion Lodge.

double doors, so I bought an enormous bookcase for Crawley and put it over the doors; I like to have four walls around me.

Upstairs they had a lot of brass and iron beds, so, as I did at the Wilderness, I cut the heads and the feet right off and had headboards covered with chintz made to replace them. That rather freshened the rooms up. For another bedroom I got yellow wallpaper with white dots from Syrie Maugham, and I used American candlewick for curtains and to cover the bed.

The plumbing and the bathrooms were done by Mr. Brace. Mr. Brace came from Arthingworth, where he had a young wife and an idiot child. He had helped me with all sorts of jobs at Cottesbrooke, Kelmarsh and Ditchley . . . anything I wanted done Mr. Brace could do. He even made lovely stars for the Christmas tree out of tin biscuit boxes for me. He was a marvelous carpenter and an intimate friend. So when I decorated Champion Lodge, he and his son came and put in three bathrooms. The two of them lived in a tent all summer. Mr. Brace wore a hairnet on his head when he worked, to keep the hair out of his eyes. Crawley roared with laughter; he couldn't get over it.

I was more proud of Champion Lodge than I was of any other house I've ever decorated. I certainly never did another like it. But it wasn't for what I did there that I was proud, but what I didn't do. I didn't put my stamp on the house; I showed restraint. Even if it's not a style of architecture or period you like, a decorator has to have a feel for a house's personality and try not to fight against it. I like to get the juice out of a house and not spoil it.

PART TWO

The English always traveled "up to London." They went up to London even if it meant taking the overnight train down from a grouse moor in Scotland, or driving in from a country house to the east or west. What it signified was London's monumental importance in the lives of the English, no matter where they were; London was always "up" metaphorically if not physically. London was the very summit of the English race, the peak of politics, commerce and society for their nation, their empire and, to a certain extent, the entire world. Between the wars Westminster still ruled the waves and a third of the earth's surface; the City remained at the height of the global financial markets; Soho dominated the stage; while the cocktail and dinner parties of Mayfair and Belgravia were simply "the tops."

The Trees kept houses in London from the moment they were married. They rented their first, at 9 Berkeley Square, after their honeymoon and had it until the end of the summer, when they returned to Mirador.

It was a charming house right next to Gunther's, where you had tea and ice cream. Nancy Astor's butler, Lee, found servants for me, and hired all the silver and linen I would need. People did that sort of thing then. We also got a key to Berkeley Square, which was a private garden. In Mayfair all of the houses on all of the streets were private houses where families lived in those days. Now they're all offices or broken up into flats, but back then a single family would live in them with their army of servants.

Beautiful in places, London was a slightly quirky, unorganized, democratic city, one of human scale accented with magnificent displays of power and wealth; a city of trees, of squares that weren't square, of winding streets and peculiar alleyways planned seemingly without rhyme or reason other than to confound a foreigner. There were still remote country houses in the center of London. We were dinner guests of Lord and Lady Ilchester at Holland House between the wars. It was practically opposite Harrod's, but when you went through the gates there were cow pats on the drive. It was so surprising. Lord Ilchester even had a shoot on his London estate. At the same time, one might travel from one corner of London to another via the Underground, the most advanced mass transit system in the world. Indeed, London in the 1920s and '30s was a city of contrasts and contradictions brought on by the dawn of the Modern World upon the Old; it was both artifact and artifice: part brick and coal soot, part hot air; a town of brilliant flourish, of shrill steel and joyous songbirds.

The renowned London Season took place at the end of spring and beginning of summer. It had changed very little in the past decades and retained all the pomp—and all the costuming—tradition dictated. Sporting events like the Derby, Ascot, Goodwood, Henley and Wimbledon were all exquisite parades of state and fashion. The private view of the Summer Show at the Royal Academy started the Season on a highbrow note, though it was more a party than a serious contemplation of contemporary British art. It was not an event Nancy had on her calendar every year, but in 1928 the portrait Munnings painted of her and Michael was one of the pictures exhibited. The Trees also attended the Fourth of June at Eton when one of their sons was attending the school; a reunion *cum* parents' day, it consisted of picnic lunches out of the back of Rolls-Royces, a daylong cricket match, tea, the Procession of Boats, picnic suppers out of the same Rolls-Royces and a fireworks display. The opera season at Covent Garden began the first of May; Ronald sat on Covent Garden's Board of Trustees starting in 1936.

In the spring of 1935 the Trees were "commanded to attend" a ball at Buckingham Palace celebrating the Silver Jubilee of King George V and Queen Mary. Ronald was taken ill the day before and was confined to his bed. "My only recollections of the memorable day," he wrote, "are that of irritation caused to my ears by the cheers and shouts of thousands of happy citizens who surged up Birdcage Walk on their way to the Palace; and of my wife, resplendent in her aunt's . . . immense tiara, returning from the ball at Buckingham Palace."[2]

Nannie loaned me some of the Astor diamonds for the ball. We were in the middle of one of our fracases then and I was not speaking to her, so when she very kindly offered to loan me the diamonds, I said I would wear them if it only meant a temporary truce and did not mean I would have to speak to her afterwards. Magnanimously she agreed, and I sallied forth wearing a huge tiara which had the famous Sancy Diamond at its center, the diamond Charles IX of France wore on his head at the Battle of Nancy. Old Lord Astor had given it to her. I dined before the ball with the Duke and Duchess of Buccleuch, where I sat next to someone who said, "I've never seen such a beautiful diamond as the one in your tiara. What is it?" I said, "All I know is that it's legitimate, because it has two names."

Nancy Tree wearing her Aunt Nancy Astor's tiara for King George V's Silver Jubilee Ball at Buckingham Palace. "I sent a friend in Virginia the photograph of me in the tiara and she wrote to Nannie asking why Waldorf didn't give her jewelry as beautiful as the tiara Ronnie gave Nancy. I've never been so embarrassed."

Going up the steps in Buckingham Palace, I was walking with a young man who had also been at the dinner and who I had teased miserably about something or another all night. He said to me, "I must tell you, your tiara is just a little bit crooked. Here, let me straighten it." He then got me back by making it completely crooked for our entrance into the ball.

You weren't supposed to wear black to the ball, but I said, with all those diamonds, I'm certainly going to wear black. So I wore black tulle and had the Sancy Diamond on my head, diamonds as big as rocks in my ears and around my neck, and a diamond stomacher sitting on my bosom that kept pulling my dress down. People didn't show their bosom in those days, so everybody kept looking at me because the diamonds were pulling down my dress. I've never had so much stuff on in my entire life.

What I remember most about the ball itself was that the people there who were really *marvelous* were the men. The women didn't look like anything at all; they all had too much jewelry. But the men wore knee breeches on their wonderful legs and uniforms with epaulets on just one shoulder and were all draped with ribbons and medals. And their faces—the women's faces looked somehow too small for everything they were wearing—the men's faces looked like they were carved out of granite: sharp, chiseled features. I also thought the ballroom at the palace looked beautiful that night. There were tiers of bright red and this wonderful silver gilt all over the sideboards along the walls down the room. Silver on violent red. It was really lovely.

The Trees attended the coronation of King George VI and Queen Elizabeth two years later, in 1937. They had known the couple as the Duke and Duchess of York from their days hunting with the Pytchley and were included at the ceremony because Tree was a Member of Parliament. Ronald wrote: "The Coronation was a glorious occasion. Living in Queen Anne's Gate, it was only a stone's throw to the Abbey and we started off early in the morning on foot, I dressed in a black velvet court suit, feeling very self-conscious, and my wife in an evening dress and a tiara bought specially for the occasion. Blue velvet seats were provided for the guests and we sat high up over the transept."[3] The Trees saw the steady stream of formally clad dignitaries from all over the world march up the isles of Westminster Abbey. Elected officials, dynastic princes, emissaries, military officers, it was the last parade of its kind before the onset of the Second World War and one of the last great displays ever of such vivid ceremonial conceit.

After the coronation all our friends came back to Queen Anne's Gate with us for a party; because we were so close to Westminster Abbey everyone could walk; the traffic in London was horrible that day. I remember Lord and Lady Bute, who lived next door to us, returning home an hour after we did. Everybody important like the Butes rode to and from the coronation in their gold state carriages, drawn by horses. The carriages swayed so much they got seasick. I remember all of us looking out the window to see Lord and Lady Bute get out of their carriage, in their robes, both of them looking quite green and wobbly, with their coronets down over their eyes, resting on their noses.

The following summer the *Times* of London reported that "Mrs. Ronald Tree regrets that owing to absence abroad she was prevented from obeying their Majesties' Command to be present at the Garden Party yesterday afternoon." She did, however, attend the Royal Ball in June of 1938 at Buckingham Palace. "Oh how heavenly it was!" wrote Joyce Grenfell to her mother, Nora. "I have never enjoyed anything so much before."[4] It was held in the ballroom where debutantes were presented every spring, with tiers of red-brocade-covered chairs, a musicians' gallery at one end, the king's and queen's thrones at the other. As the royal couple entered the room the band played the National Anthem—"the emotion was terrific"—they then began the ball by dancing together to "Love Walked In."

All of the tradition surrounding the Season and the various royal celebrations, the weight of the ermine and the tightness of the breeches, was lifted and lightened a bit by the younger generation between the wars. This was the Trees' generation, the Bright Young Things, the sole survivors from their class of the Great War. The Prince of Wales, before his ascension to the throne and his abdication, was at their vanguard. The same deep gasp of relief, the same ecstasy, that drove the hunting field after Armistice was even more pronounced in London. Jazz was everywhere, and the lyrics of Cole Porter and Noël Coward were on everyone's lips. After the formal dinner parties and balls of the Season and the "Little Season," off they all went to the favorite nightclubs, to the Embassy, the 400 and Café de Paris, to dance the Charleston and the Black Bottom. They rarely retired before dawn. Ronald remembered MPs arriving for debates or important votes in the Commons still in white tie and tails from the night before.

Emerald Cunard and Sibyl Colefax cleverly bridged the generations between the young and their more adventurous seniors at a time when society was slowly loosening its starched collar. The "bewitching" Lady Cunard lived in a grand house on Grosvenor Square that possessed a candlelit, "rococo atmosphere." It was at her house "that the great met the gay, that statesmen consorted with society, and writers with the rich. . . . Emerald's only . . . failures," wrote Chips Channon, "were the two Queens and Lady Astor and Lady Derby."[5] Her guest list overlapped with Lady Colefax's, with whom she competed for "conquests." At the Colefaxes' Argyll House, on the King's Road in Chelsea, one might have joined Virginia Woolf, Vanessa Bell and Duncan Grant at the dining table, or sat cross-legged on the sitting room floor next to Prince Edward, Louis Mountbatten and the Coopers while Arthur Rubinstein or Noël Coward—on one evening, one after the other— played the piano. Lady Colefax got H. G. Wells and G. B. Shaw to come to the same dinner by writing to each of them that the other longed to meet him.

You would always receive postcards from Sibyl in her illegible handwriting, asking, "Will you come to my Ordinary on such and such a date?" or "Would you dine with me so and so night?" She was very kind to me and Ronnie; she took a shine to us, I suppose. She must have thought we were a perfectly nice young couple.

You never got a dull seat at Sibyl's for dinner or for lunch. She was very good at getting people together. You always found her guests fascinating. But the minute you arrived and were introduced, she would sink into the woodwork. She was completely unlike Lady Cunard who had a certain effervescence and was a genius at making her own parties go. She was like a soap bubble. Emerald Cunard had a way she drew everybody out, then turned around and was even wittier than they. You went to see Lady Cunard when you were invited to her house, but when you were invited to Lady Colefax's you went to see her guests. I imagine Sibyl spent most of the time at her dinners thinking who she was going to have next week . . . always thinking of the next postcard. She spent the whole day writing notes and getting people to lunch.

She did have marvelous food at her parties; she was a thoughtful hostess. I remember she once told me that there was nothing better when people stayed very late than to send them home with a hot cup of bouillon and the very thinnest sandwiches. She even sent her old parlor maid around to Queen Anne's Gate to show my cook how to make the thin sandwiches. One slice of brown bread and one slice of white bread with butter in between. They were very, very simple and very good.

The Trees' town house in Queen Anne's Gate was at an ideal location, along the southern boundary of St. James's Park. Its back windows looked across the Birdcage Walk onto the park's flower beds and its long, narrow lake pointing directly to Buckingham Palace; its stately brick facade, with a gargoyle mask over each of the windows, opened onto a quiet L-shaped street idyllically removed from the rest of Westminster's hurly-burly. Their house, number 28, was part of a row erected in 1704 on what had been Queen Square. The house's simple dignity, and the exquisite craftsmanship of the carved wooden canopy over the front door, underscored the quality of that period's architecture.

Eastward, down Old Queen or Lewisham Streets, across Prince's Street, St. George's Street and Parliament Square, Ronald was a quick march from his seat on the back benches of the House of Commons once he gained election. Because of this propitious position, a "division bell" was installed inside their house, designed to inform MPs of an impending vote on the floor. Because of this bell, 28 Queen Anne's Gate entered the history books as the haven where the Tory Rebels of 1938–39 met during the year before the Second World War. Also nearby were the Astors' town house, on St. James's Square, and the men's clubs along Pall Mall and in St. James's Street to which Ronald Tree belonged.

It was a wonderful place to live. It's the loveliest walk in the world across St. James Park, and early in the morning you'd hear the ducks coming from Regent's Park to the water there. It was lovely to be in London and to wake up to the ducks and to the sound of Big Ben chiming. I was thinking about Big Ben last night . . . I used to sleep virtually underneath it when we lived in Queen Anne's Gate.

Nancy decorated Queen Anne's Gate just after she decorated Kelmarsh Hall, and once again she spared nothing. Descriptions of the house read like an encyclopedia of sumptuous textures and hues, and of the finest examples in the decorative arts of eighteenth-century England and Europe. Silks, satins, linens, vellums, walnut, mahogany, fruitwood, Aubusson, Savonnerie, Bessarabian, Queen Anne, George I, Regency: The Trees' house was fitted and filled with princely discernment. At the same time, as at Kelmarsh, the myriad rooms in the four-storey house were kept relatively sparse and clutter-free. The instinct to clean house that inspired all of the arts of the day to a degree also inspired the interior of Queen Anne's Gate.

Part of it was Paul Phipps's influence; perhaps it had something to do with Lutyens, whom Paul started with. Uncle Paul always furnished that way. It was the mood of the times, to clear up the jumble. But for me it was also because I had to furnish both Kelmarsh and Queen Anne's Gate, and we just didn't have that much furniture.

When you walked in, the staircase was on the left; it was the loveliest architectural feature inside the house. Carved of dark, tobacco-colored oak, the balusters were turned into a smooth, fat swirl from top to bottom, while the hewn of the banister mimicked the wainscoting along the wall. The end bracket of each tread was carved with an abstract pattern of acanthus flowers.

I left the staircase the tobacco color but painted the paneling along the stairs a pale, pale green. On the window in the stair hall I put curtains the color of a cigar, with a fringed pelmet, and along the floor I had a very pretty Bessarabian runner with the same brown in it.

Opposite the stairs was a small room I made into a very comfortable sitting room for myself. It was painted a shiny sulfur yellow that I copied from Edith Baker's in New York. The curtains were the same color as the walls and made from satin; then I had them piped with azalea pink all around the edges. I was mad about using azalea colored pink with yellow. The pelmets were cut so they looked like little pennants hanging down, and they had an azalea-and-yellow fringe like gingham. It was very, very pretty. I had an old Aubusson carpet in front of the fireplace with pink in it as well, and I had made for the room a square coal scuttle painted with dashes of pink and yellow. For furniture there was a small sofa covered in satin and a pretty walnut desk I brought over from Mirador. I used satin and other slick fabrics for slipcovers because they don't get as dirty in London and you can dust them off.

Doors opened from my sitting room into the dining room. I painted the paneled walls white—a gray-white rather than a cream-white—and again made the curtains the same colors as the walls. I'm very keen on having the same color around a room instead of having patches of color everywhere. The floors were painted shiny black that went with the black grate. The grate had been painted in Regency times with gold acorns and leaves on a black background. I loved that old decoration, so I had the dining-room table made to match it. It was black lacquer with gold-painted bands around the legs and feet.

I copied the twelve dining chairs from an old black Regency armchair I found; it was very simple, black, with rounded legs and sloping armrests. The back of it had diamonds with gold-painted spools at the end of each angle to match the table. The only piece of furniture I didn't have made for the dining room was the wire three-tiered plant stand that I brought from Virginia. I kept it in the windows facing out the back of the house and always had it overflowing with flowering plants. The one painting we had on the wall was a mar-

The Trees' Queen Anne's Gate town house. They took over the lease in 1928 following the death of its previous tenant, the eminent queen's counsel, MP, government minister and author Lord Haldane, who had lived there since 1907. It was built in 1706 by William Paterson, the founder of the Bank of England.

velous Munnings of a mounted Life Guard. It matched the room perfectly with its black horse and white plume. We gave it to Michael for his twenty-first birthday and he went right out and sold it.

The house was narrow, with each floor one room wide. **Above my sitting room and the dining room were two rooms we had made into one long sitting room.** This was where the Glamour Boys met—Eden, Salisbury, Macmillan, Thompson, Tree, etc.—to discuss their utter disgust with the older generation in power. It went all the way through from the street side to bow windows overlooking the park. I painted this room an ivory white with a little yellow in it rather than the gray-white of the dining room. On the wooden floors I had two Bessarabian carpets with lilies of the valley, and one early Aubusson with flowers in a trellis pattern.

Because we broke down the wall, the room was left with two fireplaces along the far wall. Both were always lit. I had next to each fireplace, at either end of the room, very comfortable sofas covered in dark brown satin, and comfortable armchairs. I wasn't as much inter-

The choice of black lacquer for the Queen Anne's Gate dining room was inspired by the black charger in Munnings's painting. Three tiers of white marguerites stand in the window.

ested in balancing the room as having comfortable places to sit next to the fires. I filled the wall between the fireplaces with mirror glass and put a lovely old green-and-gold Italian table in front of it with a pair of torchères on either side. Opposite the mirror, on the near wall, I put a long sofa I had made that was covered in a lighter brown satin. I took the wavy shape for the front of the sofa from a set of four beautiful eighteenth-century chairs I bought. The room was perfect because it could be intimate when you pulled a few chairs around one of the fires, or large and open when you had a big party.

Through a door at the park end was a tiny room I made into a library. I painted it a red lacquer color, like you find in Venice in the boxes you can buy there . . . a sort of starved pink. It was a very

The rooms in the Trees' town house, including the drawing room, were decorated by Nancy in 1928. "I think one was influenced by the fact that all houses when I was growing up were overdone and overarranged," she said.

> good color and looked especially pretty with the door open from the drawing room. I bought an entire set of the Everyman Library and had all of them bound in vellum and oatmeal-colored linen. I suppose I was a little extravagant.

During the first year of the Second World War Nancy was in the country most of the time organizing her mobile canteens while Ronald was attending sessions of Parliament and carrying out his war work. "I maintained a bachelor establishment in London," wrote Tree,

> and, one by one, was joined by friends. Jim Thomas . . . was one of them. Another was David Niven, who came to stay when he got some

leave. . . . David Bruce had arrived to take charge of American Red Cross activities, and after a few days in an hotel he moved into Queen Anne's Gate. The inmates saw each other rarely: our hours seldom coincided, so we only met at breakfast or by chance for a drink before dinner, but it was pleasant to have companions in the house.[6]

Nancy was in London for her birthday in September of 1940. Ronnie gave me a dinner party at the Ritz that night, and afterwards we went back to our house. I remember sleeping in the kitchen. It was to the kitchen that we went when the air raids began. For some reason we thought it was the safest place in the house, but we later found out that that part of the house was a rather flimsy Victorian addition.

The war correspondent Ben Robertson was part of the birthday party. He wrote:

> The night developed into a hard one, into one of the very worst, and we soon found that we should be unable to make our way home; so at midnight we went to bed in beds, but after half a dozen bombs had shaken the area, we found ourselves in the basement, sleeping on satin cushions brought down from the drawing-room furniture. In one room were Ronnie Tree and Nancy and Jim Thomas . . . and I. Nancy had piled cushions beneath a table. After a time we heard her say, out of the darkness: "If anyone had ever told me I would spend my forty-first birthday under a table with three men, I never would have believed them."[7]

Not long after that night, the Trees were forced to abandon their house in Queen Anne's Gate because of the increased intensity of bombing aimed at the government buildings surrounding them. The power of one German bomb that struck nearby was so severe it not only blew out their windows, it whipped the heavy dining-room doors across the hall, shattering the house's prized staircase. The Trees left for a suite of rooms at the Ritz Hotel, which would remain their London headquarters for the rest of the war. They never returned to the town house to live; five years of war changed a great deal in their lives, as it did for many people.

RAINBOW QUEST

Everything changed—I can't begin to tell you—the whole way of life. I'm not saying things are better or worse, but a true revolution has taken place in this country in my lifetime.

PART ONE

IN THE GREAT English country houses, the contrast between the "Indian Summer" years and the immediate post–World War II era was as dramatic as night and day. Where there once had been candlelight and warm fires, there was now a cold, shuttered darkness. The vast ballrooms of the nineteenth century—gaily filled from season to season in the first forty or so years of the twentieth, despite bouts of war and the depression—were now completely empty, at least of the whirling and waltzing couples who had once flashed across their parquet dance floors. Furniture and belongings collected over generations and arrayed in endless enfilades of sitting rooms, drawing rooms, libraries, studies and boudoirs, where families took tea, entertained weekend guests or read the Sunday papers, were now either sold outright at auction or covered by dust sheets. When they weren't sold, huge dinner services remained stacked in the pantries; silver, slowly tarnishing, stayed locked in the vault in the butler's office. Servants' quarters and workrooms in the upper floors and basements of older houses or in the wings of Victorian mansions, where dozens had once lived and plied their skills, now stood void of the sounds of labor and life. Dry rot crawled into the very timbers of the edifices, while weeds shot out of clogged roof gutters and between flagstones.

They had always been symbolic; allusion had been much of their point from the start. Now, in their dereliction, the houses would remain true to this purpose by symbolizing the final decline of the ancien régime that had built and maintained them for so many centuries. Nearly everything that these institutions stood for had either irrevocably vanished or moved on to a more sterile venue. The political power that resided behind their walls evaporated in the General Election of 1945, when Churchill, the product of a country house upbringing, lost the premiership, and Conservative members like Brendan Bracken, Harold Macmillan and Ronald Tree lost their seats.[1] (Members of the Labour Party did not often live in Palladian houses on sweeping manor estates, though just a half century before, Tory, Whig and Liberal members alike—whether Government or Opposition—had all owned their own seats in the country, or at least aspired to one.) At the same time, the land and all the vaunted possessions, what the house owners had banked on as long as the United Kingdom itself had existed, lost their commercial value for lack of demand. With political power and financial assets evaporating, much of the privilege and unquestioned social position the aristocracy had taken for granted dried up as well. Out of power and out of pocket, the country house class found that the magnificent, fanciful lives they had lived were now merely a volume in English history. Harold Nicolson wrote, "I felt as if chapter after chapter was being closed, finished, put away."[2] For the time being, the great houses of Great Britain had lost their hold on the collective imagination of the country: their dominant spirit, their massive, unequivocal stature, and with that, their purpose.

These enormous changes did not occur overnight, though it might have seemed that way when the smoke first cleared. The war and the Labour Party's Welfare State, which Lady Astor called the "Farewell State," were the coups de grâce in the long-drawn-out duel between old political and social adversaries. The epithet "Indian Summer" suggests a temporary respite of warm weather in the midst of an autumn already in progress. Even so, no matter how slow the evolution and how clear the warnings, it was no easier to leave behind homes and a charmed way of life, to see countless country houses empty, boarded up or wrecklessly demolished. It was worse still to see the house one was born in turned into a lifeless museum, one's family's and friends' traditions and memories the subject of a docent's tour. Vita Sackville-West was commissioned to write the tour book for her family's Elizabethan ancestral seat after it was given over to the National Trust in 1943 by her uncle. Her father had inherited Knole and she had grown up there, but it went to her father's brother when her father died; she was not allowed to inherit when he died because she was not a man. Writing the essay was simple enough, but proofreading later what she had written broke her heart: "I can't understand why I should care so dreadfully about Knole, but I do. I can't get it out of my system. Why should stones and rooms and shapes of courtyards matter so poignantly?"[3] Everyone in England had to sacrifice after the war; everyone was rationed small but equal shares of gasoline, gas, coal and electricity. That was the shock of it, though; people of the country houses had been used to so much more than an equal share.

What happened at Knole was repeated in hundreds of different scenarios over the next decades. A few of the oldest noble families held on as they always had: The Duke of Buccleuch kept four houses, including Boughton, because his vast property was in trust and immaculately managed. He was an exception. The 11th Duke of Devonshire kept Chatsworth, but he had to sell some of his prized art masterpieces and "donate" to the nation a second house he owned, Hardwick Hall, to do so. Others, like the Marquess of Bath at Longleat and the Earl of Pembroke at Wilton, opened their gates to the public as a source of income and tax easement. They were able to keep their houses, at least, though at certain times they had to give up the free run of the state rooms and move into wings or dower houses or cordoned-off sections of the house behind velvet ropes marked PRIVATE. Many families desperately attempted these schemes; most failed. One last option existed for owners of architecturally or historically notable houses: the National Trust. As the nation began to recognize the houses for their irreplaceable cultural value— they were intrinsic parts of the Britishness of Britain—the government created a budget for the preservation of the houses either bequeathed to the country, as was Lord Lothian's Blickling, or given in lieu of death duties and taxes, as was Hardwick. Just as the Sackvilles' Knole went to the Trust, so did the Meade-Fetherstonhaugh's Uppark. They would survive, but neither would ever again be presided over by an independent landlord.

In the twenty years following the end of the Second World War, 270 "notable" houses in England and Wales and 70 more in Scotland—family homes with personal histories tucked away in their attics and closets—were demolished. (This figure did not include the smaller hunting boxes, rectories and estate outbuildings also leveled by the wrecking ball.) All their pediments, chimneys, entrance stairs, carved columns and cornices were broken and ground to rubble; all these houses with such marvelous names were gone forever. Bickley, Blankney, Blatherwycke and Bloxholm; Childwell, Chillingham, Clervaux and Cloverley; Highhead Castle, High Legh Hall, Hill Hall, Hints Hall, Horsley Hall and Hoppyland Hall; Guys Cliffs, Sheepy Magna, Scrivelsby, Twizell and Ynys-Y-Maengwyn, were among those destroyed or left derelict after the war. For the Trees, two familiar houses torn down were Brixworth Hall and Sulby Hall, where the Pytchley met when Ronald Tree was Joint Master; Fawsley Hall was left to dereliction until it was turned into a hotel forty years later. Cadland, the house belonging to Henry Field's stepfather where Henry took Nancy to stay before they were married, was demolished. Cadland's park had covered a good portion of Hampshire's coastline; it was bought and eventually developed as an oil terminal and refinery. Lord Beatty's Dingley Hall had its elegant seventeenth-century interiors removed, while Lord Hampden's seat, the Hoo, where Phyllis's husband Bob Brand had grown up, was completely razed.

Waldorf Astor sold 4 St. James's Square to the government after the war, without telling his wife beforehand. It had received a direct hit from a Luftwaffe bomb, but beyond that, he understood that Lady Astor's days of Belle-Époque entertainments were in the past. And at his and his sons' dogged insistence, Lady Astor did not stand again for her Plymouth seat. With angry resignation, she retired from the Commons after twenty-five years: "Isn't that a triumph for the men?"[4] Twenty years later, after the death of their son the 3rd Viscount Astor, Cliveden was opened to the public by the National Trust. Kelmarsh remained a home only because it was a manageable size and could be kept by its own estate and the Nottingham and Essex estates Jubie Lancaster later inherited. However, Lancaster's coal-pit leases were taken from him by the government when mines were nationalized, although he was compensated for them.

Ronald Tree held on to Ditchley for only four more years after the war ended. The home he desperately loved, "where I came to live for what I expected to be the rest of my life,"[5] proved too expensive and perhaps too empty to keep. During the war the Trees had closed down most of the largest and finest rooms and used the great hall as a family sitting room. They also lost the majority of their staff, who had run the place so seamlessly for that one extraordinary decade. Their servants, as well as most of the servants from all the big houses, left the profession during and after the war, first to join the war effort, then to take better-paid and less strenuous jobs in manufacturing and production. The great network of country houses that had been one of the largest employers in England at the turn of the century—*the* largest of women—now barely existed. With its forty bedrooms (one four-poster bed took at least two housemaids to make it properly), its four kitchens, its park, gardens and thousands of acres of farmland, Ditchley was impossible to maintain without access to a whole population of servants.

This period of dramatic social and political change in England coincided with an equally turbulent time in Nancy's life. In 1942 she suffered a severe breakdown, and after leaving Ditchley first for her own rooms at Cliveden, she left England altogether for America.

> **I certainly didn't travel back to America for a holiday; I was *sent*
> back. I used to go back to Mirador twice a year, but this time I was
> put right into a lunatic asylum. The minute I got off the ship in New
> York they took me to the Institute for Living in Connecticut; I
> didn't even visit Aunt Irene.**

It was not that I was some sort of "war casualty" . . . I wasn't worn out from war work. There were plenty of people in England who worked twenty-four hours a day, seven days a week, for five years. And though it was terrible having two sons in the army—I never stopped worrying about them—everyone was in the same boat. England went through a time people in America can't imagine, especially in the years before America joined the effort. What happened to me went further back.

It was a combination of many things. It had to do with losing both my parents in a space of two weeks when I was sixteen years old, then losing my first husband, my grandfather and, after I married Ronnie, losing a baby daughter just after she was born . . . all in seven years. It had to do with my living against the grain. All I ever wanted in my life was to live in Virginia. I said to Henry and Ronnie and anybody else who ever proposed to me, "If you want to marry me, you've got to live in Virginia." I was determined to live there; it's what I knew; that is the life I wanted. I'm not complaining about England. I've had a marvelous, blessed life here; I've been very satisfied with England and thought it was a wise choice to raise our two sons here. But the only reason I left Virginia was that Ronnie couldn't go into politics there.

Politics is a life I've never liked or enjoyed. I never even liked parties or the Season. I don't know why, because I was very pretty and everyone made a great fuss over me . . . I just didn't enjoy it very much. I used to say, "I'd rather have a baby every day than go out to dinner"; I simply loathed being mortgaged at night for three months out of every year. Politics was the same thing to me, and when we went to Ditchley it was all politics. I'm not saying there was any pressure on me—everything was made extremely easy, just as it had been at Kelmarsh, by a wonderful staff who really knew their jobs; I've always been spoiled rotten. But when we had ten or more people to stay, they weren't there to *do* things, if you know what I mean. They were there to talk politics. I hated all of that: the London Season, politics, all of what Ronnie loved. I didn't enjoy people in that way; I don't like that whole thing. So at Ditchley I felt I was living against the grain, and eventually I became very ill.

I was sent to the Institute for Living to be built up. I had my own little cabin there, and they gave me hot drinks and showed me how to grow my own strawberries. I remember there was a frightfully attractive man there at the same time; he wore just the right sort of tweed jacket with leather patches over holes in the elbows and worn-out sleeves. Very chic. He was a gent, and he took a great fancy to me. He wanted to know, would I play golf with him? I said I would. My dear, he played nine holes without a ball. He was a nut. He did all the strokes and never had a ball. I nearly died.

When Nancy arrived back in England, she did not return to Ditchley. She moved instead into a quiet mews house behind her sister's town house in Mayfair, then into a town house of her own at 18a Charles Street that Ronald found for her. Nobody could have been a better friend to me than Ronnie. There's nobody that I admired more and had a deeper affection for. I used to say, "I wish to God you were my brother." Tree was also instrumental in Nancy's buying a decorating business owned by the London hostess Sibyl Colefax. To support her passion for entertaining, Lady Colefax had created, in the manner of Mrs. Bethel and Mrs. Maugham, a small, personalized interiors firm and a reputation for having good taste.[6] Nancy was not only well acquainted with Lady Colefax socially; she had been loosely associated with the business as well: Before the war, the two had an arrangement that Nancy would buy furniture for the Colefax shop if she saw suitable pieces while she perused the English countryside for herself. Lady Colefax's son Michael offered the firm to Nancy when it came time for his mother to retire; at Ronald Tree's urging—he thought it an ideal foil for her—Nancy paid £15,000 for Sibyl Colefax Ltd. in the last year of the war.[7] Ronnie always thought I should go into business, because I kept buying so much stuff for the house and there was no place to put it. He thought it was a métier I ought to go into.

Nancy called her new firm Colefax and Fowler in deference to Lady Colefax and because she made John Fowler, previously an employee of the firm, more of a partner.[8] She chose not to use her own name because . . . my name was about to change. When her divorce from Ronald Tree was final, Nancy married Colonel Claude Granville "Jubie" Lancaster, and for a moment she resumed her place as chatelaine of Kelmarsh Hall, the one house in England where she truly felt at home. She had known Jubie since they were both in their twenties; she and Ronald had met him through Nancy's cousin Bobbie Shaw; Nancy and Jubie maintained an intimate friendship for the next twenty years. Lancaster was an entertaining man, but very tough and arrogant. He suffered no fool, was an exceptional soldier, a fighting man's man— "a bit on the uncouth side," said an aquaintance—and as stout a rider to hounds as his grandfather Sir Claude de Crespigny had been. He was not the Modern Man. "Jubie was amusing to be around," said one person who knew him well, "but he was a cad."[8]

Jubie admired his Uncle Crawley enormously, and Crawley's younger brother Norman, who was married to Chinese Gordon's daughter. They were exceptional; that ilk is gone. Jubie admired that Crawley could tell someone to "Go to the devil" and be willing to live with the consequences no matter what they were. Jubie had a lot of that in him, too, but he had a much better mind than Crawley, and he was torn between wanting to say "Go to the devil" and his career as an MP. I used to tell him, "You have to make up your mind what you want. You can't be a Crawley and get along in politics." Jubie would say "Go to the devil," then couldn't understand why he didn't get any of the perks he thought he deserved.

What I thought admirable about Jubie when I met him was that he went to work. He was a young man with quite a large income for the day who'd gone to Eton and Sandhurst and had had a life of fox-hunting and being an officer in the Blues, a spoiled life, yet he pulled himself up and learnt all about mining. He inherited the Lancasters' Lancashire mine leases when he was very young and would have been fine just living off the income. Nobody went into trade in those days in England. None of his class left their houses in the country to go live in Bestwood amongst miners, or went all over Russia and America to learn the latest technology and safety. But Jubie did. He was brilliantly clever in that way. When the Socialists nationalized the mines in the 1940s, his were the only modern ones, the only ones with pit baths and power loading and those sorts of things.

Nancy's return to Kelmarsh was short-lived—the bloom was off the rose by then, we started too late—yet during the three years she was there, she filled the traditional position of mistress of the manor house with her unique spirit and sense of humor.

I began the Women's Institute in the Kelmarsh village then. Jubie built one of those sheds like in the army that we used as a clubhouse, and we had a high old time. I didn't run it like any Women's Institute had ever been run, but the people were mad about it; we had the greatest success. I got Joyce Grenfell to come and recite for them. An Elizabeth Arden girl came down from London to show the women how to do their makeup.

She also set about freshening Kelmarsh Hall, which hadn't seen a new coat of paint for over twenty years, and brought in Geoffrey Jellicoe to make landscaping alterations. Jellicoe designed a new terrace for the back of the redbrick house, framed on either side by double rows of pleached lime trees like those at Hidcote; and, borrowing from an old print of Kelmarsh that Nancy unearthed, he planted two triple lines of chestnut trees to border the lawn that sloped down from the terrace to the lake. These additions enhanced the formal qualities Nancy always sought, but didn't take away from the easy atmosphere at Kelmarsh that appealed to her so. In one of the Kelmarsh fields she had a number of old farm buildings pulled down that she thought spoiled a particular vista, and she had a wide swath cut through an ancient spinney to extend a sight line. A neighbor said, upon seeing what she'd done, "It's lucky she doesn't mind where they put the church, or she'd have that down as well."

An ingenious stroke Nancy left behind her was having an orangery placed between the stable yard and the picturesque pasture where Lancaster grazed his Park White cattle. She bought the eighteenth-century building designed by Smith of Warwick, replete with its tall, arched windows, from the owner of Brixworth at the time they were tearing down the Hall. She had it removed stone by stone, carted up the Market Harborough Road to Kelmarsh, then re-erected in a spot where it would hide the working part of the estate—the laundry, the coachman's house, the stables—from the view of visitors coming down the main drive. "My mother wasn't really married to old Jubie," said Michael Tree; "she was married to Kelmarsh." "She genuinely loved the sort of life we lived at Kelmarsh," remarked Jeremy Tree; "her heart was always there."

PART TWO

Nancy was drawn to the palaces and "treasure houses" in Britian that had retained their personalities and aura of survival, despite the odds, just as she was to historic houses in Virginia. She admired Hardwick Hall, the Tudor mansion commissioned by Elizabeth of Hardwick, one of the most powerful women in English history alongside her contemporary Queen Elizabeth I. Each of the towers of the house was surmounted by a gigantic stone carving of her initials, "E.S." (she was the Countess of Shrewsbury); the Brussels tapestries in the High Great Chamber had not been rehung in the 350 years since "Bess" first decorated her house.[10] Another was Badminton in Avon, the Duke of Beaufort's seat, where Nancy thought, despite its stately magnificence, **inside it was more domestic than grand. Every room was lived in, and every room seemed lived in by an accumulation of many generations. That's what I love.**

Deene Park in Northamptonshire, the home of the Brudenell family since 1514, Nancy thought enchanting. Deene was a salad of styles, of Elizabethan, Jacobean, Queen Anne and Victorian architecture, the final addition being a ballroom commissioned by Lord Cardigan, the officer who led the Charge of the Light Brigade. The tail of his horse was mounted and hung in a box on a wall in the great hall. And the house at Drayton fit her criterion perfectly. By the 1930s five hundred years of wrought iron work, stone masonry, joinery and carving swirled around a fortress Sir Simon de Drayton crenellated in 1328: architectural superlatives by the hands of Talman, Webb and Gibbs and by countless named and unnamed craftsmen and builders. Succeeding owners of Drayton let stand the work of their predecessors; eventually its pieces became too old, too venerable, for even the most arrogant Whig or misguided Victorian to raze. A wondrously disordered order emerged, "like a walled medieval village" with a Baroque courtyard of swag and colonnade, the Geometric Staircase, Adam-esque dining and drawing rooms, all sheltered beneath "a veritable forest of towers, pinnacles, cupolas and chimneys."[10] And to attest to the long line of humanity that crossed Drayton's threshold, stamped in its beams, pediments and paneling were the coats of arms, ciphers and ducal coronets of those who held the house over the half-millennium.

I particularly remember a wonderful set of chairs; they were covered in marvelous needlework. I wonder if they had to sell them.

There is a place I adored in Leicestershire called Stanford. It belonged to Lord Braye. It's the most lovely William and Mary brick house with wonderful wrought iron gates . . . I thought it was the best house in England. Ronnie and I almost took it instead of Kelmarsh because Lord Braye was the first person around to have electricity. But instead of being *in* the walls, the wires were actually out against the beams. I was terrified. I also remember how astonished I was to find a Holbein hanging in a dressing room, not even in one of the grand bedrooms. It was that sort of house, very surprising.

Others were slightly off the main road: Beckley, for instance, or Brympton D'Evercy in Somerset. **Brympton was one of my favorite houses in England. Lord and Lady Ilchester took me to see it when I was staying with them in the country.** It was the kind of house impossible anywhere but in England, a romantic combination of periods and styles side by side or one on top of the other. The entrance wing was Tudor and rather imbalanced, with Henry VIII's coat of arms carved into its turret staircase; the body of the house, stretching out behind it along a lawn and lake, was 150 years younger and decidedly of provincial neoclassicism. They were joined together within the confines of an early Victorian garden and park. Christopher Hussey could think of no country house "of which the whole impression is more lovely. None that summarises so exquisitely English country life."[11]

Even during the Second World War, when motorcar travel was difficult because of gas rationing, Nancy found ways of seeing houses she heard about that intrigued her. **I read of a marvelous house called Borton-on-the-Hill in**

Country Life during the middle of the war. It was in Gloucestershire, not too far from Ditchley, so Duff and Diana Cooper and I pooled our petrol coupons and motored over uninvited. A young Irish maid answered the door wearing her black dress, starched white apron and cap, red stockings and a pair of football boots . . . we couldn't believe it. She insisted that we come in and meet the owners, so we were ushered into the dining room for tea and scones with two charming old ladies. One was married to a Madjar count and was separated from him by the war, and they were both descended from Captain Bligh of the *Bounty*. The house itself was associated with the Overbury scandal during the days of James I. I kept up my acquaintance with the two through the rest of the war. They came to Ditchley on occasion, and when my canteens took me by Borton I would drop off French novels for them to read that I had had sent to me from Paris before the war.

What I was really taken by at Borton was some of the furniture there. The minute I walked through the dining-room doors my eyes were riveted to their set of William IV chairs around the table. They were verdigris buttoned leather with brass handles on the back and reeded legs. After one of the sisters died, the contents of Borton-on-the-Hill was auctioned and I bought the chairs. I also bought a set of eighteenth-century watercolors that had been in one of the bedrooms they showed us, and portraits that hung going up the stairs in James I frames. Those chairs have gone to America now; I sometimes wonder where all the things that I loved so have gone.

It was a calling, Nancy's "Rainbow Quest."[13] I have always been on a Rainbow Quest. I have always sought beauty wherever I've gone, wherever I've lived . . . a beauty that has turned out to be as fleeting as a rainbow. True beauty is something you can't get a teaspoon full of; it's something you ruin the minute you try to capture it. At home in England, or whenever she traveled abroad, free time was consumed in driving back roads, looking over walls, scouring shops, accepting invitations and suggestions to stay somewhere special or to tour a region with friends or organizations like the *Amies du Louvre*. I took a driving tour through France with Jubie and Aunt Nannie. All Nannie wanted to see was churches, Jubie only wanted to look at battlefields and I was only interested in houses. So Jubie and I waited outside while Nannie looked at her churches, my aunt and I couldn't have cared less about Jubie's battlefields and the two of them didn't even bother getting out of the car at houses I wanted to see. In one of the Tree Rolls-Royces before the war or in a hired car following it, Nancy sallied "forrard," always looking "the height of chic," pulling along her houseguests or the hosts of the house where she was staying, to find something wonderful.

One spring after the war I stayed with Jeremy at his house in Beckhampton for a few weeks. In the afternoons I used to take the car around the Wiltshire countryside and see what I could find. Once I went up a little dirt road and at the end of it found what I thought to be the most beautiful house in the world. I jumped out of the car, raced right up to the front door, rang the bell and said, "I'm Mrs. Lancaster and I think this is the most beautiful house I've ever seen; would you mind terribly showing me around inside?" The maid or the lady of the house, whoever she was, was very obliging and gave me a tour. I always used to do that, go up to a house I liked and ask whoever was there for a look around. One trick was to find out from someone at a petrol station the name of the local aristocracy, then say to the people at the house you want to see that you were trying to find Lord and Lady This and That, then "Ooohh, what a beautiful house . . . can I come in?" It always works.

The next week I was out again in the car near Jeremy's, and again we went up an old single-track drive. At the end of it, at the foot of a marvelous lawn, I saw what I was certain really was the most beautiful house I'd ever seen. I was thrilled. Here too I marched up to the door, rang the bell and said to the woman who came, "I'm so sorry to bother you, I'm Mrs. Lancaster, I'm rather lost but I think this is the most beautiful house I've ever seen, would you show me around?" The lady seemed quite astonished but replied that she'd be happy to give the tour, though hadn't I been there the week before? "Last week you came up the front drive." It was the same house; I nearly died of shame.

I suppose what attracts me has to do with a sense of timelessness, of survival of the fittest, of hanging on against everything. That was the most romantic thing in the world to me. But in my entire life I've only seen two or three truly forgotten corners of the world, where the only thing that affected a house was its great age, the smoothing of hard corners by wear and use. Wormsley was one of those. Wormsley was a never-never land set in a fold in the Chilterns only half an hour from London. You'd go up its dirt-track roads to find fields of wildflowers, huge woods of beech trees or a small stream meandering across the drive. It was an absolutely untouched part of English country.

The villas Andrea Palladio designed along the Brenta River near Venice in the sixteenth century stirred the same elation that some of the English and Virginian houses did. Though the villas had long ago seen the last of their majes-

tic preoccupations and pageantry, the grandeur of the edifices themselves survived; indeed, they were enhanced in Nancy's eyes by their humble evolution,
by the hay stored in their noble pediments or the goats grazing right up to
their stone foundations. Palladio's villas along the Brenta and in Venice offered
another comparison with Virginia: Like the plantation houses along the James,
they showed their handsome time and weather-worn faces to the river, the
water having been the principal thoroughfare for both civilizations. History
was not only apparent in their age but written into their very design.[13]

I was mad about Venice and the Veneto. I started to go every
spring back then. I would stay at the Malcontenta [Villa Foscari]
with Bertie Landsberg, or this sort of cure place you could go to, or
I'd stay at Charlie Beistegui's palazzo in Venice. I took a book with
me of the villas and would hire a car and show the driver, who only
spoke Italian, the picture of the villa I wanted to see. We'd only go
on third-class roads . . . we'd stay off the main roads. I saw every
one of the villas. Some had gone completely to ruin.

Of all the people I've ever gone sightseeing with, anywhere in
the world, Bertie Landsberg was the best. He showed me more
beautiful gardens and houses and frescoes. . . . He had a marvelous
eye, and he knew every house on the Brenta. He would take you into
a little house that didn't seem like anything much on the outside;
then upstairs in the bedroom the walls would be painted with
trompe l'oeil Gothic bookcases and inside the bookcases books and
porcelains and things would be painted on the shelves. He knew
where to find unique and wonderful things like that, things in humble places as well as grand. He had a tremendous talent . . . an enormous knowledge of beauty.

Landsberg gave up Malcontenta because the Italians began
building factories right in front of him on the Brenta; he didn't own
the land in front. What he did at Malcontenta, though, was marvelous. He bought it in 1925, when it was a ruin, and restored the
sixteenth-century frescoes in all the rooms. It had a wonderful
atmosphere that he very cleverly did not destroy. There were very
few comforts in the old house, though. My bedroom was on the
piano nobile, but the only bathroom in the house was in the attic.
And it only had a single candle to light it.[15]

I stayed at Malcontenta for Charlie Beistegui's ball in 1951. The
ball was to celebrate his restoration of the Palazzo Labia, and its
theme was an eighteenth-century *bal masqué.* The costume I wore
was a tulle cape that I got from Schiaparelli, a three-cornered hat
and a powdered wig that I sprinkled with gold and silver. Very sim-

ple and cheap. I took the gold powder up to the bathroom at Malcontenta and sprinkled it on myself in the light of the one candle.
Because I couldn't see a thing I got some of the powder on my face,
which then turned black. I went to this magnificent ball with black
spots all over my face. After that I made a deal with Bertie. I told
him that I would give him my bathtub that I had had at Ditchley if
he would turn the little anteroom to the bedroom I used into
another bathroom.[16]

When I was in Venice for Charlie's ball, Landsberg took me to
meet the man who designed the ball. His name was Paul Rado-
canachi—he came from somewhere in Central Europe—and he was
very old at the time, in his nineties. I don't exaggerate when I say
he had the best taste in the world. This old boy taught Landsberg,
Étienne de Beaumont, Jean de Ribes and Charles de Noailles everything they knew. He invented things, for instance those wire pyramids I have in my garden to grow flowers up, ingenious things. He
invented the three-tiered flower holder I had, all sorts of flower
stands out of glass that they made at the Venetian glass factory.
They were too pretty for words. He really was a genius, and an
enormous influence on others who had a great deal of influence
themselves.

Landsberg, de Noailles, de Beistegui: they made up a very exclusive international club of tastemakers, all of them coveting furniture, houses, "forgotten places," as Nancy did, as a hobby, and as a vocation. **Charlie de Noailles
and EmilioThierry, the architect who did a lot of the work for Charlie, knew
Paris the way Landsberg knew Venice; they knew where to find marvelous
things. On Saturdays they would meet to go looking. They once took me to
see these extraordinary iron gates you would have never found if they hadn't
led you there.** Nancy was an old friend of Charles de Beistegui's. They had
met during Nancy's trip to the Far East in 1919. **I knew Charlie well . . . he
was rather keen on me.** Though their approaches to decoration and architecture were often antithetical, "taste" to both of them was a plaything as well
as a form of personal expression. **He was crazy about "taste."** Nancy's interests were primarily in the antique, while de Beistegui, who lived very much in
the mix of Parisian high society, liked to juxtapose the grandeur of the past
with the sympathies of his friends in the avant-garde. From his penthouse
apartment on the Champs-Élysées, a Le Corbusier staircase led up to an open
pavilion on the roof with a series of electronically controlled walls and
hedges. A "window" in one wall framed a vista of the Arc de Triomphe. Yet
he decorated the flat mostly in Louis XV furniture. Cecil Beaton suggested

that "the baroque chichi or surrealist rococo . . . reached its fantastic peak, exemplified by Charles de Beistegui's apartment."[17]

De Beistegui seemed to lose his interest in contemporary art movements when he decorated his country retreat outside Paris, the Château de Groussay. He favored an English country house flavor for the early-nineteenth-century mansion and surrounded it with a *jardin anglais*, the French version of an English park. "The entrance hall sets the mood of the house," wrote *Country Life*. "There is a strong suggestion of English taste, but the English house that it most recalls is Ditchley, which Beistegui is known to have greatly admired."[18] There were, however, certain twists to the decor, perhaps instances of de Beistegui subtly tipping his hat to Surrealist friends—or maybe the signature of an eccentric—because a great deal of the furniture at Groussay, as at Labia, was fake. He could have afforded the finest originals, yet he preferred copies. And trompe l'oeil was used liberally throughout the house for walls and ceilings, even in the weaving of carpets. Many of the paintings, originals in the sense that they were old, were of trompe l'oeil subjects.

I was staying at Labia when he wanted to sell it in the 1960s, and I was sitting next to an important Italian collector from Turin at dinner who said very quietly, "You know everything in this house is a fake." It wasn't all fake because I remember he bought a great deal from Moss Harris, who asked me once if "Mr. Beistegui is a Spanish *don* or a furniture dealer, because he always wants a percentage off." I said he'd find it hard to answer that question himself. But he was crazy about fakes. That's the difference between me and Charlie Beistegui; I don't think you can get the effect with fakes. I'll tell you where he *was* good: He was tremendously influenced by his friend Emilio Terry, who was a great architect. I met Terry's mother when I was a little girl traveling in Europe with my mother and Alice. It was Madame Terry who owned Chenonceaux. It's extraordinary how things come around in a long life.

PART THREE

When Nancy bought Lady Colefax's shop and business at the end of the Second World War, she became intimate friends with someone else who possessed an obsession for beautiful things and places, someone who became a co-conspirator in her rainbow quest. John Fowler had "it," whatever "it" is. Like Charlie Beistegui and a very few others, John understood beautiful things and was drawn to them like a moth to a flame. I think it must be something born into you, this love for beauty, and something that your circumstances allow you to foster. For the next decade and a half, between when she bought the firm and when they decorated her Avery Row flat, Nancy and John Fowler shared the hunt.

Fowler was Sibyl Colefax Ltd.'s most valuable asset. The "prince of decorators,"[19] as the Duchess of Devonshire called him—or as James Lees-Milne described him, "a very sympathetic man . . . [with] a large upper lip which makes him look like the duchess in *Alice in Wonderland*"[19]—he came as part of the deal, along with the shop on Brook Street and the stock of antiques and fabrics displayed there. Fowler had joined Lady Colefax around 1938 as her employee when his small furniture-painting business in the King's Road failed. Before that he had painted wallpaper for Thornton Smith, furniture for Peter Jones Ltd. and nearly joined Mrs. Bethel at Elden before her death. Both Sibyl Colefax and Syrie Maugham had vied for his services then, when, even that early on in his career, it was clear he possessed unequaled instinct with paint and fabric. Lady Colefax won John over to her shop in the end because he thought she was the less "dominant" of the two; presumably he meant both in her personality and her decoration. His eye would be freer to express itself if paired with Lady Colefax's. She was a romantic, a retro-vert and a lover of the gilded Georgian age like himself, while Mrs. Maugham's Modernist facade, her whitewashed simplicity, was the antithesis of Fowler's rococo leanings.

John wasn't terribly worldly at the start. I'm sure Sibyl Colefax and Peggy Munster—Countess Munster brought John to Colefax's in the first place—I'm sure they had some influence on him, but he had never even been out of England when he began working with me. And as far as running a business was concerned, John was the worst possible manager; I lost £8,000 every year. But he was worth every bit of it as a companion. I could never have asked for a better friend. John was a gentleman, a quality that has nothing to do with what kind of family you come from. He was very generous, never mercenary; he had a marvelous sense of humor. And above everything else John was a true artist . . . he had an enormous talent.

Decoration meant something very different to John Fowler, however, than it did to a Charles de Beistegui, a Sir Philip Sassoon or to Nancy herself, all of whom were rich and passionate amateurs in the game, living to some degree or another the fantasy they created. John was a professional artisan who supported himself by this work. While these others had grown up in and around the great houses of England, Europe and America, taking their physical beauty and the life within their walls somewhat for granted, John had studied them more from a distance. But what he lacked in direct experience he made up for in fastidious learning. Aside from the jobs and the appren-

Nancy with John Fowler, c. 1960. "John was . . . the best appreciator of beautiful places and things I have ever known," wrote the Duchess of Devonshire (Devonshire, p. 127).

ticeships he had held, John Fowler had spent hour upon hour educating himself in the archives and collections of the Victoria and Albert, hoarding every aspect and nuance of Georgian decoration the museum possessed. By the time Nancy bought the firm, John was becoming a living catalogue of Great Britain's most prolific artistic age. **John knew more about the eighteenth century than anyone I've ever met.** For instance, John dug out of dormancy eighteenth-century techniques and recipes for stippling, scumbling walls and antiquing furniture, as well as those for gathering a ruffle or picking out a cornice, all for the sake of creating the authentic eighteenth-century effect he desired. Colefax and Fowler made dragging paint a popular tool in the 1950s—dragging produced the appearance of the poorly ground pigment of eighteenth-century paint—but John actually preferred using the poorly ground pigment itself, despite the painstaking application it required.

He was the type of very sensitive, gifted man that flourished in the artistic world back then. I remember whenever we went to the country together John always wore a racing-type waistcoat—flannel

with some sort of pattern on it—and always had a Tyrolean number folded up under his arm but never on his head. It was very sporting attire for a very unsporting man.

John's whole approach to a problem was through the eyes of an artist. He looked at a room or a house in terms both specific and abstract, at both its form and its content. He thought and executed keeping in mind relationships between varying tones and hues, the effect of light and shadow in and on a room and its architecture, the role of color within the context of the overall proportion. John Fowler became an immensely sophisticated interior decorator, one who during his career was to raise the standards of what was expected in the profession from the merely charming and attractive to the sublime. They made a remarkable team, the craftsman and the woman of *haute* taste, and out of the gray austerity endemic to postwar, post-Empire England, their firm flowered.

THE SHOP ITSELF was mostly left to John and his assistants, the young "dog's bodies" who often grew up to be talented decorators in their own right, like Imogen Taylor and Nancy's niece Elizabeth Winn. As the sole owner of the business Nancy came and went as she pleased, making "appearances as dramatic as they were unexpected . . . always superbly dressed . . . bringing with her an air of a wider international world,"[21] leaving behind in her wake an aura that permeated the firm's work. She never took her proprietorship too seriously and never let professional decoration become anything more to her than an extension of what she had always found so much pleasure in pursuing. Colefax was a wonderful excuse to endeavor in the search for furniture and objects and ideas—supposedly to fill their large showroom for paying customers, but just as often for her own rooms. She loved hiring a car, its tank full of pink black-market gasoline, and a driver, then gathering John at his flat and striking out into the streets of London or back roads of the countryside.

We would head out in the morning and come back six hours later with a four-poster bed and a pair of chairs tied to the top of the car. I don't suppose any two people ever had more fun. We stopped whenever and wherever we saw something we liked. Once the two of us almost got killed on the Fulham Road. We were driving along and we both saw at the exact same time two wonderful orange-colored stoneware jars in a shop on the other side of the street. We shouted "stop" to the driver, jumped out of either side of the car, and were both nearly struck down as we rushed across. John wanted the jars for the shop and I wanted them for myself, so we raced each other. I put them on top of the bookcases in the yellow room in my flat . . . they looked marvelous.

Fortunately John and I liked the same type of furniture. Old painted pieces and English black lacquer were our specialties. I'm mad about painted furniture in white and gold. I don't really like mahogany, only fruitwood and pine. But mahogany is lovely when it's been faded in the sun. A great deal of time was spent out looking for furniture. Very often we'd go every day because we had to keep the shop full and we were the only buyers. Colefax and Fowler was more of an antiques shop than anything else in those days; we only took the rather big decorating jobs. You could get lovely things then, and we became quite well known amongst the country antiques dealers; they knew we were good, and they would save things for us they knew we would like.

Besides the antiques shops one knew, the enormous house sales so common to that era were one of our biggest sources for furniture and decorations. So many people had to sell out in those years; collections that had been in the same family for centuries were broken up in a day, or in the case of a house like Ashburnham, in three-day-long auctions that took place at the house. The first sale I went to in England was at Baldwin Park, near Chelmsford, when Ronnie and I were still living at Kelmarsh. I went because it belonged to the Tyrell family, who had relations in Virginia. Another was at Holdenby House, where the Pytchley Point-to-Point was held in our day; I bought a pair of benches and some curtains there, and a lovely fire seat I had in the library at Kelmarsh.

The sale at Hartwell in Aylesbury was an enormous event that took over four days in 1938. Queen Mary and the Dukes and Duchesses of Gloucester and Kent all attended. Hartwell was the house where Louis XVIII and his court lived in England when they were exiled by Napoleon. I bought a very unusual dining room table at Hartwell, made up of six separate sofa tables that fit together, and two wonderful full-length Kent frames for Ditchley. I also bought the Spanish screen that I had in my bedroom at Ditchley at Hartwell. It was leather with chinoiserie scenes painted on it.

There were eventually sales that we went to at Borton-on-the-Hill, Kimbolton Castle, Coleshill and Brympton d'Evercy, and the enormous sale at Ashburnham Place in 1953 after the death of Lady Caroline Ashburnham. The Ashburnham family had lived on that spot in East Sussex uninterrupted for eight hundred years; then in only three days all of their possessions were dispersed. I found it rather sad that this was the end of so many centuries of a family's survival, but John and I did buy a number of lovely things there. The two of us went off in separate directions and for two days looked through everything, making lists along the way of what we wanted. Motoring back to London after a second day of searching, we compared our lists and added up the estimates. It totaled more than £50,000 which was worth a million back then.

In the attic at Ashburnham we found the W.C. boxes left from the coaching days before railroads. When people went on long coaching trips they took *pots de chambres* with them. These were made of very pretty china and were stored in wooden boxes with crimson leather surrounds. We found three sizes—one for the father, one for the mother and one for the children—just like the three bears. We bought them all.

Lady Arundell-Lee of Dagenham Park in Essex called me and said, "I hear you like beautiful things; I have some here for sale," and she invited me around to have a look. The house was being taken over by the BBC, and she was selling the family belongings. John and I lost no time at all. I bought all of her garden statuary, three full sets of china, a set of blue painted chairs that went to Kelmarsh, a glorious rug just right for Ditchley and two eighteenth-century *bergères* painted white and gold. I remember being very amused to find a serpentine wall like we had in Virginia in Lady Arundell-Lee's garden at Dagenham. Years later her son, Sir Something Arundell-Lee, became my neighbor in Oxfordshire when he bought Tythrop Hall. I was a little embarrassed that my house was full of his family's possessions, so when I wrote to him to invite him around for lunch I told him he would feel right at home there.

THE FURNITURE Nancy chose not to keep for herself ended up in the showrooms of the Colefax and Fowler shop, of which *Harper's Bazaar* wrote:

With John Fowler, [Nancy Lancaster] works in an enchanting early-eighteenth-century house in Brook Street, Mayfair, the last of its kind with a garden intact. Its great fig trees are some of the oldest in the district and climb to the top of the roof. The house is furnished as if it were to be lived in. The ballroom, in which everything is for sale, looks like the fabulous emporiums in eighteenth-century Venetian pictures.[22]

John found the town house at 39 Brook Street in 1944, and he and Lady Cole-fax moved the business there from its original offices in Bruton Street. It comprised three storeys facing Brook Street, just down from Claridges, and two more around the corner on a narrow alleyway called Avery Row. The architect Jeffry Wyatt had lived and worked in the house from 1804 to 1840; he gained his reputation, a knighthood and a new name—Sir Jeffry Wyatville—for his work at Windsor Castle for Kings George IV and William IV and Queen Victoria. It was he who gave the town house's facade its simple Georgian grace, and the enormous "ballroom," actually his studio, its vaulted ceiling and three windows overlooking the courtyard gardens, with its flowering catalpa tree.

There was a large shop window next to the front door on Brook Street where we used to put a sampling of the furniture we had inside. John made lovely displays.[23] John's office overlooked the garden. His drawers were full of lovely bits of braid and fringe. On the wall, tied together by a long string like a laundry line, he hung bunches of colored rags that we used as color samples; we called it "the palette." It could be flung into a suitcase and carried off to a client's house where it was used on the job. We'd say "THIS red . . . or THIS red?" It might have been a piece of an undergarment or someone's pajamas, anything that had a distinctive color that we liked. We never used paint swatches. One day we left the palette in the back of a taxi and that was the end of it . . . a calamity. No one ever returned it, so we started over from scratch.

The shop and the business were tiny compared to what Colefax and Fowler is today. We were a two-man show then, instead of this vast partnership worth millions. The young people who worked there were just our bodies running around; I could send them across the street to get cigarettes or anything I liked. We must have had the prettiest girls in London working for us. But most of them only rang up their young men all day . . . used the shop as a telephone booth.

One of the "pretty girls" always sat by the front door of the shop to receive clients. "I used to always sit behind a screen by the fireplace and catch the customers as they came in," remembered Elizabeth Winn.

One day I was sitting there and in walked the Duke of Windsor. He put on this fantastic Cockney accent and said, 'Can I see Lady Cole-fax, please?' That was in the days when Lady Colefax was still alive; she had sold the firm to Aunt Nancy, but she kept a sort of courtesy room there where she could chat with her friends. That room became John's after she died. The room that was eventually Aunt Nancy's marvelous yellow drawing room was then used as a show-room and was painted two awful colors of gray-green. It was where we kept all the things we were selling.

The shop had only a skeleton staff in those days, really. There was a marvelous woman with enormous bosoms called Miss Wolf. She was a Communist and used to act in the community theater in the evenings. There was Mrs. Hourrigan, who was John's right-hand person for years and years. We had a charming American woman called Catherine Gray . . . she was what I call a "Grand American." And there was Mrs. Morant, whom I was terribly frightened of because she was rather powerful. Of course, it was John and Nancy who ran the thing, though; the rest of us were assistants and secre-taries or did the cutting and sewing.

Aunt Nancy and John had what you might call a love-hate rela-tionship over the years, though in the beginning it really was more love than hate. But she did use to say very naughty things to him. "John, I'm replanting you. I'm taking you from a small pot and putting you into a slightly bigger one." She was a great tease, like the rest of the family. He used to get absolutely livid.

I used to tease John mercilessly. I used to chase him around his office saying, "I am the bloody awful Mr. Fowler and you are the charming Mrs. Tree; you should be wearing my petticoats and I should have on your trousers." We really were devoted to each other, but I'm sure I made his life absolute hell. Part of Colefax and Fowler's success was that both John and Nancy knew instinctively how something ought to be. But what each knew so instinctively often didn't correspond; Nancy Astor used to say they were the most unhappy couple she'd ever met who weren't married.

Our rows in front of clients were famous. The Duke of Norfolk said he'd never seen anything like it. We were asked down to Arun-del Castle for lunch to look over the new house he had built for him-self and his wife in the park. John and I contradicted each other from the start. "I don't like that color." "That sofa can't go there." "You don't know what you're doing; look at the way this is made and the detail." "I don't care about picayune details; I just know it isn't right." This would go on all the time. It never bothered us, in fact we enjoyed it, but our clients were puzzled by us.

We liked the same furniture, but we had very different taste in certain other things. His taste was mostly feminine, whereas mine has always been somewhat masculine. John was terrific with details,

with tassels and fringes; he knew how to do all sorts of things. But I used to get to the point when I'd say, "I'm not interested in that; leave the damn thing alone." I'm not crazy about the "et ceteras." I think I've got a feeling for the period of a house and for scale . . . for the bigger things.

I would also say I gave John a sense of luxury that he'd never seen before. I had been very lucky that my mother steered me to these things, that when I was in France as a little girl I was cast in a role where I saw these lovely houses. And I've been very fortunate to live in the houses I've lived in. I suppose I exposed him to a wider world, gave him access to it. He had never even seen a proper bathroom; he'd never seen bathrooms like the ones at Kelmarsh or Ditchley. Probably the greatest value I had to John is that I taught him how one lived comfortably.

John Fowler would eclipse his partner in the world of professional decoration—as an expert, a craftsman, a creative restorer of historic architecture—but it was Nancy's reputation, and her wholly seductive taste, that people sought. A number of Astor relatives came to Colefax, including Lady Astor, who hired the firm to work on her town house in Hill Street that replaced 4 St. James's Square. Nancy's cousin Wissy, Lady Ancaster, hired them for Grimsthorpe Castle and Drummond Castle, her husband's ancestral seats. Fowler's work at Grimsthorpe took five years to complete. **Wissy was devoted to John; she adored him.** Michael Astor brought John in to decorate rooms at his house Bruern Abbey in Oxfordshire, and Bobbie Shaw hired John for his London house. John Fowler eventually worked for John Profumo, the Conservative cabinet minister, at his house in Regent's Park; Profumo was a friend of William, the 3rd Viscount Astor.

Mr. and Mrs. David Bruce were introduced to John by Nancy in Paris; Mr. Bruce was by marriage a cousin of Ronald Tree's, and his wife would become a lifelong client and friend of John's. When Ronald Tree gave up on Ditchley in 1949 and moved to Barbados, a friend of the Tree boys, Lord Wilton, bought the estate from him. Ronald also sold Wilton most of the house's contents, and Lord Wilton hired Colefax and Fowler to execute some badly needed refurbishing after the privations of the war. (When Wilton eventually left Ditchley and moved to Ramsbury Manor, he would hire the firm to decorate his new house as well.) The list would snowball over the next twenty years, clients recommending Colefax to other clients. Mellon, Rothermere, Harmsworth, Somerset, Angelsey, Rothschild; Boughton House, Badminton House, Château la Tour, Chequers, Clandon, a suite of rooms at the Ritz. Fowler worked on a house in Eaton Square for Sir Laurence and Lady Olivier, a town house in Eaton Place for Nancy's friend Lady Alexandra Metcalfe, a country house belonging to the Redgraves called Wilks Water. He was eventually summoned by Queen Elizabeth II to carry out decorations and restoration in the Audience Chamber of Buckingham Palace. **I used to say to John, "My, how we little aspens have grown."** There were other clients—from those leaving the large houses of their recent past and settling into small, efficient London apartments, to those who made their fortunes after the war and wished their houses, and themselves, to look somewhat more established. Some John helped successfully down a step, others he guided up, but in either case he did so with intelligence and artistry.

In many ways it was Nancy's own decorative aims that in the end shaped the firm's aesthetic. Her lavish, sweeping, fun-loving gestures became an integral part of the Colefax and Fowler "look." And through her, creating the illusion that generations had lived in a room they decorated came to be the firm's signature. The ideal was second nature to Nancy. She was born to it at Mirador, where Mr. and Mrs. Langhorne expressed their longing for the Virginia of their childhood in its decoration and the style in which they lived there. Nancy then established her own version of the sensibility first at Kelmarsh and then, to enormous acclaim, at Ditchley Park. John, as well as many decorators to follow, very much drew from this, while Nancy's wistfulness found a rapt audience in the firm's clients.

OF THE MANY clients her firm worked for over the years she owned Colefax and Fowler, Nancy got involved with very few. **When I was at Colefax and Fowler, I got bored working with the hoi polloi. Decorators, if they are any good, get very intimate with their clients. John was crazy about that, getting to know them, working people around to his plan; he was crazy about being "the charming Mrs. Tree." But I simply can't bear it.**

She made an exception if it was a personal friend or a member of the family who came directly to her and asked for the firm's advice and services. Nancy and John traveled together to Boughton when Mary, Duchess of Buccleuch, asked them to help her get the house back in order after the war. There the work was mostly rearranging the priceless collection of furniture and cleaning existing paint schemes. Nancy was also involved at Mereworth when her son Michael, who was left the house by Peter Beatty, and his wife, Lady Anne, were redecorating the almost two-and-a-half-century-old mansion. Here the Lancaster-Fowler mark was in the comfortable arrangement of furniture, especially in the Long Gallery, a room that might easily have been offputting in its grandeur.

Nevertheless, it was often a frustrating business for a perfectionist with such specific ideas of "how it ought to be and what ought to be done." Despite the success of the firm's work at Wilton House, the ancestral home of the Earls of Pembroke, Nancy was never pleased with the results. (She had known Sidney and Mary Herbert, the 16th Earl and his wife, for years. When he inherited Wilton from his father, he came to Nancy, whose taste he admired from stays at Ditchley and Nancy's second house in Oxfordshire, Haseley Court.) Wilton was one of Britain's architectural masterpieces. A triumph of the civilization's cultural history, the building included Tudor parts commissioned by the 1st Earl, an unparalleled facade and string of reception rooms by the English Renaissance architect Inigo Jones (with Isaac de Caus) and a nineteenth-century Gothic Revival courtyard and cloister designed by James Wyatt and completed by his nephew Sir Jeffry Wyatville. As interior decorators at Wilton, Colefax and Fowler joined a daunting line—four hundred years long—of distinguished contributors, including Jones, de Caus, Philip Webb, William Kent and Thomas Chippendale, as well as Van Dyck, who painted the family portraits hanging in Jones's regally gilded Double Cube Room. Nancy and John were asked in to alter the Wyatt-Wyatville cloister, where the Earls of Pembroke displayed their collection of sculptural antiquities, as well as rooms in the family's private apartments.

Their plan for the cloister hall met with the approval of the nation's highly protective and critical preservationists, to whom rooms like these seemed to now belong. Nigel Nicolson wrote, "Now that its walls and vaulting have been repainted by the present Earl in warm terra-cotta with gray ribs, it forms an adjunct to the house by which previous centuries would have been startled, but not, one likes to think, ashamed."[24] **My idea was to treat the hall the way I had seen it done in Russian houses. I wanted them to move out all the paintings and display cases, and use the hall only for statues and busts, then paint the walls a lapis lazuli or equally bright color as a background for the pale, cold marble of the sculpture. This would be instead of the usual gray or beige. We settled on a color similar to the fresco orange in the Ditchley saloon, which worked perfectly. But they wouldn't have only statues in the hall, they wanted paintings as well, and they insisted on having John only mix the color but not apply it. They wanted the estate workmen to do the painting—which I can understand—but half the success of the color was in its application, its layering, which John was an expert at.** Even without his expert touch, the hall succeeded in setting off the collection of sculpture and paintings beautifully. Despite her dissatisfaction, the cloister was a perfect example of Nancy's and John's talents interlacing when they did work together, her more abstract, ethereal ideas made real by John's practical knowledge. John devised various shades of the terra-cotta color for the walls and the beds of the ceiling vaults to give the hall a certain tonal resonance to parallel its architecture, taking Nancy's bright background color one step further.

When the Duke and Duchess of Windsor wrote to Nancy asking for her help at their mill in the French countryside, she agreed to participate. The Moulin de la Tuilerie at Giff-sur-Yvette was a different job altogether from Wilton, it being of a humble, vernacular architectural tradition and possessing none of the weighty past and ornamentation of a British treasure house. Its most important historical aspect was the master of the *moulin* himself, the former King Edward VIII of Great Britain and Emperor of India.

I had met the Prince of Wales several times over the years, but I certainly wasn't *intime* with him. I was never part of his crowd. He was much too of-the-moment for me, always having the last word of slang on the tip of his tongue. But he was always charming to me whenever I saw him. I met him in the twenties on Long Island when Ronnie and I took a house there in the summer so Ronnie could play polo. The prince was there that summer with his polo team from England, and when I gave a dance at the house we took, the prince came. He was simply mad about Pina Kruger, Bertrand Kruger's sister-in-law. Pina was very pretty: She had her hair pulled back skintight and tied in a long, pointed knot like Madame X. The prince danced only with Pina Kruger the entire night.

The first time I ever caught sight of the duchess was when I was a little girl growing up in Richmond. The girls who lived across the street from us went to Oldfield in Baltimore, where she went—she was the school leader of Oldfield—and they invited her down to Richmond one year for the German. I remember looking out the window of our house and there was a Miss Wallis Warfield of Baltimore, Maryland, walking down Franklin Street wearing spats and a monocle.

Years later Ronnie and I were asked to Sibyl Colefax's for dinner; it must have been at least ten years before I bought the firm, when Lady Colefax still had Argyll House in the King's Road. She didn't tell us who the dinner was for, but we waited dinner, waited dinner and waited dinner. Dinner was supposed to be at eight, but we waited until quarter to nine, when the door opened and in came the Prince of Wales with Mr. and Mrs. Simpson. I had never met the Simpsons before: He looked like a hairdresser with a blond mustache. There were only eight of us; all through the meal the prince paid special attention to the husband, saying, "Ernie, try this cigar, it's very good. Ernie, have a bit of this." The prince was buttering him up. After dinner, when the ladies left the table, I said to Mrs. Simpson, "Could you be the same Wallis Warfield I saw walking down Franklin Street in Richmond wearing a monocle and spats?" She said, "I am."

We were dining at Blenheim Palace the night of his abdication. It was a very sad speech. Lady Pembroke, Sidney Herbert's mother, was there that night. She and Mary Marlborough were both very tall, the two tallest women in England, and after the speech they were standing up, with their heads together, crying. The two of them looked like an enormous stepladder standing like that.

The Windsors' country home was a clump of gray stone farm buildings rather than a single house. The dining room, the drawing room and their bedrooms were in the central building; guest houses, the duke's sitting room and library, and a summerhouse were all in separate outbuildings scattered beneath a steep, tree-covered hill. A cobblestone courtyard joined together some of the buildings; flagstone paths, tumbledown walls and a rerouted stream flowed along and across their property. The Duchess hired Stéphane Boudin, the Paris decorator who had worked for the Trees at Ditchley, to paint and furnish most of the rooms at the Mill as he was doing at the same time for their house in the Bois de Boulogne. For their garden, the Windsors commissioned Russell Page, another of the Ditchley cast from twenty years before.

The first day we arrived from London, we had lunch with them at their house in Paris. I remember all of their linen matched the beautiful porcelain. We were just four, and it was a delicious lunch. They didn't eat a thing because of those waistlines, but John and I ate as if we'd never seen food before. Then we got in the car and drove out to the Mill at Giff, where we had an appointment with Russell Page; he had just started doing his own gardens in France for Vilmorin and was now working for the Windsors. As we were speaking with Russell Page in the garden, the duke emerged from the house wearing a pair of shorts, a fireman's cap and a pair of boots, and began running around the garden lifting sluices in the stream like a little boy playing in the sand. It was the most extraordinary sight.

We were shown around the main cottage; then he showed me his rooms, which were very sad. I particularly remember his sitting room, where the tables were all made from the drums of the Guards regiments he had been colonel-in-chief of when he was the Prince of Wales and the king. The walls were hung with his hunting pictures. He was very nostalgic for England.

When she showed us the dining room she wanted done up, she asked, "How would you do it?" I said, "I'd understate it." There were two ideas I had, both from rooms at the Palais des Papes in Avignon. One had Indian corn on the walls, painted on the plaster like fresco, the other painted with different birdcages. And instead of all the rich things everywhere, the furniture and pictures, I wanted to bring it down; I wanted simple furniture and rush matting on the floor. She liked that, and she liked the idea of the Indian corn. So John painted the corn on the walls and a light green trompe l'oeil lattice dado. We made green, unlined curtains the color of jade for the windows that the light shone through. It was very pretty. The furniture was rather bad, however. She had a lot of Syrie Maugham's furniture she insisted on using.

While we were there they also asked us to go shopping with them to advise them what to buy. Boudin used to do that with the duchess in Paris. I was horrified by the rudeness of the French, who didn't want to send things on approval to the Mill. They were very offhand. Whether or not they had been bad at paying, I don't know; everybody said to us we would never get paid. We were not only paid on the dot, but we each had the most marvelous personal letters of appreciation. Later they wrote to me again and said they were coming to England and would I take them shopping? They evidently liked what we did. I had a long talk with John; it was a question of whether we'd have things we liked brought to the shop, or whether we would take the Windsors out where we bought things. I thought it would be far better that we take them where we found things, but I did say, "My God, we'll have bricks thrown at us." I thought they were probably very unpopular. But people were *delighted* to see them. The difference in the manner in which the English and the French treated them was astonishing.

PART FOUR

Colefax and Fowler's illustrious clients, the firm's notable work in historically and architecturally important houses, even the commercial prospects of the business she owned and continued to invest her money in annually—all meant remarkably little to Nancy Lancaster. None of it was ever of overwhelming concern to her, except perhaps as a diversion at a time when her life was passing from one chapter to the next. Nancy was not a "professional" by nature, not a career woman and certainly not someone adept at or drawn to business. But the decoration of her own houses, unfettered by another's wishes, continued to give her great pleasure. There she worked to her own standards, and there her soul revealed itself.

Between 1945 and 1957, the years she was most involved with the shop, Nancy lived in London, spending more time in a city during that period of her life than she ever had. Ronald found 18a Charles Street for her before the end of the war; he knew of it because their friend Ruth Draper, the American diseuse, had rented it whenever she stayed in London. **Charles Street became a beehive of activity. Both my sons were returning from the army and they moved in, and also one of my nieces who had been in the Wrens stayed with me. Our dinner parties were a mixture of young and old, and afterwards we always played charades and canasta, which were then much in vogue.**[25] It was a much smaller, more personal home than the palatial Ditchley had been, and it was entirely her own. The atypical West End town house stood tall but very slender with an abbreviated front on Charles Street; its length and its entrance were actually on Chesterfield Hill. **They called it 18a because they wanted a chic Charles Street address.** Beau Brummell had lived in Charles Street in the eighteenth century, as had Edward Gibbon, Edmund Burke and the Duke of Clarence; the street, and Mayfair around it, remained almost as quiet and slow paced in the decade following the war as it had been in their day. **When I lived there, at the end of the war, I realized for the first time how enjoyable quiet weekends in London could be, when traffic seemed to disappear and one could take sightseeing walks at ease.**

The Charles Street town house had no outdoor garden, and its exterior was plain and featureless, but inside Nancy created a collage of high spirit and grace, an indoor garden of furniture, carpets, fabrics and wallpapers. It began in the entrance hall and spread up the stairs, onto the landings and into the two small, warm rooms on each of the five floors. Striped Regency wallpaper in green-yellow and white, a collection of black-framed antique silhouettes, a floor covered in green felt; the black lacquer dining-room table and chairs from Queen Anne's Gate, a sepia wallpaper of painted genre scenes, a yellow, red and black Regency gros point carpet, green linen curtains piped in red; a white lacquer writing desk, a set of fringed cocktail tables supported by blackamoor acrobats: These were a very few of the treasures in the rooms on the ground floor.

Up the steps, following the needlework squares sewn onto each tread like flagstones on a path, the second floor was treated like a single room. She filled the window bay on the landing with a rounded bamboo sofa. The red curtains were secondhand, a necessity of rationing, but because they were too small for the space, Nancy had them bordered with foot-wide strips of white and stitched with lines of red tape bows. Against the banister she placed a papier-mâché cabinet that she used as a bar—**I adored that cupboard**—and a Bessarabian rug of browns and reds. **I was always lucky in my carpets, which to me are of enormous importance.**

In her library on Charles Street, seated here and there like old friends, were a few small, beloved things from Mirador that Nancy had begun to import to England. The cushions on the sofa were covered with an old floral chintz from Mirador. Between the windows she put her Queen Anne walnut desk from home, and on the floor she had her most prized needlework rug, from her sitting room in Virginia. The rug was composed of small floral arrangements on pale blue diamond backgrounds. **A woman came up to me once when the Mirador gardens were opened to the public and said, "I don't think much of your roses, but I love the flowers in that old rug."**

The stairs climbed upward three more fights: to the floor with Nancy's bedroom and bath and a guest room and bath, to one with a guest room and a maid's room, the last with a maid's room and the cook's bedroom. **I had two maids at Charles Street who were with me forever, named Flo and Beryl, and I had a cook, a kitchen maid and an odd man. With my sons, a niece, a butler named Mr. Burgess and Hilly, my secretary, who came during the day, the house was simply bulging.** The atmosphere there was gentle, comforting, even subdued compared with Nancy's other houses, yet as bright and glamorous as ever.

Ruby Hill started with Nancy in 1947 after working abroad for the Marquess of Linlithgow when he was the Viceroy and Governor General of India, then for Winston Churchill when Lord Linlithgow's entourage returned home in 1943. She remembered their first meeting:

> I had three appointments the day Nancy interviewed me for the job: one with Nancy, one with Elizabeth Arden and one with Hardy Amies. Nancy was first; she knew the Linlithgows and a number of their friends. We talked for a few minutes, then she had to leave because she was going somewhere with Jeremy. As she got up she said, "I'm so glad you're coming to work for me." I said, "But I have two other appointments," and she replied, "Never mind about them . . . you come to me." I've never really retired. That was more than forty years ago, but she still rings me up and says, "What's the name of that man, you know. . . ."
>
> Working for Nancy was a fascinating life. You never knew what you'd have to do next or what you'd have to try and find. There were travels, there was the search for certain things that she had to have, certain bath essences and soaps. And there was an enormous amount of people in and out. But with things as well as people she often got the name wrong, so nobody could find it or them. She had a way of saying, "Let's ask that man." Well, you had no idea who she meant. But I thought she was great fun to be with.

Colefax and Fowler worked on 18a Charles Street, but the job was nothing like a collaboration; finally Nancy owned a shop that could undertake all

The entrance hall of
18a Charles Street in
London after Nancy
had it hung in green-
and-white-striped
wallpaper and her
collection of silhouettes

of the stitching and dying and upholstering that in the past she had commissioned Mrs. Bethel's and Mrs. Maugham's shops for, but the serene, elegant
"stamp" on the house was distinctly her own. Perhaps the best part for Nancy
in owning Colefax and Fowler was the pleasure of having a personal decorating service always on call to carry out every whim. She kept the shop busy
from the start with Charles Street and other tasks, like decorating the rectory
at Kelmarsh for Peter and Cecily Borwick, as well as the substantial repertoire
of work they did for her relatives.

Indeed, from 1954 to 1958 John Fowler and the staff had little time to
do anything else *but* work directly for Nancy. In 1954 Nancy found Haseley Court, a ruined mansion that would require all of her imagination and
resources to revive; then in 1957 she moved from Charles Street to her
famous "flat" in Avery Row next to the shop in Brook Street. Both took a
great deal of work, but when they were finished, these homes would become
Nancy's, and the firm's, most lauded achievements and would serve for

The library at the Charles Street town house

twenty-five years as showcases of the fantastic possibilities of interior decoration.

> **Avery Row was a lovely place to live; it was charming. I could spit into Bond Street and I could spit into Claridges, and it looked out onto the park. It was so quiet I could hear owls at night.**

Twenty-two Avery Row was not an entire house, but neither was it anything that resembled an apartment. Nancy called it her "maisonette flat" or, with tongue in cheek, her "bed-sit." But "to call where Mrs. Nancy Lancaster lives in London a 'flat,' " wrote Loelia, Duchess of Westminster, "is like calling the *Queen Mary* a 'boat.' "[26] Rather, it was an electrically composed, wondrously bejeweled pied-à-terre carved from the vaulted studio, the servants' workstations and the stables of the Wyatville house in Brook Street. Like leaving the wintry fields of Northamptonshire for Kelmarsh's glowing pink great hall, entering Avery Row from the streets of London and walking down narrow passages, up stairs and into the drawing room of gold-upon-yellow-upon-gold always stole one's breath away.

Nancy and John used sleight of hand and not a little irony to transform this labyrinth of hallways, cellars and the one grand room into such hyperbole. It began just inside the front door, a door that had once been a servants' entrance but now had its own address, a door that would now open to receive the Queen Mother or Truman Capote. (**He had heard I was a Virginian, so he came to tea dressed in a Confederate uniform. He said, "Nancy, Georgia was too small for me."**) The walls were of marble, accented with Corinthian pilasters and hung with mirrors, candle sconces and a collection of Medici family portraits. The marble, however, was trompe l'oeil and didn't pretend to be anything but; the Medici portraits were quarto-sized engravings, a fraction of the size of the oil originals they were copied from; the mirrors were to give the corridor the appearance of width. A banquette, beautifully covered in striped linen, was so shallow it was as though it had been cut in half. The whole thing was pure craft and pure trickery. In one more deception, the Medici pictures, hung one right up against another and covering the walls like wallpaper, concealed a jib door that led to a guest room and a maid's room. Nothing, then again everything, was as it seemed.

Straight ahead, underneath one miniature archway then another, was the garden door leading to the courtyard and the old catalpa tree; the door was hidden after dark by a drawn curtain. To the right were steps upstairs; at their bottom was a wall-length mirror and a fluted pedestal holding a porcelain bust of a Georgian lady. (The mirror adding length and the bust offering a terminal point were architectural devices that Nancy used both indoors and out, in *allées* made from plaster or from privet.) The stair hall itself was marbelized. **One of the Dashwoods once said to me, "You know, my trompe l'oeil is so much better than yours . . . mine is almost real." That wasn't the point. The idea is to make it crude; you don't want to pretend that something fake is real.** It was obviously fake marble, but John Fowler's and his assistant George Oakes's paintwork gave a dull, utilitarian back stair true style.

The anteroom at the top of the steps, between Nancy's bedroom and the flat's main room, very much resembled that of a Venetian villa. Here they used painted furniture, four floor-to-ceiling paintings and a vivid varnished orange on the walls. Again, not everything was as it appeared, for behind the mirror, which could be pushed up into the wall, was a window looking onto Avery Row, and hidden behind the series of romantic Italian allegories were the hall closets. Her healthy disrespect for the sanctity of fine art approached vandalism when Nancy had the paintings fitted directly to the curves and corners of

The entrance hall of 22 Avery Row was an apt introduction to the cavalcade of elegant and glamorous corridors and rooms that followed.

the walls and jib doors cut into them. **They weren't very good paintings, and they had been stored in the top floor of the shop for years unsold.** The room gave the impression of a royal cabinet, a place private and exclusive.

Nancy's bedroom, adjacent to the anteroom, relied on John Fowler's talent for the will-o'-the-wisp as well: His illusions lasted only as long as one let them, as long as one didn't look too closely. The Queen Anne wall paneling, painted by Fowler in three shades of blue, was of course not paneling at all but another example of clever trompe l'oeil. Along with the grainy, antiqued coloring, he used thin ribbons of dark blue paint to represent the paneling's insets, including the "shadows" from sunlight. Nancy's recipe of elegance *cum* comfort furnished the room: chintz, petit point, an old painted side chair, a reupholstered *bergère*, a black lacquer chest of drawers given her by Lady Beatty, a Dutch *boeketten* still life, a marquetry desk, a whole collection of gold-topped dressing table accessories and eighteenth-century gilded tortoiseshell boxes. Loelia Westminster thought Nancy's bedroom an "enchantment" and "as rural-seeming as anything this side of the Wiltshire border."[27]

The blue bedroom, the orange anteroom, the halls, the mirrors and the exquisite wall treatments acted merely as preludes to Avery Row's room of rooms, however: Nancy's decorative tour de force that she called her Butter Yellow Library. All the other rooms paled by comparison. With the help of John Fowler and George Oakes, Nancy transformed the cold gray and green Wyatville studio—quite large, at forty by fourteen feet—into a place full of invitation and spontaneity beneath a balanced framework of high decoration. Here Albemarle County hospitality married 1920s dash. It was a single room that on the one hand was "to many . . . the most glamorous room in London,"[28] yet one about which Nancy could write, "I sit in this room, I eat in it, and I wish I had my bed in it—it is so cozy and agreeable."[29]

As the only large reception room in the residence, it was asked to serve a number of functions, ones for which even Nancy's smaller houses had always had separate rooms. Sitting, withdrawing from dinner, tea, cocktails, coffee and canasta might all now be combined in a single chamber—a common sign of the times—but the room also had to answer as an intimate inner sanctum where one could read and write letters and contentedly be alone without feeling dwarfed by the remaining space. On top of this—or in spite of it—the studio also had to include the dining room, one that might seat two or twenty equally effortlessly. So the one large room, with its fireplace and its three windows overlooking the garden, needed not only to express a varied pith but to accommodate a diversity of temperaments as well.

Much of it she achieved simply through her choice and arrangement of furniture and objets d'art, as she always did. Many features in the room belonged in a museum; they provided the overall rich, aristocratic atmosphere. There were Georgian bookcases from Ashburnham Place at the room's four corners and two gilded console shelves from Chiswick House, all of enormous architectural distinction. Filled with novels and folios, they played the "library" role in the room. The Lee portraits from Hartwell, in their ornately carved Kent frames, and the mirror over the fireplace, framed in a seventeenth-century mélange of gilded beads and scallop shells, lent the room the joyously unrestrained air of the Baroque. The pair of severe, full-length countenances of Elizabethan courtiers called the Fitton sisters—hanging in the stair hall at Ditchley before the Trees bought the house—loomed over the room, tempering somewhat the outrageous extravagances of Jacobean and Whig alike. Below the aloof Lee ancestors Nancy stationed her pair of contortionist cocktail tables, so beautifully carved and painted and so exceptionally peculiar. For the fireplace she found a painted metal coal scuttle in the shape of a giant scallop shell.

Within the foursquare boundary of priceless antiques and paintings, Nancy established a circle of charmed ease. Around the fireplace—the sitting room and boudoir part of the studio—were deep, cushioned chairs and a sofa. In front of the fire Nancy kept a clover-shaped plush . . . **good to put one's feet up on, or for two people to sit on.** Against the opposite wall, across the width of the room, were two of the banquettes originally made for Ditchley's White Parlour that had found their way to the servants' bothy; and scattered throughout the room were *bergères* and side chairs in waiting, ready if the circle needed to be enlarged. Alongside the glamour and the comfort, practicality had a place as well: Tucked within one of the window recesses was the desk where Miss Hill worked during the day. The desk, the French armchair and the cabinet decorated with pleated fabric were all sympathetic with the general feel of the room; at night the curtains were drawn, and Hilly's office disappeared.

The list of the room's contents was very long because Nancy kept it filled, but the surfeit of chairs and tables, lovely boxes, porcelains, urns, jars, books, torchères, lamps and even the dog beds for her poodle and lurchers only added to the room's warmth as set against its cool architecture. It seemed as though Nancy's taste had come full circle since the day thirty years before when she had laughed aloud at the interior of Kelmarsh, before she set about ridding it of its Edwardian clutter. The differences, of course, were context and purpose, as well as the quality of the furniture. Furthermore, unlike even the most sumptuous and expensively appointed salons of the late nineteenth and early twentieth centuries, the furniture in Nancy's room was actually of secondary importance. The mood of the room, its glamour as well as its surprise, began and ended with the color.

It was Paul Phipps's idea. When I was doing up Queen Anne's Gate, he said to me, "You must have a butter yellow library someday." I copied Edith Baker's sulfur yellow there instead, but I remembered his suggestion and at Avery Row I used his deep yellow. The sulfur yellow had green in it, the butter yellow was rich creamy yellow. People say that color was John Fowler's idea: The painted paneling in my bedroom was his, but the butter yellow was Paul Phipps's.

Like an alchemist John did concoct the recipe for the color, while Colefax painter George Oakes applied it to the walls, giving it texture and depth, then glazed over it. **Paul said it ought to be slicked.** When they finished, it seemed spread rather than brushed on. The effect was "slightly shocking" but in perfect keeping with Nancy's purpose, for this yellow, variously referred to as "Pekin yellow," "gorse-yellow" and "glowing Italianate yellow," was fresh and absolutely charged yet all-the-while calming and regal in its repose. It was truly original as well. Of all the bright colors in which eighteenth-century landlords painted the rooms in their palaces, they nearly always avoided yellow; the Georgians coveted their paintings and believed yellow would take away from a picture and from the gilt frames they wrapped them in. At Avery Row, however, it proved just the opposite: The pictures stood out from the yellow while the room's gilding and furniture were gathered together within this unifying background.

The ornaments and upholstery were planned with this yellow in mind. Myriad shades and intensities shimmered down its length. Dress curtains of unlined yellow taffeta hung from rosewood poles with gilt ends. Instead of pelmets the taffeta was festooned with brown-and-yellow cords and golden tassels. An easy chair, the sofa, the banquettes and their pillows were all covered in some sort of yellow fabric or other, pale or striped or fringed; the other side chairs were almost all chosen for their gilt, and a few were given yellow seats. Nancy found a Savonnerie carpet with a yellow ground and a red-rose center for the middle of the room, and she hung pieces of Ditchley's gilded *boiseries* in the window recess opposite the fireplace. The gold in the trim of the bookcases and in John Fowler's treatment of the room's double doors at either end were more consolidating details, while the painting of the room's barrel-vaulted ceiling in sable brown, and the tan-and-gray trompe l'oeil marble wainscoting and cornice, earthed the yellow without distracting from it.

The room looked stunning on a bright day, the sunshine streaming in and setting the walls ablaze. It was beautiful after dark, with the long taffeta curtains pulled across the windows, bathed in the steady wash of incandescent light. On evenings when guests were expected, however, the Butter Yellow Library was at its most glorious. A bank of candelabra, torchères and chandeliers showered flickering gold upon the golden yellow. All were burning when guests arrived, to be met at the front door by the butler, led down the hall and up the narrow staircase, given a drink in the anteroom, finally greeted by their hostess in the library. "Nancy matched the room by dressing in shocking pink or pale gold," remembered Ruby Hill. "She really was very pretty, with those huge eyes and so much life in her face. Before they all arrived, after seeing that everything was ready, she would sit down in a chair and say, 'Well, I've had my party. I wish they all weren't coming.' Then the minute someone came through the door she was up. She lit the room like a third chandelier."

I had the Queen Mother for dinner once at Avery Row: It was to return a kindness she paid me in allowing me to screen a film about Stratford at Clarence House, where she lives. Stratford was the house in Virginia where Robert E. Lee was born; I was the director on the Board of Trustees for England and was sent the film to help raise money. I met the Queen Mother years before when she was the Duchess of York and she and the duke took the house in Naseby so he could hunt with the Pytchley; our children used to go to the same parties. She accepted my invitation and came to dine on a lovely hot summer's evening. We had drinks in the garden. There were sixteen of us at the two tables for eight. The Farrells were there, John Bowes-Lyon, Bobbity Salisbury, Jeremy, Michael and Anne; the Queen Mother sat next to one of my sons. As the only cook I had in London then was one who just cooked for me, I decided to get someone in who was supposed to be a very good caterer. The soup was all right and the sweet was all right, but I'll never forget that meat . . . it was tougher than all outdoors. I'm still chewing it.

After dinner we sat out under the catalpa tree in the garden again. It was the most lovely tree, and it was in full bloom then. It bloomed great trumpet-shaped flowers. Under the tree I had a little pool with a trickle of water coming from the mouth of a porpoise, and by the wall there were fig trees that never bore any fruit. It was perfectly lovely. She stayed until after midnight talking. Then when it was time for her to leave, I took her to the door.

The building across Avery Row from my flat was a house of ill fame; they used to call it "the Office" because any time a wife would ring up looking for her husband they could say, "He's at the Office." Avery Row was a very narrow alley with barely enough room for the Queen Mother's car, and just as we came to the door that night a man in a long trench coat came out the door of the building across the street. You should have seen the look on his face when he saw us and saw this enormous Rolls with a driver and the royal cipher blocking his escape. His eyes nearly popped out in terror. I don't know if the Queen Mother saw him, she was too polite to have said anything, but I had a very hard time keeping a straight face as I curtsied while a man in a trench coat ran hell-for-leather down the alley in the other direction.

Nancy sometimes used the yellow room for after-dinner bridge parties. Laura, Duchess of Marlborough, suggested that Nancy was not a very good bridge player. (That's the pot calling the kettle black. But I will say I had to recite the rhyme in my head the whole time I played, "Dummy to the right leads the weakest thing in sight. Highest of the partner's suit will help to pacify the brute." I recited that every time I sat down at the table.) Once she loaned the room for Lady Caroline Thynne's debut dance. It still scares me to think of the queen and Princess Margaret dancing on the rickety old floor; it's a miracle it didn't collapse. She let her niece Elizabeth Winn have "musical evenings" in the room and Ian McClellan, of the American Museum in Bath, have dinner parties there for the American tour groups he showed around English country houses.

The yellow room had historic importance, for it was here that Nancy's taste—the taste with which she had dressed so many houses and rooms in the preceding quarter-century—transcended to an acknowledged "style," to a well-defined period on the time line of the decorative arts. Referring to Avery Row, the decorator Nicholas Haslam wrote, "Nancy Lancaster decorated these rooms with such panache that they became, and have remained, the model, the very yardstick, of the English style."[30] The English Style, the English Country House Look, the Country House Style, the American Country Style—however it was labeled, its sources were exactly those Nancy had always sought and used. Beginning with a core of Virginian country gentility, she drew from the eighteenth century, from 1920s New York, from Paris and rural France; part *haute* decor, part simple elegance; a "salad" (as Nancy called it) of fabrics, colors and furniture like the layering of generations in a house that remained one family's home for centuries, "underpinnings"; the humble amongst the elevated; a nod toward the "Rules of Taste," yet an accompanying lack of regard for them as well; a balance, a sophisticated architectural preoccupation, warmth, humanity, hospitality, unself-conscious élan. From Edith Wharton and Ogden Codman writing their book about decoration in the year Nancy was born, to Elsie de Wolfe and the New York ladies creating crazes, to Lady Islington, Norah Lindsay, Colonel Cooper, Johnny Johnston,

Lady Cholmondeley, Lady Meade-Fetherstonhaugh, Sir Philip Sassoon, Oliver Messel, Stéphane Boudin, Gerald Wellington, Charles de Beistegui, Emilio Terry and Bertie Landsberg: It was a defining moment for a sensibility. John Fowler's ingenious hand polished it and took it in his own direction, while Colefax and Fowler established a formula and a market for it. By then, of course, it had to lose some of its point, its exclusive origins, but it had now found a way to survive the late twentieth century.

HASELEY COURT

*In my early life Mirador was the healing thing for me, the balm;
it healed all of my early ills. It always had that effect on me.
Haseley was the same for me later in life. Haseley too had the
power to heal whatever ailed me.*

THROUGHOUT THE WAR and for five years afterward Mirador remained
Nancy's stay. As time passed, however, she saw less and less of the redbrick
house, the cottage she was born in, the long strings of whitewashed fencing
snaking over her land, Humpback Mountain, the Blue Ridge that seemed just
outside the house's back windows. The war brought an end to an itinerary that
had her sailing back and forth across the Atlantic with such ease. Perhaps if
Jeremy or Michael Tree had wanted it, Mirador would have played a bigger
role in Nancy's life after the war, but they were Englishmen. **The next generation isn't like us. Alice and I are the last who understand it.** "I used to love
Mirador," said Jeremy Tree. "It was lovely. But I think Nanny Weir didn't
much like it, and one is always brainwashed by nannies." **I remember talking
about Mirador with Michael when he was a little boy, saying how marvelous
I thought it was. He said, "What, that old farmhouse?"**

Mirador was kept running just the same, through the 1930s and the
'40s, and lovingly looked after even in Nancy's absence by the butler, Stewart Wood, and the housekeeper, Jenny White. Though she now rarely
passed under her Grandfather Langhorne's arch, she continued to find in
Mirador a source of comfort and pleasure, knowing it was there, reflecting
on the possibility of retreat. As long as she had Mirador she was never too
far from home.

Stewart Wood was as nostalgic as the rest of the family. He wrote to
Nancy in England in January 1939:

Haseley Court, Oxfordshire, 1960

I have been so used to your being here in the Fall, in the late autumn I used to go and stand on the front porch and gaze down across the lawn and say dinner is served. I could see you, Miss Irene, my dear Miss Phyllis, Mr. Buck God bless him and Aunt Liz, [and] so many more getting up from under those maple trees coming in when the leaves had begun to turn golden and begun to fall. I would stand with tears in my eyes as big as old black fists looking for you all.[1]

Ronald wrote to Nancy from Mirador in late April 1942, having traveled to the United States for the Ministry of Information on a Pan Am Clipper:

It's boiling hot outside—and the door and the gateway are intertwined with wisteria—and the birds are chattering away happily. The sunk garden is dead white with a great wall of dogwood—easily twenty feet high. The serpentine wall is a mass of creeper and flowering shrubs with twelve- to fifteen-feet magnolia overhead. The lake is almost hidden by immense willows, and the hillside by dogwood and judas in full bloom. In the garden back of the house the apple trees that we planted only twenty years ago are almost meeting overhead and in full white bloom. We sat under their shade this morning and they sent a continuous sprinkle of white petals down on us until we were almost white. . . . In other words it was a dream. We motored down last evening . . . leaving Washington about four and getting here just as it was beginning to cool off around seven. Helen met us and seemed so pleased to see me, and I made old-fashioneds and then we had a delicious dinner and sat in the library afterwards and talked. This morning I walked round the farm with German [the caretaker] and saw that it all looked very trim and shipshape. He is selling every gallon of milk that he can produce and thinks that there will be a real demand for apples this fall.[2]

And Irene Gibson went to Mirador as often as she could, staying at her late father's old home before and during the war. In an undated letter to Nancy, she wrote:

If you could have seen Mirador, *so* lovely, *so* peaceful and *so* Mirador. My thoughts were with you and all the good lovely times we have had together, the gaiety. If I started to write about that I could fill volumes. Helen has the coziest cottage in the world and Stewart looks well, but older. Just longs for "My Miss Nancy."[3]

The Langhorne family's era at Mirador, a relationship that lasted for three generations beginning in 1890, came to an abrupt end in 1950. Though Mirador was more than three thousand miles across the sea, government policies in Great Britain forced Nancy to sell the house and the one thousand acres, just as they had helped cause British families to sell *their* ancestral seats. Along with postwar rationing, the Labour cabinet instituted a dramatic devaluation of the pound sterling. They then pushed through the Commons currency controls making it illegal to send large amounts of money abroad. The two measures made it impossible for Nancy to maintain Mirador and retain the people who had been with her family for so long. If Nancy had kept her American citizenship and her assets in the United States, nothing the British government might have decreed could have affected the fate of Mirador. During the war, however, she chose to become a Crown subject; at the same time she transferred her principal from the United States to Great Britain.

I changed my citizenship because I thought the Americans were much too slow in entering the war. As for my money, I remember Ronnie saying to me, "I can't get over it: You have two boys in the British Army and yet you keep everything in America." I *was* rather ashamed of that. So I said to the Americans, "Take back your mink."

Then I brought every sou over in 1944. I've been a pauper ever since. Most English people were sending their money as quick as they could to Canada and places like that, where it could be protected. But this fool did it the other way around.

Before I agreed, though, I made sure there would always be enough to send what was necessary to Mirador. I said to the people at the time, "Look here, you can have my money, but I don't want to sell my roots. I was born at Mirador. It's what I love most in the world." I made sure that I could keep Mirador and would have the money I needed every year to support the farm. They said, "Of course." The government agreed originally, then a later Socialist government rescinded the agreement.

They stopped me from sending money abroad without any warning and without any regard to our having loaned Mirador to the government during the war at our expense. It was just at the time we thought America was going to war over Formosa and the bottom had fallen out of the real estate market. Six months before, a man had followed me to New York and offered to pay me $350,000 for Mirador. I turned him down. I didn't want to sell Mirador. That $350,000 would be worth millions today. When they rescinded their agreement six months later, they only gave me one month to sell, and I could only get $100,000. I sold one thousand acres and a house in perfect order for $100,000.

But selling Mirador for anything nearly killed me.

It devastated Nancy Astor as well. She traveled to Virginia from England "to see about it," as she wrote in a draft of an autobiography she never completed.

Going there made me think of the day in my own childhood when Phyllis and I went with mother to Danville to see her old home. The house was in ruins, the once beautiful garden overgrown. Mother hunted for the graves of the children who had been buried there and she could not find them. She sat on the steps and cried, and Phyllis and I, who were running about enjoying ourselves, could not imagine why she was crying. But now I know. She had been a young girl there. She remembered the Yankees coming down the river, and she and her mother hastily burying the silver and what valuables they could. No one had looted Mirador. It looked peaceful and beautiful as ever—but I too could have cried.[4]

Those mountains held my world in like stays to a fat woman. I don't care about dying, but I'm sad I won't see the Blue Ridge again.

NANCY LOOKED at 150 houses before she bought Haseley Court. I looked everywhere. I even went and saw that charming rotunda folly outside of Exeter made entirely of seashells. When I wanted to see a house I'd heard about, I would wire the people first, saying I was passing through and could I come and see it. I made the answer prepaid. Before she lost Mirador, house hunting was more of an amateur pursuit, now there was a purpose to her search. Whether it was England or Virginia, Nancy Perkins Field Tree Lancaster always preferred the countryside to living anywhere else, no matter how comfortable or glamorous a house in the city might be.

I couldn't bear anybody else's mistakes. I couldn't have stood it. I had to have a house that was untouched. I've always fooled with that. Some people are crazy about building . . . I'm not. But I want to get a house with just the bones. I want to put the fat on it myself.

And I didn't want a house earlier than Charles II or later than George III. I wasn't as fond of very early houses with their low ceilings and beams and things. I happen to like houses that remind me of Virginia. The houses built in Virginia in the eighteenth century were very much like those built in England in the seventeenth century. Fashion took a long time to cross the Atlantic in those days. And I don't like houses later than George III because I don't like Adam. Adam stucco is too thin. I like seventeenth- and early-eighteenth-century houses. To me the proportions are more livable—not necessarily more beautiful than earlier or later houses—but more livable. You get a sense of proportion rather than rambling.

I wrote to the Historic Building Society, the National Trust and other groups like that and asked if there were any houses that had been offered to them that were too small for their purposes or that were off their priority lists because there wasn't enough money to keep them. They all sent me lists . . . I saw a lot of beautiful houses that way. In the spring of 1954 the Duke of Grafton wrote to me from the National Trust suggesting that I look at Tythrop in Oxfordshire, a house with a Grinling Gibbons staircase that he thought I would like. On a Sunday in late June, Michael, Jeremy and I drove out to Oxfordshire to have a look at Tythrop. Along the way, following my rather vague directions, we made a left turn instead of a right and we ended up at Haseley instead.

The first thing I said to my sons as we drove up the drive was, "I've been here before. I was in this house before the war. Tony Muirhead lived here." I had been looking for it for years. Ronnie and I had dined at Haseley. He and Tony knew each other from the Commons; Tony was an MP as well. I particularly remember Tony saying to me at dinner, "I want you to see my garden; I want you to see my primroses." To get there, he led me through a men's lavatory and a walled coal yard. I kept teasing him, "This is the funniest way to get to the garden, Tony." Driving home to Ditchley, I turned to Ronnie and said, "Why didn't you buy a house that size instead of one so grand?" I thought Haseley was lovely.

I didn't see Haseley again after that. Tony Muirhead was found shot in his bed in the first days of the war; he was supposedly depressed because he was a colonel in the Ox and Bucks but they weren't going to take him to France because he was too old. He had fought in the 1914 War. The Americans had Haseley during the war, and later it was a prisoner-of-war camp. I did hear of it again, though, before the boys and I came upon it. I knew a charming and clever Frenchwoman who worked for Pierre Balmain in London named Annette Spaines. Annette had many friends in the theatrical world like Noël Coward and my cousin Joyce Grenfell, and one afternoon she telephoned me after spending the weekend with Vivien Leigh and Laurence Olivier at their house in Oxfordshire, saying that Vivien had taken her to see a perfect, untouched eighteenth-century house nearby with a curious topiary garden. She said I should get the address from Vivien Leigh and see it. I meant to, but somehow I never did. I already had a rather long list of houses to see.

Nancy fell in love with Haseley Court the moment she saw the house again in June of 1954. She was so adamant about it she called her agent from the village that Sunday afternoon and told him to make an offer for it immediately. I was worried when I saw a couple drive up in a Bentley and get out to walk their boxer dog there. I thought too many other people knew about it. When the agent suggested she have it surveyed, she said she wanted it anyway, dry rot or not. Within a very few days Nancy owned Haseley Court and fifty acres, for which she paid £3,000. She signed the deed on a summer afternoon in what was left of the garden at Haseley, sitting on the balustrade overlooking the topiary, the one small part of Haseley Court even hinting of any former glory.

There stood a lovely early Georgian house of silver stone, deserted and in unkempt long grass where occasional garden plants like thalictrum, monkshood and daisies had seeded themselves. Rabbits and hedgehogs scuttled about. With so many trees gone—the avenues I remembered when I had been there fifteen years before had been cut down—there was now a wide horizon of fields with no houses in sight, and a view of the Chiltern Hills that reminded me of a miniature Blue Ridge Mountains.

Haseley gripped Nancy as Ditchley had Ronald Tree. There was something enormously compelling to each of them about the houses they chose, and decidedly compulsive about the way they bought them. Despite Ditchley's decadent condition, it at least had people living there when Tree took it over. There had been a continuum in its rooms, fires lit, meals served, beds made, slept in and made again. Haseley in 1954 was completely abandoned and had been for almost a decade. Christopher Hussey saw Haseley before Nancy bought it, and wrote about what he saw in a 1960 *Country Life* article: "in the dusk of a wintery evening, the first sight of Haseley . . . was not encouraging: mud, hutments, rank grass and dripping trees around a dreary grey house that was shut up. . . . [W]e peered through plate-glass windows at dim derelict rooms, in one of which the ceiling was falling on to the floor.[5]

Life had altogether left the reception rooms downstairs and the bedrooms up; no ancient butler lived there, no old family member in a dower house on the grounds. The only person who had anything to do with the stately court was the late Colonel Muirhead's gardener, who continued to bicycle to the house twice a year to keep the topiary chess set in the sunk garden trim. Haseley was a ruin. Better houses were being torn down all over Great Britain. It took a Virginian, and an admirer of the eighteenth century, to love it as Nancy did. The Virginian in her saw the ghosts and the grandeur; the Georgian recognized the same picturesque quality in ruins that the Whigs had found in the Italian countryside and in the paintings of Piranesi and Robert. But to love Haseley as a ruin was one thing, to restore it another.

The house and the estate had flourished once; indeed, Little Haseley, the settlement in which Haseley Court grew, existed at the time of William the Conqueror's invasion and was recorded in the Domesday Book of 1086 as being held for the Bishop Odo of Bayeux by Harvey de Saio. A family named Scalebrook, of Yorkshire, owned it for the next two hundred years, followed by an Adam de Louches, then a Sir Richard Adderbury. Sir Richard sold it to Thomas and Dru Barantine in 1391; Dru was successively the sheriff and Lord Mayor of London, and to honor his position the Barantines built what was probably a substantial manor house on the site of Nancy's Haseley Court. The house must have been sturdy enough, because when a subsequent owner, Edmund Boulter, purchased Haseley three hundred years later and began to

Haseley Court's condition in 1954. "I know Vivien Leigh was very interested in Haseley and thought it very romantic," said Nancy. "She wanted Laurence Olivier to leave his house and move here."

build the Queen Anne addition, he incorporated remains of the medieval building instead of tearing it down. The Barantines also built (around 1500) the stable range of buildings, half of which Nancy transformed into her Coach House cottage.

When he bought the estate, Boulter built the center of the Court's entrance front in the typical restrained and balanced style of the first decade of the eighteenth century; when James Blacknall, the next owner, bought it around 1770, he added two bays at either end to complete the very attractive, dignified front of the house. (Blacknall was the squire of Great Haseley, Little Haseley's neighbor.) Haseley, however, was Janus-faced, its backside almost completely contradicting the simple order of its front, for around 1770 Blacknall also built a "Gothick" (Gothic Revival) wing replete with crenellation and coupled lancet windows that shot perpendicularly from the Georgian addition. This wing, with its range of buttresses, covered up the last of the original Barantine fourteenth-century manor and left the north and east sides of the house wonderfully quirky and asymmetrical. The heart of Haseley remained medieval.

In 1954, piles of brick, stone, slate and other rubble—along with the remnants of Nissen huts erected by the U.S. Air Force, which occupied Haseley during the war—littered the garden and the courtyard in random heaps. The glorious avenue of trees Nancy had seen when she'd dined there with Muirhead, which had reached outward along a lawn from the facade, had been cut into planking and sold; only stumps survived. And the house itself had a dead, empty expression on its gray stone face: Thirty-two blank windows and one doorway stared out of the Georgian front. A few panes of glass were missing; some were covered over in plywood, others left open to nature. An original clerestory window in the oldest part of the house was entirely boarded over, with a plank wedged in its frame to keep it from collapsing. As stucco peeled away from the Gothick wing, exposing its brick underclothes, moss coated every horizontal stone surface. The brew house outbuildings had nearly disappeared altogether, buried as they were in overgrowth. **It would have been cheaper if I'd bought Versailles.**

Inside was worse than out, for the house could no longer defend itself from the elements. Aside from the broken windowpanes, wood frames around the windows were neither air- nor watertight, and here and there roofing slates on the 1770 addition had slipped down the steep grading, leaving gaping spaces. Someone had shorn up the flat roof over the main part of the house during the preceding decade, but only after they had stripped the lead from it and sold it. They substituted concrete for the lead. A house's worst enemies, dry and damp rot, prevailed inside walls and ceilings and in discreet corners. The air force's presence, keeping the rooms warm during the war, saved Haseley from total disaster, but once they left, the rot spread fast. The upstairs rooms were all bad in 1954. The small reception room downstairs with the Palladian window was a victim. The drawing room was the hardest hit. When rot got into the "bones" of a house, it couldn't be painted over; the bones had to be replaced.

Besides structural decay, interior doors were missing from their hinges, floorboards had separated and were worn perilously thin and what had once been wallpaper was shredded and in patches or hung loosely from the walls it had been glued to. Slabs of marble and chunks of brick and stone that surrounded the fireplaces had broken off and were now gone. Harder to replace would be the pieces of Haseley's once-elegant architectural decoration. Large sections of cornice, wainscoting and skirting were missing in the dining room and the library, along with the base of a pilaster and snippets of tiny egg-and-dart fretwork. And rubble was piled up inside as well. In 1954 Haseley was an attractive, captivating, romantic ruin, but a heatless, waterless, lightless ruin as well.

Yet where most found Haseley half empty, Nancy recognized it as half full. Someone more pragmatic perhaps noticed the broken pieces, whereas Nancy saw marvelous details that survived from the fifteenth and sixteenth centuries. In one room downstairs, instead of the damp rot, filth or absent sections of woodwork, Nancy gravitated toward the fluted pilasters and Corinthian capitals of the Palladian window. The skeleton was there, and that's what she had been hunting. Haseley possessed a staircase, perhaps not as delicate as a Gibbons, but nonetheless of gracefully turned wooden balusters. In the room she would make her library there was an interesting Gothick bow window. In the hall stood a "vigorously carved stone fireplace" of about 1710 with "a Baroque overmantel and broken pediment . . . , delicately carved Rococo details of garlands, shells, and drapery."[6] These were just the sort of architectural exclamation points Nancy adored. "We used to motor down after dinner in the summer when it wasn't too dark," remembered Ruby Hill, "and we would crawl about all over the house with torches. Nancy would arrange the furniture in her imagination as we went. She'd say, 'I'll put such and such bed in here, and that table that I love in there,' It was all rather ghostly. Outside the window you'd see owls in the moonlight . . . and there was a nightingale." Instead of broken glass or missing mortar, Nancy saw ideal proportion and a suitable scale—grand but not too grand.

John Fowler once said to her, "Decorating is your root and passion; you'll never give it up." Nancy's true passion really lay in the actual houses themselves. Decoration—what she did with a house she "felt," the uncanny amount of effort and concentration she expelled on it—was the outpouring of that passion, not the passion itself. Decoration was a way of embracing a house, of making it hers. She was struck with passion for Haseley the moment she saw it again, and when she was finished with its restoration and decoration—it took her just over a year—this passion was evident everywhere, indoors and out, on the walls of the building and the walls of her garden, about each bedroom and flower bed. Cecil Beaton, a guest there a number of times, wrote of Haseley that it "could not be more beautiful to the spirit . . . every nook and corner is of an offhand perfection."[7]

To reach that state, Haseley required an enormous burst of creativity, from Nancy, from her collaboration with John Fowler and George Oakes and from anyone who did any work for Colefax and Fowler. There would be a thousand choices to consider, a number of mistakes to make, historical research to undertake. Plans were drawn up practically overnight by a Mr. Page of Essex for architectural and structural renovations to the five empty reception rooms, eleven neglected bedrooms, antiquated kitchens, draughty hallways and uninhabitable staff quarters: plans for the plumbing, the heating and electricity, plans for the eight bathrooms Nancy installed, plans for the missing ceiling of the Palladian Room and the existing vaulted ceiling of the long room in the Gothick wing.

That autumn Nancy, Miss Hill and John Fowler drove to Haseley from London two or three times a month to check on the builder's progress and to make decisions about the house's decoration. "We took a picnic with us that we ate in the smallest room on the ground floor," recalled Miss Hill. "Sometimes we lit a fire in the fireplace." **How cold we were as we collected sticks from the jungle outside, but the thickness of Haseley's woods made it perfect for a ladies room.** "There was no water laid on then," Ruby Hill continued; "one had to go in the bushes. And you had to take the dishes back to London to wash. I carried a lot of towels with me to wrap the old china in when we were finished with lunch." Nancy converted part of the medieval barn into a cottage so that by springtime she would be able to stay at Haseley and oversee the progress herself. "I don't think Nancy realized that workmen had to have an hour off in the middle of the day, because one day she went up to an upstairs bedroom and found them all sitting around with their backs against the wall, smoking their cigarettes and eating their lunches. She said, 'I hope you're comfortable. Would you like some mattresses?' They all worked pretty hard, though, and it was finished very quickly. In the evenings they all used to play football in the yard around an old discarded bathtub and all the rubble."

FROM THE PERPLEXING amount of structural work—the patching of walls, the sculpting of bathrooms from what had been dressing rooms and closets, the plumbing, heating and wiring, the scrubbing of ancient tile floors

The early eighteenth-century Rococo fireplace in the great hall was one of the finer architectural details left intact through Haseley's years of dereliction.

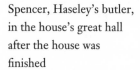

Spencer, Haseley's butler, in the house's great hall after the house was finished

and the restoration of wooden ones, the crafting of ceiling-high bookshelves in the library and the installation of modern appliances in the kitchens—they turned next to adding the colors and textures to the parade of whole, clean, empty rooms. Depending on the architecture of the room and what furniture and rugs she had decided would go into each, some rooms were painted, others papered, another stretched with fine silk. The walls were the backdrops of Nancy's decorative compositions; color was their centerpiece.

The entrance hall she painted a soft, mottled, sandy white, similar to the color she had painted the hall at Mirador, while the passageways leading through the upper floors were a pure white. She decided on the "palest beige" trimmed in white and gold leaf for the panels in her dining room, a soft, gray-green for the eighteenth-century panels of her boudoir and a lovely light blue silk to cover the walls of the drawing room. **I no doubt would have painted the walls of the drawing room, but I put silk on them instead because by that time I had bought from Lord Wilton the wonderful Chippendale carvings from the Tapestry Room at Ditchley, as well as some extremely grand eighteenth-century brocade pelmets and blue-colored satin curtains. I also bought the painted cornices from Ditchley that the pelmets hung on. With all of that, the room needed something special for the walls; that's why I used the silk.** Fowler painted the ceiling in the two-storey drawing room, picking out the existing plaster details in gold.

Nancy found the wallpaper for the small Palladian Room at Drottning-holm Palace in Sweden. **My Aunt Nancy was always asking me to go on a trip with her. Not being that interested, I teasingly tried to put her off by saying, "Only if you visit royalty." It seemed a safe reply; however, within a few weeks she called me to say, "We are invited to stay with the King of Sweden in his summer palace." I'd been to Sweden once before, with the Duke of Wellington, Ralph Dutton and Sonia Cubitt, and I was enchanted by its palaces and the arrangement of their museums, which seemed smaller and more personal than in most countries.**

Thinking we would be staying in one of these palaces, I took all my glad rags, my jewelry and my tiara. But when we arrived by air, we were met by the king in socks and shorts: He had spent the morning bicycling. He then drove us himself to his villa by the sea, where he enjoyed relaxing. It was more like a Victorian boardinghouse on the coast of Maine than a palace. The queen was there, with a very old lady-in-waiting on sticks, and the king's equerry: With us, that was the entire household. At meals, which were delicious, we helped ourselves. Dinner was at six-thirty so that the footman and the butler could enjoy their summer. I was rather ashamed of the wardrobe I'd brought with me; I hid my tiara in the *pot de chambre*.

She spotted the wallpaper when they toured the king's palace. Covering the walls of the Prima Donna's Dressing Room in Drottningholm's private theater, which dated back to the 1760s, it was hand painted in narrow strips, a vine growing up each panel with exotic birds resting on its stock. **The king took enormous trouble. He not only sent me a sample piece of the wallpaper when he learned how much I liked it, but he got his fine arts people to tell exactly what the color should be and above all what sort of paper to use.** John Fowler copied the one strip seventeen times to make enough to dress Nancy's Palladian Room. He painted each piece freehand, without tracing. **He copied it so perfectly you can't tell which is the original. Not even the king could tell the difference when he came to lunch at Haseley.**[8]

The walls of the eleven bedrooms on the upper floors of Haseley received a variety of treatments. There was the White Bedroom, with eighteenth-century paneling original to Haseley; the Mauve Bedroom; and the room Nancy referred to as "the Shooting Gallery"—it had been the previous owner's bedroom—which she painted the color of forget-me-nots. The *Paul et Virginie* Bedroom, or the Tobacco Bedroom, as it was also called, was hung with a French sepia wallpaper from around 1820 that depicted the love story of *Paul et Virginie* in beautifully rendered figures, palm trees and mountains in a ring around the small room.

Nancy's own bedroom, the Gothick Bedroom—the long "ark" that stretched from the Georgian wing out into the back garden—had the boldest painting. The room had been created when the tall fourteenth-century chapel (part of the Barantine medieval manor) was horizontally bisected in the eighteenth century into kitchens below and this room above. Its ceiling was vaulted, and when Nancy bought the house it was decorated with Gothick paneling. She removed the paneling, assuming she would find something older and better beneath; **when I found nothing at all, I sat down with John and we decided we could make it however we liked.** "However we liked" meant John and George Oakes reproducing on the walls the pumpkin orange Nancy had found in the saloon at Ditchley when she scraped with a coin, then painting panels in the hipped ceiling a lighter apricot orange.

As there was no original plaster molding in the ceiling or above the fireplace other than the Strawberry Hill Gothic corbel table, Nancy asked John and George to create trompe l'oeil decorations for it instead. **I specifically wanted trompe l'oeil; we couldn't have it plaster. I went off to Virginia then and left it in their hands. John and George Oakes—George has the most marvelous taste and is really very good at painting—worked together on that room like Tweedledee and Tweedledum. But when I returned from Virginia, I took one look at what they'd done and became furious. I said, "Damn John . . . he's gone ahead and done exactly what I told him not to, he's put** stucco on the walls." I really was livid. That's how convincing their trompe l'oeil was. The only thing that didn't quite work was the woman over the fireplace . . . her bosom hung down to her breadbasket. I used to threaten to expose myself to teach them. They covered the walls of the adjoining bath-room with powder blue wallpaper and strips of golden needlework.

With the painting completed, floors covered or restored and not a hint of Haseley's recent dereliction evident, a number of huge trucks pulled up the drive and parked before the front door. They were filled with furniture from Mirador, from Kelmarsh, from Ditchley and from London that had all been in store. I wept as I watched them unpack and carry things inside. I wept with joy *and* sadness. I felt as though these were my arms and legs pouring from the vans; my whole life seemed to be right there in front of me.

I directed the placing of each piece without going inside the house. I sat outside on the terrace and told them where to go. It was a miracle: Everything from my past fit perfectly into the rooms of Haseley. I never moved a stick of furniture from that day on.

HASELEY *was* a sort of miracle—not only how Nancy rescued the house, but how close she brought it to her ideal. It began with the architecture of the house itself that then melded with her sense of nostalgic beauty, with her sense of how one should decorate one's life.

The entrance hall at Haseley told a visitor everything about the house and about the world they were going to enter for a week or the weekend. The stately fireplace and cornice reminded one that the manor, and its chatelaine, could be rather grand; the ever present sprays of fresh cut flowers suggested their liveliness and flair, while the two high-backed chairs surrounding the wood fire were a prelude to Haseley Court's never ending array of creature comforts. Red twill curtains that came from Kelmarsh Hall were draped over the windows. A pair of nineteenth-century hall stools from Dagenham Park, their seats carved of wood to look like cloth, stood against the wall opposite the front door. Dutch Delft porcelains ornamented the mantelpiece. In the corner by the door rested a collection of walking sticks, as well as a plywood poodle and a carved pig with a boot-scrape for a belly.

Mr. Spencer, the butler at Haseley, dressed in his dark suit, opened the door and met each houseguest. He was an extraordinarily fine-looking man; no doubt he's related in some way to the Princess of Wales. He was Lord Carnarvon's valet, and when the two of them went to America, Spencer looked so much better bred that everybody in America addressed him as "Lord Carnarvon." They'd invite Spencer through the front door and expect the earl to go through the back.

Haseley was run the way Ditchley had been, only I had fewer working there. I didn't have a footman: Spencer had a hallboy but did most of the job of a footman himself, like waiting table. The hallboy was the man who brought in the coal and did the shoes and the knives. He was really an odd man because he did the odd jobs, but before the war the same position was called hallboy because he waited table in the servants' hall. I only had a couple in the kitchen at Haseley instead of three or four; the man was my chef, and his wife was kitchen maid. Then I had two housemaids and my own maid, Winnie, who looked after me. Whenever Nancy Astor came to stay, she brought her maid with her and a footman, because I always had to entertain more people for her. I also had a chauffeur to drive the car, but he did a little more than that because I didn't do much driving.

Spencer was very fond of my Aunt Nancy. When she became quite old, he used to help her around the garden. He once did a rather wonderful thing: She had handed him as a tip £100 and he gave it back, not to her but to her secretary. He sent it to her secretary with a note saying, "It's a pleasure to do anything for Lady Astor but I can't accept this," and all without telling me, which I think is very chic.

Depending on what time a guest arrived at Haseley, they either would be shown by Spenser into tea while their suitcases were taken upstairs and unpacked, or would be led by him to their bedroom to dress for dinner. Each bedroom at Haseley had lovely rugs (for instance, the early-nineteenth-century Savonnerie carpet of wreaths and bouquets in the South Bedroom), each had easy chairs (a Georgian provincial wing chair covered in chintz with odd pad feet in Bedroom No. 5), each had tables (a nest of three Chinese black lacquer coffee tables with lyre-shaped ends in the Mauve room) and each had a desk or a writing table (a George III mahogany kneehole writing table in No. 6). Each also had a dressing table, at least one chest of drawers or highboy, side and desk chairs, perhaps a sofa or a chaise longue, bedside tables on either side of the bed (a particularly fine pair of painted traveling tables with trompe l'oeil marble pilasters flanked the bed in the White Bedroom), any number of fine mirrors and lamps, and a painted coal scuttle. And each was liberally endowed with objets d'art, *objets de virtu* and good pictures (the eighteenth-century portrait of Lady Tara in the Mauve Bedroom) and prints (a pair of colored engravings of Ditchley in No. 5).

As the beds were the focal point of every guest room, they were, without exception, rare and valuable. The Mauve and South bedrooms each had one of the regal four-poster canopy beds Nancy bought at the Kimbolton sale: The former was George III, and was hung with printed linen curtains and a deep valance, while the latter had one with fluted baluster posts, a tester printed with feathers and a green silk taffeta canopy and curtains. Bedroom No. 3 had a painted Regency bed with trompe l'oeil painted posts, while a guest in No. 5 slept on a divan of the Empire style with a green painted headboard. The smaller guest rooms on the top floor, numbered instead of named, were as carefully and extravagantly decorated as the larger bedrooms on the second floor. All eleven bedrooms were part sleeping quarter, part boudoir, but entirely embracing: delightful bastions of privacy in a house full of people. They all had personalities of their own, but all had Nancy's indelible style in the arrangement, details and furnishings she had chosen. (Most had a *pot de chambre* somewhere in the room—hidden discreetly in a table or under a bed step—despite there being a bathroom attached to almost every bedroom: a touch attributable to Nancy's sense of tradition and history as well as humor.) Cecil Beaton hated leaving his room for the day's activities; he preferred reading "under a huge white eiderdown"[9] while the others played croquet outside his window.

Nancy called the bedroom with the *Paul et Virginie* wallpaper the Tobacco Room because of the snuff-colored ground in the rose-and-ribbon Brussels carpet, and the sepia tones of the wallpaper. The four-poster bed, from Ashburnham Place, was draped in nineteenth-century cotton hangings, pleated around the valance and trimmed in linen galloon. The light, white material wafted and drifted in a breeze when the window was opened. At each side of the bed was a Regency satinwood cupboard with a pleated-silk front and a white marble top. Against the wall were a pair of spoon-shaped, chintz-covered Victorian chairs and a Georgian mahogany writing table. The rich browns of the wood, the wallpaper and the carpet gave it all a subdued elegance, while the carpet's pattern and the hangings on the bed combined to create a most romantic effect.

I had all the curtains in the upstairs bedrooms, the curtains that weren't so grand, done the same way I had at Kelmarsh. I put a sewing machine in a top-floor room and had an old woman who worked in a shop in Oxford come and make them up there. One day I said to her, "You must have known this house very well, living so close by. . . ." Madame Bountiful was I. She said, "I don't know it, but my family lived here in the fourteenth century." She was related to the people who built the house . . . she was a Barantine! It had gone down since the fourteenth century and she was the woman now doing the curtains, and here I am saying in a way quite patronizing, "I suppose you know this house. . . ." I'll never forget it.

One of the Haseley spare rooms, called the White Bedroom, before and after restoration

Nancy originally decorated the White Bedroom for herself and offered the immense Gothick room to Lady Astor, who so often stayed at Haseley after she gave Cliveden to her son. But Lady Astor thought the Gothick Bedroom too big, and she wanted to be closer to her lady's maid, Rose Harrison. The White Bedroom had its own bathroom and an attached dressing room with a bed for Rose, so it was given to Lady Astor. Nancy Astor was the last surviving Langhorne sister. **I was the only person left in the family whom she could share her memories with. If she said, "Who was that woman who lived on the corner of Franklin Street?" I could say "Miss Jones." But if her sisters had been living, she probably wouldn't have spoken to me. Jakie and David's generation don't know . . . the blood is very diluted by the time it's got past my generation. They haven't got any of that family feeling. I suppose that life was closer in my day. You didn't have cars to go one hundred miles for lunch; you didn't have the Concorde.**

Besides a Louis XVI bed with a canopy and lace drapery, Nancy decorated the White Bedroom with flowered-chintz curtains hung from a pair of painted pelmet boards she bought at Coleshill. On the floor were two of the best rugs in a house full of best rugs: The larger was eighteenth-century English needlework embroidered with bouquets of flowers, the smaller a green-and-ivory hooked rug that Nancy brought from Mirador. And alongside the Louis XV gilt fauteuils, a Venetian toilet box and an eighteenth-century Dutch japanned commode, was one of the finest pieces of furniture in Nancy's collection: Resting against a far wall she placed one of a pair of black-and-gold Chinese lacquer *secrétaires* (its mate was in the South Bedroom) that she bought from Mereworth Castle. The cabinet was delicately adorned with scrolled leaves, flowers, grapevines, butterflies and painted mirrored doors, all surmounted by pediments with bird crests. All in all, the White Bedroom was very grand—well suited to the first woman to sit in the British Parliament, a friend of prime ministers and monarchs—yet arranged with the same Old Dominion ease of a room at Mirador, where both Nancys had been little girls and young ladies.

The Gothick Bedroom, which Lady Astor thought too big for her liking, actually was the size of a drafty chamber in a musty gothic novel. Valentine Lawford described it, after Nancy finished its decoration, as "less like a bedroom than a cross between a private oratory, an inspired operatic hunting lodge, and an ark, or galleon, floating high above the garden's sea of flowers."[10] One did not expect such a thing of the mistress's bedroom in a traditional English country house. It was Nancy Lancaster at her most bold and iconoclastic, but also at her most ingenious. Not only did she take a largely useless and obsolete space left from another era—a room that might have, in other contemporary conversions, been torn down or ended up as storage for discarded ice skates, kitchen chairs and horsehair mattresses—and make something marvelous of it. She also took a rather awkward space and actually gave it charm and a wholly convincing aura of intimacy.

Once the initial astonishment wore off, the pumpkin orange color for walls made sense, because it softened, brightened and bound together the many pieces of the room. It worked just as the same color had in the Ditchley saloon, where pumpkin orange helped it become the most welcoming room in that very formal house. The bed came from Ditchley, one of the four *lits à la polonaise* left in the house by Viscount Dillon. Gracefully curved iron rods supported a carved, painted cupola; ivory-colored silk trimmed in blue fringes dripped luxuriantly from the crowning pinnacle. The bedspread was French embroidered linen from the eighteenth century. Hanging from the ceiling were a pair of Victorian ormolu chandeliers. Also in the room were a pair of painted chinoiserie bedside tables circa 1800 with tiny blue bells hanging from the tops, a pair of rare Louis XIV side tables with Brescia marble tops and carved lambrequins in their stands, and an early Chippendale wall mirror with a squirrel and a ho ho bird carved in its frame. And a particularly outstanding feature among a long list of them was a seventeenth-century Spanish screen by the fireplace that Nancy had had in her bedroom at Ditchley: Standing nearly ten feet high and divided into six folds, it was made of leather and painted in gouache with scenes of life in China. The room's inventory listed fifty-five pieces of furniture, not including porcelains and other *virtus*, much of it priceless, all of it beautifully made, most of it noteworthy. A pair of carved-wood stag trophies on the wall came from Brympton d'Evercy—another wink at Ditchley's saloon.

Nancy ate her breakfast in her bedroom every morning, as she always had, and read the mail and the newspaper that came up with it on the tray. Her bed was placed across the window at the far end of the room instead of against a wall. A feature of the Barantines' manor still visible, the window reached from floor to ceiling and had a pointed pinnacle and a finely coffered soffit. As the bed had no set head or foot—the boards at both ends were of equal height and the cupola was over the middle—the housemaids could make it so that it faced either direction. **It was lovely because I could lie in bed in the winter and face the fire; then in the summer they'd turn it around so I could see the garden.** She had a sofa, a daybed and a number of old stuffed chairs to choose from if she wanted to read or simply retire from the rest of the house.

NANCY PAID great attention to all of the hallways and stair halls at Haseley, treating them like rooms, with silk curtains beautifully cut and draped, suites of pictures, Chinese paper screens, Chippendale wall mirrors, bookcases, hall tables, hall chairs and lamps. She covered the floors and steps with rush matting. **I didn't invent rush matting, but I probably made it chic. I always underemphasized wealth rather than flaunted it . . . I went for the humbler coverage.** Pamela Berry was horrified when she saw the matting. **"How *can* you have matting?"** She had had wonderful carpets made in Spain for her house. But **I was quite used to matting. In the summer in Virginia everybody took up their carpets and stored them in mothballs, then put down Japanese matting for the heat. You have to water it so it doesn't dry out completely. I removed it from the steps at Haseley eventually and put carpet there because I was afraid my aunt would catch her heels in it.** The pictures she hung in the stair hall rising to the second floor were a set of "Frye's Heads," mezzotint portraits of fashionable eighteenth-century ladies by Thomas Frye.

Where the drawing room was perfectly Palladian, with its neoclassical proportions, the library was asymmetrical, the bow window jutting incongruously out into the north courtyard. Nancy's library had actually been Muirhead's dining room, and her dining room was a sitting room. **If I had my way, I'd eat in a different room every night anyway, like they did at Lancut in Poland, where Ronnie and I stayed with the Potockis before the war.** Nancy's toy poodle Joe ran freely through Haseley, going wherever he wanted. "You never knew what to expect with Nancy; you never knew what she was going to say. She was completely unpredictable."[11] Haseley had a number of false windows in its facade, partly to balance on the outside what was wonderfully erratic in, and partly to fool the Georgian government that created a window tax. "I was staying at Haseley one weekend when there was another guest there who was rather a stiff English lady. Nancy made it her weekend-long quest to shock that poor woman. What did it was when Nancy very casually disrobed down to her undergarments in the drawing room while the ladies had coffee after dinner, and sat there as though nothing at all was amiss."[12]

"It carried on at Haseley as it had at Ditchley," remembered Lady Alexandra Metcalfe. "On Friday and Saturday nights you would put on your prettiest evening dress. In the winter the men wore lovely, warm velvet dinner jackets, dark green or dark blue. It was magical. She really created the same atmosphere at Haseley that they had at Ditchley before the war." The dining room was candlelit at night by a Spanish chandelier of rolled-iron branches and cut-glass baubles, and the candelabra on the side tables. Around the round gateleg oak table were buttoned verdigris leather chairs she bought from Borton-on-the-Hill and, placed opposite each other, two wing chairs covered in quilted chintz. **I tried to make it not like a dining room but like a breakfast room. I thought that more attractive and comfortable. And I like sitting around a round table.** A George II chimney glass, in the house when Nancy bought it, was poised above the fireplace.

"Maybe I made the dining room too comfortable. I remember being rather shocked when someone came down to breakfast in his nightclothes and dressing gown. Men generally came to breakfast dressed."

The library at Haseley illustrated how Nancy's earlier convictions about a room being sparingly furnished had come full circle.

The library, next to the dining room, was an ideal corner for a small group to retire to for their coffee. It seemed a tan cocoon, woven of old leather, faded silks, cottons, chintzes, linens and needlework; mellowed rosewood, walnut, mahogany and oak; and a red-rose-and-ribbon Brussels carpet well worn throughout the nineteenth and twentieth centuries. It was a room as pleasant to the eye—with its soft colors, the sloping back or dipped arm of its chairs, the upward curving of the side table—as it was to the body.

Nancy used nineteenth-century paper dress curtains for pleated lampshades in the library—**I thought they were so chic**—and hung over the fireplace an eighteenth-century portrait by Henry Thompson, R.A., of Master George Mainwaring wearing a red frock coat, brandishing a fishing rod and a trout basket. On all of the tables were antique painted metal and fruitwood boxes, as well as family portraits of the Langhornes, their children and cousins. The bookshelves were lined with more than three thousand volumes: complete sets of Wilde, Dickens, Balzac and Tolstoy, Repton on landscape gardening, Paxton's botany magazine, William Curtis's *Flora Londinensis* from 1798 and Henry Curtis's *Beauty of the Rose* from 1853. The room was peaceful, but it was never plain, for Nancy's greenhouses always provided a stroke or two of color—a forced yellow laburnum on the piano, perhaps a cascade of red roses.

The small Palladian Room on the other side of the hall, with its handpainted wallpaper, was designated the card room, particularly for bridge and canasta. "I remember a lot of canasta in those days, before and after dinner," said Elizabeth Winn, "with a lot of screaming and yelling. That was the sort of canasta that went on." Lawford wrote that "non-players are likely to be even more sensitive than players to the beauty of [the room's] displays of Meissen, Minton, Worcester, Derby, Bow and Chelsea china."[13] Nancy the voracious collector was personified in the Palladian Room: Its shelves—like the shelves and tables in every bedroom, bathroom and reception room in the house—were covered with everything from soup and melon terrines to Chelsea vegetables, Derby ewes, Dresden ducks and a pair of Japanese glazed pigeons. In the winter the Palladian Room often seconded as a breakfast room, and in the summer, when cards were played on the terrace, it was used as a writing room. Letterhead, pens and ink were set out on the apple green tablecloth; above hung the flowers and hart's-tongue leaves of a glass chandelier.

Rooms that Nancy decorated in her own houses were in some ways, often in every way, exceptional, but a few stood out. The pink hall at Kelmarsh was one, and the "soul of blue" saloon. At Ditchley, where the very grand rooms and their stucco embellishments were so domineering and restraint was so

The Palladian Room was named for its Venetian window. "Throughout the Georgian rooms Mrs. Lancaster's furnishing and decoration," wrote Christopher Hussey, ". . . play up to their character appropriately, yet with an essentially visual scale of wit and taste" (*Country Life*, February 18, 1960).

vital, the card and writing rooms in the towers existed as tiny, dazzling jewels. The Yellow Library at Avery Row was undoubtedly *the* masterpiece of Nancy's career and was often referred to as a "Mecca" for the interior decorator's craft. Haseley Court was the last big house Nancy decorated for herself or anyone else. John Fowler, after declaring decorating Nancy's "root and passion," had added, "and you'll never give it up." Following Haseley Court, however, then two years later 22 Avery Row, she completely quit decorating on a large scale and happily "retired" to country life and to her garden without a regret. But her last great English country house was also her greatest success from the viewpoint of pure decoration. Haseley Court was her "swan song"; empty rooms practically furnished themselves, so unequivocally did she know what Haseley needed.

Of all the rooms there, the drawing room, with its sky blue shantung walls, was Haseley's masterpiece. A dinner guest remembered the Manhattan he sipped by the fireplace in the drawing room, or the conversation he had with another guest seated on the damask-upholstered settee before Spencer announced dinner. He might not recall the subject of the tête-à-tête, nor the sweet Vermouth in the cocktail, but he remembered where he drank it and spoke it, the texture of the fabric, the grace of the gilded Chippendale rocaille on the walls, the scent of flowers, the snapping of the fire, the overall glow of the room.

Satin curtains and carved pelmets, the chandelier from Clamber—**the Victoria and Albert said it was the most perfect Waterford chandelier they'd ever seen**—the indescribable Rococo wall appliqués from the Tapestry Room at Ditchley, the mid-Georgian settee with its painted-and-gilt frame carved with shells and flowers, the eleven-foot-long carved side table, the mirror from Wardour Castle over that table: These and a number of other irreplaceable works of the decorative arts were at the center of the drawing room's cast, establishing its ambiance. If this had been all that was in the room, however, there should very well have been a velvet rope across its doorway: furniture to be looked at from a safe distance, never touched. But around, about and between, the elements that always made a room Nancy's own put the fancy pieces at their ease. She did with a room what both she and her Aunt Nancy did with a pompous old fool: She brought it closer to earth. **The drawing room was not only the grandest room in the house; it was the most lived in.**

I was interested in scale and color, but I was mostly interested in comfort. I like people to be comfortable, so I used in the drawing room the comfortable chairs that had once been in the bedrooms and dressing rooms at Ditchley and Kelmarsh during Victorian times. They were often of funny shapes: I was always looking for

chairs like that, comfortable to sit in, a little unusual in shape, that weren't precious. I used old chintzes that I'd collected to cover them. So there were old faded Victorian chintzes along with the shantung silk, the satin and silk damask, and the faded yellow Aubusson carpet. I like things to be like a salad. I don't like one thing to overpower another.

At the center of the room, underneath the chandelier, I put a Victorian whatnot, what you call a "conversational" or a "sociable." The thing I had laughed at when I first went to Kelmarsh I must have digested over the years, because in my mind it had become a chic little number. But what I think really made the drawing room was the two Elizabethan portraits that I hung above the two sofas. They were the same ones I had in my Yellow Room at Avery Row. The man who bought them from the Dillons had loaned them to the Tate, and when he died they were put up at auction at Christie's. They were of the two Fitton sisters: the one, Mary, being a lady-in-waiting to Queen Elizabeth I and supposedly the "Dark Lady" of Shakespeare's sonnets. They were painted in long-waisted white dresses that they had worn for a mask ball held in honor of the queen at Northampton. I remember John Fowler's horror when I left a bid on them—Tudor pictures were not very desirable then, especially for a Georgian drawing room—but I assured John they were like Goyas and far preferable to anything else I could afford to buy. These paintings, as out of place as John may have thought, absolutely made the room.

She did it all over Haseley, but most noticeably in the drawing room. Solving unequivocally this dichotomy was Nancy's most obvious contribution to the decorator's oeuvre and the history of interior decoration, not to mention true style in general. What fifty years before had been unthinkable, even in Lady Astor's day, that grandeur and elegance could be comfortable as well as slightly relaxed, has become part of what the late twentieth century actually defines as "good breeding": crumpled glamour, easy charm. It was what the Lost Generation, the Swell Set of the 1920s, grew up to be, and it was all that differentiated the old world and its money from the new.

I really lived in the drawing room. I would sit in there in the summertime with the doors and windows open. It was simply lovely. And you could walk right through to the garden. All of Haseley was that way. You could open it up end to end and let the summer air go right through. That house was very lived in, the whole thing.

The Victorian tablecloth from the Chinese Room at Ditchley was used in the corner of the Drawing Room at Haseley.

BY THE 1960S, so much of what Nancy and her contemporaries were born into at the turn of the century was nearly unrecognizable; their lifetimes coincided with *the* century in human history of technological, political and moral upheaval. Besides the most obvious, cataclysmic events—the world wars and the revolutions—the day-to-day and the mundane had become inextricably altered as well, reshaping all of their lives. For instance, the weeklong transatlantic passage, the keystone of international life just yesterday, now took only a matter of hours by air. Jet lag replaced seasickness, and an immediate time change supplanted the gradual sea change.

Though nostalgia for certain things was an inborn sentiment, Nancy Lancaster was very realistic about "peanuts and past recollections," never becoming completely ensnared by the debilitating tangle of looking backwards at what had been. There was always too much to do, and too many

Haseley's Drawing Room as Nancy found it in 1954 and after she decorated it

people to see. She did, though, continue to be an adamant letter writer and still referred to a trip abroad as a "crossing." (And she remained barred from the Royal Enclosure at Ascot because she was a divorcée.) She was a product of her day and her generation, and because of that certain details of how life had once been did live on at Haseley Court. Customs like guests' suitcases being unpacked by a maid or the butler when they arrived or formal dress at dinner remained de rigueur in Nancy's home. Women continued to get up from the table after dinner and go to another room for their coffee, leaving the men alone for their brandy and port. This old-fashioned segregation of the sexes was among the traditions disappearing elsewhere but was established at Haseley even though the landlord was a lady. Such manners never seemed out of place or the slightest bit forced at Haseley, even to the young who stayed there.

Something else that did not change at Haseley was the relationship between Nancy and the people who worked for her. They remained very close, just this side of intimate; she depended on them completely, and she never let them forget that she knew it. **I've liked some of them far more than I've ever liked my friends.** "One thing Nancy had very much in common with my mother is her way of treating all people in one way . . . exactly the opposite of snobbishness," said David Astor. "They were friendly to all people, but at the same time they never allowed any false grandeur or false pride. It had to be on the level with them, no matter who you were. As a result of that, they treated everybody well, including their own staffs, who they always made a great fuss over. My mother and Nancy always lived quite close to their staffs, which must have something to do with their being raised in Virginia. When the Duchess of York visited Nancy the other day, Nancy introduced her to the cottage's little staff. My mother would have done that, too."

A fellowship existed at Haseley of people who lived side by side in a house, on an estate, year in and year out. There was, of course, a respectful distance in both directions: Nancy was "Madame" to her indoor and outdoor servants—"We refer to her as 'Our Madame' between us"—and conversely: **I always used to make a great deal of noise whenever I entered the kitchens or somewhere else in the servants' part of the house to let them know I was coming.** Depending on their rank and position, Nancy called some of them by their first name, some "Mr." or "Mrs." and the gardener by his surname, as gardeners always had been called. In the early 1960s Nancy gave an enormous garden party at Haseley for past and present staff members of hers and Lady Astor's; over fifty attended.

Observing the age-old rural prerogative, Nancy jumped right into the village life of the two Haseleys even though she was new to the area. Little

Haseley and Great Haseley in the late 1950s were "still part of 'elmy England,' " wrote Lawford, "a rural landscape of green and grey and cobalt blue, miraculously undefiled. In Little Haseley village, golden stone cottages, half-buried in honeysuckle, peer from beneath fringes of thatch."[14] Nancy's role as she lived it reflected a tie familiar to her between the big house and the people of the village: She recognized traditions and duty, as well as purpose, and she was charged by the joy of seeing other people well fed and amused. Nancy possessed an abiding sense of community—and hierarchy—once again, very much against the contemporary grain.

> We started having the Horticulture Show at Haseley; it was for the people and the farmers of the two Miltons and the two Haseleys. I was the president of it and I used to open it; we'd have it out in front of the house and in the fields. I still give a cup every year for the smallest vegetable. I call them "unborn vegetables"; they call it "Household's Choice." Now our village is full of people who use it as a second home from London, but in those days it was full of workingmen and their wives.
>
> I used to give a three-course dinner at Christmas in the village hall for people over sixty-five. I'll never forget one year an old woman asking me if I minded if she took her plate of food home with her; "I forgot my teeth," she said. Lady Astor was wonderful at those dinners. She would get all dressed up in her pearls and her furs. They loved it. She worked very hard at things like that and was the life and soul of the party. She would regale them all with old stories from Virginia like "Uncle Remus," not that anyone could understand a word she said in that accent. At one party I remember her saying she felt cold and asking could she have her fur. An admiring old workman put his arm on her shoulder and said, "It's not a shawl you want, Milady." After dinner we always had music and singing, and because they all were so old we played musical hats instead of musical chairs.

Lady Astor, in her eighties but almost as spry and absolutely as game as ever, was a mainstay to life at Haseley Court. She used to play golf, always looking very smart. She had a net out at the end of the terrace in front of the house, and she would hit the ball into it over and over again. She'd swing her clubs all day long. And she would walk and walk—she had the most marvelous figure and always wore tight stays—she walked around the garden and down into the village, where she would visit the neighbors.

> Nannie knew everything about everyone in the village. Everybody adored her. I had only lived at Haseley for four years when a

"She came whenever she wanted, arriving in a Rolls-Royce with her footman and her maid," said Nancy Lancaster of her aunt Nancy Astor, the last surviving Langhorne sister. "We had a great deal of fun together."

delegation from the village came and said they wanted Lady Astor to open the Horticulture Show. I told them I couldn't possibly ask her. It was midsummer and she was at her summer house in Sandwich-by-the-Sea and she was over eighty. I told them I'd get them Vivien Leigh instead. They said, "We'd rather have Lady Astor." They thought she belonged to them. She had that marvelous quality I've never seen in another person.

"I think my mother relied on my cousin Nancy a great deal in her final years," said David Astor. "I suppose they got along well because in many ways they are similar. They were amused by the same things. They made fun of each other, themselves and other people. And neither ever stood on dignity; I mean, Nancy's jokes are made largely at her own expense. My mother was the same. And both were very high-spirited. As soon as one of them was in the room, you knew it." (David Astor's always been in love with me. He used to stare at me when he was a little boy. I remember him sitting under the table the day I married Ronnie, not able to take his eyes off me. I said to him, "You're in love with me, aren't you?")

Nannie was the staunchest person to have behind you if you were in any kind of trouble . . . and not just in the family. If you went to Nannie and asked for help, no matter who you were, she would drop everything. When we were at Kelmarsh Michael became very ill; he was seven and had internal bleeding. We had all the specialists come down from London but they said, "This boy is going to die and there isn't anything more we can do," and they got up and went away. Nancy Astor dropped everything she was doing—she was giving one of her most important speeches in Parliament that night—and got into a little sporting car and drove herself over icy roads to come down and see him. She came down and sat by him all night long. She did her Christian Science work with him; she said later that she saw death passing over that boy's face. She wouldn't let me or Nanny Weir into the room because she said we were full of fear. I was upstairs dancing naked in front of the mirror, I was so upset by it. It was the most extraordinary thing. She had this ability of feeling for you and putting aside whatever was important she was doing to come and help.[15]

There was quite a family row in 1945 when it was clear that she ought to retire from the Commons. She wanted nothing to do with retiring, but all of us who loved Nannie thought she should get out. She had been in for twenty-five years by then and simply loved it, but she was getting old and she was becoming a nuisance in the House. She interrupted everybody's speeches, not just Winston's. Uncle Waldorf couldn't bear for her not to win the next election if she stood, but he didn't feel he would be able to back her up. He was also ill at the time.

Years later she was furious at Harold Macmillan for not putting her in the House of Lords when he was prime minister. But they weren't putting many women in the Lords then, and they wanted people who wouldn't be a disruption. If Nannie were in the House of Lords, she'd have been doing cartwheels down the aisle the whole time.

Peter Wilson, Nancy and Frederick Ashton in Haseley's Drawing Room in 1961

The two Nancys developed a relationship over the years both close and stormy. By the time Nancy Lancaster owned Haseley and Nancy Astor was her regular guest there, it had survived passionate disagreements and political maelstroms on two continents for more than half a century. A family skin thickened by generations of merciless needling and lightning repartee allowed for a certain freedom of expression between them, and a certain cheek. Michael Astor wrote that his cousin "did not hold my mother in awe, but loved her and sometimes, even, treated her like a child."[16] At Haseley they were often more like sisters, indeed schoolgirls, with each other rather than a respectable former MP in her dotage and a fawning niece. "Lady Astor and

On warm afternoons a card table was carried to the terrace outside the Drawing Room. John Stuart, Nancy and Rosie Kerr in 1961.

Nancy used to fight all the time at Haseley without a second thought," remembered Jack Pierrepont, an American guest. "They could be downright abusive to each other, especially Lady Astor. But neither of them seemed to notice it." **She was wicked, but she also never took offense.** "I remember Lady Astor pulling me aside at Haseley and saying, 'Don't listen to my niece Nancy. She lies a lot.'" **She always used to say that; you could hear her at the other end of the table: "My niece Nancy lies for pleasure."**

We're a family that says everything and says anything but never goes to bed angry. Tears and screams, then laughter and kissing. But other people are simply horrified by it. When Christopher Hussey and his wife came to stay, Mrs. Hussey took me aside and said, "I can't get over how horribly your aunt talks to you, and how wonderfully patient you are." It never *occurred* to me she was saying anything horrible to me. She was saying just the sort of things I say to Alice, which annoy Alice very much because she's more tactful than I am.

Nannie and I got on very well and I enjoyed her company. When I think of all the grand houses and interesting people that had surrounded her all her life, I'm amazed how she settled in at Haseley and took as much interest in its comings and goings. She never dwelt on the past in a melodramatic way, no "big me" and "little you." And I never stopped being astounded by her ability to make friends with all sorts and all ages. She was crazy about children. She'd drive children into a frenzy of excitement.

When my son Michael sold Mereworth, he, his wife and two daughters, Isabella and Esther, their maid, nurse and butler, all moved in at Haseley for a year. That was a very happy year for me. The children were here all week, then the parents came for the weekends. And Reggie and Alice used to spend all their weekends in the cottage. On Friday nights we had my neighbor Colonel Richardson in for bridge, hilarious bridge, with cards flying across the room.

Another of the twentieth century's most prominent tastemakers, Charles de Noailles, with Nancy in the doorway of Haseley's Walled Garden

Summer days seemed longer and brighter at Haseley, the doors and windows opened to the air, the gardens, the fields beyond and the steady, operatic chorus of songbirds. Everyone played croquet on the grass in front of the house or in the walled garden on turf kept like a fairway, and flirted with lawn tennis. Lunch was always outdoors then: the same elegant place settings as indoors, the same exquisite three courses.

When autumn arrived, Nancy still shot as often as she could with the matched pair of shotguns that General de Crespigny gave her. **I didn't have my own shoot at Haseley, so there was no more "I'll scratch your back if you'll scratch mine." I belonged to the syndicate at Wormsley, or I shot elsewhere if someone invited me. I kept shooting and riding until I was more than eighty, then I had a heart attack. When I was in the hospital, they discovered a frightful lump next to my shoulder and were going to operate immediately to remove it when they found after more tests that it was callus that had built up from all my years of shooting. I suppose they'd never seen such a thing on a woman.** For the long winter nights at Haseley, its many rooms—fires aglow, some candlelit, all of them sweetened with flowers—actually were warmer, more embracing, than rooms anywhere else. Guests who had tasted the pleasures of the great country houses before the war found something wonderfully familiar about Haseley Court. It was not simply a saccharine-laced dream; its savories and its stream of rapier-sharp dialogue were too vivid to be purely wistful. Yet its tone was clearly born somewhere other than 1960s England or 1970s Oxfordshire. It came from wherever Nancy's imagination lived.

Mirador's spirit of delight and pleasure was reborn at Haseley Court. The lovely plantation house in Albemarle County possessed Grandfather and his four-in-hand; Nanere and her sugar cakes; the aunts, their maids, trunks and beaux; and the uncles, with their charm and earthbound sense of living. It had the Langhornes' wide-open hospitality. Haseley had only Nancy; her will and her efforts kept it real, tangible. Nancy knew how to make a certain kind of magic. **I squeezed all the juice out of the lemon.**

IN THE FIRST YEAR she owned it she turned the interior of Haseley Court into a true ideal, both as a home and as an act of the decorator's craft; over the next ten years, with the same dash and equal extravagance, she created gardens that surpassed even the house for sheer pleasure and delight. If any art might be called Nancy Lancaster's "root and passion," it was her gardening.

What set the gardens apart from the house as an achievement was that outdoors Nancy started with nothing. The grounds of Haseley in 1954 were not only a blank canvas but a raw canvas, less gesso, stretcher and frame. Aside from the house itself at its center, a few outbuildings and the topiary chess pieces in a weed-strewn sunk garden, nothing but rubble, tree stumps, a broken wall or two and a flat terrain existed on her new property. Haseley offered her no stream, no lake, hardly a vista and no eighteenth-century landscaper's drawings discovered in a brittle bundle of old papers. She was entirely on her own. Like the masters of other media, she fashioned something extraordinary simply from an intangible muse. The result inspired Lanning Roper to write in 1963, "A number of gardens have been made since the war, but I know of none so imaginative as that of Haseley Court."[17]

There were two ways of entering Haseley's garden: the way Nancy walked into it each morning, and the way everyone else did. Visitors turned their cars left onto the drive from Little Haseley, well along a winding track from any of Oxfordshire's trunk roads. A sense of coming upon somewhere special, a place of tranquillity and expectation, began immediately with the fenced pastures either side and the wide swaths of crocuses, snowdrops and, later in the spring, yellow and white daffodils. Midsummer, a canopy of green from the double row of plane trees overhead enshrouded the drive. Two hundred yards ahead came a clearing, a sharp left-hand turn, then straight in front—at the top of a square *tapis vert* and a raised gravel-and-flagstone terrace—the house's Queen Anne/Georgian facade appeared in one spectacular shot: the culmination of the journey and an introduction to another world. Nancy, with the now renowned landscape artist Geoffrey Jellicoe, here made a statement of architectural impact in the French tradition. Even those who knew this scene and what lay behind it were still caught unawares each time they reenacted it. A pair of sculpted lions with putti on their backs framed the steps up to the pedimented front entrance of the house.

Nancy, on the other hand, came to her garden from the inside. She woke up every morning enveloped by its verdure and its sweet scents; she lived among its branches and box hedges. She also cultivated it continually, for Haseley's garden became a large measure of Nancy's life itself. Long after the conception of vistas, allées and lists of plants, and though there were gardeners to execute the day-to-day work, she spent afternoons planting flats of perennials propagated in her greenhouses, weeding a far corner of the *potager* or simply surveying what nature presented anew each morning. Haseley's garden was ongoing, always evolving in her mind as well as in the soil itself. Inside the house the furniture was never moved from the day the vans were unloaded, but the garden was in a perpetual state of transformation.

The various rooms of Haseley's garden were interconnected by corridors, a series of axes leading the eye along the vistas and the feet along to the next stop. A short walk to the east lay the Grand Terrace and the topiary chess set. There had been topiary at Haseley since the beginning of its time. "[At] Lit-

Ronald Tree, MFH, painted by Sir Alfred Munnings

From High Victorian to *haute style* in Ditchley's saloon: Lord Dillon's arms and armor gave way to Nancy's unabashed palette.

The Great Hall when Lord Dillon owned it and after Nancy decorated it. William Paley said, "Nancy Tree had the reputation of having the best taste of almost anyone in the world" (Smith, *In All His Glory*, p. 206).

In Nancy's transformation of the Tapestry Room, the fantastic Rococo *boiseries* moved from the background to center stage. On a snapshot taken of the room in the mid-1930s, she wrote in the margin below simply, "My New Room!"

A distinguished scholar and an utter recluse, the last Lord Dillon to live at Ditchley spent most of his time alone among his books in one of his two libraries. For the Trees, however, the Ditchley library was a meeting place where they and their many house guests gathered in the evening.

The Blue and White Bedroom. Ditchley was "the country house in England most admired for its combination of past and present," wrote John Cornforth, "of enthusiasm for the 18th century and appreciation of modern comfort" (*Country Life*, October 1985, p. 1173).

The Yellow Bedroom, where the prime minister slept at Ditchley. Winston Churchill wrote in his memoirs that he stayed at Ditchley when there was a full moon because it was safer than Chequers. "What he has not recorded," wrote Valentine Lawford, "is that it was incomparably more attractive and comfortable" (*Vogue's Book of Houses, Gardens, People*, p. 91).

ABOVE: Loelia Westminster thought Nancy's bedroom at Avery Row an "enchantment" and "as rural-seeming as anything this side of the Wiltshire border." BELOW: Looking from the anteroom through to the Yellow Library. "Her love of colour, her flower sense, and her feeling for comfort," wrote Cecil Beaton about Nancy, "have brought a welcome touch to many an English house so sorely in need of such ministrations" (*Glass of Fashion*, pp. 279–80).

The Yellow Library at Avery Row

"John and I made our swan song together at Haseley, which I think was a successful job." John Fowler's craft and Nancy Lancaster's taste combined perfectly in her bedroom at Haseley, the Gothick Room.

The box hedges, lavender swatches, weeping mulberries and flint paths of the Stone Garden portion of Haseley's Walled Garden. Nancy was helped with the planting plan by Vernon Russell-Smith.

Walled Garden borders with the Coach House in the background. "I found it awfully difficult to work with Nancy," said Sir Geoffrey Jellicoe, "because she was such a master in her own field."

ABOVE: "Nancy Lancaster has been the most influential
English gardener since Gertrude Jekyll," proclaimed designer
David Hicks (*House Beautiful*, November 1993, p. 119).
BELOW: The laburnum arch at Haseley in full bloom

"Lady Astor's Canal" in the mid-1960s

tle Haseley master Barantine hath a right fair mansion and marvelous fair walkes *topiarri operis*, and orchards and pooles," wrote the Tudor antiquarian John Leyland in 1540.[18] Nancy re-created the "poole" and replanted the orchards, but the topiary was there when she bought the house, though it was not the original bushes that Leyland saw. Her yew, box and Portuguese laurels were planted in the mid-nineteenth century, then sculpted into pawns and rooks by Lionel Muirhead, "a true artist and a great Chess player."[19] They survived the dereliction that beset the rest of the estate following Anthony Muirhead's death because his gardener, Mr. Shepherd, continued to bicycle to Haseley occasionally to clip them. Shepherd referred to the larger than human figures as "my Kings and Queens."

Nancy had the chess pieces placed on a pattern of lavender and santolina shorn close to the ground like a carpet. **I planted gray and silver stuff that crept; it was Victorian bedding, I suppose. I had wanted to create a chess-**

board for them, but the sunk garden wasn't perfectly square. "This garden is one of my favorite layouts in the country," wrote Lanning Roper, "for it is completely satisfying in design, in the low-key colouring of the greens and greys and in the repetition of the simple, bold, sculpted shapes."[20] The balustraded Grand Terrace, a few steps up from the sunk garden, was where Spencer set up the luncheon table among the luxuriously drooping trumpets of potted datura and boxed oleanders, lemon trees and lemon verbena. It was Italianate in its nature, "redolent," wrote Lawford, "as a greenhouse in the fitful sun."[21] Roses grew up from a border below the balustrade; lilies, peonies and standard daisies overgrew.

To the west of the chess set was a plain turf lawn with an ancient cedar of Lebanon shading a corner of it. To its east an afternoon's stroll continued along paths and the grass-carpeted Woodland Walks Nancy designed. She built a papier-mâché gothic folly in a grove of poplars at the extreme end of the garden. **It was entirely believable looking, and as money was a little short then after all the work I'd done, you should have seen the look on my sons' faces when I told them I had had it carved of stone.** Patches of spring bulbs like blue anemones shot up among the trunks of the trees and the scented shrubs like pink viburnum. **I sold a portrait of the boxer Jim Molineaux that I'd only recently bought, and with the profits floodlit the garden and the woods as if they were moonlit. The lights were on the roof of the house and hidden by the trees, which gave a lovely effect.**

Nancy had her "poole" dug parallel to the woodland on the same north–south axis as the house's Georgian front. A long rectangular slip of water she called Lady Astor's Canal, it reflected on its glassy surface the various hues of green in the profusion of shrubs growing on either side of it. The mouth of a grotesque mask from the Brenta, placed in a rough-hewn wall at the near end, slowly dribbled water into the waterway, sending the slightest ripples among the dappled foliage. A small rowboat rested on one bank; old, pale carp drifted languorously beneath the mirrored picture.

The garden took up a relatively small area of land, perhaps ten acres, yet there seemed so much of it and to it, it was more like a palace garden than a manor's in what it encompassed. Walking back toward the house, along one of the Box Parlour's flower-bordered flint paths, a Gothick doorway in the adjacent wall led through to a tiny privy garden with an astrolabe sundial at its center. Across this short lawn and through a door at the other side—between the main house, its outbuildings and a long stone wall—a large gravel courtyard emerged, looking like the lake of a Capability Brown park. Another important trait of the planning, and subsequently the garden's effect, was the rhythm between ease and intensity, open space and density. Though mostly utilitarian—it was here that deliveries were made—this courtyard was minded as carefully as any other aspect of Haseley. Its walls were hung with billowing old climbing roses, clematis and tree lupins; narrow beds were packed with euphorbias, sages, a scattering of species geraniums that seeded themselves outward into the gravel.

By 1965 some of the young trees and shrubs Nancy planted had started to peek over the top of the long wall at the north side of the courtyard, tantalizingly hinting at what might be behind it. Ten years before, all that existed through that door was the wreckage of what had once been a kitchen garden—only a bed of asparagus still flourished there—while beyond it lay open fields. Now, however, the door led through to what seemed a dream. The transformation was hallucinatory: the colors, the scents, the life abounding, all mirage. Nancy Lancaster's Walled Garden at Haseley was truly one of England's most splendid places. Held captive by the patchwork stone wall and a pair of arbor tunnels was a fantastic world, as Lawford described it, of "lawn and flowers, vegetables and fruit, where roses, lilies, and delphiniums are interspersed with raspberries and strawberries, red currants and weeping mulberries, chives, lettuces, artichokes, and beets. The flower smells are indescribable: a combination of Canterbury bells, rosa mundi, and buddleia, shot through with lavender and pinks."[22]

There was a distinctly French element about the Walled Garden, reflected in its designer's natural regard for *échelle*, or scale. One particular portion of the garden was the ideal of the *jardin potager*. If one looked at the whole again, it also possessed an air of the Italian Baroque: Nancy originally called it her Baroque Garden. There were wonderful surprises at the end of each path, but especially Italian was the sculpted boy residing in the small, arched grotto. A pipe installed in the stone ceiling over his head provided an irregular drip, drip, drip, like groundwater in a subterranean cavern. The overgrowth Nancy allowed to overtake the garden suggested the great Italian villa gardens of the Renaissance—not in their "prime," but as English travelers saw them in the eighteenth century, fifty or a hundred years later. By then neglect was pervasive; rampant was the "venerable impression of the hand of time"[23] that Nancy loved. This sort of dereliction is repeated time and time again in human history as a once vital society falls out of step; Nancy's re-creating its effect at Haseley found a sympathetic audience in postwar Britain.

What pulled the Walled Garden's disparate influences together physically was an unbending credo: **I like a formal layout and informal planting. Of the two the most important to me is the layout, the form. A very formal layout is like bone structure to a face; once you have it, you can put whatever fat on it you like. Bone structure lasts longer. A strong layout, then the softness of informal planting.**

I used box for a lot of the garden's formal lines. I'm crazy about box. I like box because Virginian gardens had box. I love the smell of it. Mirador had box, but my grandfather hated it because he said it smelled like a wet dog. He pulled it all up and put in roses and other bushes. When I bought Mirador, I pulled up his roses and planted box again. I love the smell of wet dog.

I divided the Walled Garden into four squares and decided that there should be a different design in each square. I paid Russell Page to plan the squares, but I never used his plans because I thought they were too fussy. Instead, each square sort of took shape gradually as I went along. In the first evolution I planted one of them with vegetables in a lovely pattern. That was absurd, though. Every time I ate a lettuce, I upset the pattern. It's really better to have a vegetable garden in straight lines. Now that corner and the one catercornered to it have grass centers.

In one of the two lawns, topiary swirls near each corner accented the outline of the square. In the other, Nancy used to the same purpose lattice pyramids that white roses or clematis climbed, and espaliered fruit trees with branches trained in the shape of wineglasses. The latter square was often used for croquet.

The Stone Garden within the Walled Garden was the square most elaborately conceived. **I got patterns I used from old prints and photographs. Someone sent me a picture postcard of the Roman pavement at Torcello and said wouldn't this make a marvelous garden plan? It's four fishhooks. I made the paths in the shape of the hooks out of flint stone from a quarry near here. Later I added box.** The four flint fishhooks radiated from a wagon wheel, with a hub and spokes grown from box hedges. In the beds between the spokes Nancy had rugs of lavender, while planted in each of the four hook loops was a weeping mulberry. The outer beds had a variety of standard rosebushes, annuals and perennials flowering for three seasons out of four.

Food for the eye as well as for the palate thrived in the final square. The ornamental cabbages were purely decorative, as were the sweet peas, but raspberries, *fraises des bois*, gooseberries and quince were grown to eat; a medlar tree at the square's center bore fruit that, once it went bad, made a good jam. In this quarter of the garden Nancy used a circle in the square, a form she had used in remodeling the library of Kelmarsh Hall. Round grass paths ringed the medlar; the deep beds at the outside had curved interior lines and squared exteriors bordered by box.

Without any planting the Walled Garden became a beautiful earthwork sculpture in itself. During the winter—the most telling time of year, when nearly everything was shorn of foliage—a gray, brown and green framework remained. The forms of the various beds were clearer then. The strong shape of the summerhouse, stripped of roses, stood out against the sky. The bare branches of fruit trees reached gnarled fingers upward, while those of the mulberry pointed sadly, limply, toward the cold ground.

Of course, the garden looked its best brimming with greenery and bright flowers. The other half of her design formula advocated anarchy. I love a garden that is like a crowded shoe . . . and one that's seeded itself all over the place. Haphazard. Unexpected. An exuberance. I've never done a color scheme in my life . . . I did my garden here as I went. I want to be surprised. I like to see a violet at the back and a hollyhock coming out in the path; not like an herbaceous border, where everything is lined up front to back according to height. Herbaceous borders are too set and dated. I want surprises; I like to be surprised by a garden. I want planting to go haywire, for a plant to fight for its place by taking over its neighbor's. It doesn't please me to see some rare thing from Shanghai or somewhere treated like something special.

I'm not a horticulturalist; I don't know a thing about plants and I don't really care. But I know what I like. For instance, I remember when I was a widow going to see a garden made by an old man outside Richmond. I drove all the way there from Mirador to see his border because it was so thick you couldn't see the ground. I said to him, "How do you *get* it this thick?" and he said, "I plants it so thick that no weeds can come up." That's what I like. Everywhere things growing through everything else. Some people think it's "bad" for the plants, or they say, "This is too shady a corner and too cold for such and such a thing." Horticulturalists are apt to think too much about how happy the plants are going to be. As one friend said after watching me plant, "Instead of putting them in the ground with love and tenderness as they tell you to, you plant them with a curse, 'Get in, damn you, and lie down.'" I remember the first bulbs I ever planted were for Aunt Phyllis at Mirador. There were three hundred of them, and I planted every one upside down. But they righted themselves and bloomed beautifully.

My favorite plants and flowers are the ones that have been around for a long time. I like old-fashioned flowers that you saw in old gardens rather than these new horticultural varieties they brought back from out-of-the-way places. I don't want that sort of garden at all. I rather like things that I'm used to, things that I saw as a child in Virginia. In Virginia we cook with heat in the summer and freeze with cold in the winter. They are obviously going to be rather common plants that can stand that sort of climate. That's the sort of flowers I'm used to. I filled my borders full of hollyhocks, delphiniums, sweet william, wallflowers and different salvias that go with the old roses. I love pinks. There's a garden I know where the pinks have got so small because they've been there so long . . . they look like blades of grass now. Nobody's fed them or looked after them. They just keep coming up and each year getting smaller and smaller. I find that rather romantic.

One of the first things I planted was old-fashioned roses, species roses that came out in the time of Empress Eugénie in the nineteenth century. I put them all around the four squares but mostly along the south wall. I specialized in old roses. I suppose I associate them with my childhood, too. They were all over Virginia. Bushes that people brought over from England with them were left behind whenever they moved on, and they kept growing in the garden.

The whole Walled Garden grew into a spectacular demonstration during its high-summer peak, a revolution trying to get loose from a predisposed order. Weaving in and out of those favorite roses were great heaps of everything from black-eyed Susans to alchemilla mollis, from sedums, phlox and salvias to euphorbias, campanulas, achillia, daylilies, columbines, artichokes (gone to flower and seed), foxgloves, clumps of dill weed and even a patch of pampas grass: all of it elbowing and kicking for sunlight and breathing room. So much violence created so much beauty; her informal, absolutely unexpected planting damn near breaking free from its formal layout.

Another Virginian, Thomas Jefferson, was a dedicated gardener. He wrote in a letter to the painter Charles Willson Peale that "no occupation is so delightful to me as the culture of the earth, and no culture comparable to that of a gardener."[24] Something in that "rich spot of earth" inspired cultivation and a fervent vision of Paradise. And just as Monticello has been referred to as Jefferson's autobiography—that one could learn all one wanted about the man from the house he built—the same can be said of Nancy Lancaster and her gardens at Haseley Court. She was born into a most formal of backgrounds—Victorian Virginia and Edwardian England—and thrived within its evolving constrictions. Yet the color in her life was entirely unexpected, surprising, unpredictable and overflowing. The spirit of Haseley was Nancy's own spirit transposed into the soil.

> *I loafe and invite my soul,*
> *I lean and loafe at my ease observing a spear of summer grass.*

Haseley was Nancy's "Song of Myself": expansive, generous, sensual, independent.

> *Houses and rooms are full of perfumes, the shelves are crowded with perfumes,*
> *I breathe the fragrance myself and know it and like it,*
> *The distillation would intoxicate me also, but I shall not let it.*[25]

*I have lived a particular period of history, and I seem to be the
only thing left from that period. I'm like half the ham sandwich;
I'm the only one left.*

THEY DEMOLISHED the Perkins house on Franklin Street in Richmond
to make room for an expanding Commonwealth Club. In 1927 Ogden Codman sold the town house at 7 East Ninety-sixth Street that Ronald and Nancy
Tree rented from him in New York and moved to the South of France. After
various owners and purposes, the Parisian-style building now houses the
Manhattan Country School. Its round dining room, now an office, seems very
cold without the gilded decoration it was designed for, and most of the original woodwork has been painted over and over again; the house survives, however, with its character defiantly uninstitutional.

Cliveden, the Astor house that Nancy Perkins first visited during the
First World War, was opened to the public as a museum by the National Trust
in 1966; in 1986 it was converted into a luxury hotel, where one might sleep
in the "Lady Astor Suite" or the "Prince of Wales Suite." The stunning portrait of Nancy Astor, painted by John Singer Sargent when she was Mrs.
Robert Gould Shaw, hangs in the lobby of the hotel. A round blue enamel
plaque on the enormous building at 4 St. James's Square reminds passersby
that this was once the London home of the first woman to sit in Parliament.
Lady Astor died in 1964 at Grimsthorpe Castle. "She went to the grave certain that Damn Yankee was one word," said a friend of hers from Virginia.

Cottesbrooke Hall, the Trees' first full-time home in England, continues as a private house. Major and the Hon. Mrs. MacDonald-Buchanan, who
for years had been hunting with the Pytchley and renting hunting boxes in
Guilsborough, bought the estate in 1933 when Robert Brassey put it on the

Nancy with her granddaughters Isabella and Esther Tree in Greece in 1972

market. They made the one dramatic alteration to the house of the twentieth century: turning the great redbrick pile back to front. What had been the
entrance facade, flanked by Palladian-style wings, now became the back of
the house, while the former garden facade was installed with a new front
door and entrance stair. Lord Gerald Wellesley—later "the Architect Duke"
of Wellington—rendered the changes for Major MacDonald-Buchanan.
"The advantage of this," wrote Gordon Nares, "was that the whole of the
south front could be given over to the more formal family living-rooms,
while the sunless north front could be used for the entrance hall and the
principal reception-rooms."[1] The MacDonald-Buchanans later hired Geoffrey Jellicoe to design a formal box garden that would fill what had been the
entrance courtyard. The portrait Ronald Tree commissioned Alfred
Munnings to paint of Frank Freeman and his horse Pilot, which once hung

in the great hall at Kelmarsh and the library at Ditchley, now hangs at Cottesbrooke Hall.

Cottesbrooke's neighbor Kelmarsh Hall remains a private house as well, though modern Britain has been far more intrusive upon its tranquillity. Built so conveniently for the eighteenth century along the Northampton–to–Market Harborough carriageway, Kelmarsh now sits alongside a traffic artery on which cars speed along at seventy miles per hour, their drivers only peripherally aware of the rhododendrons that Nancy planted when she lived there and that still flower magnificently every spring. Lord Bateman's digging out of the road in the mid-nineteenth century guaranteed that juggernauts passing by cannot be seen, but they can be heard, their roar breaking through the songbirds' daily recital. Ground was broken in 1990 for a six-lane motorway running east to west—to connect Cambridge with the M1—cutting through Scotland Wood, a woodland only a mile from the Hall. (Farther on, the new road dissects the previously untouched site of the Battle of Naseby.) Kelmarsh Hall is used by the pilots of the RAF and the USAF as a landmark on training missions. The screech of obsolete jet fighters banking turns a mere hundred meters overhead is unbearable, not only in the house but even more so in the village of Kelmarsh.

The Hall is kept lovingly by Colonel Lancaster's sister Valencia. The stables are empty, the old laundry derelict, and the Pytchley is no longer invited to meet there, but the Constable-like picturesqueness of the fields, the Park White cattle and the old stone church remain as sublime as ever. The collaging of fencing—an overlapping of split-wood beams, Victorian cast iron and kinked barbed wire—seen all over the three-thousand-acre estate is a poignant remark on the passing decades.

The elm trees Nancy loved at Kelmarsh were killed in the mid-1970s by Dutch elm disease, but her triple avenues of chestnuts have reached marvelous heights. And while it is impossible for two full-time gardeners to keep the pleasure grounds immaculate, spectacular colors appear all summer in the flower borders, as if Norah Lindsay herself maintained them. The pleached limes and topiary shapes are still kept closely cut.

Number 28 Queen Anne's Gate became five floors of offices: The Trees' long dining and drawing rooms were divided into small pieces, so the ceiling cornices now disappear into new walls and reappear next door. Champion Lodge—more than ever an architectural monster, without the personality of the de Crespignys to fill its halls and rooms—is a nursing home. The family, with no direct male heirs following the general, would have been gratified that the name of the Sporting Baronet's house was changed as well.

Uppark, given to the National Trust by the Meade-Fetherstonhaughs, burned to the ground in 1989. Some of its paintings and furniture survived because family members and neighbors carried as much as they could, as long as they could, out of the burning house and onto the lawns, but the aura of Sir Matthew, his dairymaid and the young Emma Hart is gone forever. The National Trust has rebuilt the house in its entirety, however, using the undertaking to experiment with and strengthen restoring techniques.

I wouldn't go back to Kelmarsh or Ditchley or any of the places I've loved if they paid me. I wouldn't go for anything. I remember them as they were . . . lovely.

After helping Colefax and Fowler redecorate Ditchley for Lord Wilton in the early 1950s, Nancy went there again just once. She drove with some Virginian friends across Oxfordshire from Haseley and up Ditchley's drive. But she waited at the gatehouse, out of view of the house, while her guests toured the estate.

Ditchley still exists as a meeting place rather than a lifeless museum, though certainly not in the rich vein of Ronald and Nancy Tree's day there. Coincidentally, it continues to advance the cause most important to Ronald Tree's wartime political career: During the Second World War his greatest efforts were spent on the Anglo-American bond, the allying of the two cultures he was a product of. David Wills, who bought Ditchley from Lord Wilton, turned the house over to the Ditchley Foundation, an organization dedicated to Anglo-American understanding. For twenty weekends a year the Gibbs mansion, replete with Nancy's orange saloon and many of the Lee portraits, though little of the celebrated furniture and extravagance, is once again filled with voices and movement. Every room in the house is lit again, and the men wear black tie for Saturday dinner. The conversation revolves more than ever, however, around politics.

Ronald Tree married Marietta Peabody FitzGerald in 1949. The second Mrs. Tree found, when she arrived at Ditchley, "lined up from the door and reaching far back into this huge, pale and gilded space were the indoor staff who served in this palace numbering over thirty people. . . . Never did I think I would walk into my next house with my beloved and sweet little daughter Frances FitzGerald . . . into what looked like the first scene of 'Marie Antoinette Comes to Versailles.' "[2] Upon leaving Ditchley shortly afterward, Ronald and Marietta moved to Sutton Place in New York and to Heron Bay in Barbados, the latter a house that Ronald commissioned Geoffrey Jellicoe to design for him "with the same Palladian grace and dignity" as Ditchley.[3] Ronald died in 1976; Marietta, along with his sons Michael and Jeremy Tree, placed a plaque in his honor in a neoclassical summerhouse in Ditchley's park.

John Fowler worked for the National Trust after his retirement from Colefax and Fowler in 1969, bringing to the Trust his vast experience in restoration and his imaginative taste in decoration. **I really thought John ought to be knighted. He was very ill with cancer by then, but he had done more for houses in England than anyone. The National Trust was very strong at that time, and he did a great deal. I felt that if they gave a knight-hood to Cecil Beaton they really should give one to John. Antony Head, who had gotten it for Cecil, told me I had to go through a member of Parliament. I thought at once of Thorneycroft,[4] who I knew very well, and he agreed that there was no one more worthy. Thorneycroft then sent me a letter saying that Harold Wilson had agreed to have John knighted. He would have been on the honors list in January, but he died in the hospital that November. And the sad thing is he didn't know it when he died. We couldn't tell him, because he would have been furious if he had thought I had pulled strings for him. But he would have been delighted to have it . . . and I could have teased him all the more.**

NANCY CONTINUED to travel back to Virginia long after she sold Mirador, staying in Richmond or somewhere in Albemarle County. "She used to slip off in the afternoons without telling anyone and look in on these extra-ordinary characters who had worked for her and her family," said a friend whom she used to visit. "She was absolutely dedicated to these people, and they to her." She saw cousins still living there and visited with old friends like Mrs. Bessy Martin and their children. "Seeing Nancy talk to her friends in Richmond was like watching a Broadway show," thought her cousin Phyllis Langhorne Draper, Uncle Buck's daughter. In one house where she stayed, "she danced the huck-a-buck" so energetically "the ceiling plaster in the room below fell to the floor." She collected a few new admirers as well, including one man who organized for her, when she was in her eighties, a trip across Virginia by car. The tour was only along the back roads and was painstakingly planned to avoid signs of modern life.

"She wore pantsuits here in the 1950s," remembered Robert Carter, whose mother, Alice, was a contemporary of Nancy's. "Ladies wearing trousers were unheard of in Virginia back then, but Nancy could get away with it, and did so with style." Carter's family had been from Redlands, a house and plantation in Albemarle County not far from Mirador, for almost two hundred years. The Georgian house, constructed of red bricks baked on the plantation, remains filled with his ancestors' portraits (by Stuart and Sully), his ancestors' furniture and, as one writer put it, his ancestors' "easy and generous life which has flowed unbroken through the old house" for so long.[5] When the BBC made a dramatized version of Nancy Astor's life, they used Redlands to portray Mirador, because it was one of the last that still evoked the ambiance of the Old Dominion. **The house was perfect, but they** made the atmosphere luxurious in the Yankee sense. They had the Mirador butler in livery, which was perfectly ridiculous.

The last time I went to Richmond, Alice Carter wanted to give me a lunch party at the country club, but I told her I'd much rather go up to Redlands to stay. There I was put in a bedroom over that beautiful oval drawing room: the bedroom with the bay window and a bathroom practically in the room with you. At Redlands "bathrooms have been cunningly inserted in convenient spaces . . . [and] in the big bedrooms are not only antique four-post beds complete with testers, but these are frequently supplemented by a single bed or even two, and also a cradle or crib."[6] I love the bedrooms in Virginia houses: They were always ready for a four-in-hand full of relatives to arrive. Mirador has changed hands three times since Nancy owned it.

AN ILLUSTRATED BROCHURE printed by an English realtor in the early 1970s proclaimed the availability of "a magnificent Queen Anne house fully restored and modernised . . . in a secluded parkland setting on the edge of a small hamlet." The proposal offered a hall, five reception rooms, ten bedrooms, "domestic offices and self-contained staff annexes," as well as "well-stocked and maintained formal gardens," a hard tennis court, parkland and pasture, and a Coach House, "with vacant possession except for the Coach House and two cottages." There were four pages of dull gray photographs of the interior and exterior of the main house, and twelve more of clinically written descriptions detailing the fixtures from the "Wastemaster disposal unit" and "Aga cooker" in the kitchens to the "open fireplace with painted wood surround, herring-bone cheeks and stone hearth" in the library. It was Haseley Court they were selling. But the room-by-room sketches were counting radiators rather than rendering the special essence of the house as it was in the short decade and a half Nancy Lancaster lived there.

I spent far too much doing it up . . . especially my gardens. There was a brief effort to take "paying guests" at Haseley to stave off disaster. That pamphlet, composed by Cadogan Travel in London with sharper, more evocative photographs and passages, suggested that "today, when so many famous English Country Houses are open to the public, Haseley Court remains shut away in a secret, enchanting, private world of its own. . . . To be asked to stay at Haseley Court is an invitation few would decline, and most people would accept eagerly; and now it is possible to stay there for a week, a weekend or even longer, from May to September." Aimed at Americans, the pamphlet extolled "chauffeur-driven cars . . . arranged to take guests to nearby golf courses or to Sulgrave, ancestral home of George Washington."

For £20 a day they got a delicious tea with scones and cakes, a room with Porthault sheets on the bed, a maid and a man to unpack, two cocktails before dinner, a dinner that consisted of three courses with wine and brandy, and a whiskey and soda before they retired. Breakfast was served to the lady in bed and in the dining room for the gent, and there was an itinerary for sightseeing with lists of gardens, houses and museums on it. They were expected to eat lunch out and then return in time for tea. The problem was, all the people who came were friends of mine. At once my house was a beehive of my friends and their friends. We had a high old time that summer . . . they ate me out of house and home. They wanted to pay, but they were the people that I lived with for months on end whenever I went to America, so quite rightly I refused their money.

I don't at all regret the way I did Haseley. They were the happiest years for me. It was a house full of sun and life, with fires always lit and eight people always staying. It was nice to live like that . . . I was very lucky. Now I'm so old I wouldn't even know eight people to have to stay.

The final blow to Haseley was a fire in the early spring of 1974. The house was saved, as the fire was confined to the bedrooms above the drawing room and the drawing room itself, but the cost of the repairs forced Nancy in the end to sell her home. **All houses that age instead of having steel girders had a big oak beam over the flue. As I liked to have a fire here in the drawing room every day almost all year round, the oak beam began to smolder. I had noticed a funny smell, and I had the architect out to have a look. He and his man got into the thing and said everything was fine. That was two weeks before the fire.**

It was March and a day with quite a wind. The wind must have ignited the smoldering beam. I was out in the garden at about half past ten in the morning. Michael and Anne's children luckily were at play school: The nursery was on the third floor of the house, and if it had happened at night they would have been smothered. From the garden I saw the odd man limping about madly . . . he was a lame Irishman. I said, "What *are* you doing?" He said, "There's smoke." I said, "Don't be silly; they're burning leaves down in the woods." He said, "Oh, no, the hall is full of smoke." So I went in and sure enough the hall was full of smoke. Michael was in the library painting, and I rushed in and said, "The house is on fire." He said—without stopping his painting—"Have you telephoned the insurance people?" I'll never forget that. "Have you telephoned the insurance people?" I said, "I haven't even got the fire brigade yet."

I was very lucky, because Spencer used to call out the firemen and make them do fire drills, so when they arrived fifteen minutes after I called, they knew there was water in the moat. If he hadn't done that, the whole house would have gone, because they didn't have enough chemicals for it. It's only a small fire company. Where they had terrible difficulties, though, was with the roof, which was made of cement. The firemen couldn't get through it. They had to call the American Air Force base, which was on the other side of Oxford, because they were the only people with the drills or the saws to cut through the cement. So we had the Air Force there that day as well.

I got so nervous with all this going on that I went out into the topiary garden with a little hose and started watering the topiary. The firemen kept coming to me and saying, "I think we can save it." I said, "I don't care if you can save it or not, but don't come and tell me about it . . . just let me be." A reporter from the Oxford newspaper came to interview me about the fire, and I slapped his face. I said, "How dare you ask me questions while my house is burning? Get in there and help. Get in there and help bring out furniture."

They brought out as much as they could. Michael got the Fitton sisters out of the drawing room, but while he was carrying one of them my wonderful Waterford chandelier fell and missed killing him by an inch. I had it on a cable that was attached to the floor of the bedroom above the drawing room so it could be lowered and cleaned. That was the part of the house on fire, and it burned the cable.

The bed in that room from Kimbolton was burnt, and all the furniture from Mirador that I had in there was destroyed. I had a very pretty walnut highboy and a very pretty walnut desk. And I had a perfectly charming dressing table covered with white lily of the valley muslin. It was Marie Antoinette's muslin that we had copied . . . I was very fond of that muslin. Two bookcases that I had made for Kelmarsh and brought with me were also destroyed, and a lovely French chair, a beautiful Chippendale mirror, some very good china, a wonderful rug from Ditchley: They were all gone. A very pretty sofa. It was a very pretty room with awfully pretty things in it. That was really the only damage to the house, though—they got the fire out—the rest was water damage to the rooms on the top floor.

They were also able to carry out from the drawing room my Waterford glass candelabra. They brought them out very carefully and gently lined them up next to each other on the terrace outside the front door. I was thrilled they could be saved. Then a gust of wind came and knocked them all down like dominoes, and they were ruined.

Over the next year I repaired the damage done to the house by the fire . . . I knew by then that I'd have to sell Haseley, but I couldn't sell it in that condition. For a year I lived there with that part of the house boarded off as they did the repair work. I couldn't keep it. I didn't have income. I'd lived on my capital, and my capital had gone. That's what killed it. I've lived too long and I've lived too well.

Lord Hereford bought Haseley Court from Nancy. **He told me he was tired of saying, "I'm Hereford from Hereford in Herefordshire."** Most of her furniture, all of the very grand pieces she thought appropriate only for a very grand house, were sold piecemeal through the Colefax and Fowler shop and at auction. **I should have had a house sale . . . you get much better prices when you sell things that way.** Five years later the Desmond Heywards bought Haseley Court from Lord Hereford.

I was born in a cottage, and it seems as though I'm going to end my life in one. Much of the gaiety and the elegance—as well as a few small whispers of the grandeur—Nancy somehow shoehorned into the tiny Coach House at Haseley. **I decided, against the advice of everyone, not to move. I was far too old to start afresh. I liked my neighbors, and I still had a gun in the syndicate at Wormsley. So an arrangement was made that once I sold the house and the land I could keep the Coach House free of rent for the rest of my life, and with it the walled part of my garden and the orangery I had added onto the laundry. I also kept a gardener's cottage, a garage and half the greenhouses, and I put up two portable houses for staff. I put a wooden floor and a false ceiling in the orangery and made it my library and summer sitting room.** Her presence was very strong at Haseley until the day she died in August 1994 at age ninety-six, partly in the beauty of the place and partly because Nancy, even when she was in her nineties, could not remain sitting by the fire too long without getting up to work in her garden or walk the dogs.

The Coach House was just a stone shed when I bought Haseley . . . probably fifteenth century. I put in the floors and the windows when I did it up the first time, while we were working on the big house. Then I made other improvements when I was going to live here. I added two bathrooms downstairs, then a pantry, a room for my maid and a staff hall, by using space in the old stable building that is connected to the cottage. I put in an extra window in the

Nancy Lancaster's last house, the Coach House, Little Haseley, Oxfordshire, September 1994

sitting room and another in my bedroom to get the cross lighting. Now there are two bedrooms upstairs, mine and a guest room. The guest room has a dressing room and its own bathroom. Another small room I made for cupboards and pressing. The windows upstairs are all dormer windows.

I put a French window on the end of the cottage facing the courtyard. It leads right into my sitting room and is used more often than the front door. I painted the sitting room white, to make it seem larger, and as there was no cornice or molding, I had a two-inch strip of paper painted blue, then put it along all the corners of the walls and where the walls meet the ceiling. I did a similar thing with the beige hair carpet; I had them sew a three-inch strip of blue fabric all around the outside.

The Coach House had a lightness to it, though it was completely stuffed with Nancy's things. Every surface was covered, both horizontal and vertical. Walls were packed with pictures, engravings of formal gardens, silhouettes,

At Stratford Hall, the birthplace of Robert E. Lee, Nancy Lancaster, right, and her sister, Alice Winn

all of different shapes and sizes. The mirror over the fire had photographs and postcards wedged all around its frame: a card of Gilbert Stuart's "Skater," photos of Nancy's dogs, her sons and her grandchildren. The firewood in the basket was cut small to fit the cottage fireplace, and the bark was removed like the crusts of sandwiches. There was as much furniture in the sitting room that could fit without seeming claustrophobic. Nancy sat to the right of the fireplace in a pale blue-and-white wing chair.

There is blue and white throughout the room. I have one of the corner sofas from the farmhouse at Ditchley; it's covered in white with blue piping. All the comfortable chairs and the other sofa are covered in a blue-and-white striped dress material I bought in Greece—it had to be backed in cotton to make it strong enough— and I have blue-and-white Delft china above the bookcases and Williamsburg plates by the fire. The walls are covered with framed Kip's views of gardens and houses from the seventeenth century. Something I got from the Duchess of Windsor at their Mill was the idea for my curtains. They are white cotton, but instead of being lined in white, they were lined in chintz. You see the chintz from the outside of the cottage. That's what she had at the Mill. I think it's very pretty.

The dining room is very small. If we are more than four, we seem to be sitting on each other's laps. The table was made for the farmhouse at Ditchley and seats four comfortably but can be extended for six or even eight. It is marbleized wood on a column stand. The walls are white, and as this room too has no molding, I had them paint trompe l'oeil Queen Anne paneling like in my bedroom at Avery Row. I'm crazy about fake Queen Anne paneling. There is an unusual white porcelain chandelier above the table that I bought in Germany but I think is Swedish, a lovely carved mirror on one wall, and some very good Chinese blue-and-white plates arranged inside the "panels." I bought the sideboard in France. It's really a commode and is painted an ivory color, decorated with gold fish and has a reddish marble top.

I use a set of rather fragile painted side chairs at the table that I borrowed from the shop twenty years ago and never returned. I panic every time a large luncheon guest sits on them, thinking if I have to send it to the shop to be repaired they'll remember the loan. I usually put male guests at the head or foot of the table in the small wing chairs that are covered with blue-patterned lining chintz.

My bedroom is papered with that French paper called Angoulême: It's like the French china of the same name. The curtains and bed hangings are made of a linen Sybil Connolly had copied for me in Ireland from the wallpaper. Bed curtains hang from a ruched crown on the ceiling and are lined with blue-patterned chintz. The room is sunny and light, with a wonderful view of the walled kitchen garden.

The gardens were open for the National Garden Scheme the other day, and we had over six hundred visitors. There were so many old people with white hair that when I looked out my bedroom window into the garden, I thought I was growing cotton.

My favorite room in the Coach House is my bathroom. I use a chest of drawers as my dressing table; its drawers are all painted Cambridge blue. All over the walls are huge white frames with blue paper on which I have made collages of photographs from my Kodak books. I lie in my bath and look at all the favorite people and places in my life spread out before me. It's also the perfect solution for Kodak books, which never get looked at and bore to tears anyone who's not in them.

I haven't got nostalgia for what I've lost. My neighbors think it's extraordinary that I don't talk about the big house, but as a matter of fact I don't even think about it. I think about my cottage and my family and the people who work for me, not about the past. I'm now living the life of a village woman.

When I look at myself in the mirror, I think I look like old Mr. Getty. I'm not sad about it . . . I think it's frightfully funny. I used to be quite pretty when they dolled me up, and look at me now. There were a lot of people who were much better looking than I, though, and who had real talent. I have no talent and can *just* read and write. So it's quite amazing to me how my way has fallen into quite pleasant places when I'm not an exceptional person at all.

NOTES

BIBLIOGRAPHY

INDEX

ILLUSTRATION CREDITS

NOTES

MIRADOR

Acknowledgments: Nancy Lancaster's memories of her childhood at Mirador are mostly taken from transcriptions of interviews with the author, with some additions coming from handwritten notes and an unpublished autobiographical manuscript provided to the author by her. Her descriptions of Irene Gibson's voice practice, and her garden in Maine, come from an article she wrote for the July 1984 *Down East* magazine. The facts of Chiswell Langhorne's military service during the Civil War come mostly from Alice Winn's book *Always a Virginian*.

1. Sykes, Christopher, *Nancy: The Life of Lady Astor*, p. 14.
2. Astor, Michael, *Tribal Feeling*, p. 22.
3. From an unpublished, undated letter from Nancy Lancaster to her uncle the Hon. Robert Brand.
4. Sykes, p. 62.
5. Lancaster, Nancy, "Splendid Summers on Seven Hundred Acre Island," in *Down East*, July 1984, p. 160.
6. Sykes, p. 28.
7. Downey, Fairfax, *Portrait of an Era*, p. 222.
8. *Time* magazine, March 28, 1927, p. 24.
9. Lancaster, *Down East*, p. 160.
10. Mrs. Lewis C. Albro, quoted in "Lady Astor, from Virginia," in *The New York Times* magazine section, November 16, 1919, p. 1.
11. Ibid.
12. Astor, p. 72.
13. Sykes, p. 220.
14. Ibid. p. 224.
15. Ibid. p. 225.
16. Ibid. pp. 225–26.
17. Winn, Alice, *Always a Virginian*, p. 32.
18. From an undated article, "The Hon. Mrs. R. H. Brand, A Tribute."
19. Ibid.
20. Winn, p. 32.
21. Sykes, p. 571.
22. From an unpublished, undated letter to Nancy Tree from Irene Gibson.
23. From Nancy Lancaster's unpublished manuscript.

"ALWAYS A VIRGINIAN"

Acknowledgments: Nancy Lancaster's description of her mother, Elizabeth Langhorne, comes from interviews with the author and from an unpublished, undated letter from Nancy Lancaster to her uncle, the Hon. Robert Brand.

1. Smith, Captain John, *Works: 1608–31*, p. 48.
2. Dickens, Charles, *American Notes for General Circulation*, p. 18.
3. Ibid., pp. 21–2.
4. Quoted in Dabney, Virginius, *Richmond*, p. 114.
5. Dashiell, Margaret, *Richmond Reverie*, p. 1.
6. Poindexter, Charles, *Richmond, Virginia: Her Advantages and Attractions*, p. 15.
7. Winn, Alice, *Always a Virginian*, p. 83.
8. Dabney, *Richmond*, p. 221.
9. Dabney, Virginius, *Virginia*, p. 264.
10. Quoted in Dabney, *Richmond*, p. 287.
11. See acknowledgments note.
12. Lancaster, Robert, *Historic Virginia Homes and Churches*, p. 217.
13. Malone, Dumas, *Jefferson the Virginian*, p. 21.
14. Lancaster, p. 168.
15. McLaughlin, Jack, *Jefferson and Monticello*, p. 291.
16. Adams, William Howard, *Jefferson's Monticello*, p. 33.
17. McLaughlin, p. 269.
18. Adams, *Jefferson's Monticello*, p. 34.
19. Ibid.
20. McLaughlin, p. 32.

1910 TO 1920

Acknowledgments: General sources other than the author's interviews with Nancy Lancaster include her original manuscript and the handwritten notes she provided for the author, and the author's interviews with Alice Winn. Some of the material for Islesboro was taken from Nancy Lancaster's article in *Down East* magazine, July 1984. Some of the information about Cliveden came from *Tribal Feeling* by Michael Astor, *The Search for a Style* by John Cornforth, *Nancy: The Life of Lady Astor* by Christopher Sykes and the British National Trust's guidebook, *Cliveden*.

1. Nancy wrote to her brother, Chillie, from Dinard St. Enoga, "I've been to Mont St. Michel. It is really wonderful, though I must admit that from how people talked of it I expected it to reach nearly to the sky, and I would say I was a little bit disappointed. . . . I suppose you know that I was thirteen on the tenth of September."
2. From an unpublished letter to Thomas Moncure Perkins from Nancy Perkins, dated 1910.
3. Sykes, Christopher, *Nancy: The Life of Lady Astor*, p. 92.
4. Orkney was governor of Virginia in 1714.
5. The National Trust, *Cliveden*, p. 16.
6. He moved the building materials over in the winter when the bay was frozen.
7. Roth, Leland M., *McKim, Mead & White Architects*, p. 266.
8. Chiswell Dabney Langhorne died in February 1919. The Richmond *Times Dispatch* of Saturday, February 15, 1919, eulogized him as "famed as the father of Mrs.

Charles Dana Gibson, the original 'Gibson Girl,' and the father of America's most beautiful women, millionaire railway builder, sportsman and gentleman of the Old Virginian School."

A HOUSE OF HER OWN: MIRADOR REVISITED

Acknowledgments: A source for research information about Ogden Codman was *Ogden Codman and the Decoration of Houses*, edited by Pauline C. Metcalf, specifically chapters "From Lincoln to Leopold" by Metcalf and "The Making of a Colonial Revival Architect" by Christopher Monkhouse.

1. Tree, Ronald, *When the Moon Was High*, p. 30.
2. The Murphys were the inspiration for F. Scott Fitzgerald's characters Dick and Nicole Diver in *Tender Is the Night*.
3. From an unpublished letter from Nancy Tree to her sister, Alice, October 1922.
4. Hewitt, Mark Alan, *The Architect and the American Country House*, p. 176.
5. Ibid., p. 25.
6. Delano, like Stanford White before him, was commissioned to design pavilions for Thomas Jefferson's University of Virginia campus.
7. On her list their first year at Mirador were *Arctotis*, balsam, Canterbury bells, various euphorbias, gypsophila, annual larkspur, snapdragon, various calendulas, cornflower, *Scabiosa*, Siberian wallflower, African daisy, annual chrysanthemum, globe amaranthus, *Nigella*, Virginian stock (*Malcolmia maritima*), mignonette, *Lavatera*, *Malva Moschata* alba, nicotiana, *Salvia farinacea* and cosmos, marigold and different zinnias. Nancy also filled her garden with forsythia, lilac, peonies, irises, *Eremurus*, Michaelmas daisies and pinks, as well as roses—in the rose garden and climbing vines—and the trees.
8. From an unpublished letter to Nancy Tree from Irene Gibson, circa 1935.
9. From an unpublished letter to Nancy Tree from Irene Gibson dated 1937.
10. From an unpublished, undated letter to Nancy Tree from Phyllis Brand.
11. From an unpublished, undated letter to Nancy Tree from Irene Gibson.
12. Birkenhead, Earl of, *The Earl of Halifax*, p. 484.
13. Halifax, Lord Edward, *Fullness of Days*, p. 279.

KELMARSH HALL

Acknowledgments: Author's interviews with Mrs. Cecily Borwick, Colonel Sir Rupert and Lady Hardy, Captain and Mrs. John MacDonald-Buchanan and Mrs. Patsy Whetstone. Also Eric Beck, Nancy Lancaster's second horseman in the late 1920s, and Andy Menzies, the contemporary head gardener at Kelmarsh Hall.

1. Astor, Michael, *Tribal Feeling*, pp. 79–80.
2. Paget, Sir Thomas Guy, *Rum 'Uns to Follow*, p. 114.
3. Usually scarlet in color, they were called pink coats for a tailor in London named Pink, who at one time made the best. Ronald Tree's, while Joint Master of the Pytchley, was actually a claret coloring called Lowther-red, named for the famous hunting family and worn to single the Masters and hunt servants out from the rest of the men in the field.
4. The Duke and Duchess of York's daughter, who would one day become Queen Elizabeth II, had her first "day out" with the Pytchley. She was five years old, rode

on the back of a small pony and was very closely piloted by a family groom (from "Sabretache," *Monarchy and the Chase*, pp. 152–3). Her Majesty's uncle, Edward VIII, had his first day hunting with the Pytchley as well, in 1920.

5. Buxton, Meriel, *Ladies of the Chase*, p. 78.
6. The 7th Earl Spencer, the grandfather of Diana, the Princess of Wales, was the Pytchley Hunt Committee Chairman when Ronald Tree was Joint Master.
7. Cottesbrooke Hall is thought to be the Northamptonshire manor house from which Jane Austen fashioned her Mansfield Park.
8. Freeman was the professional "fox catcher" employed by the Pytchley from 1906 to 1932 and was universally considered "the greatest huntsman of the present century if not of all time" (*Country Life*, February 25, 1933, p. 191). **He was a genius**. Seemingly born to the craft, he possessed the uncanny ability to play with his fox as if he had it on a line, then kill it, using his pack with all the precision of a rod and reel in the hands of an expert fly fisherman.
9. This quote and following extract from Munnings, Sir Alfred, *Second Burst*, p. 305.
10. The painting Munnings did of Nancy in front of Cottesbrooke appeared in the Summer Show at the Royal Academy that year. *Punch* printed a cartoon of it with a caption that read "Darling, do keep your pony in step. Look at Dear Gilbert." Gilbert was supposed to be the greyhound. The Royal Academy borrowed the painting again in 1956 for a retrospective of Munnings's paintings.
11. *Country Life*, Feb. 25, 1933, p. 200.
12. James Gibbs wielded considerable influence over Virginia builders through his *Book of Architecture* (1728), which included an early plan for Kelmarsh, and his *Rules for Drawing the Several Parts of Architecture* (1732). Both books were in the libraries at the College of William and Mary and at Westover.
13. The system of paging the servants harkened to another era. A complicated series of ropes and pulleys behind the walls culminated in a bank of old bells. One bell for each room in the house hung at the top of the wall in the crescent-shaped service passageway. The bell cords were attached to metal coils like enormous watch springs; once one had been pulled somewhere in the house and a bell rung, the cord would continue to wobble on its coil until the footman or maid had a chance to see which room they were required in.
14. Phipps also worked for the Astors at 4 St. James's Square and Hever Castle; and, probably through the influence of Nancy Astor, he received the commission to build the Seventh Church of Christ Scientist in Kensington, London.
15. Great Britain's cavalry officers had trained at the Weedon School of Equitation for more than a century. **Because of Weedon there was never a shortage of young men out hunting. Every smart young cavalry officer in England was at the school. They went like Billy-O across country.**
16. Munnings, p. 303.
17. She wrote it on the back of a black-and-white print of the room that was published in *Country Life* magazine, February 25, 1933.
18. According to Stephen Calloway in *Twentieth-Century Decoration*, Maugham's room was created in 1929–30.
19. Lindsay, Norah, "The Manor House I, Sutton Courtney Berks.," *Country Life*, May 16, 1931, p. 610.
20. Ibid.
21. *Sporting Life*, May 20, 1932.

22. Ibid.

23. The Pytchley's collar was white. I was always very proud of the Pytchley collar; I always wore it no matter where I was hunting. It was considered a great honor to have it on your jacket, as it was only awarded to regular members. It was also very attractive, because it made your neck look longer.

24. *Northampton Echo*, January 11, 1929.

25. Ibid.

DITCHLEY PARK

Acknowledgments: Author's interviews with Sir Geoffrey Jellicoe, Edith Bridges, Sarah Baring, Lady Alexandra Metcalfe, David Astor, the Duke and Duchess of Devonshire and Elizabeth Winn; the Duchess of Devonshire's introduction to Nancy Lancaster's original manuscript; Sotheby's catalogue of the sale of Ronald Tree's estate; Jellicoe's *Garden History* essay; the Ditchley Foundation.

1. Bradford, Sarah, *George VI*, p. 130.

2. Tree, Ronald, *When the Moon Was High*, p. 32.

3. Ibid., p. 34.

4. Market Harborough *Advertiser*, March, 1935.

5. Tree, p. 36.

6. Ibid., p. 40.

7. Ibid., p. 38.

8. In England then there were five or six Italian master *stuccatores* going from house to house, job to job. Their paths could be traced in the ledger books of their employers, where increases in the outlay for red wine were often recorded during their stays.

9. Nicolson, Nigel, ed., *Diaries and Letters of Harold Nicolson*, vol. 2, p. 129.

10. Lyttleton, Oliver, *The Memoirs of Lord Chandos*, p. 169.

11. Quoted in Smith, Sally Bedell, *In All His Glory: The Life and Times of William S. Paley and the Birth of Modern Broadcasting*, p. 206.

12. Lees-Milne, James, *Midway on the Waves*, p. 66.

13. Tree, p. 40.

14. Oswald, Arthur, "Ditchley, Oxfordshire, I," *Country Life*, June 9, 1934, p. 590.

15. Author's interview with Nancy Lancaster.

16. *Country Life*, June 14, 1941, p. 520.

17. Ibid.

18. Tree, p. 42.

19. Mrs. Lybbe Powys, a ubiquitous eighteenth-century house guest and diarist who turned up at country seats all over England, agreed about the velvet. She wrote in 1778 while staying with the Earl and Countess of Lichfield that the "bed chamber with hangings, bed and furniture of crimson and yellow velvet, is shown as a great curiosity, but I think [it] ugly. The pattern is all pagoda." Quoted in Oswald, Arthur, "Ditchley, Oxfordshire, II," *Country Life*, June 16, 1934, p. 627.

20. I did almost buy back one of the tapestries. Lord Ancaster, my cousin Wissy's father-in-law, bought one of them from the Dillons, restored it and hung it at Normanton, where he had others from the same period. I sat next to him at a dinner party one night and wouldn't let him alone until he agreed to let me buy it back. After all that, once I saw it, I decided I didn't really want it.

21. Cornforth, John, "Leeds Castle," *Country Life*, April 14, 1983, p. 925.

22. On the other hand, an engraving of Ditchley in James Gibbs's *Book of Architecture* of 1728 shows an entrance stair descending from the east side of the house down to Lyon's Court and the stable block—a stair and doorway no longer discernible by 1933. The house and its rooms' functions had been switched around for other than financial reasons, speculated the architectural historian John Cornforth in *Country Life*, November 17, 1988, and with that, their decorations.

23. **They call lavatories in England "loos." I always thought loo was a slang name, like in Virginia, where they call outhouses "johnny houses." But it turns out they were called loos for a parson at the court of Louis XIV named Père Bourdaloue, whose sermons were so long ladies kept bedpans under their skirts.**

24. From author's interview with the duchess and from her introduction to Nancy Lancaster's original manuscript.

25. From the duchess's introduction to Nancy Lancaster's original manuscript.

26. Tree, p. 41.

27. Ibid., p. 134.

28. Harrison, Rosina, *Gentlemen's Gentlemen*, pp. 195–96, this quote and following. Ditchley's servants' rooms were in sharp contrast with those common to country houses. A servant at Chiswick House wrote, "My room was in the attic. There was a little iron bed in the corner, a wooden chair and a wash stand. It was a cold, bare, utterly cheerless room. At night I used to climb the dark stairs to the gloomy top of the house, go over to my bed, put the candle on the chair, fall on my knees, say my prayers, and crawl into bed too tired to wash." (Bennett, Arnold, *Riceyman Steps*, part 4, ch. 7, quoted in Hibbert, Christopher, *The English: A Social History*, p. 505).

29. Tree, p. 47.

30. Ibid., p. 45.

31. **The whole Ditchley basement was stone flagging when we bought the house. Because they were so uneven and so hard under the servants' feet, I took them out and used them elsewhere.**

32. The Trees were among the first in a long line of clients of Russell Page's that included Marcel Boussac of Dior, Prince Aly Khan, the Duke and Duchess of Windsor, Count Theo Rossi di Montelera and Mrs. William Paley. Geoffrey Jellicoe wrote in the Oxford *Companion to Gardens* that he thought Page an ideal partner because of what he called his "sense of plant forms. . . . Page was primarily an artist and only secondarily an expert horticulturist, following in the tradition of Gertrude Jekyll." Page met Stéphane Boudin while the two worked for the Trees at Ditchley; from then until Boudin's death, in the 1960s, Page would often design the gardens for houses Boudin was commissioned to decorate, while in turn Page suggested Boudin to his own clients.

33. Most were perennials, with the more delicate herbs surviving throughout the year in the mild English climate and establishing themselves in great semihardwood clumps. Others, like coriander and zea, were renewed each spring. Page added extra dashes of color—bergamot, calendulas, lupin, foxgloves and iris—weaving them in with the lavender, the pink-blossomed sweetbrier and the brilliant blue of globe artichokes left to seed. Along the outside and inside walls where there was exposure to the sun and protection from the harshest weather were trained espaliered fruit trees that flowered in the spring and produced fresh plums and pears during the summer.

34. Jellicoe, Sir Geoffrey, "Ronald Tree and the Gardens of Ditchley Park," *Garden History: The Journal of the Garden History Society*, vol. 10, no. 1, p. 88.

35. Beaton, Cecil, *The Wandering Years*, p. 316. The photographer went on to say, "I hardly knew anything of my host and hostess, but automatically warmed to them for this treat." Beaton had met Nancy a decade before, when he was commissioned to take her portrait.
36. Tree, p. 68.
37. Ibid.
38. *Vogue*, July 7, 1937.
39. Tree, p. 69.
40. *Vogue*, July 7, 1937.
41. Ibid.

"WHEN THE MOON IS HIGH"

Acknowledgments: Author's interviews with Jeremy Tree, Michael Tree, David Astor, Lady Soames, Sir John Martin, Lord Wilton, Baroness Edwina D'Erlanger, the Duke and Duchess of Devonshire, Sarah Baring, John Bowes-Lyon, Lady Alexandra Metcalfe and Elizabeth Winn.

1. Quotes in this paragraph from author's interview with the Duchess of Devonshire; author's interview with Sarah Baring; Tree, Ronald, *When the Moon Was High*, p. 46; author's interview with the Duchess of Devonshire; author's interview with Sarah Baring.
2. Quotes in this paragraph from a letter from Dorothea, Viscountess Head to John Cornforth, parts of which were published in Cornforth, John, "Ditchley Revisited," *Country Life*, October 24, 1985; author's interview with Lady Alexandra Metcalfe.
3. Grenfell, Joyce, *Darling Ma: Letters to Her Mother*, p. 33.
4. Lady Apsley, "Woman's Part in the Shooting Field."
5. Nancy shot with a matched pair of sixteen-bore side-by-side shotguns made by Boss and Company of London. The bag at Grantully Castle on August 19, 1933, was 242 brace of grouse, a snipe and 2 rabbits. Seven guns participated—Admiral Earl Beatty, Viscount Borodale, the Hon. Peter Beatty, Ronald, Nancy, Sir Matthew Wilson and Lord Cochran—on a day of "very stormy weather." The next day they took 141½ brace of grouse, 1 snipe and 57 hares; on the third day, 133 brace of grouse, 4 blackgame, 1 snipe, 25 hares and 4 rabbits. On August 26, members of the family were joined by the Duke of Rutland, the Earl of Dalkeith and Captain D. E. Wallace; they killed 280½ brace of grouse, 2 blackgame, 25 hares and 3 rabbits.
6. A clear appraisal of the existence or not of a fascist "Cliveden Set" appears in Sykes, *Nancy: The Life of Lady Astor*, chapter 18.
7. Tree, pp. 130–1.
8. Ibid., p. 135.
9. Ibid., pp. 132–3.
10. Lothian died shortly after his return to his post in Washington, leaving the negotiations at a brief standstill. The prime minister replaced him with Lord Halifax, who was replaced as Foreign Secretary by Anthony Eden.
11. Gilbert, Martin, *Winston S. Churchill*, vol. 2, p. 357.
12. Cooper, Lady Diana, *Trumpets from the Steep*, pp. 60–1.
13. Churchill, the shrewdest of politicians, was certainly aware when he chose Ditchley as a house for moonlit weekends that its owner was not only a sympathetic colleague in Parliament but an American as well, with a dashing American wife.

Ditchley was a house where visiting Americans unused to the British and British ways would feel at home.

14. Colville, John, *The Fringes of Power: Downing Street Diaries, 1939–55*, p. 331. Colville kept a diary against strict government regulations.

15. Titled *That Hamilton Woman* in America.

16. Grenfell, *Darling Ma: Letters to Her Mother*, p. 186, 3*n*.

17. Robertson, Ben, *I Saw England*, p. 39. Shortly after the publication of his book, Robertson was killed when the Pan Am Clipper in which he was a passenger crashed in Lisbon.

18. Ibid., pp. 192–3.

OTHER HOUSES

1. He hurtled over Niagara Falls inside a wooden barrel, was the first man to cross the North Sea in a hot-air balloon and even beat Bay Middleton—the most lauded horseman in Victorian England—in a steeplechase. Sir Claude was in his early eighties when Nancy met him—still fit, lean, with hollow cheeks and piercing blue eyes, and always up to his knees in riding boots.

2. Tree, Ronald, *When the Moon Was High*, p. 59.

3. Ibid., p. 67.

4. All quotes this paragraph from Grenfell, Joyce, *Darling Ma: Letters to Her Mother*, p. 46.

5. Channon, Sir Henry, *Chips: The Diaries of Sir Henry Channon*, quoted in McLeod, Kirsty, *A Passion for Friendship*, p. 88.

6. Tree, pp. 125–7.

7. Robertson, Ben, *I Saw England*, pp. 133–4.

RAINBOW QUEST

Acknowledgments: Author's interviews with Elizabeth Winn, Ruby Hill, Imogen Taylor, George Oakes, John Bowes-Lyon and Laura, Duchess of Marlborough. John Fowler's person and work were brought to life in an interview with John Cornforth, as well as in his books and articles about Fowler. The Windsors' Mill is described in Suzy Menkes's book *The Windsor Style*.

1. Macmillan was returned to Parliament in a November by-election.

2. Nicolson, Nigel, ed., *Diaries and Letters of Harold Nicolson*, vol. 3, p. 31.

3. Quoted in ibid., p. 110.

4. Quoted in Sykes, Christopher, *Nancy: The Life of Lady Astor*, p. 555.

5. Tree, Ronald, *When the Moon Was High*, p. 47.

6. Cecil Beaton, one of Lady Colefax's regular guests at lunch and dinner, wrote of her house in the King's Road that her rooms were marked with "an overall discretion." "Everything appeared to be immaculately swept and varnished: on the well-polished oak table, the glass vases of jasmine would be freshly filled with water that was still full of oxygen bubbles." When Lady Colefax turned professional, however, Beaton thought her taste became stale. "Room after room would be decorated in what John Betjeman has called 'ghastly good taste': somewhat sparsely furnished, with a couple of delicate black and gold chairs, a settee, striped curtains and a colour scheme of yellow and grey" (Beaton, Cecil, *The Glass of Fashion*, p. 210).

7. Nancy was adamant that it was she, and not Ronald Tree, who paid for Sibyl Colefax, Ltd. It has been suggested that the shop was a gift from Tree to her, "a parting act

of generosity." The £15,000 may have been paid with one of Tree's checks; nonetheless, according to Nancy Lancaster it was her own money.

8. This derivation of the Colefax and Fowler name is according to Nancy; papers belonging to Colefax and Fowler suggest it was named "Sibyl Colefax and John Fowler Limited" by "special resolution of the shareholders" in April 1939.

9. Nancy Lancaster's obituary in *The Times* of London, August 20, 1994, stated, "The Trees' marriage was in trouble long before it formally ended shortly after the war. For some years she had been involved with another Conservative MP, Colonel C. G. "Juby" [sic] Lancaster, who was the owner of Kelmarsh and had continued to live nearby while the Trees were his tenants in the house. He was also invited [to] Ditchley, before and during the war, though his presence was always offensive to Tree."

10. Nancy first saw Hardwick between the wars as the guest of the 10th Duke of Devonshire, who had inherited it through his Cavendish ancestors.

11. Both quotes from Norwich, John Julius, *The Architecture of Southern England*, p. 455.

12. Quoted in the house's contemporary guidebook. The beauty of Brympton d'Evercy, as Nancy saw it in the 1930s, was to prove fleeting. When this house like so many others became difficult to keep, the family held a sale and dispersed their ancient possessions. Nancy attended the auction and bought for herself deer trophies from Brympton's Tudor past, and a stack of nineteenth-century paper dress-curtains she collected to make into pleated lampshades.

13. "Rainbow Quest" was the name of a horse Nancy Lancaster's son Jeremy Tree trained, which went on to win the *Prix d'Arc de Triomphe*.

14. **Thomas Jefferson was very much influenced by Palladio and brought his architecture to Virginia. I've always felt that the Virginian interpretations of Palladio, made of red brick and white wood and sitting under sunny blue skies at places like Bremo or the University of Virginia, were much more true to Palladio and much more suitable than the cold, damp palaces in England.**

15. In an article for *Architectural Digest* in December 1980, Nancy wrote that much of Malcontenta's pleasure was that "he hadn't overdone the restoration." The frescoes were by Zelloli and Battista Franco, but a preceding owner had whitewashed over them, the white soaking into the porous plaster of the frescoes. When Landsberg stripped the whitewash to restore the paintings, an opaque film was left behind that Nancy thought gave the paintings a "mother-of-pearl quality."

16. The Palazzo Labia, the backdrop for the *bal masqué*, was a late-seventeenth-century palace on the Canareggio, lavishly restored over a three-year period by de Beistegui. For the ball, some of the seventy footmen attending to the party, wearing the original yellow livery that the Duke of Richmond's footmen wore at his ball on the eve of the Battle of Waterloo, helped ashore hundreds of guests as they disembarked from gondolas at the palace's grand entrance. Guests proceeded through the ballroom, where they were acknowledged by their host—who was dressed in the powdered wig, silken robes and eight-inch platform soles of an eighteenth-century Venetian Procurate—then up to the *piano nobile* and its twelve reception and state rooms. Lady Diana Cooper was part of a choreographed entrée at one a.m. that celebrated the Tiepolo painting of Antony and Cleopatra in the palace's ballroom; Lady Diana was Cleopatra to the Baron de Cabrol's Mark Antony. Arturo Lopez dressed as the Emperor of China and arrived with his entourage of twenty in an

authentic Chinese junk; his entrée had supposedly cost £50,000. International society from Orson Welles to Clementine Churchill came to Venice for the ball; and Alexandre Serebriakoff, who painted watercolors of Ditchley for Ronald Tree, was commissioned by de Beistegui to document it.

17. Beaton, p. 220.
18. Aslet, Clive, "Château de Groussay: The House of Jean Beistegui," *Country Life*, June 18, 1987, p. 160.
19. Devonshire, Duchess of, *The House: A Portrait of Chatsworth*, p. 127.
20. Lees-Milne, James, *Prophesying Peace*, pp. 33–4.
21. Cornforth, John, *The Inspiration of the Past*, p. 127.
22. *Harper's Bazaar*, October 1948.
23. **At the sale at Kimbolton Castle I bought two dozen of the most beautiful Wedgwood sauceboats, and when we got them back to London, we put them in the shop window. I thought they would make very pretty flower holders. One afternoon the Duke of Wellington came into the shop and asked me why on earth I had a lot of male urinals in the window and were they something I was now collecting?**
24. Nicolson, Nigel, *Great Houses of Britain*, p. 133.
25. Quoted from Nancy Lancaster's original manuscript.
26. Westminster, Loelia Duchess of, "A Secluded, Spectacular House Seventy Yards from Bond Street," *House and Garden* [Great Britain], December 1960.
27. Ibid.
28. Cornforth, p. 129.
29. *Architectural Digest*, December 1980.
30. Haslam, Nicholas, "The Last of the 'Buttah-Yellah' Library," *Interiors*, September 1982.

HASELEY COURT

Acknowledgments: Author's interviews with Jeremy Tree, Ruby Hill, Lady Alexandra Metcalfe, Lady Bolker, Elizabeth Shonnard, Vernon Russell-Smith, Elizabeth Winn and Mary, Duchess of Buccleuch. Some of the general historical information about Haseley Court came from Christopher Hussey's two 1960 *Country Life* articles about the house.

1. From an unpublished letter to Nancy Tree from Stewart Wood, dated January 1939.
2. From an unpublished letter to Nancy Tree from Ronald Tree, dated April 26, 1942.
3. From an unpublished, undated letter to Nancy Tree from Irene Gibson.
4. Quoted in Sykes, Christopher, *Nancy: The Life of Lady Astor*, p. 500.
5. Hussey, Christopher, "Haseley Court, Oxfordshire, II," *Country Life*, February 18, 1960, p. 328.
6. Pevsner, Nikolaus, and Jennifer Sherwood, *The Buildings of England: Oxfordshire*, p. 686.
7. Unpublished extract from the diary of Sir Cecil Beaton, © the Literary Executors of Sir Cecil Beaton Deceased. The entry in Beaton's diary, for Whitsun 1959, continued, "As for me I stayed on longer than most. The post mortem on the other guests was kindly and agreeably funny—and the analyses of Nancy were wise and broad-minded. She is a woman of great character, artistic creativeness, complete lack of vulgarity and independence—and the fact that she is rich makes everything seem so much more easy and agreeable."

8. Drottningholm was a source for Charles de Beistegui as well. He copied one of the palace's painted Chinese pavilions for Groussay.

9. Unpublished extract from the diary of Sir Cecil Beaton, © the Literary Executors of Sir Cecil Beaton Deceased.

10. Lawford, Valentine, "Mrs. Nancy Lancaster and Her House and Garden at Haseley Court, Oxfordshire," *Vogue's Book of Houses, Gardens, People*, p. 95.

11. Author's interview with Mary, Duchess of Buccleuch.

12. Author's interview with Lady Bolker.

13. Lawford, p. 94.

14. Ibid., p. 91.

15. **She was not the best of motorcar drivers, though she was fearless. When driving from her Christian Science church in Maidenhead back to Cliveden one night, she was approached by a furious policeman whom she had roared past and who said, "Didn't you see me put up my hand?" Nannie replied, "If you knew who was driving you would have held both hands up."**

16. Michael Astor, *Tribal Feeling*, p. 26.

17. Roper, Lanning, "A Garden of Contrasting Forms: Haseley Court, Oxfordshire," *Country Life*, May 30, 1963, p. 1230.

18. Quoted in Hussey, Christopher, "Haseley Court, Oxfordshire, I," *Country Life*, February 11, 1960, p. 268.

19. From an unpublished letter from Mrs. Katherine M. Sturt, granddaughter of Lionel Muirhead and cousin of Anthony Muirhead, to Christopher Hussey, April 2, 1960.

20. Roper, p. 1231.

21. Lawford, p. 92.

22. Ibid., pp. 92–3.

23. Adams, William Howard, *Nature Perfected: Gardens Through History*, p. 109.

24. Quoted in ibid., p. 283.

25. Whitman, Walt, "Song of Myself," v. 1, ll. 4–5; v. 2, ll. 1–3.

EPILOGUE

Acknowledgments: Author's interviews with Mr. and Mrs. Robert Carter, Roberta Bocock, Phyllis Langhorne Draper and Vernon Edenfield.

1. Nares, Gordon, "Cottesbrooke Hall, Northampton II," *Country Life*, March 24, 1955.

2. Quoted in the foreword by Daniel P. Davidson of catalogue 7520; Christie, Manson & Woods International, Inc.; for a sale dated October 17, 1992; p. 5.

3. Geoffrey Jellicoe was honored with a knighthood for his contributions to the art of landscape design and his work for the British royal family. In the 1970s and '80s he undertook with Lady Anne and Michael Tree to design the gardens at their house, called Shute, in Wiltshire.

4. Peter Thorneycroft, former Chancellor of the Exchequer and Chairman of the Conservative Party.

5. Rothery, Agnes, *Houses Virginians Have Loved*, p. 178.

6. Ibid.

Adams, William Howard. *Nature Perfected: Gardens Through History.* New York: Abbeville, 1991.

———. *Jefferson's Monticello.* New York: Abbeville, 1983.

———. *Jefferson and the Arts: An Extended View.* Charlottesville: University of Virginia Press, 1976.

———, ed. *The Eye of Thomas Jefferson.* Washington: National Gallery of Art, 1976.

Astor, Michael. *Tribal Feeling.* London: John Murray, 1963.

Baldwin, Charles. *Stanford White.* New York: Dodd, Mead, 1931.

Beaton, Cecil. *The Wandering Years.* London: Weidenfeld and Nicolson, 1961.

———. *The Glass of Fashion.* London: Weidenfeld and Nicolson, 1954.

Becker, Stephen. *Marshall Field III.* New York: Simon and Schuster, 1964.

Birkenhead, Earl of. *The Earl of Halifax.* London: Hamish Hamilton, 1965.

Blow, Simon. *Fields Elysian: A Portrait of Hunting Society.* London and Melbourne: J. M. Dent, 1983.

Bradford, Sarah. *George VI.* London: Weidenfeld and Nicolson, 1989.

Buxton, Meriel. *Ladies of the Chase.* London: The Sportsman's Press, 1987.

Calloway, Stephen. *Twentieth-Century Decoration: The Domestic Interior from 1900 to the Present Day.* London: Weidenfeld and Nicolson, 1988.

Castle, Charles. *Oliver Messel.* New York: Thames and Hudson, 1986.

Cecil, Lord David. *Lord Melbourne.* London: Constable, 1954.

Charmley, John. *Duff Cooper.* London: Weidenfeld and Nicolson, 1986.

Churchill, Winston. *The Second World War.* Vol. II, *Their Finest Hour.* Boston: Houghton Mifflin, 1949. Vol. III, *The Grand Alliance.* Boston: Houghton Mifflin, 1950.

Coats, Peter. *Great Gardens of Britain.* New York: G. P. Putnam's Sons, 1967.

Colville, John. *The Fringes of Power: Downing Street Diaries, 1939–55.* London: Hodder and Stoughton, 1985.

Cooper, Duff. *Old Men Forget.* London: Hart-Davis, 1953.

Cooper, Lady Diana. *Trumpets from the Steep.* London: Hart-Davis, 1960.

———. *The Rainbow Comes and Goes.* London: Hart-Davis, 1958.

Cornforth, John. *The Search for a Style: Country Life and Architecture, 1897–1935.* London: Andre Deutsch, 1988.

———. *The Inspiration of the Past.* London: Viking/Country Life, 1985.

Cornforth, John, with John Fowler. *English Decoration in the 18th Century*. London: Barrie and Jenkins, 1978.

Cowles, Virginia. *The Astors*. New York: Alfred A. Knopf, 1979.

Dabney, Virginius. *Richmond: The Story of a City*. Garden City, New York: Doubleday, 1976.

———. *Virginia: The New Dominion*. Garden City, New York: Doubleday, 1971.

Dashiell, Margaret. *Richmond Reverie*. Private printing, 1942.

de Crespigny, Sir Claude Champion, Bart. *Memoirs*. London: Lawrence and Bullen, 1896.

Devonshire, Duchess of. *The House: A Portrait of Chatsworth*. London: Macmillan, 1982.

Dickens, Charles. *American Notes for General Circulation*. New York: Harper, 1842.

Downey, Fairfax. *Portrait of an Era*. New York: C. Scribner's Sons, 1936.

Faber, Walter. *Wit and Wisdom of the Shires*. Leicester: Edgar Backus, 1932.

Farrar, Emmie Ferguson. *Old Virginia Houses: The Mobjack Bay Country and Along the James*. New York: Bonanza, 1955.

Flood, Charles Bracken. *Lee, the Last Years*. Boston: Houghton Mifflin, 1981.

Foreman, John, and Robbe Pierce Stimson. *The Vanderbilts and the Gilded Age: Architectural Aspirations, 1879–1901*. New York: St. Martin's Press, 1991.

Fraser, Antonia. *King Charles II*. London: Weidenfeld and Nicolson, 1979.

Friedman, Terry. *James Gibbs*. New Haven and London: Yale, 1984.

Gilbert, Martin. *Winston S. Churchill*. Vol. 7, *Road to Victory, 1941–1945*. London: Heinemann, 1986.

Girouard, Mark. *Life in the English Country House*. New Haven and London: Yale, 1978.

Gotch, J. Alfred. *Squires' Homes and Other Old Buildings of Northamptonshire*. London: B. T. Batsford, 1939.

Graves, Robert, and Alan Hodge. *The Long Weekend: A Social History of Great Britain, 1918–1939*. London: Faber and Faber, 1940.

Greaves, Ralph. *Foxhunting in Leicestershire*. London: Field Sports Publications, 1962.

Grenfell, Joyce. *Darling Ma: Letters to Her Mother*. Ed. by James Roose-Evans. London: Hodder and Stoughton. 1988.

———. *Requests the Pleasure. . . .* London: Macmillan, 1976.

Halifax, Lord Edward. *Fullness of Days*. London: Collins, 1957.

Harrison, Rosina. *Gentlemen's Gentlemen: My Friends in Service*. London: Arlington Books, 1976.

———. *My Life in Service*. London: Cassell, 1975.

Hewitt, Mark Alan. *The Architect and the American Country House*. New Haven and London: Yale University Press, 1990.

Hibbert, Christopher. *The English: A Social History, 1066–1945*. London: Grafton Books, 1987.

Hussey, Christopher. *English Country Houses: Early Georgian, 1715–1760*. London: Country Life, 1955.

———. *English Country Houses Open to the Public*. London: Country Life and Scribners, 1953.

Jackson-Stops, Gervase, and James Pipkin. *The Country House Garden: A Grand Tour*. London: Pavilion Books, 1987.

———. *The English Country House: A Grand Tour*. London: The National Trust and Weidenfeld and Nicolson, 1985.

Jones, Chester. *Colefax and Fowler: The Best in English Interior Decoration*. Boston: Little, Brown, 1989.

Jourdain, Margaret. *English Decorative Plasterworks*. London: B. T. Batsford, 1927.

Kendrick, Alexander. *Prime Time: The Life of Edward R. Murrow*. London: Dent, 1970.

Lambert, Angela. *1939: The Last Season of Peace*. New York: Weidenfeld and Nicolson, 1989.

Lancaster, Robert A. *Historic Virginia Homes and Churches*. Philadelphia: J. B. Lippincott, 1915.

Lane, Mills. *Architecture of the Old South: Virginia*. Savannah: Beehive Press, 1987.

Lansdale, Maria Horner, and Jules Guerin. *The Chateaux of Touraine*. New York: Century Co., 1906.

Lees-Milne, James. *Midway on the Waves*. London: Faber and Faber, 1985.

———. *The Country House*. Oxford: Oxford University Press, 1982.

———. *Prophesying Peace*. London: Chatto & Windus, 1977.

Lloyd, Nathaniel. *The History of the English Country House*. London: The Architecture Press, 1949.

Lutz, Earl. *A Richmond Album*. Richmond: Garrett and Massie, 1937.

Lysaght, Charles Edward. *Brendan Bracken*. London: Allen Lane, 1979.

Lyttelton, Oliver. *The Memoirs of Lord Chandos*. London: Bodley Head, 1962.

Malone, Dumas. *Jefferson the Virginian*. Boston: Little, Brown, 1948.

Massie, Susanne Williams, and Francis Archer Christian, eds. *Homes and Gardens in Old Virginia*. Richmond: J. W. Fergusson and Sons, 1930.

Masters, Brian. *The Dukes*. London: Blond and Briggs, 1975.

McLaughlin, Jack. *Jefferson and Monticello: The Biography of a Builder*. New York: Henry Holt, 1988.

McLeod, Kirsty. *A Passion for Friendship: Sibyl Colefax and Her Circle*. London: Michael Joseph, 1991.

Meade-Fetherstonhaugh, Margaret and Oliver Warner. *Uppark and Its People*. London: George Allen and Unwin, 1964.

Menkes, Suzy. *The Windsor Style*. London: Grafton Books, 1987.

Metcalf, Pauline C., ed. *Ogden Codman and the Decoration of Houses*. Boston: Atheneum and David R. Godine, 1988.

Moore, John Hammond. *Albemarle, Jefferson's County, 1727–1976*. Charlottesville: University Press of Virginia, 1976.

Munford, Robert, Jr. *Richmond Homes and Memories*. Richmond: Garrett and Massie, 1936.

Munnings, Sir Alfred. *The Second Burst*. London: Museum Press Ltd., 1951.

Neale, J. P. *Views of Seats*. Vol. III. London: W. H. Reid, 1820.

Nicolson, Nigel, ed. *Diaries and Letters of Harold Nicolson*. Vol. 2, *The War Years, 1939–1945*. New York: Atheneum, 1967. Vol. 3, *The Later Years, 1945–1962*. New York: Atheneum, 1968.

Nicolson, Nigel. *Great Houses of Britain*. London: Weidenfeld and Nicolson, 1965.

Niven, David. *The Moon's a Balloon*. London: Hamish Hamilton, 1971.

Norwich, John Julius. *The Architecture of Southern England*. London: Macmillan, 1985.

Page, Russell. *The Education of a Gardener*. Newton Abbot: Gardeners Book Club, 1973.

Paget, Sir Thomas Guy. *The Life of Frank Freeman*. Leicester: Edgar Backus, 1948.

———. *History of the Althorp and Pytchley Hunt*. London: Collins, 1937.

———. *Rum 'Uns to Follow* (by "Dick Heathen"). London: Country Life, 1924.

Pevsner, Nikolaus. *The Buildings of England: Northamptonshire.* 2nd ed., rev. by Bridget Cherry. Harmondsworth: Penguin, 1973.

Pevsner, Nikolaus, and Jennifer Sherwood. *The Buildings of England: Oxfordshire.* Harmondsworth: Penguin, 1974.

Priestley, J. B. *The English.* London: Heinemann, 1983.

Reiff, Daniel D. *Small Georgian Houses in England and Virginia.* Newark: University of Delaware, 1986.

Richmond, Capital of Virginia: Approaches to Its History, by "Various Hands." Richmond: Whittet and Shepperson, 1938.

Robertson, Ben. *I Saw England.* New York: Grosset and Dunlap, 1940–41.

Roth, Leland M. *McKim, Mead & White Architects.* New York: Harper and Row, 1983.

Rothery, Agnes. *Houses Virginians Have Loved.* New York: Rinehart, 1954.

"Sabretache." *Monarchy and the Chase.* London: Eyre and Spottiswoode, 1948.

———. *A Gentleman and His Hounds.* London: Eyre and Spottiswoode, 1935.

Scully, Vincent. *Architecture: The Natural and the Man-made.* New York: St. Martin's Press, 1991.

Shepherd, Robert. *A Class Divided.* London: Macmillan, 1988.

Sitwell, Sacheverell. *British Architects and Craftsmen.* London: Batsford, 1945.

Smith, Joan. *Elsie de Wolfe: A Life in High Style.* New York: Atheneum, 1982.

Smith, Captain John. *Works: 1608–31.* Westminster: Archibald Constable and Co., 1985.

Smith, Sally Bedell. *In All His Glory: The Life and Times of William S. Paley and the Birth of Modern Broadcasting.* New York: Simon and Schuster, 1990.

Soames, Mary. *Clementine Churchill.* London: Cassell, 1979.

Somerset, Anne. *Elizabeth I.* New York: Alfred A. Knopf, 1991.

Spens, Michael. *Gardens of the Mind: The Genius of Geoffrey Jellicoe.* Suffolk: Antique Collectors' Club, 1992.

Stanard, Mary Norton. *Richmond, Its People and Its Story.* Philadelphia and London: Lippincott, 1923.

Steegman, John. *The Rule of Taste.* London: Macmillan, 1936.

Strong, Roy, M. Binney and J. Harris. *The Destruction of the Country House.* London: Thames and Hudson, 1974.

Sykes, Christopher. *Nancy: The Life of Lady Astor.* Frogmore, St. Albans, Herts.: Granada, 1979.

Tipping, H. Avery. *English Homes.* Period V, Early Georgian, 1714–1760. London: Country Life, 1921.

Tree, Ronald. *When the Moon Was High: Memoirs of Peace and War 1897–1942.* London: Macmillan, 1975.

Vogue's Book of Houses, Gardens, People. New York: Viking Press, 1968.

Wall, Rev. J. Clifford. *Kelmarsh: A Parochial History.* Market Harborough: Green and Co. Booksellers, 1927.

Waterman, T. T. *Mansions of Virginia.* Chapel Hill: University of North Carolina, 1945.

———. *Domestic Colonial Architecture of Tidewater Virginia.* New York: Charles Scribner, 1932.

Weinreb, Ben, and Christopher Hibbert, eds. *The London Encyclopaedia.* New York: St. Martin's Press, 1983.

Wharton, Edith, and Ogden Codman. *Decoration of Houses*. New York, Scribners, 1897.

Wilson, Michael I. *William Kent: Architect, Designer, Painter, Gardener 1685–1748*. London: Routledge and Kegan Paul, 1984.

Winn, Alice. *Always a Virginian: The Colorful Langhornes of Mirador, Lady Astor, and Their Kin*. Lynchburg: Kenmore Association, 1982.

Ziegler, Philip. *King Edward VIII*. New York: Alfred A. Knopf, 1991.

PUBLICATIONS

Aslet, Clive. "Château de Groussay: The Home of Jean de Beistegui." *Country Life*, June 18, 1987.

Becker, Robert. "A Fond Last Look." *House Beautiful*, January 1995.

Binney, Marcus. "Eydon Hall, Northamptonshire: The Home of Sir Edward and the Hon. Lady Ford." *Country Life*, January 21, 1971.

Brympton d' Evercy guidebook, n.d.

Cliveden. The National Trust, 1978.

Cornforth, John. "Ditchley Park, Oxfordshire, I and II. The Property of the Ditchley Foundation." *Country Life*, November 17, 1988.

———. "Ditchley Revisited." *Country Life*, October 24, 1985.

———. "Boudin at Leeds Castle, I and II." *Country Life*, April 14 and 21, 1983.

———. "Prince of Humble Elegance: John Fowler I." *Country Life*, April 28, 1983.

———. "Comfort and Pleasing Decay: John Fowler II." *Country Life*, May 19, 1983.

———. "Boughton House, Northamptonshire, I, II, III, and IV. A Seat of the Duke of Buccleuch and Queensbury." *Country Life*, September 3, 10 and 17, 1970, February 25, 1971.

"Ditchley, Oxfordshire. The Seat of Lord Dillon." *Country Life*, October 22, 1904.

"F." "Hartwell House, Buckinghamshire, I and II. The Seat of Mrs. Edward Lee." *Country Life*, March 14 and 21, 1914.

Gomme, A. H. "Architects and Craftsmen at Ditchley." *Architectural History* 32 (1989): 85–104.

Haslam, Nicholas. "The Last of the 'Buttah-Yellah' Library." *Interiors*, September 1982.

Hussey, Christopher. "Wilton House, Wiltshire, I, II and III. The Seat of the Earl of Pembroke and Montgomery." *Country Life*, May 9, 16 and 23, 1963.

———. "Haseley Court, Oxfordshire, I and II. The Home of Mrs. C. G. Lancaster." *Country Life*, February 11 and 18, 1960.

———. "Heron Bay, Barbados: The Home of Mr. Ronald Tree." *Country Life*, November 5, 1959.

———. "Uppark, Sussex, I, II and III. The Home of Admiral the Hon. Sir Herbert Meade-Fetherstonhaugh, GCVO, CB, DSO" *Country Life*, June 14, 21 and 28, 1941.

———. "Cliveden, Buckinghamshire, I and II. The Seat of Lord Astor." *Country Life*, July 11 and 18, 1931.

Isham, Giles. "The Langhams of Cottesbrooke Hall." Correspondence, *Country Life*, April 14, 1955.

Jellicoe, Sir Geoffrey. "Ronald Tree and the Gardens of Ditchley Park: The Human Face of History." *Garden History: The Journal of the Garden History Society*, vol. 10, no. 1, 1982.

Jourdain, Margaret. "Boughton House, Northamptonshire, I and II. A Seat of the Duke of Buccleuch." *Country Life*, November 26 and December 3, 1932.

"Lady Astor, from Virginia." *The New York Times* magazine, November 16, 1919.

Lancaster, Nancy. "Splendid Summers on Seven Hundred Acre Island." *Down East*, July 1984.

Lindsay, Norah. "The Manor House, I and II, Sutton Courtney, Berks. The Residence of Mrs. Harry Lindsay." *Country Life*, May 16 and 23, 1931.

"M. F." "Famous Hunts and Their Countries: The Pytchley." *Country Life*, February 25, 1933.

Nares, Gordon. "Cottesbrooke Hall, Northampton, I and II. The Home of Major and the Hon. Mrs. R. N. MacDonald-Buchanan." *Country Life*, March 17 and 24, 1955.

Osler, Mirabel. "Perfectly Squared." *House Beautiful*, November 1993.

Oswald, Arthur. "Cottesbrooke Hall, Northamptonshire, I and II. The Seat of Captain R. B. Brassey." *Country Life*, February 15 and 22, 1936.

———. "Ditchley, Oxfordshire, I and II. The Seat of Mr. Ronald Tree," *Country Life*, June 9 and 16, 1934.

———. "Kelmarsh Hall, Northamptonshire. The Property of Capt. C. G. Lancaster." *Country Life*, February 25, 1933.

Poindexter, Charles. "Snapshots at Richmond, Virginia, USA," from a booster pamphlet, *Richmond, Virginia: Her Advantages and Attractions*, printed by J. L. Hill Co., Richmond, 1896.

Roper, Lanning. "A Garden of Contrasting Forms: Haseley Court Oxfordshire." *Country Life*, May 30, 1963.

Schuyler, M. "The New York House," *Architectural Record* 19 (February 1906).

Tipping, H. Avray. "Ashburnham Place, Sussex, I and II. A Seat of the Earl of Ashburnham." *Country Life*, January 22 and 29, 1918.

Uppark. The National Trust, 1976.

Westminster, Loelia Duchess of. "A Secluded, Spectacular House Seventy Yards from Bond Street." *House and Garden* [Great Britain], December 1960.

INDEX

Page numbers in *italics* refer to illustrations.

407

ILLUSTRATION CREDITS

From the personal collection of Nancy Lancaster: 4, 5, 8, 9, 12, 20, 23, 26, 27, 28, 30, 37, 45, 46, 47, 54, 62, 88, 94, 98, 99, 101, 103, 108, 121, 122, 125, 126, 129, 130, 131, 132, 133, 134, 135, 136, 138, 142, 143, 145, 151, 178, 179, 181, 183, 185, 188, 218, 233, 236, 237, 239, 240, 243, 246, 250, 251, 252, 255, 256, 260, 262, 263, 266, 267, 274, 275, 277, 280, 286, 287, 288, 305, 319, 320, 340 (bottom), 360, 362, 363, 364 and 384

From the collection of the Valentine Museum, Richmond; gifts of Nancy Lancaster: 18, 24, 34, 35, 36, 42, 74 and 81

Courtesy of Mrs. Alice Winn: 61

Reproduced by permission of *Country Life* magazine: 77, 78, 80, 82, 148, 154, 162, 166, 168, 172, 173, 226 (bottom), 227, 330 and 350 (bottom)

From the collection of the Clifton Waller Barrett Library of American Literature, Special Collections Department, University of Virginia Library: 102

Courtesy of the Metropolitan Museum of Art; gifts of the Estate of Ogden Codman, Jr., 1951: 110, 112 and 113

Courtesy of the Ditchley Foundation: 226 (top)

Photographs by Sir Cecil Beaton, reproduced by permission of Sotheby's, London: 230, 356

Photographs by Millar and Harris: 322, 336, 340 (top), 346, 350 (top), 351, 353 and 357

Photograph by Valerie Finnis, reproduced by permission of Valerie Finnis: 367

Courtesy of Mrs. Kitty Abbott Johnson: 375

Reprinted by permission of *House Beautiful*, copyright © January 1995, The Hearst Corporation. All rights reserved. Michael Dunne, photographer: 383

Color illustrations between pages 110 and 111: Hoffbaur painting of Mirador from the personal collection of Nancy Lancaster; Mirador interiors painted by Scaisbrooke Langhorne Abbott, photographed by Jonathan Pilkington, from the personal collection of Nancy Lancaster.

Color illustrations between pages 366 and 367: *Ronald Tree, MFH* by Sir Alfred Munnings © the Sir Alfred Munnings Art Museum, Dedham, Essex, England; interior watercolors of Ditchley Park by Alexandre Serebriakoff, photographed by Mark Fiennes; black-and-white photographs of Ditchley's saloon and Tapestry Room reproduced by permission of *Country Life* magazine; black-and-white photographs of Ditchley's Great Hall and library courtesy of the Ditchley Foundation; bedroom, anteroom and the Yellow Library of 22 Avery Row photographed by Derry Moore, reproduced by permission of Derry Moore; black-and-white photograph of the Gothick Bedroom by Millar and Harris; color photograph of the Gothick Bedroom by Horst, reproduced by permission of Horst; Haseley's Stone Garden, Walled Garden and laburnum arch, and the portrait of Nancy Lancaster in the Haseley garden all photographed by Valerie Finnis, reproduced by permission of Valerie Finnis.

A NOTE ON THE TYPE

This book was set in Janson, a typeface long thought to have been made by the Dutchman Anton Janson, who was a practicing type-founder in Leipzig during the years 1668–1687. However, it has been conclusively demonstrated that these types are actually the work of Nicholas Kis (1650–1702), a Hungarian, who most probably learned his trade from the master Dutch typefounder Dirk Voskens. The type is an excellent example of the influential and sturdy Dutch types that prevailed in England up to the time William Caslon (1692–1766) developed his own incomparable designs from them.

Composed by North Market Street Graphics,
Lancaster, Pennsylvania

Printed and bound by Quebecor Printing Martinsburg,
Martinsburg, West Virginia

Designed by Iris Weinstein